THE SHAPE OF THINGS TO COME

How will man adapt to his environment
in the future?

Will nations continue to fight each other
thus destroying themselves and the world
in the hopeless futility of war?

What sort of cultural and technical
revolutions must occur in the ceaseless
advance of civilisation?

WHAT ARE THE SHAPE OF
THINGS TO COME?

SF TITLES SPECIALLY SELECTED TO APPEAR IN

CORGI
SF COLLECTOR'S
LIBRARY

MORE THAN HUMAN   by Theodore Sturgeon*
FANTASTIC VOYAGE   by Isaac Asimov*
DRAGONFLIGHT   by Anne McCaffrey*
FAHRENHEIT 451   by Ray Bradbury*
THE GOLDEN APPLES OF THE SUN   by Ray Bradbury*
THE ILLUSTRATED MAN   by Ray Bradbury†
EARTH ABIDES   by George R. Stewart*
REPORT ON PLANET THREE   by Arthur C. Clarke*
THE CITY AND THE STARS   by Arthur C. Clarke*
REACH FOR TOMORROW   by Arthur C. Clarke†
THE MENACE FROM EARTH   by Robert Heinlein*
A CANTICLE FOR LEIBOWITZ   by Walter M. Miller*
THE SHAPE OF FURTHER THINGS   by Brian Aldiss*

* Published by Corgi Books
† To be published by CORGI BOOKS

The Shape of Things to Come

H. G. Wells

CORGI BOOKS

A DIVISION OF TRANSWORLD PUBLISHERS LTD

THE SHAPE OF THINGS TO COME

A CORGI BOOK 0 552 09532 X

Originally published in Great Britain by
Hutchinson & Co. (Publishers) Ltd.

PRINTING HISTORY

Hutchinson edition published 1933
Corgi edition published 1967
Corgi edition reissued 1974

This book is set in Times 10/11 pt.

Corgi Books are published by Transworld Publishers Ltd.,
Cavendish House, 57–59 Uxbridge Road, Ealing,
London, W.5.

Made and printed in Great Britain by
Richard Clay (The Chaucer Press), Ltd., Bungay, Suffolk.

CONTENTS

INTRODUCTION

BOOK THE FIRST

TO-DAY AND TO-MORROW: THE AGE OF FRUSTRATION DAWNS

BOOK THE SECOND

BOOK THE THIRD

BOOK THE FOURTH

THE MODERN STATE MILITANT

BOOK THE FIFTH

THE MODERN STATE IN CONTROL OF LIFE

THE SHAPE OF THINGS
TO COME

THE DREAM BOOK OF DR. PHILIP RAVEN

The unexpected death of Dr. Philip Raven at Geneva in November 1930 was a very grave loss to the League of Nations Secretariat. Geneva lost a familar figure—the long bent back, the halting gait, the head quizzically on one side —and the world lost a stimulatingly aggressive mind. His incessant devoted work, his extraordinary mental vigour, were, as his obituary notices testified, appreciated very highly by a world-wide following of distinguished and capable admirers. The general public was suddenly made aware of him.

It is rare that anyone outside the conventional areas of newspaper publicity produces so great a stir by dying; there were accounts of him in nearly every paper of importance from Oslo to New Zealand and from Buenos Aires to Japan—and the brief but admirable memoir by Sir Godfrey Cliffe gave the general reader a picture of an exceptionally simple, direct, devoted and energetic personality. There seems to have been only two extremely dissimilar photographs available for publication: an early one in which he looks like a blend of Shelley and Mr. Maxton, and a later one, a snapshot, in which he leans askew on his stick and talks to Lord Parmoor in the entrance hall of the assembly. One of his lank hands is held out in a characteristic illustrative gesture.

Incessantly laborious though he was, he could nevertheless find time to assist in, share and master all the broader problems that exercised his colleagues, and now they rushed forward with their gratitude. One noticeable thing in that

11

posthumous eruption of publicity was the frequent acknow-ledgments of his aid and advice. Men were eager to testify to his importance and resentful at the public ignorance of his work. Three memorial volumes of his more important papers, reports, memoranda and addresses were arranged for and are still in course of publication.

Personally, although I was asked to do so in several quarters, and though I was known to have had the honour of his friendship, I made no contribution to that obituary chorus. My standing in the academic world did not justify my writing him a testimonial, but under normal circum-stances that would not have deterred me from an attempt to sketch something of his odd personal ease and charm. I did not do so, however, because I found myself in a position of extraordinary embarrassment. His death was so unfore-seen that we had embarked upon a very peculiar joint under-taking without making the slightest provision for that risk. It is only now after an interval of nearly three years, and after some very difficult discussions with his more intimate friends, that I have decided to publish the facts and the substance of this peculiar co-operation of ours.

It concerns the matter of this present book. All this time I have been holding back a manuscript, or rather a collection of papers and writings, entrusted to me. It is a collection about which, I think, a considerable amount of hesitation was, and perhaps is still, justifiable. It is, or least it professes to be, a Short History of the World for about the next century and a half. (I can quite understand that the reader will rub his eyes at these words and suspect the printer of some sort of agraphia.) But that is exactly what this manu-script is. It is a Short History of the Future. It is a modern Sibylline book. Only now that the events of three years have more than justified everything stated in this anticipatory history have I had the courage to associate the reputation of my friend with the incredible claims of this work, and to find a publisher for it.

Let me tell very briefly what I know of its origin and how it came into my hands. I made the acquaintance of Dr.

Raven, or, to be more precise, he made mine, in the closing year of the war. It was before he left Whitehall for Geneva. He was always an eager amateur of ideas, and he had been attracted by some suggestions about money I had made in a scrappy little book of forecasts called *What is Coming?* published in 1916. In this I had thrown out the suggestion that the waste of resources in the war, combined with the accumulation of debts that had been going on, would certainly leave the world as a whole bankrupt, that is to say it would leave the creditor class in a position to strangle the world, and that the only method to clear up this world bankruptcy and begin again on a hopeful basis would be to scale down all debts impartially, by a reduction of the amount of gold in the pound sterling and proportionally in the dollar and all other currencies based on gold. It seemed to me then an obvious necessity. It was, I recognise now, a crude idea—evidently I had not even got away from the idea of intrinsically valuable money—but none of us in those days had had the educational benefit of the monetary and credit convulsions that followed the Peace of Versailles. We were without experience, it wasn't popular to think about money, and at best we thought like precocious children. Seventeen years later this idea of appreciating gold is accepted as an obvious suggestion by quite a number of people. Then it was received merely as the amateurish comment of an ignorant writer upon what was still regarded as the mysterious business of 'monetary experts'. But it attracted the attention of Raven, who came along to talk over that and one or two other post-war possibilities I had started, and so he made my acquaintance.

Raven was free from intellectual pompousness as William James; as candidly receptive to candid thinking. He could talk about his subject to an artist or a journalist; he would have talked to an errand boy if he thought he would get a fresh slant in that way. 'Obvious' was the word he brought with him. 'The thing, my dear fellow'—he called me my dear fellow in the first five minutes—'is so obvious that everybody will be too clever to consider it for a

13

moment. Until it is belated. It is impossible to persuade anybody responsible that there is going to be a tremendous financial and monetary mix-up after this war. The victors will exact vindictive penalties and the losers of course will undertake to pay, but none of them realise that money is going to do the most extraordinary things to them when they begin upon that. What they are going to do to each other is what occupies them, and what money is going to do to the whole lot of them is nobody's affair.'

I can still see him as he said that in his high-pitched remonstrating voice. I will confess that for perhaps our first half-hour, until I was accustomed to his flavour, I did not like him. He was too full, too sure, too rapid and altogether too vivid for my slower Anglo-Saxon make-up. I did not like the evident preparation of his talk, nor the fact that he assisted it by the most extraordinary gestures. He would not sit down; he limped about my room, peering at books and pictures while he talked in his cracked forced voice, and waving those long lean hands of his about almost as if he was swimming through his subject. I have compared him to Maxton plus Shelley, rather older, but at the first outset I was reminded of Svengali in Du Maurier's once popular *Trilby*. A shaven Svengali. I felt he was *foreign*, and my instincts about foreigners are as insular as my principles are cosmopolitan. It always seemed to me a little irreconcilable that he was a Balliol scholar, and had been one of the brightest ornaments of our Foreign Office staff before he went to Geneva.

At bottom I suppose much of essential English shyness is an exaggerated wariness. We suspect the other fellow of our own moral subtleties. We restrain ourselves often to the point of insincerity. I am a rash man with a pen perhaps, but I am as circumspect and evasive as any other of my fellow countrymen when it comes to social intercourse. I found something almost indelicate in Raven's direct attack upon my ideas.

He wanted to talk about my ideas beyond question. But at least equally he wanted to talk about his own. I had

14

more than a suspicion that he had, in fact, come to me in order to talk to himself and hear how it sounded—against me as a sounding-board.

He went on to discuss various collateral suggestions of mine, which were also, he said, of the 'obvious' class. He offered me a series of flattering insults. He said he found a certain mental simplicity I possess very refreshing. He was being tormented by the way things were going behind the fronts—and behind the scenes. Everybody, he declared, was busy fighting the war or planning to best our enemies or allies after the war; everybody was being so damned subtle that they were forgetting every clear realisation they had ever had, and nobody, with the exception of a few such onlookers and outsiders as myself, was putting in any time in working out the broad inevitabilities of the process. With these others it is always what trick X will play next, and what will be Y's dodge and whether the Z's will stand this, that or the other thing that is put upon them—if it is put in this, that or the other way to them. But, of course, none of this was essential. In the long run only the essentials mattered.

'In the long run,' said I.

'In the long run. And not such a very long run either in these days.'

I accepted that.

Gradually I warmed to this intellectual glow. What were the essentials? On that issue I was as keen as, if less outspoken than he. 'What is *really* happening now?' I asked.

'Yes,' he agreed, in manifest delight. 'What is *really* happening now? Damn them! Not one of them asks that question. That's where you are so good, that's where you are worth while. The others all think they know so well that they can afford to be shut and sly about it. They can't.'

He called me then a Dealer in the Obvious, and he repeated that not very flattering phrase on various occasions when we met. 'You have,' he said, 'defects that are almost gifts: a rapid but inexact memory for particulars, a quick grasp of proportions, and no patience with detail. You hurry

15

on to wholes. You have to see things simply or you could not see them at all. Consequently you cannot endure any conventional elaborations, any side-shows, needless complexities, indirect methods, diplomacies, legal fictions and tactful half-statements. It's a joy to rattle on to you and feel there's no complications. It isn't, I think, that you have the power to take up all those things in your stride; I won't flatter you like that; no—but you have the intuitive sense to drop them in your stride. There's the secret of your simplicity; you come as near to stupidity as wisdom can. How men of affairs must hate you—if and when they hear of you! They must think you an awful mug, you know—and yet you get there! Complications are their life. *You* try to get all these complications out of the way. You are a stripper, a damned impatient stripper. I would be a stripper too if I hadn't the sort of job I have to do. But it is really extraordinarily refreshing to spend these occasional hours stripping events in your company.'

The reader must forgive my egotism in quoting these comments upon myself; they are necessary if my relations with Raven are to be made clear and if the spirit of this book is to be understood. I met him upon an unusual side that he could afford to reveal to very few other persons. That is my point. 'If I generalised to other people as I do to you,' he said, 'if I talked as plainly, my reputation as an expert would go up—like a battleship hit in the magazine.'

I was, in fact, an outlet for a definite mental exuberance of his which it had hitherto distressed him to suppress. In my presence he could throw off Balliol and the Foreign Office—or, later on, the Secretariat—and let himself go. He could become the Eastern European Cosmopolitan he was by nature and descent. I became, as it were, an imaginative boon companion for him, his disreputable friend, a sort of intelligent butt, his Watson. I got to like the relationship. I got used to his physical exoticism, his gestures. I sympathised more and more with his irritation and distress as the Conference at Versailles unfolded. My instinctive racial

16

distrust faded before the glowing intensity of his intellectual curiosity. We found we supplemented each other. I had a ready unclouded imagination and he had knowledge. We would go on the speculative spree together.

Finally it may be he started out to take me on the greatest speculative spree of all. I am quite open to the idea that this book is nothing more than that. It is well to bear that in mind in weighing what I have next to tell about this anticipatory History of his.

Among other gifted and original friends who, at all too rare intervals, honour me by coming along for a gossip is Mr. J. W. Dunne, who years ago invented one of the earliest and most 'different' of aeroplanes, and who has since done a very considerable amount of subtle thinking upon the relationship of time and space to consciousness. Dunne clings to the idea that in certain ways we may anticipate the future, and he has adduced a series of very remarkable observations indeed to support that in his well-known *Experiment With Time*. That book was published in 1927, and I found it so attractive and stimulating that I wrote about it in one or two articles that were syndicated very extensively throughout the world. It was so excitingly fresh.

And among others who saw my account of this *Experiment with Time*, and who got the book and read it and then wrote to me about it, was Raven. Usually his communications to me were the briefest of notes, saying he would be in London, telling me of a change of address, asking about my movements and so forth; but this was quite a long letter. Experiences such as Dunne's, he said, were no novelty to him. He could add a lot to what was told in the book, and indeed he could *extend* the experience. The thing anticipated between sleeping and waking— Dunne's experiments dealt chiefly with the premonitions in the dozing moment between wakefulness and oblivion— need not be just small affairs of to-morrow or next week; they could have a longer range. If, that is, you had the habit of long-range thinking. But these were days when scepticism had to present a hard face to greedy superstition,

17

and it was one's public duty to refrain from rash statements about these flimsy intimations, difficult as they were to distinguish from fantasies—except in one's own mind. One might sacrifice a lot of influence if one betrayed too lively an interest in this sort of thing.

He wandered off into such sage generalisations and concluded abruptly. The letter had an effect of starting out to tell much more than it did. 'Are you coming through Geneva on your way to Italy?' it wound up. 'If so, we might talk.'

When, however, I talked to him in Geneva—it was hot and we took a motor launch and had dinner at a pleasant restaurant on the lake shore beyond the waterspout—he would say scarcely a word about any glimpses he had had into futurity. He was dull and depressed that day. I never found out exactly what it was had robbed him of his customary exuberance. I asked him at last outright whether he hadn't something to tell me about seeing into the future. He semed to have forgotten his letter altogether. '*What* is there to see in the future?' he asked, hunched in his chair. 'I haven't the guts for it.

'These people here mean nothing,' he vouchsafed. 'Nothing at all.'

Afterwards we fell talking about the speculative boom that was then at its height in America. He said it was essentially an inflation of credit by bulling securities. While it lasted there would be a kind of prosperity, but there was nothing behind it but faith. At any time somone might start a selling that would collapse the whole thing. 'And once they start a collapse over there ...'

He let a grimace and a gesture of his lean long hand finish his sentence.

'It's a card castle,' he said, and then with a groan of a tired man: 'I can't even find a metaphor to-day. It's a card castle that will fall—like ten million tons of bricks.'

And I remember another sentence of his.

'What I cannot understand is the levity of human beings —their incurable levity. This Geneva is the home of Calvinism. I used to think the Calvinists at least had some

18

conception of the seriousness of life.'

He shook his head slowly and suddenly a gleam of humour lit up his sombre eyes for a moment. 'It was liver,' he said. 'Everyone who comes to Geneva gets liver.'

'So that's what's the matter!' said I.

'Liver and lethargy. Predestination. Do nothing. Attempt nothing. And burn any heretic who attempts salvation by works. . . . *You* hope by nature, you know. It's just the luck of your glands. They would have burnt you here without hesitation three centuries ago.'

Between endocrines and theology, whatever experiments with time he had been making were forgotten.

Afterwards I thought of the Dunne idea again, and I connected it so little with Raven's abortive confidences that I made up a short story. *Brownlow's Newspaper*, about a man into whose hands there fell an evening journal of fifty years ahead—and of all the tantalisingly incomplete intimations of change, such a scrap of the future would be sure to convey. Brownlow, whom I imagined as a cheerful and self-indulgent friend, came home late and rather alcoholic, and found this paper stuck through his letter-slit in the place of his usual *Evening Standard*. He found the print, paper and spelling rather queer; he was surprised by the realism of the coloured illustrations, he missed several familiar features, and he thought the news fantastic stuff, but he was too tired and muzzy to see the thing in its proper proportions, and in the morning when he awoke and thought about it, and realised the marvellous glimpse he had had into the world to come, the paper had vanished for ever down the dust-chute. This story was published in a popular magazine—the *Strand Magazine*, if I remember rightly—and Raven saw it. He wrote to me at once.

You are joking about a serious possibility [he wrote].
You are making a fairy tale of something that can happen.

Then he turned up in London, dropped into my study unexpectedly and made a clean breast of it.

19

'This Dunne business,' he began.

'Well?' said I.

'He has a way of snatching the fleeting dream between unconscious sleep and waking.'

'Yes.'

'He keeps a notebook by his bedside and writes down his dream the very instant he is awake.'

'That's the procedure.'

'And he finds that a certain percentage of his dream items are—sometimes quite plainly—anticipations of things that will come into his mind out of reality, days, weeks and even years ahead.'

'That's Dunne.'

'It's nothing.'

'But how—nothing?'

'Nothing to what I have been doing for a long time.'

'And that is ...?'

He stared at the backs of my books. It was amusing to find Raven for once at a loss for words.

'Well?' I said.

He turned and looked at me with a reluctant expression that broke into a smile. Then he seemed to rally his candour.

'How shall I put it? I wouldn't tell anyone but you. For some years, off and on—between sleeping and waking—I've been—in effect reading a book. A non-existent book. A dream book if you like. It's always the same book. Always. And it's a history.'

'Of the past?'

'There's a lot about the past. With all sorts of things I didn't know and all sorts of gaps filled in. Extraordinary things about North India and Central Asia, for instance. And also—it goes on. It's going on. It keeps on going on.'

'Going on?'

'Right past the present time.'

'Sailing away into the future?'

'Yes.'

'Is it—is it a *paper* book?'

'Not quite paper. Rather like that newspaper of your

20

friend Brownlow. Not quite print as we know. Vivid maps. And quite easy to read, in spite of the queer letters and spelling.'

He paused. 'I know it's nonsense.'

He added, 'It's frightfully real.'

'Do you turn the pages?'

He thought for a moment. 'No, I don't turn the pages. That would wake me up.'

'It just goes on?'

'Yes.'

'Until you realise you are doing it?'

'I suppose—yes, it is like that.'

'And then you wake up?'

'Exactly. And it isn't there!'

'And you are always *reading*?'

'Generally—very definitely.'

'But at times?'

'Oh—just the same as reading a book when one is awake. If the matter is vivid one *sees* the events. As if one was looking at a moving picture on the page.'

'But the book is still there?'

'Yes—always. I think it's there always.'

'Do you by any chance make notes?'

'I didn't at first. Now I do.'

'At once?'

'I write a kind of shorthand. . . . Do you know—I've piles of notes *that* high.'

He straddled my fireplace and stared at me.

'Now you've told me,' I said.

'Now I've told you.'

'If I had known this before, I wouldn't have written *Brownlow's Newspaper*.'

'Naturally. My fault for not telling you plainly sooner.'

His lank hand waved all that aside.

'Can't I see some of the notes?'

'Illegible, my dear sir—except to me. You don't know my shorthand. I can hardly read it myself after a week or so. But lately I've been writing it out—some I've dictated.'

'You see,' he went on, standing up and walking about my room, 'if it's—a reality, it's the most important thing in the world. And I haven't an atom of proof. Not an atom. Do you——Do you believe this sort of thing is possible?'

'*Possible?*' I considered. 'I'm inclined to think I do. Though what exactly this kind of thing may be, I don't know.'

'I can't tell anyone but you. How could I? Naturally they would say I had gone cranky—or that I was an impostor. You know the sort of row. Look at Oliver Lodge. Look at Charles Richet. It would smash my work, my position. And yet, you know, it's such credible stuff.... I tell you I believe in it.'

'If you wrote some of it out. If I could see some of it.'

'You shall.'

He seemed to be consulting my opinion. 'The worst thing against it is that I always believe in what the fellow says. That's rather as though it was *me,* eh?'

That in effect was our conversation. I was left half incredulous, half attracted. My disposition was to believe that between sleeping and waking he did not actually see this book, but that it was not in any sense a real book: it was the creation of his own hard thinking about man's past and present and future. He was, I supposed, projecting his own speculations. His bold, far-ranging mind, severely repressed and kept within narrow limits in his official work, was escaping in this fantasy, was indulging in the free play of its possibilities. I was only the recipient of a fraction of his mental overflow. This was the rest. He was not content with simply answering my original question, What is really happening? If one knows what is really happening one knows what is going to happen. His brain was taking the business out of his hands and carrying interpretation on to prophecy. It is a logical development. That is still the most acceptable explanation of this history that follows. Even as a speculation it merits attention. But, I must insist, it is not a perfect explanation. There are one or two little things that do not fit into that.

He did not send me any of his notes, but when next I met him, it was at Berne, he gave me a spring-backed folder filled with papers. Afterwards he gave me two others. Pencilled sheets they were mostly, but some were evidently written at his desk in ink and perhaps fifty pages had been typed, probably from his dictation. He asked me to take great care of them, to read them carefully, have typed copies made and return a set to him. The whole thing was to be kept as a secret between us. We were both to think over the advisability of a possibly anonymous publication. And meanwhile events might either confirm or explode various statements made in this history and so set a definite value, one way or the other, upon its authenticity.

Then he died.

He died quite unexpectedly as the result of a sudden operation. Some dislocation connected with his marked spinal curvature had developed abruptly into an acute crisis.

As soon as I heard of his death I hurried off to Geneva and told the story of the dream book to his heir and executor, Mr. Montefiore Renaud. I am greatly indebted to that gentleman for his courtesy and quick understanding of the situation. He was at great pains to get every possible scrap of material together and to place it all at my disposal. In addition to the three folders Raven had already given me there was a further folder in longhand and a drawerful of papers in this peculiar shorthand evidently dealing with this History. The fourth folder contained the material which forms the concluding book of this present work. The short-hand notes, of which even the pages were not numbered, have supplied the material for the penultimate book, which has had to be a compilation of my own. Generally Raven seems to have scribbled down his impressions of the dream book as soon as he could, before the memory faded, and as he intended to recopy it all himself he had no consideration for any prospective reader. This material was just for his own use. It is a mixture of very cursive (and inaccurate) shorthand and, for proper names and so forth, longhand. Punctuation is indicated by gaps, and often a single word stands for a whole sentence and even a paragraph. About a third of the shorthand stuff was already represented by longhand or typescript copy in the folders. That was my Rosetta Stone. If it were not for the indications conveyed by that I do not think it would have been possible to decipher any of the remainder. As it is, I found it impossible to make a flowing narrative, altogether of a piece with the opening and closing parts of this history. Some passages came out fairly clear and then would come confusion and obscurity. I have transcribed what I could and written up the intervals when transcription was hopeless. I think I have made a comprehensive story altogether of the course of events during the struggles and changes in world government that went on between 1980 and 2059, at which date the Air Dictatorship, properly so called, gave place to that world-wide Modern State which was still flourishing when the history was published. The reader will find large gaps, or rather he will find large abbreviations, in that portion, but none that leave the main lines of the history of world consolidation in doubt.

And now let me say a word or so more about the real value of this queer 'Outline of the Future'.

Certain minor considerations weigh against the idea that this history that follows is merely the imaginative dreaming of a brilliant publicist. I put them before the reader, but I will not press them. First of all this history has now received a certain amount of confirmation. The latest part of the MS. dates from September 20th 1930, and much of it is earlier. And yet it alludes explicitly to the death of Ivar Kreuger a year later, to the tragic kidnapping of the Lindbergh baby, which happened in the spring of 1932, to the Mollison world flights of the same year, to the American debt discussions in December 1932, to the Hitlerite régime in Germany, the Japanese invasion of China proper in 1933, the election of President Roosevelt II and the World Economic Conference in London. These anticipations in detail I find a little difficult to explain away. I do not think that they are of such a nature that they could have been foretold. They are not

24

events that were deducible from any preceding situation. How could Raven have known about them in 1930?

And another thing that troubles me much more than it will trouble the reader is the fact that there was no reason at all why Raven should have attempted a mystification upon me. There was no reason on earth or in heaven why he should have lied about the way in which this material came to him and he wrote it down.

If it were not for these considerations, I think I should be quite prepared to fall in with what will no doubt be the general opinion, that the writing of this History was deliberately chosen by Raven as an imaginative outlet. That it is indeed a work of fiction by a late member of the Geneva Secretariat with unusual opportunities for forming judgments upon the trend of things. Or, let us say, a conditional prophecy in the Hebrew manner produced in a quasi-inspired mood. The style in which it is written is recognisably Raven's style, and there are few of those differences in vocabulary and locutions that one might reasonably expect in our language a hundred and seventy-odd years from now. On the other hand, the attitude revealed is entirely inconsistent with Raven's fully conscious public utterances. The idiom of thought at least is not his, whatever the idiom of expression. Either his marginal vision transcended his waking convictions or we have here a clear case of suppressions making their way to the surface.

The centre of perspective in this history is as remote from Geneva as it can well be. It floats in a rarer and wider air than the tired atmosphere of that mountain-girdled lake. Its scope is extravagantly wider and uncompromising, and Geneva is above all a place for arrangements and bargaining. Officially Raven was a believer in and a supporter of the League of Nations. The writer of the history details the life and death of the League of Nations with unconcealed contempt and tells of its inglorious end. The attitude towards existing institutions and the leading personalities of to-day affects me as outrageous. My editorial pen has had some prolonged hesitations between what I consider to be my

25

duty to my author and my regard for one or two distinguished friends. The reader may well ask in dismay: 'Is this what posterity will think of them?'

Or alternatively: 'Is this what Raven really thought of the world?' One name alone among those who have been prominent in our time escapes to a certain extent the indictment of this history—the name of Nicolai Lenin. And this although this grim history presently reveals the arrest and relative failure of the creative impulse in Russia. An immense pity pervades this long record of the battle of reason with ignoble folly—there is no other book in the world so full of pity, unless it be Winwood Reade's *Martyrdom of Man*—but all the admiration is for obscure dispositions in ordinary minds and for the work and sacrifices of anonymous men and women. This is a history of unknown heroes Is that what history is going to be?

There are three possible views about this book. Either it may be a cold-blooded fabrication of Raven's, which he tried to cheat me into accepting as a sort of revelation—this I reject absolutely—or it is largely a product of his subconscious mind, a work of inspiration, as our fathers would have called it, which came up precisely as he said it came up, to his consciousness between sleeping and waking, perplexing him just as much as I am perplexed by its vividness and assurance. Or, thirdly, it is really what he believed it to be, a part of a universal history for students of the year A.D. 2106. I cannot decide between the two latter alternatives. But one thing is certain: the third choice, a real history from the perspective of that year, is the form in which it is presented. That is what it claims to be. That, I think, is the spirit in which it can be read most agreeably.

Accepting it then as a real history, it is still difficult to imagine the type of reader aimed at by the writer (or writers). It is elementary; it is explicit; but it is not written down to a quite young and unfurnished intelligence. It may be designed for use in what a Scottish educationist would call the 'college' stage. It seems to me to be addressed to a student much better trained in the elements of philosophy and biological science, graver, more alert and keener to learn, than the average youth of to-day. But it is often quite frankly instructive in its manner. Such a higher level of learner is only what is to be expected from the substance of the record. And there is much more attention given to operating forces and much less to mere events than would be the case in a contemporary students' history. (It is tantalising, for instance, to learn of a great London land-slide and fire in 1968 only in various passing allusions.) There are studies of typical personalities, but it is relatively very free from anecdotalism. It is much more scientific. There are gaps in this history, but they are not enigmatic gaps. I have made only the barest intimations where these gaps occur. The reader will notice ever and again little jumps of a dozen or a score of years or so.

I must admit that at first, while I was still under the impression that the whole thing was a speculative exercise, I was tempted to annotate Raven's text rather extensively. I wanted to take a hand in the game. In fact I did some months' work upon it. Until my notes were becoming more bulky than his history. But when I revised them I came to the conclusion that many of them were fussy obtrusions and very few of them likely to be really helpful to an intelligent and well-informed contemporary reader. The more attracted he was by the book, the more likely he was to make his observations for himself; the less he appreciated it, the less he was likely to appreciate a superincumbent mass of education. My notes might have proved as annoying as the pencillings one finds at times in public-library books to-day. If the history is merely a speculative history, even then they would have been impertinent; if there is anything more in it than speculation, then they would be a very grave impertinence indeed. In the end I scrapped the entire accumulation.

But I have had also to arrange these chapters in order, and that much intervention was unavoidable and must remain. I have had indeed to arrange and rearrange them after several trials, because they do not seem to have been read

27

and written down by Raven in their proper chronological sequence. I have smoothed out the transitions. Later on I hope to publish a special edition of Raven's notes exactly as he left them.

We begin here with what is evidently the opening of a fresh book in the history, though it was not actually the first paper in the folders handed to me. It reviews very conveniently the course of worldly events in recent years, and it does so in what is, to me, a novel and very persuasive way. It analyses the main factors of the Great War from a new angle. From that review the story of the 'Age of Frustration', in the opening years of which we are now living flows on in a fairly consecutive fashion. Apart from this introduction the period covered by the actual narrative is roughly from about A.D. 1929 to the end of the year 2105. The last recorded event is on New Year's day 2106; there is a passing mention of the levelling of the remaining 'skeletons' of the famous 'Skyscrapers' of Lower New York on that date. The printing and publication probably occurred early in the new year; occurred—or should I write 'will occur'?   H. G. W.

28

TO-DAY AND TO-MORROW: THE AGE OF FRUSTRATION DAWNS

TO-DAY AND TO-MORROW: THE AGE OF FRUSTRATION DAWNS

§ 1. *A Chronological Note*

In the nineteenth and twentieth centuries the story of mankind upon this planet undergoes a change of phase. It broadens out. It unifies. It ceases to be a tangle of more and more inter-related histories and it becomes plainly and consciously one history. There is a complete confluence of racial, social and political destinies. With that a vision of previously unsuspected possibilities opens to the human imagination. And that vision brings with it an immense readjustment of ideas.

The first phase of that readjustment is necessarily destructive. The conceptions of life and obligation that have served and satisfied even the most vigorous and intelligent personalities hitherto, conceptions that were naturally partial, sectarian and limited, begin to lose, decade by decade, their credibility and their directive force. They fade, they become attentuated. It is an age of increasing mental uneasiness, of forced beliefs, hypocrisy, cynicism, abandon and impatience. What has been hitherto a final and impenetrable background of conviction in the rightness of the methods of behaviour characteristic of the national or local culture of each individual becomes, as it were, a dissolving and ragged curtain. Behind it appear, vague and dim at first, and refracted and distorted by the slow dissolution of the traditional veils, the intimations of the type of behaviour necessary to that single world community in which we live today.

Until the Chronological Institute has completed its present

labour of revision and defined the cardinal dates in our social evolution, it is best to refer our account of the development of man's mind and will throughout this hectic period of human experience to the clumsy and irrelevant computation by centuries before and after the Christian Era that is still current. As we have explained more fully in a previous book [*Nothing of this is to be found in Raven's notes.*—ED.], we inherit this system of historical pigeon-holes from Christendom; that arbitrary chequerwork of hundred-year blocks was imposed upon the entire Mediterranean and Atlantic literatures for two thousand years, and it still distorts the views of history of all but the alertest minds. The young student needs to be constantly on his guard against its false divisions. As Peter Lightfoot has remarked, we talk of the 'eigtheenth century', and we think of fashions and customs and attitudes that are characeristic of a period extending from the Treaty of Westphalia in 1642 C.E. [Christian Era] to the Napoleonic collapse in 1815 C.E.; we talk of the 'nineteenth century', and the pictures and images evoked are those of the gas-lighting and steam-transport era, from after the distressful years of post-Napoleonic recovery to the immense shock of the World War in 1914 C.E. The phase 'twentieth century', again calls forth images of the aeroplane, the electrification of the world and so forth; but an aeroplane was an extremely rare object in the air until 1914 (the first got up in 1905), and the replacement of the last steam railway train and the last steamship was not completed until the nineteen-forties. It is a tiresome waste of energy to oblige each generation of young minds to learn first of all in any unmeaning pattern of centuries and then to correct that first crude arrangement, so that this long-needed revision of our chronology is one that will be very welcome to every teacher. Then from the very outset he or she will be able to block out the story of our race in significant masses.

The Chronological Institute is setting about its task with a helpful publicity, inviting discussion from every angle. It is proposing to divide up as much of the known history of our race as is amenable to annual reckoning into a series of eras of unequal length. Naturally the choice of these eras is the cause of some extremely lively and interesting interchanges; most of us have our own private estimates of the values of events, and many issues affecting the earlier civilised communities remain in a state of animated unsettlement. Our chronology is now fairly sure as to the year for most important events in the last 4,000 years, and, thanks largely to the minute and patient labours of the Selwyn–Cornford Committee for Alluvial Research, to the decade for another hundred centuries. So far as the last 3,000 years are concerned, little doubt remains now that the main dividing points to be adopted will be *first* the epoch of Alexander and the Hellenic conquests which will begin the phase of the great Helleno-Latin monetary imperialism in the Western World, the *Helleno-Latin Era.* This will commence at the crossing of the Hellespont by Alexander the Great and end either with the Battle of the Yarmuk (636 C.E.) or the surrender of Jerusalem to the Caliph Omar (638 C.E.). *Next* will come the epoch of Moslem and Mongol pressure on the West which opened the era of feudal Christendom vis-à-vis with feudal Islam: the *Era of Asiatic Predominance.* This ends with the Battle of Lepanto (1571 C.E.). Then *thirdly* there will follow the epoch of the Protestant and the Catholic (counter) Reformations, which inaugurated the era of the competing sovereign states with organised standing armies: the *Era of European Predominance,* or, as it may also be called, the *Era of National Sovereignty.* Finally comes the catastrophe of the World War of 1914, when the outward drive of the new economic methods the Atlantic civilisations had developed gave way under the internal stresses of European nationalism. That war, and its long-drawn sequelae, released the human mind to the potentialities and dangers of an imperfectly Europeanised world—a world which had unconsciously become one single interlocking system, while still obsessed by the Treaty of Westphalia and the idea of competing sovereign states. This mental shock and release marks the beginning of the *Era of the Modern State.* The opening phase of this latest era is this Age of Frustration with which we are now about to deal. That is the first age of the Era of the Modern State. A second age, but not a new era, began with the Declaration of Mégève which was accepted by the general common sense of mankind forty-seven years ago. This closed the Age of Frustration, which lasted therefore a little short of a century and a half.

The date upon the title-page for the first publication of this History is 2106 C.E. Before many editions have been exhausted that will be changed to Modern Era (M.E.) 192 or M.E. 189 or M.E. 187, according to whether our chronologists decide upon 1914, the date of the outbreak of the Great War, or 1917, the beginning of the social revolution in Russia, or 1919, the signing of the Treaty of Versailles, as the conclusive opening of the Age of Frustration and the conflict for world unity. The second date seems at present to be the more practicable one.

In 1914 C.E. the concept of an organised world order did not seem to be within the sphere of human possibility; in 1919 C.E. it was an active power in a steadily increasing proportion of human brains. The Modern State had been conceived. It was germinating. One system, the Soviet system in Russia, was already claiming to be a world system. To most of the generation which suffered it, the Great War seemed to be purely catastrophe and loss; to us who see those hideous years in perspective and in proportion to the general dullness and baseness of apprehension out of which that conflict arose, the destruction of life and substance, unprecedented as they were, has none of that overwhelming quality. We see it as a clumsy, involuntary release from outworn assumptions by their reduction to tragic absurdity, and as a practically unavoidable step therefore in the dialectic of human destiny.

§ 2. *How the Idea and Hope of the Modern State First Appeared*

The essential difference between the world before the Great War and the world after it lay in this, that before that storm of distress and disillusionment the clear recognition that a world-wide order and happiness, in spite of contemporary distresses, was within the reach of mankind was confined to a few exceptional persons, while after the catastrophe it had spread to an increasing multitude, it had become a desperate hope and desire, and at last a working conviction that made organised mass action possible.

Even those who apprehended this idea before the epoch of the Great War seem to have propounded it with what impresses us to-day as an almost inexplicable timidity and feebleness. Apart from the great star of Shelley, which shines the brighter as his successors dwindle in perspective, there is a flavour of unreality about all these pre-war assertions of a possible world order. In most of them the Victorian terror of 'extravangance' is dominant, and the writer simpers and laughs at his own suggestions in what was evidently supposed to be a very disarming manner. Hardly any of these prophets dared believe in their own reasoning. Maxwell Brown has recently disinterred a pamphlet, *The Great Analysis,* dated 1912, in which a shrewd and reasoned forecast of the primary structure of the *Modern State,* quite amazingly prescient for the time, was broached with the utmost timidity, without even an author's name. It was a scheme to revolutionise the world, and the writer would not put his name to it, he confesses, because it might make him ridiculous.*

* Here for once the editor knows better than the writer of the history. This pamphlet was written by William Archer, the dramatic

35

Maxwell Brown's entertaining *Modern State Prophets Before the Great War* is an exhaustive study of the psychological processes by which this idea, which is now the foundation of our contemporary life, gradually its opposite of combative patriotism and established itself as a practicable and necessary form of action for men of good-will a century and a half ago. He traces the idea almost to its germ; he shows that its early manifestations, so far from being pacific, were dreams of universal conquest. He tells of its age-long struggle with everyday usage and practical common sense. In the first of his huge supplementary volumes he gives thousands of quotations going back far beyond the beginnings of the Christian Era. All the monotheistic religions were, in spirit, World-State religions. He examines the Tower of Babel myth as the attempt of some primordial cosmopolitan, some seer before the dawn, to account for the divisions of mankind. (There is strong reason now for ascribing this story to Emesal Gudeka of Nippur, the early Sumerian fabulist.)

Maxwell Brown shows how the syncretic religious developments, due to the growth of the early empires and the official pooling of gods, led necessarily to monotheism. From at least the time of Buddha onward the sentiment of, if not the living faith in, human brotherhood always existed somewhere in the world. But its extension from a mere sentiment and a fluctuating sympathy for the stranger to the quality of a practicable enterprise was a very recent process indeed. The necessary conditions were not satisfied.

In the briefer studies of human innovations that preceded his more important contributions to human history Maxwell Brown has shown how for the past ten thousand years at least, since the Cro-Magnards stamped their leather robes and tents, the art of printing reappeared and disappeared again and again, never culminating in the printed

critic, and reprinted under it's author's name with a preface by Gilbert Murray in 1931. Apparently the book collectors of the years ahead are going to miss this book.—ED.

book and all its consequences, never obtaining a primary importance in human doings, until the fifteenth century (C.E.); he has assembled the evidence for man's repeated abortive essays in flying, from the fourth dynasty gliders recently found in Bedrashen, the shattered Yu-chow machine and the interesting wreckage, ornaments and human remains found last year in Mirabella Bay. (These last were first remarked in 2104 C.E. after an earthquake in the deep-sea photographs of the survey aeroplane *Crawford*, and they were subsequently sought and recovered by the divers of the submarine *Salvemini* belonging to the Naples Biological Station. They have now been identified by Professor Gullio Marinetti as the remains of the legendary glider of Daedalus and Icarus.) Maxwell Brown has also traced the perpetual discovery and rediscovery of America from the days of the Aalesund tablets and the early Chinese inscriptions in the caves near Bahia Coqui to the final establishment of uninterrupted communications across the Atlantic by the Western Europeans in the fifteenth century C.E. In all there are sixteen separate ineffectual discoveries of America either from the east or from the west now on record, and there may have been many others that left no trace behind them.

These earlier cases of human enterprise and inadequacy help us to understand the long struggle of the Age of Frustration and the difficulty our ancestors found in achieving what is now so obviously the only sane arrangement of human affairs upon this planet.

The fruitlessness of all these premature inventions is very easily explained. First in the case of the transatlantic passage; either the earlier navigators who got to America never got back, or, if they did get back, they were unable to find the necessary support and means to go again before they died, or they had had enough of hardship, or they perished in a second attempt. Their stories were distorted into fantastic legends and substantially disbelieved. It was, indeed, a quite futile adventure to get to America until the keeled sailing ship, the science of navigation and the

37

mariner's compass had been added to human resources.

Then again, in the matter of printing, it was only when the Chinese had developed the systematic manufacture of abundant cheap paper sheets in standard sizes that the printed book—and its consequent release of knowledge—became practically possible. Finally the delay in the attainment of flying was inevitable because before men could progress beyond precarious gliding it was necessary for metallurgy to reach a point at which the internal combustion engine could be made. Until then they could build nothing strong enough and light enough to battle with the eddies of the air.

In an exactly parallel manner, the conception of one single human community organised for collective service to the common weal had to wait until the rapid evolution of the means of communication could arrest and promise to defeat the disintegrative influence of geographical separation. That rapid evolution came at last in the nineteenth century, and it has been described already in a preceding chapter of this world history. [*Not recorded by Raven.*— ED.] Steam power, oil power, electric power, the railway, the steamship, the aeroplane, transmission by wire and aerial transmission followed each other very rapidly. They knit together the human species as it had never been knit before. Insensibly, in less than a century, the utterly impracticable became not merely a possible adjustment but an urgently necessary adjustment if civilisation was to continue.

Now the cardinal prominence of the Great War in history lies in this, that it demonstrated the necessity of that adjustment. It was never considered to be necessary before. Recognition lagged behind accomplishment. None of the pre-war World-State Prophets betrays any sense of necessity. They make their polite and timid gestures towards human unity as something nice and desirable indeed but anything but imperative. The clearest demand for world-wide cooperation before the war came from the Second International. And even after the war, and after the vague and vacillating adumbration of a federal super-state by the

38

League of Nations at Geneva, most of even the most advanced writers seem to have been still under the impression that the utmost adjustment needed was some patching up of the current system so as to prevent or mitigate war and restrain the insurrectionary urge of the unprosperous.

Even the Communist movement, which, as we had told already, had been able by a conspiracy of accidents to seize upon Russia and demonstrate the value of its theories there, lapsed from, rather than advanced towards, cosmopolitan socialism. Its theories, as we have shown, were hopelessly inadequate for its practical needs. The development of its ideology was greatly hampered by the conservative dogmatism imposed upon it by the incurable egotism of Marx. His intolerance, his innate bad manners, his vain insistence that he had produced a final doctrine to put beside Darwinism, cast a long shadow of impatience and obduracy upon the subsequent development of Communism. He was bitterly jealous of the Utopian school of socialism, and so, until Lenin faced the urgencies of power, the 'orthodox' Marxist took a quite idiotic pride in a planless outlook. 'Overthrow capitalism,' he said, and what could happen but millennial bliss? Communism insisted indeed upon the necessity of economic socialisation, but—until it attained power in Russia—without a glance at its technical difficulties. It produced its belated and ill-proportioned Five Year Plan only in 1928 C.E., eleven years after its accession to power. Until then it had no comprehensive working scheme whatever for the realisation of socialism. Thrown back on experiment, it was forced to such desperately urgent manoeuvres, improvisations and changes in front, and defended by such tawdry and transparent apologetics, that the general world movement passed out of its ken.

The reader of this world history knows already how the moral and intellectual force of the Communist Party proved unequal, after the death of Lenin, to control or resist the dictatorship of that forcible, worthy, devoted and limited man, the Georgian, Stalin. The premature death of the creative and adaptable Lenin and the impatient suppression by

39

Stalin of such intelligent, troublesome, but necessary types as Trotsky—a man who, but for lack of tact and essential dignity, might well have been Lenin's successor—crippled whatever hope there may have been that the Modern State would first emerge in Russia. Terrible are the faithful disciples of creative men. Lenin relaxed and reversed the dogmatism of Marx, Stalin made what he imagined to be Leninism into a new and stiffer dogmatism. Thereafter the political doctrinaire dominated and crippled the technician in a struggle that cried aloud for technical competence. Just as theological disputes impoverished and devastated Europe through the long centuries of Christendom, and reduced the benefits of its unifying influence to zero, so in Russia efficiency of organisation was prevented by the pendantries of political theorists. The young were trained to a conceit and a xenophobia, indistinguishable in its practical effects from the gross patriotism of such countries as France, Germany, Italy or Scotland.

Because of this subordination of its mental development to politics, Russia passed into a political and social phase comparable, as Rostovtzeff pointed out at the time in his *Social and Economic History of the Roman Empire*, in its universal impoverishment and its lack of any critical vigour to the well-meaning but devitalising autocracy of the Emperor Diocletian. From its very start the Russian revolution failed in its ambition to lead mankind. Its cosmopolitanism lasted hardly longer than the cosmopolitanism of the great French revolution a dozen decades earlier.

This almost inevitable lag of the constructive movement in Russia behind Western developments was foreseen by the shrewd and penetrating brain of Lenin even in the phase of its apparent leadership (*see* No. 3090 in the thirteenth series of the Historical Documents Collection, *Left Wing Communism*). But his observation found little or no echo in the incurably illiberal thought of the Marxian tradition.

It was in Western Europe especially that the conception of the organised and disciplined World-State as a revolutionary objective ultimately grew to its full proportions. At first it grew obscurely. In 1933 any observer might have been misled by the fact of the Fascist régime in Italy, by the tumult of the Nazi party in Germany, by similar national-socialist movements in other countries, and by the increase in tariff barriers and other restraints upon trade everywhere, to conclude that the cosmopolitan idea was everywhere in retreat before the obsessions of race, creed and nationalism. Yet all the while the germs of the Modern State were growing, everywhere its votaries were learning and assembling force.

It needed the financial storm of the years 1928 and 1929 C.E. and the steadily progressive collapse of the whole world's economic life, of which this storm was the prelude, to give the World-State prophets the courage of their convictions. Then indeed they began to speak out. Instead of the restrained, partial and inconclusive criticism of public affairs which had hitherto contented them, they now insisted plainly upon the need of a world-wide reconstruction, that is to say a world revolution—though 'revolution' was still a word they shirked. The way in which this increased definition of aim and will came about is characteristic of the changing quality of social life. It was not that one or two outstanding men suddenly became audible and conspicuous as leaders in this awakening. There were no leaders. It was a widespread movement in human thought.

In a second huge supplementary volume Maxwell Brown has assembled the substance of a precise study of fifty typical writers and speakers in Europe and America, and he gives a list of nearly two thousand who yield parallel results which remain filed for reference in the Encyclopaedia Library. In each case, guarded, limited and tentative suggestions give place to more and more outspoken and lucid statements of the world situation. For ten years from 1917 onward these typical people are saying mildly what might be done; then suddenly they begin to say more and more plainly what had to be done. It was a general movement of opinion affecting all the more intelligent people in the world. Whatever interchange of ideas occurred is now untraceable.

The development was too rapid to establish priorities. Opinion appears now to have moved in line abreast.

The conclusions upon which all these intelligent people were converging may be briefly stated. They had arrived at the realisation that human society had become one indivisible economic system with novel and enormous potentialities of well-being. By 1931 C.E. this conception becomes visible even in the obstinately intellectualist mind of France —for example, in the parting speech to America of an obscure and transitory French Prime Minister, Laval, who crossed the Atlantic on some now undiscoverable mission in that year; and we find it promtply echoed by such prominent loud speakers as President Hoover of America and Mr. Ramsay MacDonald, the British Prime Minister.

That idea at any rate had already become sufficiently popular for the politicians to render it lip service. But it was still only the intelligent minority who went on to the logical consequences of its realisation; that is to say, the necessity of disavowing the sovereignty of contemporary governments, of setting up authoritive central controls to supplement or supersede them, and of putting the production of armaments, the production of the main economic staples, and the protection of workers from destructive under-payment beyond the reach of profit-seeking manipulation.

Yet by 1932–33 this understanding minority was speaking very plainly. These immense changes were no longer being presented as merely desirable things; they were presented as urgently necessary things if civilisation was to be saved from an immense catastrophe. And not merely saved. The alternative to disaster, they saw even then, was not just a bleak and terrified security. That was the last thing possible. There was no alternative to disorder and wretchedness, but 'such an abundance, such a prosperity and richness of opportunity', as man had never known before. (These words are quoted from a Scottish newspaper of the year 1929.) Enlightened people in 1932 C.E. were as assured of the possibility of world order, universal sufficiency and ever-increasing human vitality as are we who live to-day in ample possession of our lives amidst the practical realisation of that possibility.

Clearness of vision did not make for the happiness of the enlightened. Their minds were tormented not simply by contemporary fears and miseries, but by the sure knowledge of a possible world of free activity within the reach of man and, as it were, magically withheld. They saw hundreds of millions of lives cramped and crippled, meagerly lived, sacrificed untimely, and they could not see any primary necessity for this blighting and starvation of human life. They saw youthful millions drifting to lives of violence, mutilation and premature and hideous deaths. And beyond was our security, our eventfulness and our freedom.

Maxwell Brown, in a chapter called 'Tantalus 1932', cites forty instances of these realisations. But the lengendary Tantalus was put within apparent reach of the unattainable by the inexorable decrees of the gods. Mankind was under no such pitiless destiny. The world-wide Modern State shone bright upon the living imaginations of our race within a decade of the Great War, absurdly near, fantastically out of reach. For a century of passionate confusion and disorder that Modern State was not to be released from potentiality into actuality.

It is to the story of these battling, lost and suffering generations, the 'generations of the half-light', that we must now proceed.

For the first time in history the mind of man was really attempting to control his destiny, Hitherto usage, tradition, external necessity, accident, had furnished the unchallenged framework within which he had devised his explanations and his consolations. He had resisted any clear knowledge of his own nature and romanced about his destiny. He had evaded responsibility for his stresses and disasters by putting his faith in over-ruling gods; he had clung to arbitrary rules of conduct against all reason, and he had persecuted and sought to destroy every sceptical thinker, every heretical experimentalist in conduct, who disturbed the equanimity of his submission. He preferred familiar miseries to the mental torture of novel effort. Now through a complex of enlightening accidents, and especially through the jumbling together of a hundred different and discordant cultures in one world-wide mutuality of discredit and destruction, the vision of reality was forcing itself upon him. And with an ever-widening sweep of change even his mean submissiveness gave him no sense of security any more. Effort was before him and the goad behind. He was compelled to ask in spite of himself what indeed he was, and with that, in spite of his deep conservatism, he began to realise all that he might be.

When now we look back to the scattered and diverse individuals who first give expression to this idea of the modern World-State which was dawning upon the human intelligence, when we appraise their first general efforts towards its realisation, we need, before we can do them anything like justice, to attempt some measure of the ignorances, prejudices and other inertias, the habits of concession and association, the herd love and the herd fear, with which they had to struggle not only in the society in which they found themselves, but within themselves. It is not a conflict of light and darkness we have to describe; it is the struggle of the purblind among the blind. We have to realise that for all that they were haunted by a vision of the civilised world of to-day, they still belonged not to our age but to their own. The thing imagined in their minds was something quite distinct from their present reality. Maxwell Brown has devoted several chapters, and a third great supplementary volume, to a special selection of early Modern State Prophets who followed public careers. He showed conclusively that in the third and fourth decades of the twentieth century (C.E.) there was a rapidly increasing number of men and women with a clear general conception of the possibilities of the modern world. He gives their written and spoken words, often astoundingly prescient and explicit. And then he traces out the tenor of their lives subsequent to these utterances. The discrepancy of belief and effort is a useful and indeed a startling reminder of the conditioned nature of the individual life.

As he writes: 'In the security and serenity of the study, these men and women could see plainly. In those hours of withdrawal, the fragile delicate brain matter could escape from immediacy, apprehend causation in four dimensions, reach forward to the permanent values of social events in the spacetime framework. But even to the study there penetrated the rumble of the outer disorder. And directly the door was opened, forthwith the uproar of contemporary existence, the carnival, the riot, the war and the market, beat in triumphantly. The raging question of what had to bo done that day scattered the fine thought of our common destiny to the four winds of heaven.'

Maxwell Brown adds a vivid illustration to this passage. It it the facsimile of the first draft by Peter Raut, the American progressive leader, of the Revolutionary Manifesto of 1937. It was indisputably a very inspiring document in its time, and Raut gave the last proof of loyalty to the best in his mind by a courageous martyrdom. But in the margin of this draft one's attention is caught by a maze of little figures; little sums in multiplication and addition. By his almost inspired gift for evidence and through the industry of his group of research assistants, Maxwell Brown has been able to demonstrate exactly what these sums were. They show that even while Raut, so far as his foresight permitted, was planning our new world, his thoughts were not wholly fixed on that end. They wandered. For a time the manifesto was neglected while he did these sums. He was gambling in industrial equities, and a large and active portion of his brain was considering whether the time had arrived to sell.

A more illuminating instance of what social psychologists have called the 'divided mind' of the intellectuals in the twentieth century of the Christian Era could scarcely be imagined. In the middle years of the nineteenth century there was a primitive form of entertainment in Western Europe and America called 'Dissolving Views'. Crudely coloured pictures were thrown on a screen by a double-barrelled arrangement of lenses called a 'Magic Lantern'. A picture would be projected first by the right-hand lens of the contraption and then the light would be shifted to the left-hand side, so that the picture cast by one half of the apparatus faded as the other became brighter. The real became a phantom and vanished and the faint intimations of its successor became at length the only reality visible. Apparently this is where our ancestors found the 'magic' effect. At a certain phase it must have been hard to determine which details were advancing and which were receding realities, or of any part of the ensemble whether it was real. It was very much after the fashion of this artless Victorian wonder-toy that faith in established institutions and usages faded and the idea of the Modern State dawned upon the intelligence of mankind.

§ 3. *The Accumulating Disproportions of the Old Order*

But this analogy of the Age of Frustration to the old-fashioned Dissolving View must not be carried too far. The Modern State was indeed becoming conscious of itself and consciously endeavouring to realise itself, but the sixty-odd sovereign states which divided the world among themselves were by no means disposed to dissolve away in its favour. It was not a case of one thing always growing stronger and another always growing weaker. In the opening decade of the twentieth century there did indeed seem to be some intimations of such a pacific orderly supersession; there were many things that could be interpreted as the gradual establishment of a world community amidst the formal patchwork of governments and cultures. But they were superficial and secondary in relation to the preoccupations that were presently to resist and reverse them.

Let us consider some of the main appearances that disposed many minds to expect a world community in those days. In the first place a very considerable financial unity had been achieved. The credit of the City of London ran to the ends of the earth, and the gold sovereign was for all practical purposes a world coin, exchangeable locally for local expenditure within relatively slight fluctuations. Economic life was becoming very generalised. Over great areas trade moved with but small impediments, and the British still hoped to see their cosmopolitan conception of Free Trade accepted by the whole world. The International Institute of Agriculture in Rome was developing an annual census of staple production and reaching out towards a world control of commodity transport. Considerable movements and readjustments of population were going on, unimpeded by any government interference. Swarms of Russian Poles, for instance, drifted into Eastern Germany for the harvest work and returned; hundreds of thousands of Italians went to work in the United States for a few years and then came back with their earnings to their native villages. An ordinary traveller might go all over the more settled parts of the earth and never be asked for a passport unless he wanted to obtain a registered letter at a post office or otherwise prove his identity.

A number of minor but significant federal services had also come into existence and had a sound legal standing throughout the world, the Postal Union for example. Before 1914 c.e. a written document was delivered into the hands of the addressee at almost every point upon the planet, almost as surely as, if less swiftly than, it is to-day. (The Historical Documents Board has recently reprinted a small book, *International Government*, prepared for the little old Fabian Society during the Great War period by L. S. Woolf, which gives a summary of such arrangements. He lists twenty-three important world unions dealing at that time with trade, industry, finance, communications, health, science, art, literature, drugs, brothels, criminals, emigration and immigration and minor political affairs.) These world-wide co-operations seemed—more particularly to the English-speaking peoples—to presage a direct and compara-tively smooth transition from the political patchwork of the nineteenth century, as the divisions of the patchwork grew insensibly fainter, to a stable confederation of mankind. The idea of a coming World-State was quite familiar at the time —one finds it, for instance, as early as Lord Tennyson's *Locksley Hall* (published in 1842); but there was no effort whatever to achieve it, and indeed no sense of the need of such effort. The World-State was expected to come about automatically by the inherent forces in things.

That belief in some underlying benevolence in uncon-trolled events was a common error, one might almost say *the* common error, of the time. It affected every school of thought. In exactly the same fashion the followers of Marx (before the invigorating advent of Lenin and the Bolshevist reconstruction of Communism) regarded their dream of World Communism as inevitable, and the disciples of Her-bert Spencer found a benevolent Providence in 'free com-petition'. 'Trust Evolution,' said the extreme Socialist and the extreme Individualist, as piously as the Christians put their trust in God. It was the Bolshevik movement in the twentieth century which put will into Communism. The thought of the nineteenth-century revolutionary and re-actionary alike was saturated with that confident irrespons-ible laziness. As Professor K. Chandra Sen has remarked, hope in the Victorian period was not a stimulant but an opiate.

We who live in a disciplined order, the chastened victors of a hard-fought battle, understand how superficial and unsubstantial were all those hopeful appearances. The great processes of mechanical invention, which have been described in our general account of the release of experi-mental science from deductive intellectualism, were increas-ing the power and range of every operating material force quite irrespective of its fitness or unfitness for the new occasions of mankind. With an equal impartiality they were bringing world-wide understanding and world-wide massacre into the range of human possibility.

It was through no fault of these inventors and investigators that the new opportunities they created were misused. That was outside their range. They had as yet no common culture of their own. Nor, since each worked in his own field, were they responsible for the fragmentary irregularity of their discoveries. Biological and especially social invention were lagging far behind the practical advances of the exacter, simpler sciences. Their application was more difficult; the matters they affected were so much more deeply embedded in ordinary use and wont, variation was more intimate, novelties could not be inserted with the same freedom. It was easy to supplant the coach and horses on the macadamised road by the steam-engine or the railway, because it was not necessary to do anything to the road or the coach and horses to bring about the change. They were just left alone to run themselves out as the railroad (and later the automobile on the rubber-glass track) superseded them. But men cannot set up new social institutions, new social and political and industrial relationships, side by side with the old in that fashion. It must be an altogether tougher and slower job. It is a question not of ousting but of reconstruction. The old must be converted into the new without ceasing for a moment to be a going concern. The overrunning of the biologically old by the mechanically new, due to these differences in timing, was inevitable, and it reached its maximum in the twentieth century.

A pathological analogy may be useful here. In the past, before the correlation of development in living organisms began to be studied, people used to suffer helplessly and often very dreadfully from all sorts of irregularities of growth in their bodies. The medical services of the time, such as they were, were quite unable to control them. One of these, due to what is called the Nurmi ratios in the blood, was a great overproduction of bone, either locally or generally. The sufferer gradually underwent distortion into a clumsy caricature of his former self; his features became course and massive, his skull bones underwent a monstrous expansion; the proportions of his limbs altered, and the leverage of his muscles went askew. He was made to look grotesque; he was crippled and at last killed. Something strictly parallel happened to human society in the hundred years before the Great War. Under the stimulus of mechanical invention and experimental physics it achieved, to pursue our metaphor, a hypertrophy of bone, muscle and stomach, without any corresponding enlargement of its nervous controls.

Long before the Great War this progressive disproportion had been dimly recognised by many observers. The favourite formula was to declare that 'spiritual'—for the naïve primordial opposition of spirit and matter was still accepted in those days—had not kept pace with 'material' advances. This was usually said with an air of moral superiority to the world at large. Mostly there was a vague implication that if these other people would only refrain from using modern inventions so briskly, or go to church more, or marry earlier and artlessly, or read a more 'spiritual' type of literature, or refrain from mixed bathing, or work harder and accept lower wages, or be more respectful and obedient to constituted authority, all might yet be well. Beyond this sort of thing there was little recognition of the great and increasing disharmonies of the social corpus until after the Great War.

The young reader will ask, 'But where was the Central Observation Bureau? Where was the professorial and student body which should have been recording these irregularities and producing plans for adjustment?'

There was no Central Observation Bureau. That did not exist for another century. That complex organisation of discussion, calculation, criticism and forecast was undreamt of. Those cities of thought, full of serene activities, came into existence only after the organisation of the Record and Library Network under the Air Dictatorship between 2010 and 2030. Even the mother thought-city the World Encyclopaedia Establishment, was not founded until 2012. In the early twentieth century there was still no adequate estimate of economic forces and their social reactions. There were only a few score professors and amateurs of these fundamentally important studies scattered throughout the earth. They were scattered in every sense; even their communications were unsystematic. They had no powers of enquiry, no adequate statistics, little prestige; few people heeded what they thought or said.

Maybe they deserved nothing better. They bickered stupidly with and discredited each other. They ignored or wilfully misunderstood each other. It is impossible to read such social and economic literature as the period produced without realising the extraordinary backwardness of that side of the world's intellectual life. It is difficult to believe nowadays that the writers of these publications, at once tediously copious and incredibly jejune, were living at the same time as the lively multitude of workers in the experimental sciences who were daily adding to and reshaping knowledge to achieve fresh practical triumphs. From 1812 C.E., when public gas-lighting was first organised, to the outbreak of the Great War, while the world was being made over anew by gas, by steam, by oil and then by the swift headlong development of electrical science, while the last *terrae incognitae* were being explored and mapped, while a multitude of hitherto-unthought-of elements and compounds and hundreds of thousands of new substances were coming into use, while epidemic diseases were being restrained and driven back, while the death rate was being halved, and the average duration of life increased by a score of years, the social and political sciences remained practically stagnant and unserviceable. Throughout that century of material achievement there is no single instance of the successful application of a social, economic or educational generalisation.

Even the attempt to bring social institutions within the range of genuine scientific enquiry did not begin until after the Great War. It is on record that a chair of 'Social Biology' was set up in the London School of Economics and

51

political science in 1930, and there are some allusions to a chair of Social Psychology in the same college. But here our sources are obscure. In the great London landslip of 1968, due to the weight of new buildings piled up on the northern slope, when the bed of the Thames buckled up and the Second Fire of London ensued, a vast mass of material perished, including the irreplaceable treasures of the British Museum, and among other grave, if lesser, losses were all the records of this interesting institution in Clare Market. But certainly that chair of Social Biology was the first of its kind in the European world.

Because of this belatedness of the social sciences, the progressive dislocation of the refined if socially limited and precarious civilisation of the more advanced of the eighteenth- and nineteenth-century sovereign states went on without any effectual contemporary understanding of what was straining it to pieces. The Europeans and the Americans of the early twentieth century apprehended the social and political forces that ravaged their lives hardly more clearly than the citizens of the Roman Empire during its collapse. Plenty and the appearance of security *happened*; then débâcle *happened*. There was no analysis of operating causes. For years even quite bold and advanced thinkers were chased by events. They did not grasp what was occurring at the time. They only realised what had really occurred long afterwards. And so they never foresaw. There was no foresight, and therefore still less could there by any understanding control.

§ 4. *Early Attempts to Understand and Deal with these Disproportions: The Criticisms of Karl Marx and Henry George*

There are, however, one or two exceptions to this general absence of diagnosis in the affairs of the nineteenth and twentieth century of the Christian Era which even the student of general history cannot ignore. Prominent among them is the analysis and forecasts of economic development made by Karl Marx and his associates.

In any case Marxism would have demanded our attention as a curious contemporary realisation of the self-destroying elements in the business methods of the nineteenth century; but its accidental selection as the ostensible creed of revolutionary Russia after the Tsarist collapse gives it an almost primary importance in the history of kinetic ideas.

Karl Marx (1818–83) was the son of a christianised Jewish lawyer of Treves, of considerable social pretensions; he had an excellent university career at Bonn and Berlin, assimilated the radical thought of his time and became the lifelong friend of the far more modest and gifted Friedrich Engels (1820–95), a Lancashire calico-dealer. Under the inspiration of Engels and the English socialist movement of Robert Owen, Marx elaborated the theory of economic development which is the substance of Marxism. It is embodied in a huge unfinished work, *Das Kapital*, and summarised in a *Communist Manifesto* (1848) drawn up by Engels and himself. (These, and indeed all his writings, together with an able digest and summary, are to be found in the *Library of Historical Thought*, vols. 17,252–59.) His chief merit lies in his clear recognition of the ultimate dependence of social and political forms and reactions upon physical necessity ('the Materialist Conception of History'). His chief fault was his insane hatred of the middle

53

classes (bourgeoisie), due mainly to his pose as a needy aristocrat and embittered, it may be, by his material and intellectual dependence on the trader Engels. His own attempts to apply his theories by conspiracy and political action were inept and futile. He died in London a disappointed and resentful man, quite unaware of the posthumous fame that awaited his doctrines. It was the organisation of his followers into the disciplined Communist Party and the modernisation of his doctrines by the genius of Lenin that made his name a cardinal one in history.

It is interesting to consider his general propositions now in the light of accomplished events and note the hits and misses of those heroic speculations—heroic, that is to say, measured by the mental courage of the time.

Nowadays every schoolboy knows that the essential and permanent conflict in life is a conflict between the past and the future, between the accomplished past and the forward effort. He is made to realise this conflict in his primary biological course. Therein he comes to see and in part to understand the continual automatic struggle of the thing achieved, to hold the new, the new-born individual, the new-born idea, the widening needs of the species, in thrall. This conflict, he is shown, runs through all history. In the old classical mythology Saturn, the Conservative head-god, devoured all his children until at last one escaped to become Jove. And of how Jove bound Prometheus in his turn every lover of Shelley can tell. We need only refer the student to the recorded struggles in the histories of Republican Rome and Judaea between debtor and creditor; to the plebeian Secessions of the former and the year of Jubilee of the latter; to the legend of Joseph in Egypt (so richly interpreted now through the minute study of contemporary Egyptian documents by the students of the Breasted Commemoration Fund); to the English Statute of Mortmain; to Austen Liverwright's lucid study of *Bankruptcy Through the Ages* (1979), to remind of this perennial struggle of life against the creditor and the dead hand. But Marx, like most of his contemporaries, was profoundly ignorant of historical science, and addicted to a queer 'dialectic' devised by the pseudo-philosopher Hegel; his ill-equipped mind apprehended this perennial antagonism only in terms of the finance of the industrial production about him; the entrepreneur, the capitalist, became the villain of his piece, using the prior advantage of his capital to appropriate the 'surplus value' of production, so that his share of purchasing power became more and more disproportionately great.

Marx seems never to have distinguished clearly between restrictive and productive possessions, which nowadays we recognise as a difference of fundamental importance. Exploitation for profit and strangulation for dominance, the radical son and the conservative father, were all one to him. And his proposals for expropriating the profit-seeking 'Capitalist' were of the vaguest; he betrayed no conception whatever of the real psychology of economic activities, and he had no sense of the intricate organisation of motives needed if the coarse incentive of profit was to be superseded. Indeed, he had no practical capacity at all, and one is not surprised to learn that for his own part he never earned a living. He claimed all the privileges of a prophet and all the laxity and indolence of a genius, and he never even completed his great book.

It was the far abler and finer-minded Lenin (1870–1924, in power in Russia after 1917), rather than Marx, who gave a practical organisation to the revolutionary forces of Communism and made the Communist Party for a time, until Stalin overtook it, the most vital creative force in the world. The essential intellectual difference between these two men is explained very clearly by Max Eastman (1895–1980), whose compact and scholarly *Marx and Lenin* is still quite readable by the contemporary student. In his time Lenin had to pose as the disciple and exponent of Marx; it was only later that criticism revealed the subtle brilliance of his effort to wrest a practical common sense out of the time-worn doctrines of the older prophet.

Another nineteenth-century writer, with perhaps a clearer

realisation of the strangulating effect of restrictive property as distinguished from the stimulating effect of exploitation, was Henry George (1839–97), an American printer who rose to great popularity as a writer upon economic questions. He saw the life of mankind limited and dwarfed by the continual rise in rents. His naïve remedy was to tax the landowner, as Marx's naïve remedy was to expropriate the capitalist, and just as Marx never gave his disciples the ghost of an idea for a competent administration of the expropriated economic plant and resources of the world, so Henry George never indicated how, in the world of implacable individualism he advocated, the taxing authority was to find a use for its ever-increasing tax receipts.

We can smile to-day at the limitations of these early pioneers. But we smile only because we live later than they did, and are two centuries and more to the good in our experience. We owe them enormous gratitude for the valiant disinterestedness of their life work.

Our debt is on the whole rather for what they got rid of than for what they did. The broad outlines of the world's economic life are fairly simple as we see them frankly exposed to-day, but these men were born into an atmosphere of uncriticised usage, secrecy, time-honoured misconceptions, fetishisms, working fictions—which often worked very badly—and almost insane suppressions of thought and statement. The very terms they were obliged to use were question-begging terms; the habitual assumptions of the world they addressed were crooked and only to be apprehended with obliquity and inconsistency. They were forcing their minds towards the expression of reality through an intricate mental and moral tangle. They destroyed the current assumption of permanence in established institutions and usages, and, though that seems a small thing to us now, it was a profoundly important release at the time. The infantile habit of assuming the fixity of the Thing that Is was almost universal in their day.

The Marxist doctrines did at least indicate that a term was necessarily set to economic development through profit-seeking, by the concentration of controlling ownership, by the progressive relative impoverishment of larger and larger sections of the world population and by the consequent final dwindling of markets. The rapid coagulation of human activities after 1928 c.e. was widely recognised as a confirmation of the Marxian forecast and, by one of those rapid mental leaps charactistic of the time, as a complete endorsement of the Communist pretension to have solved the social problem.

Unembarrassed as we are now by the mental clutter of our forefathers, the fundamental processes at work during the distressful years of the third and fourth decades of the century appear fairly simple. We know that it is a permanent condition of human well-being that the general level of prices should never fall, and we have in the Currency Council a fairly efficient and steadily improving world-organ to ensure that end. A dollar, as we know it to-day, means practically the same things in goods, necessities and satisfactions from one year's end to another. Its diminution in value is infinitesimal. No increase is ever allowed to occur. For the owner of an unspent dollar there is neither unearnt increment nor unmerited loss. As the productive energy of our species rises, the dollar value of the total wealth is arranged to increase steadily in proportion, and neither is the creditor enriched nor robbed of his substantial expectation nor the debtor confronted with payments beyond his powers.

There remains no way now of becoming passively wealthy. Gambling was ruthlessly eradicated under the Air Dictatorship and has never returned. Usury ranks with forgery as a monetary offence. Money is given to people to get what they want and not as a basis for further acquisition, and we realise that the gambling spirit is a problem for the educationist and mental expert. It implies a fundamental misunderstanding of life. We have neither speculators, shareholders, private usurers or rent lords. All these 'independent' types have vanished from the earth. Land and its natural resources are now owned and administered,

57

either directly or by delegation, by a hierarchy of administrative boards representing our whole species; there are lease-holding cultivators and exploiting corporations with no right to sublet, but there is no such thing as a permanent private ownership of natural resources making an automatic profit by the increment of rent. And since there is, and probably always will be now, a continual advance in our average individual productive efficiency by which the whole community profits, there follows a continual extension of our collective enterprise, a progressive release of leisure, and secular raising of the standard of individual life to compensate for what would otherwise be a progressive diminution in the number of brains and hands needed to carry on the work of the world. Human society, so long as productive efficiency increases, is *obliged* to raise its standards of consumption and extend its activities year by year, or collapse. And if its advance does not go on it will drop into routine, boredom, viciousness and decay. Steadfastly the quantity and variety of things *must* increase.

These imperative conditions, which constitute the ABC of the existing order, seem so obvious to-day that it is with difficulty we put ourselves in the place of these twentieth-century folk to whom they were strange and novel. They were not yet humanised *en masse*; they still had the mentality of the 'struggle for existence'. It is only by a considerable mental effort, and after a careful study of the gradual evolution of the civilised mentality out of the chaotic impulses and competition of an originally very unsocial animal, that we can even begin to see matters with the eyes of our predecessors of a century and a half ago.

§ 5. *The Way in Which Competition and Monetary Inefficiency Strained the Old Order*

In the twentieth century of the Christian era there was still no common currency by which to measure and carry on the world's economic exchanges. Those transactions were not merely apprehended inexactly because of this; they were falsified, and it did not seem possible that there would ever be an effective simplification. It is true that during what is known as the First Period of General Prosperity, from 1850 C.E. until 1914, there was a kind of working world-system of currency and credit, centring upon the City of London and based on the gold pound; but this was a purely accidental growth, made workable by successive gold discoveries which prevented too disastrous a fall in prices as productive efficiency increased, and by the circumstances that gave the insular English a lead in the development of steam transport on land and sea and real incentives towards a practical propaganda of world free trade.

That first gleam of cosmopolitan sunlight waned as it had waxed, without any contemporary apprehension of the real forces at work, much less any attempt to seize upon them and organise them in permanence. The financial ascendancy and initiative of the City of London crumbled away after the war and nothing appeared to take its place. In any case, this quasicosmopolitan system based on the gold sovereign, and owing its modicum of success to continual increments in the available gold, would have wilted as the world's gold supplies gave out, but the strangulation of the world's industry after the war was greatly accelerated by the gold hoarding of the Americans and French.

And during all that phase of opportunity there was no substantial effort to take hold of the land, sea and natural resources of the planet and bring them from a state of fragmentary, chaotic and wasteful exploitation into a general scheme. There remained sixty-odd 'sovereign' governments, each claiming a supreme control of all the natural wealth of the areas within its frontiers, and under these governments, under conditions that varied with each, there were private corporations and individuals with a right to deal more or less freely with the fragment upon which they had established a grip. Everywhere the guiding principle in the exploitation of the minerals, sunshine and power resources of the globe was the profit of single or associated private individuals, and the patchwork governments of the time interfered in the profit scramble only in favour of their nationals against their foreign rivals. Yet for nearly a hundred years, because of the fortunate influx of gold and inventions, this profit-seeking system, linked to the metallic monetary system, sufficed to sustain a very great expansion and enlargement of human life, and it was hard to convince the mass of men, and still harder to convince the prosperous manufacturers, traders, miners, cultivators and financiers who dominated public affairs, that this was not a permanent system and that the world already needed very essential modifications of its economic methods. A considerable measure of breakdown, a phase of dismay, fear and distress, was necessary before they could be disillusioned.

The nineteenth century had for its watchwords 'individual enterprise and free competition'. But the natural end of all competition is the triumph of one competitor. It was in America that the phenomena of Big Business first appeared and demonstrated the force of this truism; at a score of points triumphant organisations capable of crushing out new competitors and crippling and restraining new initiatives that threatened their predominance appeared. In Europe there was little governmental resistance to industrial alliances and concentrations in restraint of competition, and they speedily developed upon a scale that transcended political frontiers, but in the United States of America there was a genuine effort to prevent enterprises developing on a monopolistic scale. The conspicuous leader of this preventive effort was the first President Roosevelt (1858–1919) and its chief fruit the Sherman Anti-Trust Act (1890), which proved a rich mine for lawyers in the subsequent decades.

These great consolidations, which closed the phase of free competition, were so far effective in controlling trade and arresting new developments that Hilary Hooker, in his *Studies in Business Coagulation During the First Period of General Prosperity*, is able to cite rather more than two thousand instances, ranging from radium and new fruits and foodstuffs to gramophones, automobiles, reconstructed households, artificial moonlight for the roadways by the countryside, and comfortable and economical railway plant, in which ample supplies or beneficial improvements were successfully kept off the market in the interests of established profit-making systems. After 1900 C.E. again there was a world-wide cessation of daily newspaper initiative and a consequent systole of free speech. Distribution, paper supply and news services had fallen into the hands of powerful groups able and willing to crush out any new types of periodical, or any inimical schools of public suggestion. They set about stereotyping the public mind.

These same profit-making systems in possession also played a large part in arresting competition from countries in which they were less completely in control, by subsidised political action for the maintenance of protective tariffs. Long before the world breakdown became manifest, the experience of the ordinary consumer so far belied the sanguine theory that free competition was a mode of endless progress that he was still living in a house, wearing clothes, using appliances, travelling about in conveyances, and being fed with phrases and ideas that by the standard of the known and worked-out inventions of the times should have been discarded on an average, Hooker computes, from a quarter to half a century before. There was labour unemployed and abundant material available to remedy all this, but its utilisation was held up by the rent-exacting and profit-earning systems already in possession.

This lag in modernisation added greatly to the effects of increased productive efficiency in the disengagement of those vast masses of destitute unemployed and unemploying people which began to appear almost everywhere, like the morbid secretion of a diseased body, as the twentieth century passed on into its third decade.

§ 6. *The Paradox of Over-Production and its Relation to War*

This so-called 'paradox of over-production' which figures so largely in the loose discussions of the 'post-war' period was in its essence a very simple affair indeed. Just as the inevitable end of a process of free competition was a consolidation of successful competitors and an arrest of enterprise, so the inevitable end of a search for profit in production was a steady reduction of costs through increased efficiency—that is to say, a steady decrease of the ratio of employment to output. These things lie so much on the surface of the process that it is almost incredible to us that, wilfully or not, our ancestors disregarded them. Equally inevitable was it that these necessary contractions of enterprise and employment should lead to an increase in the proportion of unemployable people. Geographical expansion and a rising standard of life among both the employed and possessing classes, together with the stimulating effect of a steady influx of gold, masked and tempered for half a century this squeezing-out of an increasing fraction of the species from its general economic life. There were nevertheless fluctuations, 'cycles of trade' as they were called, when the clogging machinery threatened to stall and was then relieved and went on again. But by the opening of the twentieth century the fact that the method of running human affairs as an open competition for profit was in its nature a terminating method was forcing itself upon the attention even of those who profited most by it and had the most excuse for disregarding it, and who, as a class, knew nothing of the Marxian analysis.

We know now that the primary task of world administration is to arrest this squeezing-out of human beings from active economic life by the continual extension of new collective enterprises, but such ideas had still to be broached at that time. The common folk, wiser in their instincts than the political economists in their intellectualism, were disposed to approve of waste and extravagance because money was 'circulated' and workers 'found employment'. And the reader will not be able to understand the world-wide tolerance of growing armaments and war preparations during this period unless he realises the immediate need inherent in the system for unremunerative public expenditure. Somewhere the energy economised had to come out. The world of private finance would not tolerate great rehousing, great educational and socially constructive enterprises on the part of the relatively feeble governments of the time. All that had to be reserved for the profit accumulator. And so the ever-increasing productivity of the race found its vent in its ancient traditions of warfare, which admitted the withdrawal of a large proportion of the male population from employment for a year or so and secreted that vast accumulation of forts, battleships, guns, submarines, explosives, barracks and the like which still amazes us. Without this cancer growth of armies and navies the paradox of over-production latent in competitive private enterprise would probably have revealed itself in an overwhelming mass of unemployment before even the end of the nineteenth century. A social revolution might have occurred then.

Militarism, however, alleviated these revolutionary

stresses by providing vast profit-yielding channels of waste. And it also strengthened the forces of social repression. The means of destruction accumulated on a scale that wellnigh kept pace with the increase in the potential wealth of mankind. The progressive enslavement of the race to military tyranny was an inseparable aspect, therefore, of free competition for profits. The latter system conditioned and produced the former. It needed the former so as to have ballast to throw out to destruction and death whenever it began to sink. The militarist phase of the early twentieth century and the paradox of over-production are correlated facets of the same reality, the reality of the planless hypertrophy of the social body.

It is interesting to note how this morbid accumulation of energy in belligerence and its failure to find vent in other directions became more and more evident in the physiognomy of the world as the twentieth century progressed. The gatherings of mankind became blotched with uniforms. Those admirable albums of coloured pictures, *Historical Scenes in a Hundred Volumes*, which are now placed in all our schools and show-places and supplied freely to any home in which there are children, display very interestingly the advent, predominance and disappearance of military preoccupations in the everyday life of our ancestors. These pictures are all either reproductions of actual paintings, engravings or photographs, or, in the case of the earlier volumes, they are elaborate reconditionings to the more realistic methods of our time of such illustrations as were available. Military operations have always attracted the picture-maker at all times, and there are plentiful pictures of battles from every age, from the little cricket-field battle of the Middle Ages to the hundred-mile fights of the last Great War, but our interest here is not with battles but with the general facies of social life. Even in the war-torn seventeenth century the general stream of life went on without any manifest soldiering. War was a special occupation. While the battles of the English Civil War, which set up the first English Republic (1649-60), were in progress, we have evidence that hunting and hawking parties were busy almost within sound of the guns. The novels of Jane Austen (England, 1775–1817) pursue their even way without the faintest echo of the land and sea campaigns in progress. Goethe in Weimar (the German literary 'Great Man' during the 'Great Man' period of literary thought in Europe, 1749–1832) could not be bothered by requests for supplies of wood and food for the German troops before the battle of Jena, and was very pleased to meet his 'enemy alien' Napoleon socially during that campaign.

We rarely see the monarchs of the eighteenth century depicted in military guise; the fashion was for robes and majesty rather than for the spurs and feathers of the Bantam warrior-king. It was the unprecedented vehemence of the Napoleonic adventure that splashed the social life of Europe with uniforms, infected feminine fashions, and even set plump princess colonels, frogged with gold lace and clutching bare sabres, joggling unsteadily at the heads of regiments. There was a brief return towards civilian attire with the accession of the 'domesticated monarchs', Louis Philippe in France and Victoria in Great Britain; they marked a transient reaction from Napoleonic fashions; but from the middle of the nineteenth century onward the prestige of the soldier resumed its advance and the military uniform became increasingly pervasive. Flags became more abundant in the towns and 'flag-days' dotted the calendar. There was never a crowd pictured in Europe after 1870 without a soldier or so.

The Great War greatly intensified the military element in the street population, not only in Europe but America. Various corps of feminine auxiliaries were enrolled during that time and paraded the world thereafter in appetising soldierly outfits. In the United States, except at Washington, or when there was a parade of civil war veterans, a soldier in uniform had been hitherto the rarest of birds. He would have felt strange and uncomfortable. He would have offended the susceptibilities of a consciously liberated people. The Great War changed all that. When Germany was disarmed after the war, a Nazi movement and a Reichs-banner movement supplied the needed colour until a German's freedom to get into properly recognised livery was restored. The pattern of half-military, half-civilian organisations in uniform had already been spread about the world between the South African War (1899–1901) and the Great War by the Boy Scout movement.

Of the Nazi movement, the Italian Fascisti and the Polish Brotherhood at least there will be more to tell later. The black and brown shirts may be cited here as instances of the visible breaking down of the boundaries between military and civil life that went on during and after the World War.

Hitherto war had been a marginal business, fought upon 'fronts', and the ordinary citizen had lived in comparative security behind the front, but the bombing, gas-diffusing aeroplane and later the long-range air torpedo, changed all that. The extended use of propaganda as a weapon, and the increasing danger of social mutiny under war stress, had also its share in making the entire surface of a belligerent country a war area and abolishing any vestiges of civil liberty, first during actual warfare and then in view of warfare. The desirability of getting everyone under orders, under oath and subject to prompt disciplinary measures, became more and more manifest to governments.

So within a century the appearance of the human crowd changed over from a varied assembly of inco-ordinated free individuals to a medley of uniforms. Everybody's dress at last indicated function, obligation and preparedness. The militarisation of the European multitude reached a maximum during the Polish wars. About 1942 gas masks, either actually worn or hanging from the neck, were common for a time, and so, too, were the small sheath-knives which were to be used in disposing of fallen aviators who might still be alive. Patella metal hats and metal epaulettes to protect the head and body against a rain of poisoned needles also appeared. Some civilians became far more formidable-looking than any soldiers.

The military authorities of those days were much perplexed by the problem of giving the general population protective apparatus and light weapons that would be effective against the military enemy and yet useless for the purposes of insurrection. For in spite of the most strenuous suppression of agitation in those troubled decades, the possible revolt of humanity against warfare, the possibility of complete 'loss of morale', however illogical and incoherent, was felt by the professional soldiers as an increasing menace.

Along the streets of most of the old-world cities there presently appeared the characteristic yellow (or in France blue, and in America red-and-white-striped) air-raid pillars with their glass faces, only to be broken into and used after an official alarm, which contained respirators and first-aid sets for possible gas victims. It is also to the same period we have to ascribe the multiplication of vivid and abundant direction signs at every street corner, set so as to throw a minimum of light upward and pointing the way to gas chambers and hospitals. It was a 'gas-minded' world in the 'forties. The practical suppression of other vivid and illuminated street signs was a natural corollary to this preoccupation.

In the first half of the twentieth century the cities blazed with advertisement. It was the period of maximum advertisement. The pictures of the Great White Way of New York, Piccadilly Circus, the Grands Boulevards of Paris and so forth, with their polychromatic visual clamour, still strike us as distractingly picturesque. There was much flood-lighting after 1928. Then progressively the lights were turned down again and that visual clamour died away. As the air threat returned, 'lights out' became at last imperative, except for the vivid furtive indications of refuge and first aid we have just mentioned.

War fear spread very rapidly after 1930. Darkness recaptured the nocturnal town. 'Night-life' became stealthy and obscure, with an increasing taint of criminality. All civil hospitals and all private doctors had disappeared from the world by 1945, and the health services were only legally

67

demilitarised again after 2010. The amalgamation of the military and civil hospital and medical services began in France as early as 1933. By 1945 every doctor in the Old World was, in theory at least, on a quasi-military footing; he wore a distinctive uniform, was subject to stringent discipline, and his premises, as well as the hospitals, bore the characteristic black and yellow chequer-work. All nurses were similarly enrolled. Finally the general public was enrolled for health treatment as common patients under oath. By 1948 in such towns as had sufficiently survived the general social demoralisation to enforce such regulations, it was impossible to take a chill or break an ankle without at once falling into the category of patients and being numbered, put into a black-and-yellow uniform and marched or carried off for treatment. Theoretically this system of treatment was universal. In practice neither the uniforms nor the doctors were available. For regulation and militarisation were going on in that period against an immense counter-drive towards social disintegration. The more humanity got into uniform, the shabbier the uniforms became.

Before the Polish struggle, general architecture was very little affected by military needs. The militarisation of costume preceded the militarisation of scenery. Even barracks and suchlike army buildings were erected by army architects as a simple vulgarisation of ordinary housing patterns, a mere stiffening up, so to speak, of the common 'jerry-built' house. There still survive for our astonishment pictures of Victorian Military Gothic and Victorian Military Tudor, produced under the British War Office. They display homes fit for drill-sergeants. The military mind had to be roused by the experiences of the Polish conflict to the profound reconstruction of the ordinary town that had become necessary if it was still to be taken seriously. Before then, fortification scarcely affected the urban scene at all, even in the case of a fortified town. Previously a fortress had been just an ordinary civil town surrounded at distances of from three to fifty miles by forts, strong points, trench systems and the

68

like. Now it was realised, first in Berlin, and then in Danzig, Warsaw, Paris and Turin, and after that by the whole world, that air warfare demanded not merely fortification round a town, but, much more imperatively, fortification *over* a town. The world, which had been far too stupid to realise in 1930 that the direct way out of its economic difficulties lay in the modernisation and rebuilding of its houses, set itself, in a state of war panic after 1942, to as complete a revision of its architecture in the face of bombs and gas as its deepening impoverishment permitted. What it would not do for prosperity, it attempted belatedly out of fear.

The first most obvious undertaking was the construction of those immense usually ill-built concrete cavern systems for refuge, whose vestiges are still to be visited by the curious tourist at Paris and Berlin (the London ones have all fallen in, the collapse beginning after the great landslip and fire), and close upon this came the cessation of tall building and the concentration of design upon the vast (and often dangerous) carapace roof and its gigantic supporting pillars and foundation rafts. Only the ever-deepening poverty, the increasing industrial disorganisation and the transitoriness of that last war-phase saved all the towns in the world from being thrust completely under such squat massive coverings.

So strong were the influences of that time that even up to 2020 the tendency of architectural design was to crouch. Hardly any mass of buildings erected between 1945 and the end of the century lifts up its head and looks the world in the face. That period has been called, not unjustly, Second Egyptian. And this was so in spite of the multiplying opportunities for grace and lightness afforded by the supersession of steel-frame buildings by the strong and flexible neo-concrete materials that were already available. How timidly they were used! We grovel no longer, because we are ceasing to fear each other. The soaring, ever important homes in which we live to-day would have sent our great-grandfathers scurrying to their cellars in an ecstasy of terror.

§ 7. The Great War of 1914–18

There is a monstrous tedious accumulation of records concerned with the World War. The Catalogue of Historical Material stored at Atacama gives a list of 2,362,705 books and gross files, up to date, and of these over 182,000 deal exclusively or largely with the causation of the war. Nothing could bring home to the student the profound difference in mental equipment between ourselves and the men and women of that period than a visit to the long silent galleries of that great library of dead disputes and almost completely forgotten records. He will see hardly a visitor along the vistas of that shining framework of shelves; a quiet cleaner or duster perhaps will be visible, scrutinising the condition of the material, or a young revisionist student patiently checking some current summary—or a black cat. For the rest, above, below, to right and left is a clean and luminous stillness; papers at rest.

In one large section of this sere honeycomb the student will find the records of the 'war guilt controversy' that agitated the world for decades after the Peace of Versailles. Let him draw out a set anywhere and take down a file or so at hazard and turn over its pages. He will be able to read almost all of it nowadays, whatever the original language, because practically all the collection has now been interleaved with translations into Basic English. And it will seem to him that he is reading the outpourings of lunatics, so completely have the universal obsessions of that time been exorcised since.

Had 'Germany' planned the war? Was 'France' the guilty party? Had 'Britain' much to answer for? With difficulty will the student let down his mind into the fantastic world

70

of extinct imaginations in which these strange personifications, as monstrous and incredible as the ancient gods of India, were treated as real and morally responsible individuals, hated, trusted, feared and loved. The war was, in immediate fact, an aimless and fruitless slaughter upon the altars of these stupendous deities, the wounding and mutilation of perhaps twenty million human beings, and a vast burning-up of material wealth. In the crazy fancy of our ancestors it was a noble and significant struggle. Happily we need not revive their craziness here. The question of 'war guilt' was never settled. It ceased to be pursued, it was neglected, it floated away into the absurd, and little but those three hundred feet or so of forgotten books and gross files remain to testify to its vanished importance.

The causation of the struggle was, indeed, perfectly simple. It arose naturally and necessarily from that irregular disproportionate growth of human appliances as compared with the extension of political and social intelligence we have already described.

The new means of communication and transport, and the new economic life which demanded the products of every zone and soil for its purposes, were necessitating the reorganisation of human affairs as a World-State, and since the world was already parcelled up among sixty-odd competing sovereign governments there were only two possible courses open to mankind, either to arrange the coalescence of these governments by treaty and rational arrangements to meet the new need, or to allow a steadily intensified mutal pressure to develop into more or less thinly disguised attempts at world conquest. In the decades before the war the British, French, German, Russian, Japanese and American systems were all, as the word went then, 'imperialist'— all, that is, attempting to become World-States on a planet on which obviously there was room only for one single World-State. Nothing of the sort had been apparent when the methods of European statescraft had been devised. These vaster possibilities had yawned open afterwards. The eighteenth and nineteenth centuries were centuries of small restricted wars for limited advantages. In the twentieth century the scale of war expanded beyond any limit and the advantages to be won by it disappeared. But the politicians and diplomatists played their time-honoured game against each other with a sort of terrified inevitability. They were driven; they had no control, or at least none of them seemed to have had the vigour and imagination to attempt a control. They were driven by the economic necessity we have explained in the previous section. They had to arm preposterously. They had to threaten. They had to go through with the business.

These forces account for the outbreak and universality of the Great War, but they do not account for its peculiar frightfulness. For that it is necessary to realise that, though governments expanded only against an enormous pressure of mutual restraint, no limitations had been set to the hypertrophy of financial and industrial enterprises. These last were under the sway of a relentless and unrestrained progress; they expanded, invented, urged and sold; they brought weapons of a strange and terrible effectiveness to the settlement of what were in comparison small and antiquated disputes. To that hypertrophy of the armour we will return presently, because the Great War was really only a first revelation of this peculiar disproportion between economics and politics, and the evil still went on in an exaggerated form after the formal conclusion of the struggle at the Peace of Versailles (1919). But let us first tell what needs to be known of the details of the Great War.

How little that is now! There is a vast literature both of fiction based on experience and of personal reminiscence about it, and some of it is admirably written; almost any of it may be read for interest and edification, and hardly any of it need be read with scholarly precision. The picture of the outbreak of the war still touches us. There was a curious unconsciousness of the grossness of the menace in events, even on the part of myriads doomed to suffer and die in a few months' time. Many of the stories told begin with a holiday party or a country-house gathering or some such

72

bright setting. The weather that August (1914) was exceptionally fine.

The details of the struggle itself were as horrible and distressing as they were inconsquent, and there is no need whatever for anyone but the specialist to master their sequence in detail. The old-fashioned history, with its lists of names, dates, battles and so on, was designed rather to supply easily marked material for examinations than to give any sense of the historical process. Examinations have long passed out of educational practice; they have gone to join the 'globes' and the abacus, the slate and the cane in the scholastic limbo, but their memory is preserved in the popular game of 'examination papers', when people write down as fast as they can and as much as they can about some suddenly selected subject.

Few of us could write even a brief account now of the World War. The names of such generals as Haig, Kitchener, French, Joffre, Foch and Ludendorff, to take their names at random, and such battles as Tannenberg, the Marne, the Somme, Passchendaele, the Falkland Isles, Jutland and so forth, mean nothing and need mean nothing to the ordinary citizen to-day. He does not know whether French was really French or not, nor whether Foch was a Frenchman or a German. He inclines to the latter view. He does not know who won or lost these conflicts and he does not care. He has not even a sporting interest in it. They were not lively fights. Nearly all the commanders concerned had dull and unattractive personalities and the business was altogether too unwieldy for them. Most of their operations were densely stupid, muddled both in conception and execution. One would as soon listen to a child reciting not very accurately and at endless length the deals and tricks of some game of cards it has played, or imagines it has played, as read their memoirs—packed as they often are with self-exculpation, personal resentments and malice. Faint, faded, immense far-off tragedies, these struggles that were to have astounded posterity have already gone far towards complete effacement in any but a few specialising minds, are hardly more vivid now in our collective consciousness than the battles of the Peloponnesian War—or the campaigns and conquests of Tamerlane. They had nothing of the primary historical importance and strategic splendour which have restored the gigantic military conceptions of Genghis Khan to an integral place in our ordinary educational curriculum.

For the rodomontade of the conflict the curious cannot do better than glance through the eager narrative of Winston Churchill's *World Crisis*. There one finds all the stereotyped flourishes and heroisms of nineteenth-century history from the British point of view; the 'drama of history' in rich profusion, centred upon one of the most alert personalities in the conflict. He displays a vigorous naïve puerility that still gives his story an atoning charm. He has the insensitiveness of a child of thirteen. His soldiers are toy soldiers and he loves to knock over a whole row of them. He enjoyed the war. He takes himself and all the now forgotten generals and statesmen of the war with a boyish seriousness. He passes grave judgments on their tragic fooleries and distributes compliments and blame, often in the most gracious manner, convinced that he is writing for a meticulously admiring and envious posterity. They would read, they would marvel. He was the sort of man who believed that when he begot children he created an audience. He was misled by the excitement of his own reading of history. He not only measures for us the enormous gulf between the mentality of his times and our own, but he enables us to bridge that gulf with an amused and forgiving sympathy.

A less attractive spirit displays itself in the memoirs of such figures as Ludendorff, Bülow, Clemenceau, Fisher, Foch and so through the whole category of war leaders. The war was the supreme event in the lives of most of these men, and apparently they were never able to think of anything else afterwards. They had none of the recuperative innocence of Churchill, his terrier-like interest in everything. They all took to writing furiously in their declining years and no other pens could have damned them so completely.

They are grown-up and yet underdeveloped persons; as adult as old chimpanzees; they cannot claim Churchill's benefit of schoolboy, and there is a real horror in their wrinkled meannesses and envies, their gross enthusiasms and their sincere bloodthirstiness and hate. Most of their mutual recriminations are too incomprehensive to be of the slightest interest now; spite and twaddle are still spite and twaddle even if drenched with blood. The most accessible sample for the contemporary reader is *The Life and Diaries of Field-Marshal Sir Henry Wilson, Bart., G.S.B., D.S.O.*, a lean, unsightly man of infinite energy, gusto and vanity, who played a very prominent rôle in bringing about and carrying out the catastrophe. It is the latest reprint in the Historical Documents Series; it is richly illustrated and abundantly annotated, and with it are bound up the brilliantly scornful criticisms of Wilson's contemporary, Sir Andrew MacPhail, and Stephen Freudheim's more scientific analysis of him as the supreme type of the 'soldierly mind'.

For the grimmer actualities of the struggle there is a vast and sombre literature. It has been summarised in the last fifteen years by the Historical Bureau in its *War Pictures for Posterity by Pen, Pencil and Camera*. Everyone should turn over those strange incredible records of endurance, callousness, devotion and insane courage to learn something of the extremes to which men and women like ourselves can be pushed by the grim forces of social compulsion.

The earlier volumes deal chiefly with the psychology of the more than half civilised citizens of the Atlantic and North European states suddenly precipitated into a maelstrom of destruction. We see the urban crowds demonstrating and cheering in the streets of the capital cities, the floods of youths coming from their work to 'join up', the wonder and unimaginative fierceness and heroism of the opening stage. Then come the first contacts, villages in flames, the wild shooting of curious bystanders as spies and guerillas, realisations of horror and a wave of fear, the invaded populations in flight, black crowds with their pitiful impedimenta streaming along darkling roads, going they know not whither. The rifles and machine-guns rattle, the guns thud, and the cheering adventurousness of the advancing armies as they blunder heavily into contact passes into a phase of astounded violence and hardship. The new war was like no war that had ever been before. The French upon their eastern front went forward to the attack with immense élan, in bright uniforms and to the historical inspiration of the 'Marseillaise'. They were massacred. They lost a third of a million men in three weeks. The Germans poured through Belgium, more than a million strong, to be stopped and stunned with Paris almost within their grasp. The pictures show the smiling landscape of eastern Belgium, France and east Prussia in July 1914, and the same country-side a couple of months later—torn, scored and trenched, defiled with bloody heaps of litter that were once clothed bodies, an anguish of countless thousands of unclean, hungry, exhausted, cruelty-wrung human beings.

These bands of contact, these regions of filthy pain and tumult, spread. Presently there were 'war zones' reaching from the North Sea to the Alps and across Eastern Europe, strange regions in which every house was a ruin, every tree a splintered trunk, where millions of crouching men went to and fro in trenches and ditches furtively like rats, and the ragged dead lay unburied. There day and night the superfluous energy of a profiteering economic system, denied all other outlet by its own preconceptions and the rigid historical traditions in which it was blinkered, blew itself away in the incessant concussions of mines, bombs and guns and a continual destruction of human life.

Presently newly invented weapons, hitherto untried, came to extend and intensify the struggle. The aeroplane, and that primitive 'navigable' the Zeppelin, carried the war behind the fronts and attacked the civilian population in the cities. We see the explosive and incendiary bombs bursting into the dirty little urban homes of the time, blowing to rags the bed-rid grandmother and the baby in the cradle; we see the panic-stricken crowds seeking the shelter of cellars and excavations and the drainlike railway 'tubes' of the time. In the early stages of the air-war only explosives and inflammatory substances were used, but as the struggle progressed the art of using gas bombs developed, and an agonising suffocation was added to the nocturnal chances of flame and explosion and death among fallen ruins for the non-combatant at home. The submarine, also, was a novelty of the Great War, and a very searching novelty. It was used first to sink fighting ships, and then it was turned against all sea-going craft. We have vivid descriptions of the sinking of the *Lusitania* without warning and the drowning of 1,198 men, women and children. She was, by the standards of the time, a great and luxurious ship, and a sort of symbolism was found by the writers of this period in this sudden descent from light, comfort and confidence into a desperate and hopeless struggle in the waters of the night. All the achievements of the nineteenth-century civilisation seemed to many to be following in the downward wake of the *Lusitania*.

Service in these early submarines strained men to the breaking point. They were essentially engines of war, they had all the defects of inventions at an early stage, and none of the security and comfort of the great submarine barges that are used to-day for the Mediterranean and Atlantic Ridge mines and for general deep-sea exploration. These, with their beautifully adjusted pressure systems and their limitless vertical range, are calculated rather to mislead than enlighten us as to the capabilities of the primitive submarines of the Great War. The latter were able to descend safely only to a depth of a hundred metres; below that the pressure became too much for them and their plates gave and leaked. When they leaked the salt water was apt to affect the accumulators and chlorine gas was released to torment and suffocate the crews. Below a hundred and fifty metres these fragile contrivances crumpled up altogether and were destroyed. The air in them became foul when they submerged, in spite of the compressed oxygen they carried, and the continual condensation of exhaled

77

moisture gave them a peculiar clammy discomfort. They could move about under water for a couple of days by means of their electric batteries, but then it was necessary to come to the surface and run their oil-combustion engines for some hours to recharge. Armed with guns and packed with mines, bombs, torpedoes and other explosives, they set out to harass and destroy the surface shipping of the enemy.

It was a difficult and almost fantastically dangerous task. Submerged, they were invisible, but also they were blind. Near the surface they could get a limited view of what was going on by means of a periscope. On the surface they had the range of outlook of any other surface boat, but all the risks a surface boat must take. So under conditions of extreme discomfort and partial asphyxiation the crews of these strangely formidable and strangely fragile contrivances groped their way towards their victims. To see the quarry fairly they had to come to the surface, and that exposed them to gunfire. If their thin steel skins were pierced by a single shot they could no longer go under. Often when submerged they betrayed their whereabouts unwittingly by bubbles of gas and escapes of oil.

At first, in spite of their limitations, the submarines proved a very deadly weapon, more particularly in the hands of the Central European Powers. They destroyed a great multitude of ships and drowned many score thousands of men. Then slowly the methods used against them improved. They were hunted by a special flotilla, and among other ships by the 'Q' boats, armed vessels diguised as harmless merchantmen. These lured them to the surface and then let down sham bulwarks and opened fire upon them, so that after a time they no longer dared emerge to challenge even the most harmless-looking craft. Explosive mines were moored in their possible tracks and mine-armed nets across harbours and channels. They were also watched for by aeroplanes and special airships whose signals guided the destroyers to their quarry. Ingenious listening contrivances were invented to locate them. They were shot at on the surface, rammed, and pursued by 'depth-charges' which could strain their plates and disable them even when exploded scores of metres away.

Such, briefly, were the conditions of submarine warfare in the years 1917–18. And yet to the very end of the war men could be found to carry it on, to destroy and drown and be in their turn hunted and destroyed. The building and launching of submersibles never ceased. Men went down in them to chilly confinement, to the perpetual anxiety of mine or ram, to the quivering menace of the distant depth-charge, to the reasonable probability of a frightful death beyond all human aid. Few submarines returned to harbour ten times; many went out new upon their first voyage never to return. Two hundred of them were lost by the Germans alone; each loss a tragedy of anguish and dismay in the deeps. Towards the end it was claimed by their antagonists that the crews were losing morale. Once or twice an undamaged submarine that had been cornered surrendered, and the new commanders showed a growing tendency to return to port for minor repairs or other slight pretexts. But on the whole, such is the unimaginative heroic submissiveness of our species, the service was sustained. The Germans supplied most of the flesh for this particular altar; willing and disciplined, their youngsters saluted and carried their kit down the ladder into this gently swaying clumsy murder-mechanism which was destined to become their coffin.

Their obedience brings us to one of the most fundamental lessons that the Great War has for us: the extreme slowness with which the realisation of even the most obvious new conditions pierces through the swathings of habitual acceptance. Millions of human beings went open-eyed to servitude, bullying, hardship, suffering and slaughter without a murmur, with a sort of fatalistic pride. In obedience to the dictates of the blindest prejudices and the most fatuous loyalties they did their utmost to kill men against whom they had no conceivable grievance, and they were in their turn butchered gallantly, fighting to the last. The *War*

79

Pictures volumes dismay our imaginations by portraying a series of wholesale butcheries, many of them on a stupendous scale, of men who died facing their enemies. After the great slaughter of the French at the outset of the war, a mighty killing of Russians at the Battles of Tannenberg and the Masurian Lakes, there was during what was called the deadlock period, the period of trench warfare, a diminution of the losses upon the West. Hostilities sank down to a gusty conflict of shell-fire, rifle assassinations, and raids with bombs and bludgeons. In the East, however, the Russians ran out of ammunition, and held their trenches only by a great martyrdom of men; they lost well over a million before the end of 1914, and yet they continued to obey orders. A series of minor campaigns broke out in regions remote from the main centres of contact. There is a horrible account in the *Pictures* of the sufferings of some thousands of British common soldiers taken prisoner at Kut, in Mesopotamia. (Their generals and other officers, however, who had arranged that particular capitulation, were honourably and comfortably entertained by their captors the Turks.) There is no effective expression of resentment by the British troops on record.

In 1916 and 1917 there were spasmodic renewals of hostilities on a large scale by the British and French in France. Newly trained British armies were made to advance in close formation by generals who, unless they were imbeciles, could have had no doubts of the fate to which they were sending their men. If they were not imbeciles then they were criminally unwilling to learn and soul-blind to suffering and waste. The mentality of the men is still a matter for discussion. The poor boys they commanded were marched forward shoulder to shoulder in successive waves of attack, and so advancing they were shot to pieces by the enemy machine-guns. Out of battalions of six or seven hundred, perhaps a hundred would struggle through the defensive fire and come to bomb-throwing, bayonet-thrusts and surrender in the German trenches. Small isolated groups of them in shell-holes and captured positions fought on for days. So perished the flower of an entire school generation, collected from hundreds of thousands of homes, more or less loved, more or less cared for and more or less educated; it had been enlisted, trained, sent out to the battlefields at enormous cost, to be left at last in the desolated spaces between the armies, lying in heaps and swathes to rot and be rat-eaten. For months afterwards, as the photographs show, thousands of them were to be seen sprawling in formation as they fell, just as if their ranks were still waiting to leap again to the attack. But as the observer drew nearer he realised their corruption. He discovered bony hands, eyeless sockets, faces far gone in decay.

The British Commander-in-Chief in his despatches did not fail to extol the courage of his lost battalions and to represent this monstrous exploit as a victory. Some mile or so of ground had been gained in that July offensive and less than 12,000 prisoners had been taken. Twice as many British were left prisoners in German hands, but this the despatches ignored.

The appalling nature of this particular disaster leaked out only very slowly. The British censorship at least was efficient and the generals, however incapable in other respects, lied magnificently. The Channel crossing made it particularly easy to hide events from the British public. And it had a peculiar effect on the British troops; it gave them a feeling of being in another and a different world from 'home', a war-world in which such cruel and fantastic things could be natural. This monstrous massacre was, indeed, contrived and carried through, not simply without a revolt, but with scarcely an audible protest on the part of either the parents, relations, friends or surviving comrades of those hosts of wasted victims.

The commanders of the Russian armies in Austria, Armenia and elsewhere were announcing equally costly and heroic triumphs and the Germans and Austrians were issuing the most valiant and excessive contradictions of their claims. They, too, were losing hideously enough, though in a lesser proportion than their opponents. The next

81

year (1917), the British, gallant and docile as ever, with only very slightly improved tactics, were going again into great offensives.

But now the French troops began to manifest a livelier intelligence. They were amidst familiar things, nearer their homes and less cut off from subversive influences than the British. A certain General Nivelle, at that time French Commander-in-Chief, made what Churchill calls an 'experiment', which resulted altogether in the loss of nearly a couple of hundred thousand men. It involved the advance of masses of infantry into intense fields of fire. In an hour said Lieutenant Ybarnegaray (in a debate in the French Chamber, June 1917), they were reduced to a crowd 'running like madmen', all formations and distinctions lost. Provision had been made for less than 15,000 wounded. There were seven times as many. Most of the casualties never received the most elementary attention for three days. The result was gangrene, amputation and death for thousands. Then came the first intimation that there were limits to human obedience. A French division ordered into action to continue this futile holocaust refused to march. Churchill says this was 'deeply disquieting' to the authorities, and no doubt it pained and distressed every intelligent amateur of war. This particular division was cajoled into a change of mind. It took part in the fighting, says Churchill, 'without discredit', but the spirit of its resistance spread.

The next sign of insanity in this world torture was the collapse of the grotesque Russian autocracy. We have already told of the mental and moral decay of the Tsardom in our general study of the degeneration of monarchy. [*Non inventus.*—Ed.] Abruptly this profoundly rotten government collapsed into nothing; its vast domains became a various disorder, and for some months phantom imitations of Western revolutionaries, inspired by memories of the first French revolution or by legends of British parliamentary wisdom, occupied the capital. The one certain fact in the situation was the accumulated disinclination of the Russian people for any further warfare. But this first republican government under an eloquent lawyer politician, of no great directive force, Alexandre Kerensky, was unable either to carry on the war or to end it. A subdued but spreading clamour for 'peace by negotiation' in all the combatant countries ensued, a clamour that active repression and the most rigorous concealment in the Press failed to silence. There was an attempt to call a sort of peace conference of Radicals at Stockholm, and then a second revolution in Russia which carried a small and resolute Communist organisation to power—carried it to power simply and solely because there was no other organised alternative, and because it promised peace plainly and surely—peace on any terms. The Russian armies melted away at its signal; the men streamed home. The German military authorities in the East found the trenches before them undefended and with every courtesy of war, as one soldier to another, welcomed the Russian officers of the old régime, taking refuge from the belated resentment of their own men.

In 1917 mankind seemed already to be awakening from the war-nightmare. Mutinies broke out in sixteen separate French army corps, 115 regiments were involved, divisions elected soldiers' councils and whole regiments set out for Paris to demand a reasonable wind-up of the struggle. The one last hope of the despairing soldiers, said Pierre Laval, had been Stockholm. That disappointment had made life unbearable. But the storm abated with the entry of the United States of America into the war, and the powers in control of the Western World were still able to pursue their dreadful obsessions for another year.

War Pictures for Posterity by Pen, Pencil and Camera devotes a whole volume (xxi) to the tragedy of a special Russian infantry corps in France. Fifteen thousand Russians had been sent thither in 1916 to be equipped and armed and put into the line with the French armies. Many of these poor lads scarcely knew the difference between a Frenchman and a German, and the ostensible objects of the war were quite beyond their understanding. But they heard of the revolution in their own country and they resolved to consider their attitude with regard to it. They elected representatives and put it to the vote whether they should continue to fight, which meant for them to take part in that 'experiment' of Nivelle's known to be in preparation at the time. They chose what seemed to them the generous part and went into the battle. The French command used them ruthlessly, and nearly 6,000 were killed or wounded. The rest came out of the line and mutinied. They would fight no more. Thereupon these defenceless men were surrounded by trustworthy French troops, a great concentration of guns was assembled, fire was opened upon them suddenly and they were massacred. Horrible photographs of the details of this—photographs hidden away at the time from the authorities and brought to light later— are given in the summary already cited.

For nearly a year the French lost confidence in the morale of their own men and dared make no more great attacks, but their allies offered up another 400,000 men in the battle of Passchendaele and accounted for 300,000 Germans, and in the spring the Germans made a vast multitudinous attack in the West which succeeded at first and then collapsed, whereupon their antagonists, reinforced by new armies from America, waded back through blood to a dreadful final victory. The last nine months of the conflict saw more slaughter than any preceding year. From March 21st 1918, to November 11th in the same year the British suffered 830,000 casualties, the French and Belgians 964,000 and the Germans 1,470,000. There were also 2,000,000 American troops brought to Europe before the end, and of these more than half were actually engaged in the fighting. Their casualties were certainly not less than 350,000. Portuguese and other contingents from the most unexpected quarters also contributed to that culminating death-roll, but it is impossible for us now to give exact numbers for these minor forces.

These are the gross figures of warfare. But *War Pictures* devotes three volumes, perhaps the most horrible of all, to the presentation of various details of the fighting in which these vast multitudes suffered and perished. These three volumes are like the microscopic slides in a specimen book of anatomy, which show us from a selected scrap of tissue the texture of the whole. Little figures stand out enlarged, chosen by the hazard that they wrote or talked or carried a camera, to represent the nameless millions who have left no record. We have accounts of men who were left to lie out for days between the lines, tortured by thirst and stifled by the stench of their own corruption, and yet who survived to tell the tale. We have the stories of men who fell into heaps of rotting dead, and lay there choking, and of men who were gassed. The tortures of gas were already many and various, and most of the mixtures then used left tormenting weaknesses in the system for the rest of life. We have descriptions of the rude surgery of the time and abstracts of the mental disorders through which minds fled from reality. There are also some dreadful pictures of mutilated men, faceless, crippled, grotesquely distorted and an autobiography of one of the blinded (*Outstaying My Welcome*, by Fritz Schiff, 1923). Scores of thousands of unhappy fragments of humanity had to be hidden away in special institutions until they died, they were at once so terrifying and so pitiful and hopeless. The world forgot them even while they lived.

The distortion of souls was even more dreadful than the distortion of bodies. One of the most lurid items in that dreadful assemblage of realities is a lecture on the use of the bayonet, which chanced to be printed, reprinted later by anti-war propagandists and so preserved for us, delivered by a certain sergeant-major to a class of English cadets in training. To us he is incredible in his ferocity; we are almost forced to believe he was drunk or mad, until we realise from the 'laughter' that punctuated his utterances, from the hearty thanks of his commanding officer, and the 'three cheers' which rewarded him at the conclusion of his discourse, that he was merely expressing the spirit of war service as it was then understood.

'If you see a wounded German,' he said, 'shove him out

and have no nonsense about it.'

He was all against taking prisoners—and for murdering them after surrender. He told with sympathy and approval of how a corporal under him butchered a group of German boys. 'Can I do these blokes in, sir?' asked the corporal, pointing to a bunch of disarmed enemies.

'Please yourself,' said the sergeant-major. . . .

When they had been 'done-in', the honest corporal, a released convict from Dartmoor prison, came back to the sergeant-major very gratified and honoured, and, still in favour, discussed the technical difficulties of withdrawing a bayonet quickly in order to be ready for the 'next fellow'.

That was, that is, the spirit to which war brings a human being. That gallant sergeant-major had abundant equivalents in every army engaged. We were able to quote an English document, freely published. Participants in many other countries had less freedom. On the whole the English were as gentle as any other soldiers. But fear and bloodlust, it is plain, wipe out all the slowly acquired restraints and tolerance of social order very quickly and completely from any breed of men. History must not be written in pink and gilt. Prisoners and wounded were not simply neglected and ill-treated and 'shoved out'. Many were actually tortured to death—either by way of reprisals or in sheer wanton cruelty. There is also a series of photographs of foully mutilated bodies, mutilated and indecently displayed while they were dying or immediately after they were dead. Those millions marched indeed right out of civilisation, right out of any sort of human life as we know it to-day, marched down to something viler than mere bestiality, when they marched into the war zone.

After the summer of 1918, which brought with it the certainty of ultimate defeat, the combatant energy of Germany evaporated. Everywhere there was distress and hunger due to a rigorous blockade. The discipline of the land relaxed; the country behind the front was infested by stragglers; the Higher German Command found itself now, like its antagonists, unable to rely upon the men to advance, found itself unable to rely upon their resistance to an enemy attack. They became eager to surrender—taking the off-chance of meeting experimental corporals from Dartmoor on the way.

Wherever there was still loyalty and obedience, however, men were still callously sacrificed by the Higher Command *War Pictures* (vol. xxvii, 23,842 *et seq*.) show the German machine-gunners in their pits, on the defensive against advancing British and American troops. These men allowed themselves to be drugged and chained to their weapons, and so continued to fire and kill until the attack came up to them. Then they found small mercy. They were bayoneted or their brains were beaten out. They paid for the inventions of their masters. They paid for the hatred of Germany the introduction of poison gas had evoked in every attacking army. Such residues of senseless devotion availed nothing against the massive pressures that were at last exhausting Germany. In November the Kaiser, the War Lord, was in flight; a humiliating Armistice had been concluded and the German armies were streaming home in disorder, incoherently revolutionary.

Upon that phrase, 'incoherently revolutionary', our account of the main war may very well end. Here we will only allude to the defeat and demoralisation of the Italian armies after the battle of Caporetto, when 800,000 were either killed, wounded, taken prisoner or (sensible fellows) 'went home'. Nor will we describe the naval battles, of which the chief and last was Jutland. It was the last, because afterwards the German admirals were faced by the threat of mutiny if they essayed another fight. Whether it was or was not a victory for the British was never exactly determined. The controversy died out during the Polish wars.

The *War Pictures* volumes give many photographs and accounts of these naval encounters. We have, for example, a whole series of snapshots of a British cruiser in the Battle of Jutland, the *Defence* steaming at full-speed-ahead to attack and finish up a smashed and sinking German battleship, the *Wiesbaden*. The onrush of that fierce mechanism is terrific. It seems invincible and overpowering. It has an undeniable splendour. Then suddenly a series of blinding flashes show the *Defence* has been hit by the fire of some other German battleship coming to the help of her sister ship, and in a moment she has blown up and gone; she is no more than a mounting unfolding column of smoke and flying fragments, including, we realise with an effort, the torn and scalded bodies of eight hundred men. Then a welter of littered tumbled water....

There is no end of the multitude of such pictures.

But let us return to our phrase 'incoherently revolutionary'. That is the key to the whole human situation at that time. The distaste for the war throughout the world was enormous, if not in its opening phases, then certainly before the second year was reached. It bored; it disgusted. Its events had none of the smashing decisiveness that seizes the imagination. Even the great naval battle of Jutland was, from the point of view of spectacle, a complete failure. None the less, for a very simple reason a comparatively small minority of resolutely belligerent persons was able to keep this vast misery going. On the one hand the war was in accordance with the ruling ideas of the time, while on the other the hundreds of millions whose astonishment and dismay deepened daily, as horror unfolded beyond horror, had no conception of any alternative pattern of life to which they could turn as a refuge from its relentless sequences.

To cry, 'End the war!' ended nothing, because it gave no intimations of what had to replace belligerent governments in the control of human affairs. The peace the masses craved for was as yet only a featureless negative. But peace must be a positive thing, designed and sustained, for peace is less natural than warfare. We who have at last won through to the Pax Mundi know how strong and resolute, how powerfully equipped and how vigilant, the keepers of the peace must be.

§ 8. *The Impulse to Abolish War: The Episode of the Ford Peace Ship*

One quaint expedition, grotesque and childish and yet an augury of greater things to come, flits very illuminatingly across the dreadful record of these war years. It is the voyage of a passenger steamship from New York to Norway. The dark curtains of oblivion fall in heavier and heavier folds before the thundering battleships of the twilit Battle of Jutland; their forgotten names sink back into a vague general impression of huge flame-spouting masses that rush through smoke and mist to their fate; only a specialist can tell us now whether the *Lützow* or the *Friedrich der Grosse*, the *Lion*, or the *Iron Duke*, the *Vanguard* or the *Colossus* perished with its complement of men or staggered out of that battle. They have become monstrous irrelevances. There is nothing but their size, and the smashing and drowning of hundreds of men in them, to make them more significant to us now than an exploding casket of fireworks. But steaming its way across the Atlantic a few months before Jutland was fought came this other ship, a passenger boat of the Scandinavian–American line, the *Oscar II*, whose voyage remains to this day important and interesting, because in the most simple and artless fashion it mingled the new conceptions of life that were coming into being with all the prevalent weaknesses of the time. The *Oscar II* is better known in history as the Peace Ship of Henry Ford. It is a gleam of tragic comedy amidst the universal horror.

This Henry Ford was a very natural-minded mechanical genius, without much education or social sophistication, a great friend of, and kindred spirit with, that Edison whose career has been traced in the chapter of human history dealing with the development and exploitations of inventions at

89

the close of the nineteenth and the beginning of the twentieth century. Born and brought up in a period of economic expansion, Ford took economic expansion as if it were a necessity inherent in things, and never began to doubt continual progress until he was a man of over seventy. That was his good fortune. That gave him the confidence to design an automobile as sound and good and cheap as could be done at that time, and to organise the mass production of his pattern with extraordinary energy and skill because his mind was untroubled by the thought that there could be a limit to the number of possible purchasers. He marketed his 'flivver', or 'tin lizzie', as it was affectionately called, in enormous quantities, and in consequence he revolutionised the road transport and town planning of America. He changed the shape of every growing town by enabling the small householder to live further from the work and business centre than had ever been possible before. He did more than any other single man to drive the horse not only from the road but, by making farm tractors, from the fields. He created factories at Dearborn that even to-day seem vast. He became enormously rich and an outstanding 'character' in the world, and particularly in America. And he remained curiously simple and direct in his outlook upon life.

The first effect of the Great War upon him, as on a vast proportion of the English-speaking peoples, was incredulous amazement. He had known there were armies and sovereign nations in the world, but apparently he had never supposed they would fight. He felt there must be some mistake. He exchanged views with other Americans in a similar phase of astonishment. By the beginning of 1915 they had accumulated a sufficient mass of evidence from the belligerent countries to convince them that great masses of people in these countries were as amazed and as anxious to end the widening bloodshed and brutalisation as the neutral onlookers. There had been deputations to the President (President Wilson), who was at that time, in harmony with his country, highly pacificist, and there was a widespread ambition that the United States should evoke some sort of

90

permanent arbitration council alone, or in concert with the other Powers still neutral, which should stand, so to speak, on the edge of the battlefield and continue to offer its mediatory services to the warring governments until they were accepted. There was the suggestion of a deputation to Europe to further this idea, and the question arose how should it go across the Atlantic. Ford offered to charter a ship to take it.

Then his peculiar imagination seized upon his own offer. He would make this ship a spectacular ship; it should be the 'Peace Ship'. It should take a complement of chosen delegates to Europe in such a blaze of publicity that at its coming the war would be, as it were, arrested, to look at it. Its mere appearance would recall infuriated Europe to its senses. 'I want to get those boys out of the trenches,' said Ford. 'They don't want to fight, and would be only too glad to shake hands with each other.' At the back of his mind there seems to have been an idea of calling a general strike at the fronts. 'Out of the trenches by Christmas, never to return again,' was his brief speech at a public meeting in Washington in November. All sorts of eminent and energetic people were invited to join the mission. He sought the overt approval of the President, but the President was far too seasoned a politician to squander his publicity upon this 'gesture' of Henry Ford's. He was meditating a gesture of his own later on.

American life at that time had its conspicuous popular stars, who embodied its ideals of greatness and goodness. Some of them are still for various reasons remembered by the historian, Jane Addams and Thomas Edison, for example, William Jennings Bryan (the 'Last Creationist') and Luther Burbank. These names are still to be found even in the Lower School Encyclopaedia. Ford tried to include them all in one meteoric shipload. The governors of all the states in the Union were also invited, groups of representative university students, and so on. The Historical Collection at Atacama has gathered all the surviving originals or replicas of Ford's invitations and the replies in which these

91

outstanding individuals hesitated over or evaded his proposals. Several were only prevented by sudden attacks of ill-health at the very last moment from joining him. And there was a number of newspaper reporters, cinema operators and other photographers, stenographers, typists, translators, interpreters, baggage masters and publicity agents who made no trouble about coming. A certain Madame Rosika Schwimmer, an Hungarian lady, gleams forth and vanishes again from history as the organising spirit of this selection. A vast multitude of adventurers and crazy people offered to assist when Ford's project was made public, and many were only prevented with the utmost difficulty from coming aboard the *Oscar II*.

There is still material for a great writer in the details of that expedition, but our interest here is neither with the expedition as a whole nor with Ford or the other persons concerned in it as personalities, but with this idea that flamed and faded, this idea of *an appeal against war to human sanity*. And with the vicissitudes of that idea.

The first thing to note is that it evoked response and a very wide response. Eminent people, both in America and Europe, with their popularity to consider, found it advisable to be sympathetic, even if unhelpful. President Wilson, for example, was sympathetic but unhelpful. All the pretentious weathercocks of the Western World swung round towards it. We have every indication indeed of a very considerable drive towards a world pax in these years. But presently the weathercocks began to waver and swing away.

Why did they waver? From the first there was a sustained, malignant antagonism to the project. This grew in force and vigour. The American Press, and in its wake the European Press, set itself to magnify and distort every weakness, every slight absurdity, in the expedition and to invent further weaknesses and absurdities. A campaign of ridicule began, so skilful and persistent that it stripped away one blushing celebrity after another from the constellation, and smothered the essential sanity of the project in their wilting apologies. While Ford and his surviving missioners discussed and discoursed on their liner the newspaper men they had brought with them concocted lies and absurd stories about their host—as though they were under instructions.

We know now they were under instructions. The Historical Documents Series makes this perfectly plain.

As our students disentangle strand after strand of that long-hidden story, we realise more and more clearly the tortuous dishonesty, the confused double-mindedness, of the times. The export trade of the United States was flourishing under war conditions as it had never flourished before. Munitions of every sort were being sold at enormously enhanced prices to the belligerents. Such great banking houses as Morgan and Co. were facilitating the financial subjugation of Europe to America, through debts for these supplies. It is clear that American finance and American Big Business had not foreseen this. They had no exceptional foresight. But suddenly they found themselves in a position of great advantage, and by all their traditions they were bound to make use of that advantage. And Ford in his infinite artlessness, 'butting in', as they said, 'on things that were not his business', was setting out to destroy this favourable state of affairs.

There was just enough plausibility in this endeavour to make it seem dangerous. Ford could not be ignored; his available publicity was too great for that. He was by no means beneath contempt; so he had to be made contemptible. With an earnestness worthy of a better cause, the American Press was launched against him. And it was one of the strange traditions of the American Press that a newsman should have no scruples. The ordinary reporter was a moral invert taking a real pride in his degradation. No expedient was too mean, no lie, no trick too contemptible if only it helped thwart and disillusion Ford.

And they did thwart and disillusion him. They got him wrong with himself. This half-baked man of genius, deserted by his friends, lost confidence in his project. He began to suspect his allies and believe his enemies.

We have to accept the evidence preserved for us, but

even with that evidence before us, some of the details of that Press campaign appear incredible. There are a hundred gross files of newspaper cuttings at Atacama, and some of the most amazing are reproduced in the selected Historical Documents. The reporters and writers, who were aboard as Ford's guests, invented and sent home by wireless fantastic reports of free fights among the members of the mission, of disputes among the leaders, of Ford being chained to his bed by his secretary, of mutinies and grotesque happenings. Ford was told of and could have prevented these radio messages being sent—it was his ship for the time being—but a kind of fanaticism for free opinion—even if in practice that meant free lying—restrained him. 'Let them do their darnedest,' he said, still valiant. 'Our work will speak for itself.'

But presently he caught the influenza, a lowering disease long since extinct but very rife in that period, and, under the clumsy medical attention of the day, he arrived in Europe deflated and tired, physically and morally, prepared now to believe that there was something essentially foolish in the whole affair. He had been drenched in ridicule beyond his powers of resistance, and he was giving way. He gave way.

'Guess I had better go home to mother,' said Mr. Ford, sick in bed in Christiania, and kept to his room, though all Norway was agog to greet and cheer him.

But his movement went on by the inertia it had gained. His delegation was received with great enthusiasm in Norway and subsequently in Sweden, Switzerland, Denmark and Holland, those small sovereign European states which contrived so dexterously to keep out of the conflict to the end. People in those countries were evidently only too eager to believe that this novel intervention might help to end the war. If Ford was discouraged, some of his associates were of more persistent material. They held great public meetings in Sweden, Holland and Switzerland, and the repercussion of their activities certainly had a heartening effect on the peace movement in Germany and Britain. They contrived to get speech with a number of politicians and statesmen.

and they roused the watchful hostility of the German and British war authorities—for the military chiefs of both sides regarded this mission very properly as an attack on war morale. A Neutral Conference for Continuous Mediation came into being—very precarious being—in Stockholm. It is claimed that it checked a movement to bring Sweden into the war on the side of the Germans.

Then gradually the Ford Organisation for Peace lost prominence. It was overshadowed by greater movements towards negotiation, and more particularly by the large uncertain gestures of President Wilson, who, re-elected as 'the man who kept the United States out of the war', brought his people from a phase of hypocritical pacificism and energetic armament into the war in 1917. Before that culmination the Peace Ship bladder had collapsed altogether. Its last typist and photographer and clerk had been paid off, and Ford himself was already doing all that was humanly possible to draw a blanket of oblivion over that unforgettable Peace Ship. But the records have been too much for him.

He had not led his expeditionary force in Europe, even nominally, for more than five weeks. He had kept to his Norwegian hotel, avoided his more enthusiastic associates, started a vigorous reduction of his financial commitments and finally bolted home. He deserted. He left his hotel at Christiania, stealthily, at five o'clock in the morning, and, in spite of the pleadings of those of his party who, warned at the last minute, tumbled out of bed to protest, he got away. Before the year was out he had ceased even financial support, and the various men and women who had abandoned careers and positions and faced ridicule and odium in complete faith in his simplicity were left to find their way back to their former niches or discover fresh ones.

Now what had happened to his great idea? What strange reversal of motive had occurred in the brain and heart of this Peace Crusader? There the curious historian must needs speculate, for that brain and heart have gone now beyond all closer scrutiny.

It has to be noted first that while the Peace Ship was on the Atlantic something very significant was going on at Washington. The swiftly growing munition industries of America had discovered that a home market for their products, a home market of superior solvency, might be added to the vast demands of the fighting nations overseas. America. it was argued, might keep out of the war—well and good—but nevertheless America must be 'prepared'. The United States must arm. The President had weighed this proposal with a due regard for the votes and Press support that would come to him at the next election; he had weighed it very carefully as became a politician, and after some resistance he consented that America should be 'prepared'. Munitions should be assembled, troops should be drilled. Flags began to wave—and the United States flag was a very intoxicating one—and drums and trumpets to sound. Military excitement stirred through that vast pacific population and rose.

And Ford had a mighty industrial plant hitherto engaged in pouring out motor-cars and agricultural material, but capable of rapid adaptation to the production of war material. It was his creation; it was his embodiment. It was all that made him visibly different from any other fellow in the street. His friends and family had certainly watched his abandonment of business for world affairs with profound misgiving. It may have been plain to them before it was plain to him, that if he stood out of this 'preparedness' movement as he threatened to do, other great plants would arise beside his own, to produce war material indeed at first, but capable when the war was over of a reverse transformation into great factories for the mass production of motor-cars and the like. In France this transference from munitions to automobiles was actually foreseen and carried out by the Citröen organisation. It is impossible that this prospect could have escaped Ford.

But in his haste he had declared himself against preparedness. He had threatened to hoist an 'international flag' over his works in the place of the Stars and Stripes. . . .

96

It is clear that in that one lively brain all the main forces of the time were at work. It had responded vividly and generously to the new drive towards a world pax. Lochner (*America's Don Quixote*, 1924) reports him thus on his sailing from New York:

'Have you any last word to say?' a journalist enquired.

'Yes,' he replied. 'Tell the people to cry peace and fight preparedness.'

'What if this expedition fails?' ventured another.

'If this expedition fails I'll start another,' he flashed without a moment's hesitation.

'People say you are not sincere,' commented a third....

'We've got peace-talk going now, and I'll pound it to the end.'

And afterwards came those second thoughts. When, in 1917, the United States entered the war, the Peace Ship was a stale old joke and the vast Ford establishments were prepared and ready for the production of munitions.

Ford was a compendium of his age. That is why we give him this prominence in our history. The common man of the twentieth century was neither a pacificist nor a warmonger. He was both—and Ford was just a common man made big by accident and exceptional energy.

The main thread in the history of the twentieth century is essentially the drama of the indecisions manifested in their elementary plainness by Ford on board his Peace Ship. That voyage comes therefore like a tin-whistle solo by way of overture to the complex orchestration of human motive in the great struggle for human unity that lay ahead.

§ 9. *The Direct Action of the Armament Industries in Maintaining War Stresses*

We must now say something about the direct activities of the hypertrophied 'armament firms' in bringing about and sustaining the massacres of the Great War. A proper understanding of that influence is essential if the stresses and martyrdoms of the middle years of the twentieth century are to be understood.

These 'armament firms' were an outcome of the iron and steel industry, which in a few score years between 1700 and 1850 grew up—no man objecting—from a modest activity of artisans to relatively gigantic possibilities of production. This industry covered the world with a network of railways, and produced iron and then steel steamships to drive the wooden sailing ships off the seas. And at an early stage (all this is traced in full detail in Luke Zimmern's *Entwickelung und Geschichte von Kruppismus*, 1913; *Hist. Doc.* 394,112) it turned its attention to the weapons in the world.

In a perpetual progress in the size and range of great guns, in a vast expansion of battleships that were continually scrapped in favour of large or more elaborate models, it found a most important and inexhaustible field of profit. The governments of the world were taken unawares, and in a little while the industry, by sound and accepted methods of salesmanship, was able to impose its novelties upon these ancient institutions with their tradition of implacable mutual antagonism. It was realised very soon that any decay of patriotism and loyalty would be inimical to this great system of profits, and the selling branch of the industry either bought directly or contrived to control most of the great newspapers of the time, and exercised a watchful vigilance on the teaching of belligerence in schools. Following the established rules and usages for a marketing industrialism, and with little thought of any consequences but profits, the directors of these huge concerns built up the new warfare that found is first exposition in the Great War of 1914–18 and gave its last desperate and frightful convulsions in the Polish wars of 1940 and the subsequent decade.

Even at its outset in 1914–18 this new warfare was extraordinarily uncongenial to humanity. It did not even satisfy man's normal combative instincts. What an angry man wants to do is to beat and bash another living being, not to be shot at from ten miles distance or poisoned in a hole. Instead of drinking delight of battle with their peers, men tasted all the indiscriminating terror of an earthquake. The war literature stored at Atacama, to which we have already referred, is full of futile protest against the horror, the unsportsmanlike quality, the casual filthiness and indecency, the mechanical disregard of human dignity, of the new tactics. But such protest itself was necessarily futile, because it did not go on to a clear indictment of the forces that were making, sustaining and distorting war. The child howled and wept and they did not even attempt to see what it was that had tormented it.

To us nowadays it seems insane that profit-making individuals and companies should have been allowed to manufacture weapons and sell the apparatus of murder to all comers. But to the man of the late nineteenth and early twentieth centuries it seemed the most natural thing in the world. It had grown up in an entirely logical and necessary way, without any restraint upon the normal marketing methods of peace-time commerce, from the continually more extensive application of new industrial products to warfare. Even after the World War catastrophe, after that complete demonstration of the futility of war, men still allowed themselves to be herded like sheep into the barracks, to be trained to consume, and be consumed, by new lines of slaughter goods produced and marketed by the still active armament traders. And the accumulation of a still greater and still more dangerous mass of war material continued.

There is a queer little pseudo-scientific essay by a Bengali satirist (Professor K. Chandra Sen, 1897–1942) among the *India* series of reprints, professing to be a study of the relative stupidity of the more intelligent animals up to and including man. His is concerned by the fatuity with which the mass of humanity watched the preparation of its own destruction during this period. He considers the fate of various species of penguins which were then being swept out of the world—the twentieth century was an age of extermination for hundreds of species—and infers a similar destiny for mankind. He begins with the slaughter of the penguins; he gives photographs of these extraordinary creatures in their multitudes, gathered on the beaches of Oceanic islands and watching the advance of their slayers. One sees them scattered over a long sloping shore, standing still, or waddling about, or flapping their stumpy wings while the massacre goes on. They seem to be vaguely interested in the killing of their fellows, but in no way stirred either to flight or resistance. (No thorough scientific observations, we may note, were ever made of penguin mentality, the revival of experimental psychology comes too late for that, and we are left now to guess at what went on in these queer brains of theirs during these raids. There is evidence to show that these creatures had curiosity, kindliness, sympathy and humour; and they were eminently teachable. They stood quite high in the scale of bird intelligence. And yet they permitted their own extinction.) They were not so much a-mental, Professor Sen insists, half seriously, half mockingly, as defective and wrong. They were capable of many idea systems but not of the idea of social preservation. He suggests, too, that the same was true of the sea elephants which were also very rapidly destroyed. (The last of these were murdered later 'to make a record' by a Japanese lunatic with a craving for an 'immortal Name' when the protective patrol was withdrawn during the 'revolt of the sea pirates' in 1985 C.E.) But after Professor Sen has weighed

100

every possible case, he still awards the palm for complaisant social stupidity to man.

With a fine parody of the social research methods of that time, he gives various photographs of what he calls the 'human penguins' of that early twentieth century, waddling in their sleek thousands to see battleships launched, to rejoice over reviews and parades, to watch their army aeroplanes stunting in the sky. Side by side he gives photographs of penguin assemblies that, either by happy accident or skilful rearrangement, are absurdly parallel. He gives lists of shareholders in the armament firms, including the current President of the Free Church Council, an Anglican bishop, a great multitude of other clergymen, artists, judges and every sort of gentlefolk. He quotes extensively from the Hansard records of various pre-war debates in the British House of Commons (in a debate on the Naval Estimates early in 1914, Philip Snowden, the radical socialist who afterwards became Viscount Snowden, was particularly explicit), showing that the nature of the danger was clearly seen and clearly and publicly stated. Only it was not *felt*. It is upon that little difference between factual apprehension and the kind of apprehension that leads to effective action that our interest concentrates here.

Why did humanity gape at the guns and do nothing? And why, after the Great War, after that generation had seen over twenty million human beings perish painfully and untimely, did it still go on doing nothing adequate to the occasion? With the preparations still mounting up and the horrible possibilities of war increasing under its eyes? The great Cradle of Bethlehem Steel Corporation of America in 1929 was revealed as actively opposing naval disarmament at the Geneva Conference of 1927. At any rate it was associated with three ship-building companies who were sued by a Mr. Shearer, who claimed to have been given that task, for fees alleged to be due to him. There seems to have been little dispute that he had been so employed; the case turned upon the extent of his services and the amount of his fees. Nothing was done by the penguins either to the companies concerned or to Mr. Shearer. A few expressed indignation; that was all. Just as now and then no doubt a bird or so squawked at the oil-hunters. (For a detailed account and references see *The Navy; Defence or Portent*, by C. A. Beard, 1930; reprinted Hist. Doc. Series 4,270,112.)

The clue lies in the fact that there was practically no philosophical education at all in the world, no intelligent criticism of generalisations and general ideas. There was no science of social processes at all. People were not trained to remark the correlations of things; for the most part they were not aware that there was any correlation between things; they imagined this side of life might change and that remain unaltered. The industrialists and financiers built up these monstrous armaments and imposed them on the governments of the time with a disregard of consequences that seems now absolutely imbecile. Most of these armament propagandists were admirable in their private lives: gentle lovers, excellent husbands, fond of children and animals, good fellows, courteous to inferiors, and so on. Sir Basil Zaharoff, the greatest of munition salesmen, as one sees him in the painting (ascribed to Orpen) recently discovered in Paris, with his three-cornered hat, his neat little moustaches and beardlet, and the ribbon of some Order of Chivalry about his neck, looks quite a nice, if faintly absurd, little gentleman. Those shareholding bishops and clergy may, for anything we know to the contrary, have had charming Christian personalities. But they wanted their dividends. And in order to pay those dividends, the dread of war and the need of war had to be kept alive in the public mind.

That was done most conveniently through the Press. You could buy a big newspaper in those days, lock, stock and barrel, for five or ten million dollars, and the profits made on one single battleship came to more than that. Naturally, and according to the best business traditions, the newspapers hired or sold themselves to the war salesmen. What was wrong in that? Telling the news in those days was a trade, not a public duty. A daily paper that had dealt faithfully with this accumulating danger would quite as naturally and necessarily have found its distribution impeded, have found itself vigorously outdone by more richly endowed competitors, able because of their wealth to buy up all the most attractive features, able to outdo it in every way with the common reader.

It wasn't that the newspaper owners and the munition dealers wanted anyone hurt. They only wanted to sell equipment and see it used up. Nor was it that the newspapers desired the wholesale mangling and butchering of human beings. They wanted sales and advertisements. The butchery was quite by the way, an unfortunate side issue to legitimate business. Shortsightedness is not diabolical, even if it produces diabolical results.

And even those soldiers? Freudheim, in his analysis of the soldiery mind, shows a picture of that Sir Henry Wilson we have already mentioned arrayed in shirt-sleeves and digging modestly in the garden of his villa during a phase of retirement, and the same individual smirking in all his glory, buttons, straps and 'decorations', as a director of military operations. It is an amazing leap from the suburban insignificance of a retired clerk to godlike importance. In peace-time, on the evidence of his own diaries, this Wilson was a tiresome nobody, an opinionated bore; in war he passed beyond criticism and became a god. One understands at once what a vital matter employment and promotion must have been to him. But so far as we can tell he desired no killing *as* killing. If he had been given blood to drink he would probably have been sick. Yet he lived upon tanks of blood.

These professional soldiers thought of slaughter as little as possible. It is preposterous to say they desired it, much less that they gloated over it. It might have fared better with their men if they had thought of it more. They had an age-old sentimental devotion to their country, a solemn sense of great personal worth in their services, an orgiastic delight of battle. And they did not see, nor want to see, what was beyond their occupation. Their religious teachers

103

were quite ready to assure them they were correct in all they did and were.

The senescent Christian Churches of that age had indeed a very direct interest in war. A marked tendency to ignore or ridicule the current religious observances had become manifest, but under the stresses of loss and death people turned again to the altar. It is easily traceable in the fiction of the time. The despised curate of the tea-cups and croquet lawn became the implicitly heroic 'padre' of the sentimental war stories.

The problem that confronted the growing minority that was waking up to the perils and possibilties of our species in the third and fourth decades of the twentieth century was this: How in the first place to concentrate the minds of people out of this distraction and diffusion, how to bring them to bear upon the crude realities before them, and then how to organise the gigantic effort needed to shake off that intermittent and ever more dangerous fever of war and that chronic onset of pauperisation which threatened the whole world with social dissolution.

There was no central antagonist, no ruling devil, for those anxious spirits to fight. That would have made it a straight, understandable campaign. But the Press with a certain flavouring of pious intentions was practically against them. Old social and political traditions, whatever the poses they assumed, were tacitly against them. History was against them, for it could but witness that war had always gone on since its records began. Not only the current Bishop of Hereford, and the current President of the Free Church Council, caught with their dividends upon them, but their Churches and the Catholic Church, and indeed all the Christian Churches, in spite of their allegiance to the Prince of Peace, were quietly competitive with, or antagonistic to, the secular world controls that alone could make a healthy world peace possible. The admission of the insufficiency of their own creeds to comfort or direct would have been the necessary prelude to a new moral effort.

And the idea of the naturalness and inevitability of war

was not only everywhere in the world around those few forward-looking men who knew better, it was in their blood and habits. They were seeking how to attack not a fortress, but what seemed a perpetually recuperative jungle of mixed motives, tangled interests and cross-purposes, within themselves as without.

§ 10. *Versailles: Seed Bed of Disasters*

The formal war, against the Central Powers, the 'World War', ended on November 11th 1918 C.E. in the defeat and submission of the Central Powers. There was a conference at Versailles, in the same palace in which triumphant Germans had dictated peace to France after a previous war in 1870–71. There was a needlessly dramatic flavour in this reversal of the roles of the two countries. It was now France and her allies who dictated, and naturally the ideas of a romantic restoration and a stern and righteous judgment dominated the situation. The assembled Powers sat down to right the wrongs and punish the misdeeds of their grandparents. Even at the time it seemed a little belated. But threading their proceedings we do find quite plainly evident the developing conflict between historical tradition and the quickening sense of human unity in the world. If the World-State was not present at the conference, its voice was at any rate 'heard without'.

By this time (1919 C.E.) there was indeed quite a considerable number of intelligent people in the world who had realised the accumulating necessity of a world government, and a still larger multitude, like that Henry Ford we have described, who had apprehended it instinctively and senti-

105

mentally, but there was no one yet who had had the intellectual vigour to attack in earnest the problem of substituting a world system for the existing governments. Men's
minds and hearts quailed before that undertaking. And yet,
as we know so clearly, it was the only thing for them to do.
It was the sole alternative to an ever-broadening and
deepening series of disasters. But its novelty and vastness
held them back. Irrational habit kept them in the ancient
currents of history.

To us they seem like drowning men who were willing to
attempt to save themselves by rallies of swimming, floating,
holding on to straws and bubbles, but who refused steadfastly, in spite of the proximity of a ladder, to climb out
of the water for good and all.

Hardly any of them in their ideas of a world system dared
go beyond a purely political agreement for the avoidance
of war. Five decades of human distress were still needed
before there was to be any extensive realisation that belligerence was only one symptom, and by no means the
gravest symptom, of human disunion.

The American President Woodrow Wilson, of all the
delegates to the Peace Conference, was the most susceptible
to the intimations of the future. The defects and limitations
of his contributions to that settlement give us a measure
of the political imagination of those days. He brought what
was left of the individualistic liberalism that had created
the American Republics to the solution of the world
problem. None of the other participants in these remarkable discussions—Clemenceau (France), Lloyd George
(Britain), Sonnino (Italy), Saionji (Japan), Hymans (Belgium), Paderewski (Poland), Bratianu (Roumania), Bénès
(Bohemia), Venezelos (Greece), Feisal (Hedjaz), and so on
through a long list of now fading names—seemed aware
that, apart from any consideration of national advantage,
humanity as a whole might claim an interest in the settlement. They were hard-shell 'representatives', national advo-
cates. For a brief interval Wilson stood alone for mankind.
Or at least he seemed to stand for mankind. And in that

brief interval there was a very extraordinary and significant wave of response to him throughout the earth. So eager was the situation that all humanity leapt to accept and glorify Wilson—for a phrase, for a gesture. It seized upon him as its symbol. He was transfigured in the eyes of men. He ceased to be a common statesman; he became a Messiah. Millions believed him as the bringer of untold blessings; thousands would gladly have died for him. That response was one of the most illuminating events in the early twentieth century. Manifestly the World-State had been convinced then, and now it stirred in the womb. It was alive.

And then for some anxious decades it ceased to stir.

Amidst different scenery and in different costumes, the story of Wilson repeats the story of Ford, the story of a man lifted by an idea too great for him, thrown up into conspicuousness for a little while and then dropped, as a leaf may be spun up and dropped by a gust of wind before a gale. The essential Wilson, the world was soon to learn, was vain and theatrical, with no depth of thought and no wide generosity. So far from standing for all mankind, he stood indeed only for the Democratic Party in the United States—and for himself. He sacrificed the general support of his people in America to party considerations and his prestige in Europe to a craving for social applause. For a brief season he was the greatest man alive. Then for a while he remained the most conspicuous. He visited all the surviving courts of Europe and was fêted and undone in every European capital. That triumphal procession to futility need not occupy us further here. Our concern is with his idea.

Manifestly he wanted some sort of a world pax. But it is doubtful if at any time he realised that a world pax means a world control of all the vital common interests of mankind. He seems never to have thought out his job to which he set his hand so confidently. He did not want, or, if he did, he did not dare to ask for, any such centralised world controls as we now possess. They were probably beyond the range of his reading and understanding. His project

107

from first to last was purely a politician's project.

The pattern conceived by him was a naïve adaptation of the parliamentary governments of Europe and America to a wider union. His League, as it emerged from the Versailles Conference, was a typical nineteenth-century government enlarged to planetary dimensions and greatly faded in the process; it had an upper chamber, the Council, and a lower chamber, the Assembly, but, in ready deference to national susceptibilities it had no executive powers, no certain revenues, no army, no police and practically no authority to do anything at all. And even as a political body it was remote and ineffective; it was not in any way representative of the peoples of the earth as distinguished from the governments of the earth. Practically nothing was done to make the common people of the world feel that the League was theirs. Its delegates were appointed by the Foreign Offices of the very governments its only conceivable role was to supersede. They were national politicians and they were expected to go to Geneva to liquidate national politics. The League came into being at last, a solemn simulacrum to mock, cheat and dispel the first desire for unity that mankind has ever betrayed.

Yet what else was possible then? If Wilson seemed to embody the formless aspirations of mankind, there can be no dispute that he impressed the politicians with whom he had to deal as a profoundly insincere visionary. They dealt with him as that and they beat as that. The only way to have got anything more real than this futile League would have been a revolutionary appeal to the war-weary peoples of the earth against their governments, to have said, as indeed he could have said in 1918, to the whole world that the day of the World-State had come. That would have reverberated to the ends of the earth.

He was not the man to do that. He had not that power of imagination. He had not that boldness with governments. He had the common politician's way of regarding great propositions as a means to small ends. If he had been bolder and greater, he might have failed, he might have perished;

108

but he failed and perished anyhow; and a bolder bid for world unity might have put the real issue before mankind for ever and shortened the Age of Frustration by many decades.

What he did do was to reap an immediate harvest of popular applause, to present to human hope a white face rigid with self-approval, bowing from processional carriages and decorated balconies, retiring gravely into secret conference with the diplomatists and politicians of the old order and emerging at last with this League of Nations, that began nothing and ended nothing and passed in a couple of decades out of history.

It was a League not to end sovereignties but preserve them. It stipulated that the extraordinarily ill-contrived boundaries established by the Treaty in which it was incorporated should be guaranteed by the League for *evermore*. Included among other amiable arrangements were clauses penalising Germany and her allies as completely as Carthage was penalised by Rome after the disaster of Zamia—penalising her in so overwhelmingly a way as to make default inevitable and afford a perennial excuse for her continued abasement. It was not a settlement, it was a permanent punishment. The Germans were to become the penitent helots of the conquerors; a generation, whole generations, were to be born and die in debt, and to ensure the security of this arrangement Germany was to be effectually disarmed and kept disarmed.

Delenda est Germania was the sole idea of the French (*see* Morris Henbane's *Study of Pertinax*, 1939), and the representatives of the other Allies who were gathered together in the Paris atmosphere and working amidst the vindictive memories of Versailles were only too ready to fall in with this punitive conception of their task. It was the easiest conception; it put a hundred difficult issues into a subordinate place. It always looks so much easier to men of poor imagination to put things back than to carry them on. If the French dreaded a resurrection of the German armies, the British feared a resurrection of the German fleet and of

German industrial competition. Japan and Italy, seeking their own compensations elsewhere, were content to see the German-speaking peoples, who constituted the backbone of the Continent, divided and reduced to vassalage.

The antiquated form of Wilson's ideas produced still more mischievous consequences in the multiplication of sovereign governments in the already congested European area. Deluded by the vague intimations of unity embodied in the League, Wilson lent himself readily to a reconstruction of the map of Europe upon strictly nationalist lines. The Polish nation was restored. Our history has already studied the successive divisions of this country in the eighteenth century. It is a great region of the Central Plain, whose independent existence became more and more inconvenient as the trade and commerce of Europe developed. Geography fought against it. It was a loose-knit union of individualistic equestrian aristocrats dominating a peasantry. But its partition between Russia, Prussia and Austria was achieved with the utmost amount of brutality, and after the Napoleonic wars a romantic legend about this lost kingdom of Poland seized upon the sentiment of France, Britain and America. These rude nobles and their serfs, so roughly incorporated by the adjacent states, were transfigured into a delicate, brave and altogether wonderful people, a people with a soul torn asunder and trampled underfoot by excessively booted oppressors. The restoration of Poland—the excessive restoration of Poland—was one of the brightest ambitions of President Wilson.

Poland was restored. But instead of a fine-spirited and generous people emerging from those hundred and twenty years of subjugation and justifying the sympathy and hopes of liberalism throughout the world, there appeared a narrowly patriotic government, which presently developed into an aggressive, vindictive and pitiless dictatorship, and set itself at once to the zestful persecution of the unfortunate ethnic minorities (about a third of the entire population) caught in the net of its all too ample boundaries. The real Poland of the past had been a raiding and aggressive nation

110

which had ridden and harried to the very walls of Moscow. It had not changed its nature. The Lithuanian city of Vilna was now grabbed by a *coup de main* and the south-eastern boundary pushed forward in Galicia. In the treatment of the Ukrainians and Ruthenians involved in liberation, Poland equalled any of the atrocities which had been the burden of her song during her years of martyrdom. In 1932 one-third of the budget of this new militant Power was for armament.

Not only was Poland thus put back upon the map. As a result of a sedulous study of historical sentimentalities, traditions, dialects and local feelings, a whole cluster of new sovereign Powers, Czecho-Slovakia, Yugo-Slavia, Finland, Esthonia, Latvia, Lithuania, an attenuated Hungary and an enlarged Roumania, was evoked to crowd and complicate the affairs of mankind by their sovereign liberties, their ambitions, hostilities, alliances, understandings, misunderstandings, open and secret treaties, tariffs, trade wars and the like. Russia was excluded from the first attempt at a World Parliament because she had repudiated her vast war debts—always a matter of grave solicitude to the Western creditor, and—strangest fact of all in this strange story—the United States, the Arbitrator and Restorer of Nations, stood out from the League, because President Wilson's obstinate resolve to monopolise the immortal glory of World Salvation for himself and his party had estranged a majority of his senators.

The Senate, after some attempts at compromise, rejected the Covenant of the League altogether, washed its hands of world affairs, and the President, instead of remaining for ever Prince of Everlasting Peace and Wonder of the Ages, shrank again very rapidly to human proportions and died a broken and disappointed man. Like Ford, the United States returned to normal business and the Profit and Loss Account, and the Europeans were left with the name of Wilson written all over their towns, upon streets, avenues, esplanades, railway stations, parks and squares, to make what they could of this emasculated League he had left about among their affairs.

If Russia and Germany in their character of Bad Peoples were excluded from the League, such remote peoples as the Chinese and the Japanese were included as a matter of course. It was assumed, apparently, that they were 'just fellows' of the universal Treaty-of-Westphalia pattern. The European world knew practically nothing of the mental processes of these remote and ancient communities, and it seems hardly to have dawned upon the conferring states- men that political processes rest entirely upon mental facts. The League, after much difficulty, and after some years' de- lay, did indeed evolve a Committee of Intellectual Co- operation, but so far as its activities can now be traced this was concerned with dilettante intellectualism only; there is no indication that it ever interested itself in the League as an idea.

Considering all things in the light of subsequent events, it would have been well if the League of Nations had com- mitted hari-kari directly the United States Senate refused participation, and if the European Powers, realising their failure to stabilise the planet at one blow, had set themselves at once to the organisation of a League of Conciliation and Co-operation within the European area. The League's complete inability to control or even modify the foreign policy of Japan (modelled on the best nineteenth-century European patterns) was the decisive factor in its declension to a mere organisation of commentary upon current affairs.

As its authority declined the courage and pungency of its reports increased. Some of the later ones are quite admir- able historical documents. Gradually the member govern- ments discontinued their subsidies and the secretariat dwindled to nothing. Like the Hague Tribunal, the League faded out of existence before or during the Famished Fifties. It does not figure in history after the first Polish war, but its official buildings were intact in 1965, and in 1968, and for some years later, they were used as auxiliary offices by the Western branch of the Transport Union.

The imposition of vast monetary payments upon Germany was the only part of the settlement of Versailles that dealt with the financial and economic life of our race. Astounding as this seems to us to-day, it was the most natural oversight possible to the Versailles politicians. Political life was still deep in the old purely combatant tradition, still concentrated upon boundaries and strategic advantages; and it was extraordinarily innocent in the face of economic realities. The mighty forces demanding economic unification, albeit they were, as we have shown, the real causes of the Great War, were ignored at Versailles as completely as if they had never existed.

Only one outstanding voice, that of the British economist J. M. Keynes (*Economic Consequences of the Peace*, 1919), was audible at the time in protest and warning against the preposterous dislocation of credit and trade involved in the reparation payments. There was no arrangement whatever for the liquidation of the debts piled up by the Allies *against each other* (!), and no economic parallel to the political League of Nations. No control of economic warfare was even suggested. The Americans, Wilson included, were still in a stage of financial individualism; they thought money-getting was an affair of individual smartness within the limits of the law, and the American conception of law was of something that presented interesting obstacles rather than effectual barrier to enlightened self-seeking. The contemporary American form of mutual entertainment was a poker party, and that great people therefore found nothing inimical in sitting down after the war to play poker, with France and Great Britain as its chief opponents, for the gold and credit of the world.

It was only slowly during the decade following after the war that the human intelligence began to realise that the Treaty of Versailles had not ended the war at all. It had set a truce to the bloodshed, but it had done so only to open a more subtle and ultimately more destructive phase in the traditional struggle of the sovereign states. The existence of independent sovereign states *is* war, white or red, and only an elaborate mis-education blinded the world to this elementary fact. The peoples of the defeated nations suffered from a real if not very easily defined sense of injustice in this Treaty, which was framed only for them to sign, and sign in the role of wrongdoers brought to book. Very naturally they were inspired by an ill-conceived resolve to revise, circumvent or disregard its provisions at the earliest possible opportunity. The conquering Powers, on the other hand, were conscious of having not only humiliated their defeated enemies but thrust them into a state of exasperated disadvantage. The thought of a *revanche* was equally present therefore to the victors, and instead of disarming as the Germans were compelled to do, they broke the obligations of the Treaty and retained and increased their military establishments.

The armament firms and their newspapers naturally did all they could to intensify this persistence in an armed 'security'. Any disposition on the part of the French public, for instance, to lay aside its weapons was promptly checked by tales of secret arsenals and furtive drilling in Germany. And the narrow patriotic forces that guided France not only kept her extravagantly armed against her fallen foe, but carried on a subtle but ruthless financial warfare that, side by side with the American game, overcame every effort of Germany to recover socially or economically.

Moreover, the conquering Powers, so soon as they considered their former antagonists conclusively disposed of, turned themselves frankly, in full accordance with the traditions of the sovereign state system, to the task of getting the better of each other in the division of the spoils. Their 'Alliances' had brought about no sense of community. Already within a year of the signing of the Peace Treaty of Versailles heavy fighting was going on in Asia Minor between the Greeks and the Turks. The Greeks had British encouragement; the French and Italians had supported the Turks. It was a war of cat's-paws. This war culminated in a disastrous rout of the Greeks and the burning of the town of Smyrna. This last was a quite terrible massacre; multitudes of women and children were outraged, men and boys

114

gouged, emasculated or killed; all but the Turkish quarter was looted and burnt. The quays in front of the flaming town were dense with terror-stricken crowds, hoping against hope to get away upon some ship before they were fallen upon, robbed, butchered, or thrust into the water.

A little before this the Turks had driven the French out of the ancient province of Cilicia, and had completed the extermination of that ancient people the Hittites or Armenians. During the war or after the war mattered little to the Armenians, for fire and sword pursued them still. Over two million died—for the most part violent deaths.

Fighting still went on after the Great Peace in the north and south of Russia and in eastern Siberia; and China became a prey to armies of marauders. Poland seized Vilna, invaded eastern Galicia and fought Russia in the Ukraine, and a raid of patriotic Italians expelled a mixed allied garrison from Fiume.

Presently there was a dreadful famine in south-east Russia which neither America nor Europe was able to alleviate. Always before the war a famine in any part of the world had exercised the philanthropic element in the Anglo-Saxon community. But philanthropy had lost heart. There was a faint but insufficient flutter of the old habits in America but none in Britain.

Such was the peace and union of the world immediately achieved by the Conference of Versailles.

A number of unsatisfactory appendices and patches had presently to be made to correct the most glaring defects and omissions of the Treaty. Constantinople, which had been taken from the Turks and held by a mixed force of the Allies, was restored to them in 1923 after the Smyrna massacre and some warlike gesticulation between them and the British.

In drawing the boundaries of the new and revised states of the European patchwork there was the utmost disregard of economic common sense; peasants would find themselves cut off from winter or summer pasture or from market towns which had been developed by their needs.

Great foundries and chemical and metallurgical works were separated from the ores and deposits on which they relied. Vienna, once the financial and business centre of all south-east Central Europe, was decapitated. Most fantastic and, as it proved, most disastrous of all the follies of Versailles was the creation of the free city of Danzig and what was called the Polish Corridor.

Let us note a point or so about this later tangle to illustrate the mental quality of the Conference at its worst. Here more than anywhere else did the simple romantic idea that the Germans were Bad, and that anyone opposed to the Germans was without qualification Good, rule the situation. The Poles were Good, and they were the chosen of the Allies, the particular protégés of the sentimental historian from America. He had come to put down the mighty from their seats and to exalt the humble and the meek. The hungry and eager were to be filled with good things and the rich, the erstwhile rich, were to be sent empty away. Germany, like Dives in hell, was to look up and see Poland like Lazarus in Woodrow Wilson's bosom. Not only were the Good Poles to be given dominion over Ruthenians, Ukrainians, Jews (whom particularly they detested), Lithuanians, White Russians and Germans, they were to have also something of profound economic importance—'access to the sea'.

On that President Wilson had been very insistent. Switzerland had done very well in pre-war Europe without access to the sea, but that was another story. The difficulty was that by no stretch of ethnic map-colouring could Poland be shown to border on the sea. A belt of Pomeranians and Germans stretched across the mouth of the Vistula, and the only possibility of a reasonable trading outlet to the sea, so far as Poland needed such an outlet—for most of its trade was with its immediate neighbours—was through an understanding with that belt of people. That would have been easy enough to arrange. At the mouth of the Vistula stood the entirely German city of Danzig. It lived mainly as an outlet for Polish trade, and it could prosper in no other way.

116

There was no reason to suppose it would put any difficulties in the way of Polish imports and exports. It was an ancient, honest, clean and prosperous German city. Ninety-six per cent of its inhabitants were German.

This was the situation to which the Conference of Versailles, under the inspiration of that magic phrase 'access to the sea', turned its attention. Even the profound belief of the Conquerors that there were no Germans but bad Germans could not justify their turning over Danzig itself to Polish rule. But they separated it from Germany and made it into a 'free city', and to the west of it they achieved that 'access to the sea' of Wilson's, by annexing a broad band of Pomeranian territory to Poland. (This was the actual 'Corridor' of the controversies.) It had no port to compare with Danzig, but the Poles set themselves to create a rival in Gdynia, which should be purely Polish, and which should ultimately starve the trading Germans out of Danzig.

And to keep the waters of the Vistula as pure and sweet for Poland as the existence of Danzig at the estuary allowed, the peace-makers ran the Vistula boundary between Poland and east Prussia, not in the usual fashion midway along the stream, but at a little distance on the east Prussian side. (Jacques Kayser, *La Paix en Péril*, 1931, Hist. Doc., 711,711.) So that the east German population, the peasant cultivator, the erstwhile fisherman, the shepherd with his flocks to water, was pulled up by a line of frontier posts and a Polish rifle within sight of the stream. Moreover, that eastward country was flat and low-lying an dhad hitherto been protected from floods and a relapse to marsh conditions by a line of dykes. The frontier cut that line five times, and, since the Poles had no interest whatever in these defences, they fell rapidly out of repair. Further along the boundary cut off the great towns of Garnsee and Bischofswerder from their railway station.

But we must not lose ourselves in the details of this exasperating settlement. The maximum of irritation developed in the absurd Corridor itself. The current of traffic had hitherto run to and fro between east and west, the trend of the railways was in that direction; the traffic in the north and south direction had come to Danzig along the great river. Now the Poles set themselves to obstruct both these currents and to wrench round all the communications into a north and south direction avoiding Danzig. Every German going east or west found himself subjected to a series of frontier examinations, to tariff payments, to elaborate delays, to such petty but memorable vexations as that all the windows of an express train passing across the Corridor should be closed and so forth, and the city of Danzig, cut off from German trade, found its Polish business being steadily diverted to Gdynia. French capital was poured into Gdynia and into its new railway to the south, so that French financial interests were speedily entangled in the dispute.

The indignity and menace of Danzig burnt into the German imagination. That Corridor fretted it as nothing else in the peace settlement had fretted it. It became a dominant political issue. There was an open sore of a similar character in Upper Silesia; there was a sore in the Saar Valley; there was the sore of an enforced detachment from Austria; there were many other bitter memories and grievances, but this was so intimate, so close to Berlin, that it obsessed all German life.

Within a dozen years of the signing of the Treaty of Versailles the Polish Corridor was plainly the most dangerous factor in the European situation. It mocked every projection of disarmament. It pointed the hypnotised and impotent statescraft of Europe straight towards a resumption of war. A fatalistic attitude towards war as something terrible indeed but inevitable, which had already been evident among the politicians of Europe before 1914, reappeared and spread.

History had an air of repeating itself. Nobody made any definite suggestions about any of these open sores, but there was scarcely a politician of the period who could not claim to have been very eloquent on various occasions against war—with, of course, a skilful avoidance of anything that could be considered specific, controversial, unpatriotic or likely to wound the susceptibilities of the Powers immediately concerned.

§ 11. *The Impulse to Abolish War: Why the League of Nations Failed to Pacify the World*

Before we leave that bleak and futile idealist, Woodrow Wilson, altogether, we will draw the attention of the student to the essential factors of his failure. The defects of his personality must not blind us to the impossibility of his ambition. His narrow egotism, the punitive treatment of the Central Powers and so forth, merely emphasised a disadvantage that would have been fatal to the launching of any League of Nations at that time. There had been an insufficient mental preparation for a world system to operate. No ideology existed to sustain it. The World-State, the Modern State, was still only a vaguely apprehended suggestion; it had not been worked out with any thoroughness and the League was the most hasty of improvisations.

It needed the life scheming of de Windt and his associates, which we shall presently describe; it needed a huge development and application of the science of social psychology, before the supersession of the chaos of sovereign states by a central control was even a remote possibility. Wilson thought he could get together with a few congenial spirits and write a recipe for humanity unity. He had not the slightest inkling of the gigantic proportions, the intricacy, intimacy and profundity, of the task that was opening before him. He attempted to patch up the outworn system of his time and pass it off as a new one. He did not dream of the monetary reconstruction, the need for a thorough-

119

going socialism throughout the world, and for a complete revolution in education, before the peace and security of mankind could be established. Yet, narrow and blind as he was, he seems to have been in advance of the general thought of his age.

This premature and ineffectual League was a hindrance rather than a help to the achievement of world peace. It got in the way. It prevented people from thinking freely about the essentials of the problem. Organisations of well-meaning folk, the British League of Nations Union, for example, came into existence to support it, and resisted rather than helped any effectual criticism of its constitution and working. They would say that it was 'better than nothing', whereas a false start is very much worse than nothing. In the post-war decade, the amount of vigorous constructive thought in the general mind about world politics was extraordinarily small. It was only when the insufficiency of the League had passed beyond any possibility of dispute that men begun to take up the abandoned search for world unification again.

A dozen years later the Modern State movement was still only foreshadowed in sketchy attempts to find a comprehensive set of general formulae for liberal progressive effort. The pacificists, communists, socialists and every other sort of 'ists' who gave a partial and confused expression to human discontent had still to be drawn together into understanding and co-operation. Most of their energy was wasted in obscure bickerings, mutual suspicion and petty and partial tentatives. The middle of the century had been passed before there was any considerable body of Modern State propaganda and education on earth.

§ 12. *The Breakdown of 'Finance' and Social Morale after Versailles*

The unprecedented range and destruction of the World War were, we have pointed out, largely ascribable to the hypertrophy of the world's iron and steel industry relatively to the political and social concepts of the race. But in the first 'post-war' decade the stresses of other disproportionate developments began to make themselves manifest at various other weak points in the loosely linked association of our species. The war from the economic point of view had been the convulsive using up of an excess of production that the race had no other method of distributing and consuming. But the necessities of the struggle, and particularly its interference with international trading, which had evoked factories and finishing processes in many undeveloped regions hitherto yielding only raw or unfinished materials, had added greatly to the gross bulk of productive plant throughout the world, and so soon as the open war-furnaces ceased to burn up the surplus and hold millions of men out of the labour market, this fact became more and more oppressively apparent. The post-war increase in war preparation, which went on in spite of endless palavering about disarmament, did not destroy men, nor scrap and destroy material, in sufficient quantity to relieve the situation.

Moreover, the expansion of productive energy was being accompanied by a positive contraction of the distributive arrangements which determined consumption. The more efficient the output, the fewer were the wages-earners. The more stuff there was, the fewer consumers there were. The fewer the consumers, the smaller the trading profits, and the less the gross spending power of the shareholders and individual entrepreneurs. So buying dwindled at both ends of the process and the common investor suffered with the wages-earner. This was the 'Paradox of Over-production' which so troubled the writers and journalists of the third decade of the twentieth century.

It is easy for the young student to-day to ask, 'Why did they not adjust?' But let him ask himself who there was to adjust. Our modern superstructure of applied economic science, the David Lubin Bureau and the General Directors' Board, with its vast recording organisation, its hundreds of thousands of stations and observers, directing, adjusting, apportioning and distributing, had not even begun to exist. Adjustment was left to blind and ill-estimated forces. It was the general interest of mankind to be prosperous, but it was nobody's particular interest to keep affairs in a frame of prosperity. Manifestly a dramatic revision of the liberties of enterprise was necessary, but the enterprising people who controlled politics, so far as political life was controlled, were the very last people to undertake such a revision.

With the hypertrophy of productive activities there had been a concurrent hypertrophy of banking and financial organisation generally, but it had been a flabby hypertrophy, a result of the expansion of material production rather than a compensatory and controlling development.

It is so plain to us to-day that the apportionment of the general product of the world for enterprise or consumption is a department of social justice and policy, and can be dealt with only in the full light of public criticism and upon grounds of claim and need, that it is difficult for us to understand the twentieth-century attitude of these things. We should no more dream of leaving the effectual control in these matters in private profit-seeking hands than we should leave our law courts or our schools to the private bidder. But nothing of the sort was plain in 1935 C.E. That lesson had still to be learnt.

The story of banking and money in the early twentieth century has so much in it verging upon the incredible that it has become one of the most attractive and fruitful fields for the student of historical psychology. The system had grown

122

up as a tangle of practice. It was evolved, not designed. There was never any attempt to gauge the justice or the ultimate consequences of any practice, so long as it worked at the time. Men tried this and that, did this and that, and concealed their opinions of what the results might be. Reserve was essential in the system. So little was the need for publicity in this universal interest understood that the most fundamental decisions affecting the common man's purchasing power and the credit of industrial undertakings were made in secret, and the restriction and stimulation of trade and work went on in the profoundest obscurity. Neither in the ordinary courses of the schools and universities was there any instruction in these essential facts. The right of private enterprise to privacy was respected in the Churches, the law courts and private practice alike. Men found themselves employed or unemployed, cheated of their savings or better off, they knew not why. Instead of the clear knowledge of economic pressures and movements that we have to-day, strange Mystery Men were dimly visible through a fog of baffling evasions and misstatements, manipulating prices and exchanges.

Prominent among these Mystery Men was a certain Mr. Montagu Norman, Governor of the Bank of England from 1920 to 1935. He is among the least credible figures in all history, and a great incrustation of legends has accumulated about him. In truth the only mystery about him was that he was mysterious. His portrait shows a slender, bearded man, dressed more like a successful artist or musician than the conventional banker of the time. He was reputed to be shy and, in the phraseology of the time, 'charming', and he excited the popular imagination by a habit of travelling about under assumed names and turning up in unexpected places. Why he did so, nobody now knows. Perhaps he did it for the fun of doing it. He gave evidence before an enquiry into finance in 1930 (the Macmillan Committee), and from that and from one or two of his public speeches that have been preserved it is plain that he had what we should now consider an entirely inadequate education for the veiled activities in which he was engaged. Of human ecology he betrays no knowledge, and his ideas of social and economic processes are not what we should now recognise as adequate general ideas even for an ordinary citizen. Indeed his chief qualification for his darkly responsible post was some practical experience acquired in association with various private banking firms before he entered the service of the Bank of England. This experience was acquired during what we know now to have been a period of quite accidental and transitory expansion of human wealth. Plainly he did not even bring a blank mind to his task. He had a mind warped and prejudiced by gainful banking under abnormal conditions. Yet for a time he was regarded as an 'expert' of almost magical quality, and during the convulsions of the post-war period he was able to dictate or defeat arrangements that enriched or impoverished millions of people in every country in Europe.

Another big obscure financial force in the war and post-war periods was the complex of great private banking ganglia of which Morgan and Co., with its associated firms, was the most central and most typical. This particular firm carried on its business upon a scale that completely overshadowed many minor governments. The loans it made or refused, confirmed or shattered régimes. Its founder, J. P. Morgan, a queer combination of Yankee 'gentleman' and German junker, whose innate acquisitiveness overflowed in great collections of pictures and 'art' objects generally, had died before the outbreak of the war, but a phrase he used in a dispute with President Roosevelt the First was taken up later and made into a deadly critical weapon against the whole private banking world. 'Roosevelt,' he protested, 'wants all of us to have glass pockets!'

A second President Roosevelt was presently to revive that demand.

Nothing could better betray the habit of deep gainful manoeuvrings than that phrase. Morgan was never dishonest and always disingenuous. That was the rule of his game. Opaque pockets he insisted upon, and hidden

124

motives, but also the punctual performance of a bargain. His tradition lived after him. His firm became an octopus of credit. The interweaving bargains it made hung like a shadowy group of spiders' webs about European life. It did its work of strangulation by its nature and without malice, as a spider spins. No contemporary could apprehend it. The particulars of any particular situation could only be unravelled vaguely by a normal enquirer after many months of study.

Interacting with such mystery systems as these of the banking world were other dark figures and groups, controlling vast industrial activities, obsessing and perverting spending power. There was, for example, that Mystery Man of Mystery Men, Sir Basil Zaharoff, the armaments salesman, still the delight of our schoolboy novelists, and Ivar Kreuger, who created an almost world-wide system of lucifer match monopolies, lent great sums to governments and was finally caught forging big parcels of bonds. He then staged a suicide in Paris to escape the penalty of fraud. (We have to remember that in those days the lucifer matches we now see in museums were consumed by the billion. There was no other handy source of fire, and their manufacture and distribution was on the scale of a primary industry.) Kreuger, unlike Morgan, was not a man of the acquisitive type; he neither hoarded nor collected; he kept nothing, not even the law, but he built lavishly and gave away money for scientific research. (The discovery of Pekin Man, a memorable incident in early archaeology, was, for instance, made possible by his gifts.) Morgan forestalled and accumulated; Kreuger robbed and gave. When Morgan spent his gains he bought 'Old Masters', manuscripts and suchlike indisputably genuine and valuable junk; when Kreuger dispersed the moneys that had been entrusted to him he made the most extraordinary experiments in decorative art, in electric lighting and fantastic building. But each operated unchecked. So obscure was the financial machinery of the time that for some months Kreuger was able to pass off as genuine a package of forged Italian bonds amounting to about half a million dollars, and to obtain advances upon them from reputable lenders. To-day a trick of such a character would be detected, were it possible, in the course of a single day by the ordinary checking of the Transactions Bureau. But nowadays no one would have any reason for attempting anything of the sort. The lives of these Mystery Men and of the various groups of speculators (the Balkan Gang, e.g.) who manipulated the exchanges of the various national currencies of Eastern Europe, and of a great number of other profit-seeking groups and individuals who were thrusting about amidst the machinery of exchange, are to be found in *Lives of Mischief* (Financial Volumes) taken out of the *Dictionary of Biography*. The very best of them were men who waylaid gain or sought adventures in a fog. Most of them were as active and as blind to the consequences of their activities as voles who perforate a dyke.

In the files of the financial papers of this period, when the movements of gold were of vital significance to the prices of commodities and the credit of everyone in the world, one sees such headings as 'Unknown Buyer Takes Two Millions in Gold' or, less exactly, 'Gold Bought by Unknown Buyer'. Then all the little manipulators of money would be set peering and spying and guessing and rigging their businesses to the possible shift of equilibrium this dark intimation might portend.

Other Mystery Men, Mystery Men *ex officio*, were the various Ministers of Finance, of whom perhaps the British Chancellor of the Exchequer was most typical. Every year there was a vast amount of whispering and hinting, peeping and calculating and going to and fro, about the National Budget and the readjustment of taxation for another twelve-months. An arithmetical mystery called 'balancing the Budget' had to be performed. Business would be held up as the great revelation drew near; gambling operations, insurance operations, would multiply. The wife, the family, the intimates and secretaries of the Man of Destiny, went about the world sealed, enigmatical, oracular, profoundly important with his reflected importance. At last the great day dawned. The legislature would assemble in unusual force, excited and curious. The Witch Doctor, with his portfolios of Obi, would take his place in the House of Commons, rise portentously, begin the 'Budget Speech'.

No Budget Speech was complete without its 'surprises'. Could anything witness more vividly to the chaotic casualness of the twentieth century? Anything might be taxed; anything might be relieved; anyone might shift the weights about. In the economic darkness of the time it did not seem to matter. The marvel is that the system staggered on for so long.

How amazing, how fantastic, was that condition of affairs! It is as if one of the great transatlantic liners of the period had careered across the ocean with its passenger decks and cabins brightly lit, its saloons and bars in full swing, while down below its essential machinery manifestly with something going wrong with it, had no arrangements for illumination at all and was served by men (some of them masked), working without a foreman or any general directions, by the light of an occasional match or a treasured but rather worn-out electric torch, or altogether in the dark, upon the cranks and swiftly sliding shafts that beat and circled about them.

From the very cessation of the fighting in 1918 and onward it was manifest that this machinery was seriously out of gear. The economic history of the time is a story of swerves and fluctuations of the most alarming kind, each one more disconcerting and disastrous than its predecessor. In the decades before the war, though there were certainly variations in the real value of the different currencies, they were variations within moderate limits, and the rise or fall went on through comparatively long periods, but after the war there commenced a series of movements in exchange and prices unprecedented throughout the whole period of prosperity. Currencies rose and towered above others and broke like Atlantic waves, and people found the good money in their banks changed to useless paper in a period of a few months. It became more and more difficult to

127

carry on foreign trade because of the increasing uncertainty of payment, and since there was scarcely a manufacturing industry that had not to obtain some material from abroad, the entanglement of foreign trade often involved a strangulation of production at home. Trade and industry sickened and lost heart more and more in this disastrous uncertainty; it was like being in an earthquake, when it seems equally unsafe to stand still or run away; and the multitudes of unemployed increased continually. The economically combatant nations entrenched themselves behind tariffs, played each other tricks with loans, repudiations, sudden inflations and deflations, and no power in the world seemed able to bring them into any concerted action to arrest and stop their common dégringolade.

The opening years of the second third of the twentieth century saw *Homo sapiens* in the strangest plight. The planet had a healthier and more abundant human population than it had ever carried before, and it lacked nothing in its available resources to give the whole of this population full and happy lives. That was already the material reality of the position. But through nothing in the world but a universal, various muddle-headedness, our species seemed unable to put out its hand and take the abundance within its reach. As we turn over the periodicals and literature of the time the notes of apprehension and distress increase and deepen. The war period of 1914–18 was full of suffering, but also it was full of excitement; even the dying on the battlefields believed that a compensatory peace and happiness lay close ahead. The survivors were promised 'homes fit for heroes'. But the Depression of 1930 and onward was characterised by its inelasticity; it was a phase of unqualified disappointment and hopelessly baffled protest. One lived, as one contemporary writer put it, in 'a world bewitched'.

The economic consequences of this monetary disorganisation followed hard upon it, but the deeper lying destruction of social morale and its effects were manifested less immediately. The whole world system heretofore had been sustained by the general good behaviour of common men,

128

by the honesty and punctuality of clerks, workers of every sort, traders, professional men. General security depended upon habitual decent behaviour in the street and on the countryside. But the common man behaved well because he had faith that his pay was a safe, if sometimes a scanty, assurance of a certain comfort and dignity in his life. He imagined an implicit bargain between himself and society that he should be given employment and security in exchange for his law-abiding subordination, and that society would keep faith with his savings. He assumed that the governments would stand by the money they issued and see that it gave him the satisfactions it promised him. He was not a good boy for nothing. Nobody is. But now in various terms and phrases all over the world millions of men and women were asking themselves whether it 'paid' to be industrious, skilful and law-abiding. The cement of confidence in the social fabric from 1918 onward was more and more plainly decaying and changing to dust. The percentage of criminal offences, which had been falling through all the period of prosperity, rose again.

§ 13. 1933 : *'Progress' Comes to a Halt*

So we bring the history of mankind to that great pause in social expansion which concluded the first third of the twentieth century. The year 1933 closed in a phase of dismayed apprehension. It was like that chilly stillness, that wordless interval of suspense, that comes at times before the breaking of a storm. The wheels of economic life were turning only reluctantly and uncertainly; the millions of unemployed accumulated and became more and more plainly a challenge and a menace. All over the world the masses were sinking down through distress and insufficiency to actual famine. And collectively they were doing nothing effectual in protest or struggle. Insurrectionary socialism lurked and muttered in every great agglomeration. But insurrection alone could remedy nothing without constructive ideas, and there was no power and energy yet behind any such constructive ideas as had appeared. The merely repressive forces, whatever their feebleness in the face of criminality, were still fully capable of restraining popular insurrection. They could keep misery stagnant and inoperative.

Everywhere, in everything, there was an ebb of vitality. A decline in the public health was becoming perceptible. A diminishing resistance to infections and a rise in the infantile death-rate was already very evident in the vital statistics after 1933.

War was manifestly drawing nearer, in Eastern Asia, in Eastern Europe; it loitered, it advanced, it halted, and no one displayed the vigour or capacity needed to avert its intermittent unhurrying approach.

Still the immense inertias of the old order carried things on. Under a darkling sky, the majority of people were going about their business according to use and wont. The unprofitable industries still carried on with reduced staffs; the shopkeepers opened their shops to a dwindling tale of customers; the unemployed queued up at the Labour Exchanges by force of habit and some at least got a job; the landlord's agent no longer collected the rent that was due but called for an instalment of his arrears; the unfed or ill-fed children went sniffing to chilly schools to be taught by dispirited teachers on reduced salaries, but still the schools were not closed; the bankrupt railways and steamship lines ran diminished but punctual services; hotels stayed open not to make profits but to mitigate losses; the road traffic lost something of its newness and smartness and swiftness, but still it flowed; the crowds in the streets moved less briskly, but, if anything, these sluggish crowds were more numerous, and the police, if less alertly vigilant, maintained order.

There had been a considerable if inadequate building boom after the Peace of Versailles, but after 1930 new construction fell off more and more. Yet some builders found work, necessary repairs were attended to, burnt-out houses were reconditioned, for example. In 1935 and 1937 the world was swept by influenza epidemics of unusual virulence. The lowered resistance, already noted by the statisticians, was now made conspicuous by this return towards medieval conditions; but the doctors and nurses stuck to their duties stoutly and the druggists and undertakers, whose affairs had long since been reorganised on Big Business lines, profited.

Pictures of life in the shadows during this phase of devitalisation are not very abundant, nor do they convey the essential misery into which a whole generation was born, in which it lived and died. One sees the rows of dilapidated houses, the wretched interiors and shabbily clad men and women standing about. In these pictures they seem always to be just standing about. Descriptive journalism brings the student nearer to the realities of a life without space, colour, movement, hope or opportunity. There were a number of 'enquiries' made, more particularly by the British, American and French newspapers, and the tale they tell is always of wheels slowing down to a stoppage, of factory gates being closed, of smokeless chimneys and rusting rails. Here is a vivid contemporary vignette, to show how things were with millions of human beings during this strange phase of human experience. It is from the pen of H. M. Tomlinson (1873–1969) one of the best of English descriptive writers.

'I chanced upon a little town above Cardiff last week. It was by pure chance; I had never before heard of the place. It is typical of these valleys, so never mind its name. It could have many names. Its population is, or was, about 6,000. Its people have faced trouble before—less than twenty years ago over 300 of its men perished in a mine

131

explosion. We won't say the town got over that, for I spoke to those whom the calamity is an abiding horror. It was a terrific defeat for them in the war upon Nature, but survivors returned to the struggle and said no more about it.

'When first I saw the town from a distance, with the bleak, bare uplands about it, I was reminded of the towns, once familiar, that were too near the battle-line in France. It was midday, and sunny, yet this colliery town was silent and so still that it seemed under a spell.

'As a fact, it *is* under a spell. It is, in a way, dead. But its people cling to the empty shell of it. Where else can they go?

'At first sight no people could have been there. Buildings in the foreground were in ruins. The gaunt pit-head gearing evidently had not moved for an age. The gaps in the blackened walls of the powerhouse suggested a home of bats and owls.

'The first man I met when I reached the end of its main street and saw then that the shops were not only closed, but abandoned, was standing on the kerb, a man in the middle years, shrewd, but haggard, his clothes brushed till they were threadbare.

' "What's the matter with this town?" I asked.

' "On the dole."

' "Are you out too?"

' "Of course I'm out."

' "How long?"

'He was silent. He held up five fingers.

' "Months?"

' "Years."

' "Are all the men here the same?"

' "Most of them. And won't go back."

'He led me up a mound of refuse, where a goat was eating paper, and we had a near view of the colliery itself. "That's the reason we won't go down again," he said. "How would you work it?"

'Whether by design or rust a steel footbridge had fallen

across the wide railway track which went to the pit-head. A deflected stream guttered down between the metals, which were overgrown with grass and stagnant marsh stuff. The outbuildings were a huddle of dilapidations. It looked haunted. "Some men I knew," muttered my guide, "are still down there. There they'll stop. They've been there nineteen years now. Would you call them lucky?"

'Two thousand five hundred men came out of the principal colliery five years ago. That is why the shops are shut, long rows of them with whitewashed windows and doorways filled with dust and straws. The woodwork of many houses has been taken for firewood. Even the Co-operative store is shut, as well as the pawnshop. Thrift and thriftlessness mean the same thing in this town, where I noticed that even Nonconformist chapels, with broken windows, had been left to the rats and birds.

'Worse than the dismal shops and broken buildings are the groups of shabby men, all neat and tidy, standing listless and silent at the street corners, waiting.

'Waiting for what? Nothing. There is nothing to come. . . .

'They are doomed, these parents, to watch a generation grow up with thin bones and a shadow on its mind. Their children learn the signs of the slow death about them when they should be at play; children that have no childhood.

'Their homes are in a graveyard of human aspiration. . . .'

The Press and literature of that period make curious reading. It varied between a bleak, insincere optimism and hopeless desperation. An undignified viciousness and a jeering humour invaded popular art and literature; 'strong' in manner and in flavour rather than in any grasp upon the realities of contemporary life. There was also an abundant production and consumption of reassuring and deliberately 'cheerful' books, a movement towards religious mysticism and other-worldliness and a marked tendency towards repressive puritanism. Excesses of libertinism provoke censorious and superstitious suppression; the two things are correlated aspects of a decline in human dignity. In the face

133

of its financial and political perplexities mankind was becoming neurasthenic.

All neurasthenia has apparently unaccountable elements. To us to-day, it seems incredible that the way out of all these distresses was not plainly seen and boldly taken. There was a blindness and an effortlessness that still exercise the mind of the social psychologist. The way was so plain that it was visible, it was indicated by hundreds of intelligent and detached observers as early as the 'thirties of the twentieth century. Maxwell Brown, in his study of the Modern State idea, has two supplementary volumes of citations to this effect. Such phrases, for example, as 'Cosmopolis, Inflation and Public Employment' (from a British provincial newspaper article in 1932) do state, in general terms at any rate, the line of escape for the race. These are crude, ill-defined terms, but manifestly they have in them the shape of the ultimate reconstruction. 'Cosmopolis' foreshadows our rational world controls, 'Inflation' was a plain indication of our present complete restraint upon the aggravation of debts and fluctuation of price level; 'Public Employment' was our ancestors' conception of socialist enterprise.

But before the exodus to peace and freedom could be achieved, such scattered flashes of understanding had to ignite a steadier illumination. The conception of revolutionary world reconstruction had to spread from the few to the many, spread to them not merely as an idea and as a suggestion, but in such force as to saturate their minds and determine their lives. Then, and then only, could the necessary will-power be marshalled and directed to the effective reorganisation of earthly affairs.

A struggle for sanity had to take place in the racial brain, a great casting-out of false assumptions, conventional distortions, hitherto uncriticised maxims and impossible 'rights', a great clearing-up of ideas about moral, material and biological relationship; it was a struggle that, as we shall see, involved the passing of three generations. To an analysis of the factors and decisive forces in this struggle our history must next address itself.

Something between eight and ten thousand million human lives in all were lived out during the Age of Frustration. Compared with the average lives of to-day, they were shorter and far less healthy; nearly all of them had long phases of such infection, maladjustment and enfeeblement as are now almost outside man's experience. The great majority of them were passed laboriously in squalid or dingy surroundings, in huts, hovels, cottages, tenements and cellars almost as dismal as the ancestral cave and nearly as insanitary. A minority who could command the services of 'domestics' lived in relative comfort and even with a certain freedom and luxury, at an enormous cost to the rest. This prosperous minority dwindled after 1931. It had vanished in Russia after 1917.

There was a diminishing sense of personal security in the world, an enervating fear and uncertainty about the morrow through the ensuing years. There was what we find now an almost incredible amount of mutual distrust, suspicion, irritation and quarrelling. Only a small proportion of the world's population lived to be peacefully and gracefully old in this phase of deterioration. Disease or a violent death became the common end again. One of the first general histories that was ever written was called *The Martyrdom of Man* (Winwood Reade, 1871). In the Age of Frustration it seemed to many that that martyrdom was mounting to a final hopeless agony.

Yet in the welter there were also laughter, sympathy, helpfulness and courage. Those fretted and painful lives interwove with threads of great brightness. Out of that medley of human distresses, out of the brains of men stressed out of indolence and complacency by the gathering darkness and suffering about them, there came first the hope, then the broad plan and the effort, and at last the achievement of that fruitful order, gathering beauty and happy assurance, in which we live to-day.

BOOK THE SECOND

THE DAYS AFTER TO-MORROW: THE AGE OF FRUSTRATION

THE DAYS AFTER TO-MORROW: THE AGE OF FRUSTRATION

§ 1. *The London Conference, the Crowning Failure of the Old Governments; The Spread of Dictatorships and Fascisms*

In the preceding chapters we have explained how the old order of the nineteenth century, the Capitalist System as it was called, came to disaster in the second and third decades of the twentieth century because of the disproportionate development of its industrial production, the unsoundness and vulnerability of its monetary nexus, and its political inadaptability. It had no inherent power of recovery, and there was no idea of a new order, sufficiently developed, to replace it. Necessarily therefore the tale of disaster went on.

The only mechanisms in existence for collective action, and that only in disconnected spurts, were the various sovereign governments. Most of these at the outset of the war were either parliamentary monarchies or parliamentary republics. The parliaments were elected upon a very preposterous system by the bulk or all of the population. The age was called the Age of Democracy. Democracy did not mean then what it means now, an equal opportunity for every human being according to his ability and the faculty to which he belongs, to serve and have a voice in collective affairs. Nor did it mean the fraternal equality of a small community. It expressed a political fiction of a very extraordinary kind: that every subject of the contemporary state was equally capable of making whatever collective decisions had to be made.

The great republics of a remoter antiquity, the Carthaginian, the Athenian, the Roman, for example, were all essentially aristocratic. Democratic republics, that is to say republics in which every man was supposed to share equally in the government, in the rare instances when they occurred at all before the end of the eighteenth century, were, like Uri, Unterwalden or Andorra, small and poor and perched in inaccessible places. The world at large knew nothing of them. Their affairs were equally small and well within the scope of a common citizen's understanding.

Then with the Era of European Predominance came a turning-point in human affairs, that outbreak of books and discussion in the fifteenth century, a period of great anima- tion and confusion when the destructive criticism of faiths and loyalties got loose. The release of new economic forces strained the old feudal order to breaking. Exploration and merchandising, new financial conditions, industrial develop- ment, created new types of men, uncertain of their powers, needing and demanding free play. They did not know clearly what they wanted; they did not know clearly how they differed from the men of the old order, nor had they any conception of such a structural reform of human relations as Plato had already pictured nearly two thou- sand years before them. His plan for a devoted and trained order of rulers was unknown to them, though More had tried to revive it. They were simply responding to the facts about them. They chafed under an hereditary aristocracy, and they distrusted an absolute king.

Essentially the movement that evolved the phraseology of nineteenth-century democracy was a revolt against 'birth' and 'privilege', against the monopolisation of direction and advantages by restricted and generally hereditary classes in accordance with definitely established dogmas. Because this revolt was the revolt of a very miscellaneous number of energetic and resentful individuals not definitely organised, mentally or socially, it came about that at a quite early stage of the new movement it took the form of an assertion of the equal political rights of all men.

It was not that these sixteenth- and seventeenth-century

Radicals were for government by the general mass; it was that they were antagonistic to established classes and rulers. They constituted a vigorous insurgent minority rousing, so far as it could, and trailing after it the apathetic majority of submissive mankind. That was always the character of these democratic movements of the Age of European Predominance. The multitude was supposed to be demanding and deciding—and all the time it was being pushed or led. The individuality of the popular 'leaders' of those centuries stands out far more vividly than the kings and ecclesiastics of the period. Only one or two such hereditary monarchs as William Prince of Orange, or Frederick the Great of Prussia, figure as conspicuously on the record as—to cite a miscellany of new types—Cromwell, Voltaire, Mirabeau, Washington, Gladstone, Robespierre, Bonaparte or Marx.

Later on (in England, America, Scandinavia, Germany, Finland, e.g.) in just the same way a minority of dissatisfied and aggressive women struggling for a role in affairs inflicted the vote upon the indifferent majority of women. But their achievement ended with that. Outside that sexual vindication, women at that time had little to contribute to the solution of the world's problems, and as a matter of fact they contributed nothing.

Research in social psychology is still only beginning to unravel the obscure processes by which faith in 'democracy' became for the better part of a century the ruling cant of practically all America and the greater part of Europe. There was often a profound internal disingenuousness even in those who were known as 'Thinkers' in that age. They were afraid in their hearts of stark realities; they tried instinctively to adapt even their heresies to what seemed to them invincibly established prejudices. Their primary conception of democracy was of some far-away simple little republic of stout upstanding men, all similar, all practically equal in fortune and power, managing the affairs of the canton in a folk-meeting, by frank speech and acclamation. All the old-world democracies, up to and including the

Republic of Rome, were ruled, in theory at least, by such meetings of all the citizens. The people, it was imagined, watched, listened, spoke and wisdom ensued.

The extension of this ideal to the large communities of the new world that was replacing the feudal order involved such manifest difficulties and even such absurdities that mysticism was inevitable if the people was still to be supposed the sovereign of the community. But there was so strong and widespread a dread that if this supposition was not maintained, privilege, restriction, tyranny would come back that the mystical interpretation was boldly adopted. At any cost those old inequalities must not return, said the adventurers of the dawning capitalist age, and flying from one subjugation, they hurried on to another.

They found the doctrine of man's natural virtue as expounded by Rousseau extraordinarily helpful and effective. The common man, when he is not beguiled by Priest or King, is always right. The Common People became therefore a mystical sympathetic being, essentially a God, whose altar was the hustings and whose oracle the ballot box. A little slow and lumpish was this God of the Age of European Predominance, but, though his mills ground slowly, men were assured that they ground with ultimate exactitude. And meanwhile business could be carried on. You could fool some of the people all the time and all the people some of the time, said Abraham Lincoln, but you could not fool all the people all the time. Yet for such crucial purposes as bringing about a war or exploiting an economic situation, this was manifestly a quite disastrous degree of foolability.

And the situation naturally evolved a Press of the very highest fooling capacity.

This belatedly inevitable Divinity proved now to be altogether too slow-witted for the urgent political and economic riddles, with ruin and death at hand, which pressed upon our race as the twentieth century unfolded. The experience of the futile Disarmament and Economic Conferences of 1932 and 1933, the massive resistance in every national legislature to any but the most narrow egotism in foreign

142

policy, the inability of the world as a whole to establish any unanimity of action in face of swift economic collapse, revealed the final bankruptcy of Parliamentary Democracy.

The inability of the world's nominal rulers to shake off their lifelong habit of speaking to, or at, a vaguely conceived crowd of prejudiced voters and their invincible repugnance from clear statement, frustrated every effort towards realism. They recoiled from any suggestion of definitive or novel action on the plea that their function was purely representative. Behind them all the reader feels the sprawling uneasy presence of that poor invertebrate mass deity of theirs, the Voter, easily roused to panic and frantic action against novel, bold or radical measures, very amenable to patriotic claptrap, very easily scared and maddened into war, and just as easily baffled to distrust and impotence by delays, side issues and attacks on the personalities of decisive people he might otherwise have trusted. An entirely irresponsible Press, mercenary or partisan, played upon his baser emotions, which were so easy to play upon, and made no appeal whatever to his intelligence or his conscience.

The Voter, the Mass, which was neither educated nor led, the Voter without any sincere organisations of leadership anywhere, is the basal explanation of the impotence of those culminating conferences. The World Economic Conference in London was by far the more significant of the two. Armament and disarmament are symptoms and superficial, but economic life is fundamental. This London gathering has been made the subject of a thousand studies by our social psychologists. Many of its contradictions still perplex us profoundly. The men who assembled had just as good brains as anyone to-day, and, as an exhaustive analysis by Moreton Canby of the various projects advanced at the Conference proves, they had a substantial understanding of the needs of the world situation, yet collectively, and because of their haunting paralysing sense of the Mass and Press behind them and of their incalculable impulses and resentments, they achieved an effect of fatuity far beyond the pompous blunderings of Versailles.

143

Primarily the London Conference was a belated effort to repair the vast omissions of that earlier gathering, to supplement the well-meaning political patchwork of Wilson by some readjustment of the monetary and economic dislocations he had been too limited to foresee or too weak to avoid. Wraith-like conceptions of some vague monetary League of Nations at Bâle, and some Tariff Council and Assembly, drifted through the mists of the opening meeting. And History, with its disposition to inexact repetition, made one of the principal figures of this second world assembly also a President of the United States, belonging also to the Democratic Party and according to the ritual of that Party invoking the name of Jefferson as the Communists invoked the name of Marx or the Moslim Mahomet. This was Roosevelt II. He leaves a less vivid impression than his predecessor because he did not impend for so long upon the European scene. But for some months at least before and after his election as American President and the holding of the London Conference there was again a whispering hope in the world that a real 'Man' had arisen, who would see simply and clearly, who would speak plainly to all mankind and liberate the world from the dire obsessions and ineptitudes under which it suffered and to which it seemed magically enslaved. But the one thing he failed to do was to speak plainly.,

Drawing wisdom from Wilson's personal failure, he did not come to London and expose himself and his conversation to too close a scrutiny. He preferred to deal with the fluctuating crisis in London from his yacht, *Amberjack II*, in Nantucket Harbour, through intermittent messages and through more or less completely authorised intermediaries. *Amberjack II* has become almost as significant a ship in the history of human affairs as the Ford Peace Ship. Significant equally in its intentions and in its inadequacies.

Everywhere as the Conference drew near men were enquiring about this possible new leader for them. 'Is this at last the Messiah we seek, or shall we look for another?' Every bookshop in Europe proffered his newly published book of utterances, *Looking Forward*, to gauge what manner of mind they had to deal with. It proved rather disconcerting reading for their anxious minds. Plainly the man was firm, honest and amiable, as the frontispiece portrait with its clear frank eyes and large resolute face showed, but the text of the book was a politician's text, saturated indeed with good will, seasoned with much vague modernity, but vague and wanting in intellectual grip. 'He's good,' they said, 'but is this good enough?'

Nevertheless hope fought a stout fight. There was no other personality visible who even promised to exorcise the spell that lay upon the economic life of the race. It was Roosevelt's Conference or nothing. And in spite of that disappointing book there remained some sound reasons for hope. In particular the President, it was asserted, had a 'Brain Trust'. A number of indisputably able and modern-minded men were his associates, such men as Professors Tugwell, Moley and Dickinson, men whose later work played a significant part in that reconstruction of legal and political method which was America's particular contribution to Modern State ideas. This 'last hope of mankind', it was credibly reported, called these intimates by their Christian names and they called him 'Guv'nor'. He was said to have the modesty and greatness to defer to their studied and matured opinions. Observers, still hopeful, felt that if he listened to these advisers things might not go so badly after all. He was at any rate one point better than the European politicians and heads of States who listened only to bankers and big-business men.

But was he listening? Did he grasp the threefold nature of the problem in hand? He understood, it seemed, the need for monetary inflation to reduce the burthen of debt and over-capitalisation; he was apparently alive to the need for a progressive expansion of public employment; and so far he was sound. Unless, which is not quite clear, he wavered between 'public' and 'publicly assisted', which was quite another matter. But was he sound upon the necessity that these measures should be world-wide or practically world-wide? He made some unexpected changes of attitude in these respects. Were these changes inconstancies or were they tactical manoeuvres veiling a profoundly consistent and resolute purpose? Was it wise to be tactical when all the world was in need of plain speech and simple directive ideas? His treatment took on a disconcertingly various quality. He listened, it seemed, to his advisers; but was he not also listening to everybody? He was flirting with bi-metallism. No medicine, it seemed, was to be spared.

The Conference opened with a stout determination to be brilliant and eventful; the hotels were full, the streets be-flagged, the programme of entertainments were admirable, and even the English weather seemed to make an effort. The opening addresses by the King of England and his Prime Minister Ramsay MacDonald make very curious reading to-day. They express an acute recognition of the crucial condition of human affairs. They state in so many words that the failure of the Conference will precipitate world disaster. They insist upon the necessity for world co-operation, for monetary simplification and a resumption of employment; and in all that we admit they had the truth of the matter. But they make not the faintest intimation of how these desirable ends are to be obtained. They made gestures that are incomprehensible to us unless they had an inkling of the primary elements of the situation. And then immediately they turned away to other things. That mixture of resolve and failure to attack is what perplexes us most. If they saw the main essentials of the situation they certainly did not see them as a connected whole; they did not see any line of world action before them.

Cordell Hull, the chief of the United States delegation, was equally large and fine. The grave and splendid words—shot with piety in the best American tradition—that he inscribed upon the roll of history were as follows: 'Selfish-ness must be banished. If—which God forbid!—any nation should wreck this Conference, with the notion that its local interests might profit, that nation would merit the execration of mankind.'

Again Daladier, the French Prime Minister, opened with extremely broad and sane admissions. He insisted strongly on a necessity which the two opening English speeches had minimised, the necessity, the urgent necessity, for a progressive development of great public works throughout the world to absorb the unemployment and restore consumption. The Americans in the second week seemed to be coming in line with that. But after this much of lucidity the Conference fell away to minor issues. Apparently it could not keep at so high a level of reality. The pressure of the Mass and the Press behind each delegate began to tell upon him. The national representatives began to insist with increasing explicitness that national interests must not be sacrificed to the general good, and in a little time it became doubtful if there could be such a thing as the general good. The World Economic Conference became by imperceptible transitions a World Economic Conflict just as the League of Nations had become a diplomatic bargain mart. All the fine preluding of the first seances withered to fruitlessness because the mind of the world had still to realise the immense moral and educational effort demanded by those triple conditions that were dawning upon its apprehension, and because it was still unwilling to accept the immense political pooling they indicated. The amount of self-abnegation involved was an insurmountable psychological barrier in the way of the representatives present. It would have meant a sacrifice of the very conditions that had made them. How could men appointed as national representatives accept a pooling of national interests? They were indeed fully prepared to revolutionise the world situation and change gathering misery to hope, plenty and order, but only on the impossible condition that they were not to change themselves and that nothing essential to their importance changed. The leading ideas of the Conference were cloudily true, but the disintegrative forces of personal, party and national egotism were too strong for them.

It is a very curious thing that the representative of Soviet Russia did nothing to enlighten the obscurity of the world riddle. It is still argued by many writers that the Bolshevik régime was the direct precursor of our Modern World-State as it exists to-day. But there was no direct continuity. The Modern State arose indeed out of the same social imperatives and the same constructive impulses that begot Marxism and Leninism, but as an independent, maturer and sounder revolutionary conception. The Soviet system certainly anticipated many of the features of our present order in its profession of internationalism, in its very real socialism, and particularly in the presence of a devoted controlling organisation, the Communist Party, which foreshadowed our Modern State Fellowship. But there was always a wide divergence in Russia between theory and practice and Litvinoff, who spoke on behalf of that first great experiment in planning, was too preoccupied with various particular points at issue between his country and the western world, trading embargoes and difficulties of credit, for example, to use the occasion as he might have done, for a world-wide appeal. He did nothing to apply the guiding principles of Communism to the world situation. Here was a supreme need for planning, but he said nothing for a Five Year or Ten Year Plan for all the world. Here was a situation asking plainly for collective employment, and he did not even press the inevitability of world-socialism. Apparently he had forgotten the world considered as a whole as completely as any of the capitalist delegates. He was thinking of Russia versus the other States of the world as simply as if he were an ordinary capitalist patriot.

The claims of the other delegations were even more shortsighted and uninspired. Since there was a time-limit set to their speeches, they compressed their assertions of general humanitarian benevolence to a phrase or so and then came to business. Only Senator Connolly, from the Irish Free State, protested against the blinkered outlooks of his fellow speakers and pleaded for a consideration of 'every possible theory, however unorthodox'. But his own speech propounded no substantial constructive ideas. He was too obsessed by an embargo that England had put upon Irish exports, and to that he settled down. . . .

The whole idea of the Modern World-State, Moreton Canby insists, is to be traced, albeit in a warped and sterilised form, alike in the expressed idea-systems of the Americans, the British, the French and the Russians at the Conference. In the American statements it is wrapped about and hidden by individualist phrases and precautions, in the British it is overlaid by imperialist assumptions, in the Russian it is made unpalatable by the false psychology and harsh jargon of Marxism. In the first the business man refuses to change and get out of the way, in the second the imperialist administrator, and in the third the doctrinaire party man. Athwart every assertion of general principles drive the misty emotions of patriotism, party and personal association. Yet for all that it is indisputable that the Modern World-State was definitely adumbrated at London in 1933. Like a ghost out of the future its presence was felt by nearly everyone, though the worst phases of the Age of Frustration had still to come, though generations of suffering had still to lapse, before it could appear as the living reality of human political life.

The ghost, says Canby, did not materialise, because there was no material. Every large country in the world was feeling its way towards the essentials of a permanently progressive World-State, but none was yet within reach even of its partial and local realisation. Roosevelt II and his eleventh-hour effort to reconstruct America he finds particularly interesting. The President was plainly aware of the need to relieve debt by inflation, but he was unable to check the dissipation of the liberated energy in speculation. He was dealing with men trained and saturated in the tradition of poker, to whom a solemn cunning had become a second nature, and he was asking them (with occasional fierce threats) to display an open-faced helpfulness. He had no proper civil service available to control large public works; it was impossible to change the American technicians at one blow from quasi-financial operators to a candid, devoted public salariat. So he tried to induce profiteers to forgo profits and organise their industries on altruistic lines by dire threats of socialisation which he had no managing class to enforce. And he was as ignorant of British or European mentality and as little able to get to an understanding with it as Wilson had been before him. It was a mutual misunderstanding, but his manners were self-righteous and provocative. He began to scold long before the Conference was over. By 1935 everyone was pointing to a sort of contrasted parallelism between America and Russia. Each was manifestly struggling towards a more scientifically organised state, and each was finding the same difficulty in reconciling productive efficiency in the general interest with primarily political control. Technician and politician had still to be assimilated one to the other. Each great dictatorship was at war with the speculator and the profiteer. Each professed a faint hope of cosmopolitan co-operation and then concentrated practically and urgently upon the establishment of an internal prosperity. But they started towards that common objective from opposite poles of productive efficiency and social assumption. Roosevelt started from the standpoint of democratic individualism and Stalin from that of Marxist Communism. The British system and the other intermediate countries of the world struggled to be conservative in the chaos of financial collapse. No solvent had yet been devised to synthesise the good will in the world.

The London Conference rose to no such dramatic climax as the signing of the Peace Treaty at Versailles. It rose to nothing. It began at its highest point and steadily declined. If Versailles produced a monster, London produced nothing at all. Never did so valiant a beginning peter out so completely.

There are abundant intimations in the Press of the time (see Habwright's *The Sense of Catastrophe in the Nineteen Thirties*, a summary of quotations in the Historical Documents Series, 173,192) of a realisation that the political and economic morale of that age was played out, and that almost any casual selection of men would have been at least

150

as adequate as this gathering of old-world political person-ages to face the vast impending disasters before our race. For at any rate these men had already been tried and tested and found wanting. Mr. Ramsay MacDonald indeed, the British premier, the fine flower and summary of professional politics, rolled his r's and his eyes over the Conference and seemed still to be hoping that some favourable accident out of the void might save him and his like from the damn-ing dissection of history. For a time, in the opening glow of the assembly, with the clicking photographers recording every studied gesture, with the attentive microphones spreading out and pickling for ever his fine voice and his rich accent, with bustling secretaries in sedulous attendance, with the well-trained gravity of the delegates and particu-larly well-matured high seriousness of those adepts in public appearance, the Americans, to sustain him, this last sublimation of democratic statesmanship may really have believed that some kind of favourable incantation was in progress under his direction. He must have felt that or he could not have remained there talking. Incantations had made him. By the sheer use of voice and gesture he had clambered from extreme obscurity to world prominence. If he did not believe in incantation there was nothing left for him to believe in. He must have clung to that persuasion to the end. But if that was his state of mind at the time, it could hardly have survived the comments and criticisms of the next few months. Surely then he had some sleepless nights in which even his private incantations failed.

The World Economic Conference lost its brilliance in a week or so. The City, which had been so flushed with hope that for a time its price lists, all pluses, looked like war-time cemeteries, relapsed into depression. The World Slump did not wait for the Conference to disperse before it re-sumed. At the outset London had been all blown up and distended by bright anticipations, so that it was like one of those little squeaking bladders children play with, and like one of those bladders, so soon as the blowing ceased, it shrank and shrivelled and ended in dying wail of despair.

As Habwright puts it, by July 1933 intelligent men and women everywhere were saying two things. Of the assembled rulers and delegates they were saying: 'These people can do nothing for us. They do worse than nothing. They intensify the disaster.' And in the second place it was demanded with a sort of astonishment: 'Why have historians, sociologists and economists nothing to tell us now? There may indeed be some excuse for the failure of politicians under democratic conditions. But have our universities been doing nothing about it? Is there indeed no science of these things? Is there no knowledge? Has history learnt nothing of causes, and is there no analysis of the social processes that are destroying us?'

To which the professors, greatly preoccupied at that particular date in marking honours papers in history and social and political science, made no audible reply.

Before the end of the thirties it was plain to all the world that a world-wide social catastrophe was now inevitably in progress, that the sanest thing left for intelligent men to do was to set about upon some sort of Noah's Ark to salvage whatever was salvageable of civilisation, so that there should be a new beginning after the rising deluge of misfortune had spent itself. A few prescient spirits had been saying as much for some years, but now this idea of salvage spread like an epidemic. It prepared the way for the Modern State Movement on which our present order rests. At the time, however, the general pessimism was little mitigated by any real hope of recovery. One writer, quoted by Habwright, compared man to a domesticated ape, 'which has had the intelligence and ability to drag its straw mattress up to the fire when it is cold, but has had neither the wit nor the foresight to escape the consequent blaze'. Habwright's brief summary of the financial operations that went on as the sense of catastrophe grew justifies that grim image very completely.

The conviction that Parliamentary Democracy had come to an end spread everywhere in that decade. Already in the period between the vacillation in international affairs after

Versailles and the warfare of the Forties, men had been going about discussing and scheming and plotting for some form of government that should be at least decisive. And now their efforts took on a new urgency. There was a world-wide hysteria to change governments and officials.

At its first onset this craving for decisiveness had produced some extremely crude results. An epidemic of tawdry 'dictatorships' had run over Europe from Poland to Spain immediately after the war. For the most part these adventures followed the pattern of the pronunciamentos of the small South American republics, and were too incidental and inconsequent for the student of general history to be troubled about them now. But there followed a world-wide development of directive or would-be directive political associations which foreshadowed very plainly the organisation of the Modern State Fellowship upon which our present world order rests.

The Fascist dictatorship of Mussolini in Italy had something in it of a more enduring type than most of the other super-sessions of parliamentary methods. It arose not as a personal usurpation but as the expression of an organisation with a purpose and a sort of doctrine of its own. The intellectual content of Fascism was limited, nationalist and romantic; its methods, especially in its opening phase, were violent and dreadful; but at least it insisted upon discipline and public service for its members. It appeared as a counter movement to a chaotic labour communism, but its support of the still-surviving monarchy and the Church was qualified by a considerable boldness in handling education and private property for the public benefit. Fascism indeed was not an altogether bad thing; it was a bad good thing; and Mussolini has left his mark on history.

In Russia something still more thorough and broader came into operation after 1917. This was the Communist Party. It was the invention of Lenin; he continued to modify and adapt its organisation and doctrine until his untimely death in 1924. While he lived Russia's experiment really seemed to be leading the world in its flight towards a new order from the futile negations and paralysis of Parliamentary government. It is still profoundly interesting to note the modernity of many aspects of the early Bolshevik régime.

This modernity achieved under the stress of urgent necessities and Lenin's guidance was attained in spite of many grave difficulties created by the Marxist tradition. Marx, who was a man of what the psychologist of the middle twenty-first century used to call 'blinkered originality', never saw through the democratic sentimentalities of the period in which he lived. There had been a tendency to exclude the privileged classes from the True Democracy of Common Men even at the dawn of the modern democratic idea and he and his followers intensified and stereotyped this tendency in their own particular version of defied democracy, the Proletariat. The Proletariat was just Pure Masses, and mystical beyond measure.

But at the outset the actual Russian revolution was under the control of the intensely practical and intensely middle-class Lenin, and he took care that the great social reconstruction he had in mind was equally secured against the risk of paralysis through mass inertia and the risk of overthrow through mass panic. His ostensibly 'democratic' government of Soviets, the Soviet pyramid, was built up on a hierarchic scheme that brought the administration face to face only with seasoned representatives who had been filtered through an ascendant series of bodies. Moreover, he established a very complete control of education and the Press, to keep the thought of the nominally sovereign masses upon the right lines. And to animate and control the whole machine he had his invention of the Communist Party.

This Communist Party, like the Italian Fascisti, owes its general conception to that germinal idea of the Modern State, the Guardians in Plato's *Republic*. For if anyone is to be called the Father of the Modern State it is Plato. The Members of the Communist Party were extremely like those Guardians. As early as 1900 critics of democratic institutions were discussing the possibility of creating a cult primarily devoted to social and political service, self-appointed, self-trained and self-disciplined. The English-speaking Socialist movement was debating projects of that kind in 1909–10 (see *Fabian News* in Historical Documents for those years), but it needed the dangers and stresses of the post-war European situation to produce types of workers and young people sufficiently detached, desperate and numerous to unite effectively into a permanent revolutionary control.

From its beginnings the Communist Party, though it was not divided into 'faculties' and remained political rather than technical in spirit, resembled our own Modern State Fellowship in its insistence upon continuous learning and training throughout life, upon free criticism within the limits of the party, upon accessibility (under due limitations) to all who wished to serve in it, and upon the right to resignation from its privileges and severities of all who wished to return to comparative irresponsibility. But the conditions which created the Russian Communist Party made it inevitably Marxist, and even after a thorough Leninisation Communism, that characteristic final product of middle-nineteenth-century radicalism, still retained many of its old sentimentalities, reverting indeed more and more towards them after Lenin's death and the rule of the devoted but unoriginal, suspicious and overbearing Stalin.

There was a heavy load of democratic and equalitarian cant upon the back of the Russian system, just as there was a burthen of patriotic and religious cant upon the Italian Fascist. Even the United States Constitution did not profess democratic equality and insist upon the inspired wisdom of the untutored more obstinately than the new Russian régime. Although hardly any of the ruling group of Russians were of peasant or working-class origin—there were far more politicians from that social level in the public life of Western Europe and America—there was a universal pretence of commonness about them all. They spat, they went unshaved and collarless. They pretended to be indifferent to bourgeois comfort. It was ordained that at the phrase 'Class-War' every knee should bow. When the Communist leaders quarrelled among themselves, 'bourgeois' or 'petty bourgeois' was the favourite term of abuse, none the less deadly because it was almost invariably true. Long years were to pass before any movement whatever in the direction of the Modern State system was quite free from this heritage of cant.

One unforunate aspect of this entanglement of the new experiment in Russia with the social envies and hatreds of the old order was its inability to assimilate competent technicians, organisers and educators into its direction. In its attempt to modernise, it refused the assistance of just the most characteristically modern types in the community. But since these types had a special education and knew things not generally known, it was difficult to accord them proletarian standing. In Russia therefore, as in America, the politician with his eloquence and his necessary and habitual disingenuousness still intervened and obstructed, if he did not actually bar, the way to a scientific development of a new economic and social order.

Manifestly Stalin learnt much from his difficulties with the Five Year Plan of the evil of subordinating technical to political ability and a speech of his upon the Old and New Technical Intelligentsia made in June 1931 (Historical Documents Series, *Stalinism*, XM 327,705) is a very frank admission of the primary necessity in the modern community of the 'non-party' man of science and of special knowledge. Unhappily the hand of the party politician in Russia was strengthened by the untrammelled activities of those stranger protectors of Marxist authority the Checka, which became later the G.P.U. So from 1928, the date of the First Five Year Plan, in spite of a great driving-force of enthusiastic devotion, Russia went clumsily, heavily and pretentiously—a politician's dictatorship, propaganding rather than performing, disappointing her well-wishers abroad and thwarting the best intelligencies she produced. When her plans went wrong through her lack of precise

156

material foresight, she accused, and imprisoned or shot, engineers and suchlike technical workers.

A further bad result of this ineradicable democratic taint of the Soviet system was the widening estrangement of the Russian process from Western creative effort. Instead of being allies they became opponents. As the challenge of social disintegration became more urgent in the Atlantic countries, it became plainer and plainer that such hope as there was for the salvaging of a reconstructed civilisation from a welter of disaster lay in the co-ordinate effort of intelligent, able and energetic individuals of every nation, race, type and class. A revolution was certainly needed, but not a revolution according to the time-worn formula of street battles and barricades, not a class war. A revolution in the very character of revolutions had to occur. There was no need for insurrectionary revolution any longer, since now the system was destroying itself. The phase for boldly constructive revolution had arrived, and at every point where constructive effort was made the nagging antagonism of the Class War fanatic appeared, to impede and divide. (See, for example, Upton Sinclair on this conflict, in *The Way Out*, 1933, in the series of reprints under his name, Historical Documents Series, *History of Opinion*.)

The waste of creative energy was enormous, not only in Russia but all over the world. Multitudes of young men and women in every civilised community, the living hope of the race, dissipated their generous youth and vigour in bitter conflicts upon a purely doctrine issue. The poison of nationalism was abroad to complicate their reactions. Many turned against progress altogether and sought to thrust the world back to some imaginary lost age of virtue. So they became Ku Klux Klansmen, Nationalists, Nazis. All felt the natural youthful impulse towards large, effective, vehement action. All meant well. They were one in spirit though they suffered from a confusion of tongues. The idea of the Modern State could not for a long time make itself clear to their imaginations largely because the conspicuous self-contradictions of Russia stood in the way.

Russia seemed to lead, it sought to lead in its acts and deeds, and it lied. Meanwhile, surviving very largely because of this distraction of creative forces, the elderly methods of Parliamentary Democracy and the elderly Nationalist Diplomacy remained in possession of the greater part of the Western World, and the social collapse it was powerless to arrest continued.

§ 2. The Sloughing of the Old Educational Tradition

Faber in his interesting and suggestive *Historical Analyses* (2103) discusses how far the wars, depressions, pestilences, phases of semi-famine and periods of actual starvation, in the hundred years before 2014, were necessary, and how far, with the resources then available, they might have been avoided by mankind. He takes the view that the encumbrance of tradition was so great that for all that period this martyrdom of our kind was inevitable. He argues that without the sufferings of these generations men's minds could never have been sufficiently purged of their obstinate loyalties, jealousies, fears and superstitions; men's wills never roused to the efforts, disciplines and sacrifices that were demanded for the establishment of the Modern State.

Faber applies his criticism more particularly to this so-called decadence of education after (*circa*) 1930. It has hitherto been usual to treat the ebb of school-building and schooling that took place then as a real retrogression, to rank it with the fall in the general standard of life and the deterioration of public health. But he advanced some excellent reasons for supposing that, so far from being an evil, the starvation and obliteration of the old-world teaching machinery was a necessary preliminary to social recovery.

The common school, he insists, had to be born again, had to be remade fundamentally. And before that could happen it had to be broken up and wellnigh destroyed. He sweeps aside almost contemptuously the claim that the nineteenth century was an educational century. We are misled, he argues, by a mere resemblance between the schools and universities of the past and the schools and post-school education of the modern period. Both occupy the time of the young, and we do not sufficiently appreciate the fact that what they are doing with the young is something entirely different. Our education is an introduction to the continual revolutionary advance of life. But education before the twenty-first century was essentially a conservative process. It was so rigorously and completely traditional that its extensive disorganisation was an inevitable preliminary to the foundation of a new world.

The word education has come now to cover almost all intellectual activities throughout life except research and artistic creation. That was not its original meaning. It meant originally the preparation of the young for life. It did not go on even in extreme cases beyond three or four and twenty, and usually it was over by fourteen! But we draw no line at any age, as our ancestors did, when learning ceases. The general information of the public, public discussion and collective decisions, all fall within the scope of our educational directorate. All that was outside what passed for education in the early twentieth century.

What people knew in those days they knew in the most haphazard way. The privately owned newspapers of the period told the public what their readers or their proprietors desired; the diffusion of facts and ideas by the early cinema, the sound radio and so on was entirely commercialised for the advertisement of goods in America, and controlled and directed in the interests of influential politicians in Great Britain; book-publishing, even the publication of scientific works, was mainly speculative and competitive, and there was no such thing as a Centre of Knowledge in the world.

It is remarkable to note how long mankind was able to carry on without any knowledge organisation whatever. No encyclopaedia, not even a bookseller's encyclopaedia, had existed before the seventeenth century, for the so-called Chinese Encyclopaedia was a literary miscellany, and there was no permanent organisation of record even on the part of such mercenary encyclopaedias as came into existence after that date. Nor was there any conception of the need of a permanent system of ordered knowledge, continually revised until the twentieth century was nearing its end. To the people of the Age of Frustration our interlocking research, digest, discussion, verification, notification and informative organisations, our Fundamental Knowledge System, that is, with its special stations everywhere, its regional bureaus, its central city at Barcelona, its seventeen million active workers and its five million correspondents and reserve enquirers, would have seemed incredibly vast. It would have seemed incredibly vast to them in spite of the fact that the entirely unproductive armies and military establishments they sustained in those days of universal poverty were practically as huge.

We are still enlarging this Brain of Mankind, still increasing its cells, extending its records and making its interactions more rapid and effective. A vast independent literature flourishes beside it. Compared with to-day, our species in the Age of Frustration was as a whole brainless: it was collectively invertebrate with a few scattered ill-connected ganglia; it was lethargically ignorant; it had still to develop beyond the crude rudiments of any co-ordinate knowledge at all.

But not only was general knowledge rudimentary, casual, erroneous and bad. Faber's case against the old education is worse than that. Knowledge was explicitly outside education, outside formal schooling altogether. The need for a sound common ideology is a Modern State idea. The old,

160

so called 'Elementary' schools, Faber shows, did not pretend to give knowledge. So far as directive ideas were concerned, they disavowed this intention. He quotes a very revealing contemporary survey of the situation in America by Dr. G. S. Counts (*The American Road to Culture*, 1930) in which the complete ideological sterilisation of the common schools of the Republic is demonstrated beyond question. The sterilisation was deliberate. So far as the giving of comprehensive information about life went, says Faber, there was absolutely nothing valuable destroyed during this period of educational collapse, because nothing valuable had as yet got into the curricula. The history taught in these popular schools was pernicious patriotic twaddle; the biology, non-existent or prudish and childish—the 'facts of sex', as they were called, were for example *taught* by dissecting flowers—and there was no economic instruction whatever. The nineteenth-century 'education' was not enlightenment; it was anti-enlightenment. Parents, political and religious organisations, watched jealously that this should be so. He quotes school time-tables and public discussions and gives samples of the textbooks in use.

The decline in scientific research, moreover, during this age of systole, Faber insists, has been greatly exaggerated. Although there was certainly a considerable diminution in the number of actual workers through the destruction of private endowments and what was called 'economy', and although there was also a considerable interference with the international exchange of ideas and a slacking down in pace at which ideas grew, there was no absolute interruption in the advance of ordered science even through the worst phases of the social breakdown. Research displayed a protean adaptability and indestructibility. It shifted from the patronage of the millionaire to the patronage of the war lord; it took refuge in Russia, Spain and South America; it betook itself to the aeroplane hangars, to rise again in due time to its present world-predominance. It had never been pampered under the régime of private capitalism. All through that First Age of Prosperity pure research had lived

161

from hand to mouth. As soon as it paid, says Sinclair Lewis in *Martin Arrowsmith*, it was commercialised and it degenerated. When the bad times came the parasites of science fell away, but the genuine scientific worker, accustomed to scanty supplies, tightened his belt a little more and in all sorts of out-of-the-way places stuck to his job.

What really did break up in this period between 1930 and 1950 was a systematic schooling of the masses which had developed steadily during the nineteenth century. Beyond the elements of reading, speech and counting, this was no more and no less than a drilling in tradition. There had been some reforms, more particularly in method, some advance in the teaching of infants (though this was sacrificed early in the economy flurry) and a few exceptional schools emerged, but this was the character of the typical school of the time. A progressive multiplication of this kind of school had indeed gone on in nearly every country in the world even up to the outbreak of the Great War. The proportion of 'literates' who could at least read increased steadily. After that the rate of advance (except in Russia after 1917, where popular teaching was only beginning) fell stage by stage to zero. But what was ebbing was not really knowledge or instruction at all, but a training in the binding traditions of the old society.

The story of what used to be called 'the conflict between religion and science' belong mainly to the history of the nineteenth century, and we will not tell again here how the fairly stable structure of Christian belief and disciplines were weakened by the changes in values that ensued from the revelation of geological and biological horizons in that period. Before 1850 more than ninety-nine per cent of the population of Europe and America believed unquestioningly that the universe had been created in the year 4004 B.C. Their intellectual lives were all cramped to the dimensions of that petty cellule of time. It was rather frightening for them to break out. They succumbed to mental agoraphobia. The student knows already of the difficulties experienced by the Christian ministry during those years of mental

162

release and expansion in 'symbolising' the Fall and Atonement, which had hitherto been taught as historical facts, and of the loss of confidence and authority that came through this unavoidable ambiguity. The ensuing controversies thundered and died away into mutterings and ironies, but the consequences of these disputes became more and more evident in the succeeding generations. They evinced themselves in a universal moral indefiniteness. The new and old cancelled out.

The accepted Christian world outlook, both that prescribed by the Catholic Church and that of the various dissentient Protestant sects, had carried with it a coarse but fairly effective moral imperative. Hell was the *ultima ratio* of good behaviour. The Churches, although badly damaged in argument, were well endowed and powerfully entrenched in the educational organisation. Their practical resistance to the new views proved to be more effective than their controversial efforts. People had the social habit of belonging to them and entrusting their children to them. There were no other teachers ready; no other schools. So the traditional orthodoxies were able to obstruct the development of a modern ethic in harmony with the new realisations of man's place in space and time, in spite of the loss of much of the former power of unquestionable conviction.

Gradually throughout the First Age of General Prosperity the relative value of their endowments diminished, and they lost intellectual and moral prestige. But it was only with the economic landslides of the post-war period that their material foundations gave way completely. For a time these great organisations share in the common disaster, and when at last under new auspices a restoration of production occurred they recovered nothing of their proportional importance. Their old investments had vanished. They suffered with other landlords in the general resumption of estates by the community. By 1965 C.E. it was no longer possible for an ordinary young man to get a living as a minister of any Church. Holy orders, since they implied an old-world outlook, were also a grave encumbrance for an ambitious teacher. It was extraordinary with what facility the priests and parsons changed their collars and vanished into the crowd with the progressive dissappearance of their endowments. The organised Christian Churches pass out of history at last almost as quickly as the priesthood of Baal vanished after the Persian conquest. There is considerable plausibility in Faber's contention that they could have disappeared in no other way.

It has been usual to treat the extensive destruction of social morale which characterised this period as due to the interregnum between the fading out of the Christian ethic and the moral and intellectual establishment of modern conduct. Faber questions that boldly. He admits that the morale of Western civilisation was built up very largely by Christian agencies, but he denies that they were sustaining it. He ascribes its evaporation almost entirely to the destruction of social confidence which we have noted already as a natural consequence of the wild fluctuations of economic security and monetary values at that time. Men ceased to respect society because they felt they were being cheated and betrayed by society.

§ 3. *Disintegration and Crystallisation in the Social Magma: The Gangster and Militant Political Organisations*

The dissolutions and regroupings of people that were going on through this period have always attracted the attention of the social philosopher. The common man had lost his faith in a friendly God, his confidence in social justice and his educational and social services. He was out of employment and stirred by unsatisfied appetites. The time-honoured life of work and family interests had become impossible for a growing majority.

164

What we now call social nucleation was failing; the grouping of human beings in families and working communities was not going on. They became restive and troublesome. The social confidence and discipline that had prevailed throughout the nineteenth century deteriorated very rapidly. There was a swift fall in social security.

Phases of fever have occurred time without number in human history, phases of unsettlement and confused motivation, clottings and drives and migrations of population. Periods of tranquil assurance are the exception throughout the ages. But in the past it has usually been the exhaustion of food supplies, pestilence or some cruel invasion that has broken up the social texture and made humanity lawless again. This new disintegration was of a different character. It was due in the first place to an increase rather than a diminution of material and energy in the social scheme. It was a process of expansion which went wrong through the inadequacy of traditional law and government.

The disintegrative forces were already evident in the eighteenth century; they became very conspicuous in the French revolution and the subsequent social and political disturbances, but they only rose to a plain domination of the controlling forces after the World War.

In the seventeenth century, when population was thin and hardly anyone moved about, it had been possible to keep order by means of a village constable, to try the malefactor by a local magistrate and jury which knew him thoroughly and understood his position and motives. Dogberry and Shallow sufficed. But the economic growth of the eighteenth century increased the size of towns and the traffic on the newly made roads between them without any corresponding increase in the forces of order. It produced therefore, the urban mob, the footpad, the highwayman and the brigand. The local constable was unequal to these new demands; the local magistrate as inadequate. There was a phase of increasing crime.

After the failure of a régime of savage punishment uncertainly inflicted, after the excesses of the first French revolution, after phases of mob violence in every European capital, and endless other manifestations of this outpacing of social control, the machinery of government did by an effort adjust itself to the new conditions. More or less modernised police forces appeared throughout the world and inaugurated a new phase of order and security, a phase which reached its maximum in the years before the Great War. For a time then the world, or at any rate very considerable areas of it, was almost as safe as it is to-day. An unarmed man could go about in reasonable security in most of Europe, India, China, America. Nobody offered him violence or attempted open robbery. Even the policeman in the English-speaking and Western European communities carried no weapon but a truncheon.

But the World War broke down many of the inhibitions of violence and bloodshed that had been built up during the progressive years of the nineteenth century, and an accumulating number of intelligent, restless unemployed men, in a new world of motor-cars, telephones, plate-glass shop windows, unbarred country houses and trustful social habits, found themselves faced with illegal opportunities far more attractive than any legal behaviour-system now afforded them. And now after the world slump that insanity of public ceremony which runs like a disease through the story of the age prevented any prompt enlargement and modernisation of the existing educational, legal or police organisations. The scale and prestige of the law-court and police-court dwindled as the problems presented to them by the vast irregular developments of that period of stress and perplexity increased.

So the stage was set for a lawless phase. The criminal was liberated from parochialism and reactionary economies long before his antagonist the policeman, and he experienced all the invigoration and enlargement of that release. The criminal grew big while the law, pot-bound in its traditional swathings, was unable to keep pace with him.

The criminal records of this disorderly interlude make strange reading to-day. Things that were terrible enough at

166

the time appear to us now as they recede into the past through a thickening, highly refractile veil of grotesqueness and picturesque absurdity. We read about them, as we read about medieval tortures or cannibal feasts or war atrocities or human sacrifice, with a startled incredulity. We laugh now; it is all so *impossible*. Few of us actually realise there were flesh-and-blood sufferings that living men and women went through only a century and a half ago.

The criminals of the more fortunate countries of the European system, during that First Age of General Prosperity before the World War, like the few cases of intolerable behaviour with which society deals to-day, had constituted a small abnormal and diminishing minority, for the most part mental defectives or at best very inferior types. The majority of their offences were emotional or brutish offences. There was some stealing and a steady proportion of swindling in business, not sufficient to disturb the social order at all seriously. But as the morale of the old order dissolved, this ceased to be the case. Increasing numbers of intelligent and enterprising people found themselves in conflict with society because, as they argued very reasonably, society had cheated them. Patriotism, too, they felt, had cheated them and given them nothing but poverty and war. They had never had a fair chance. They looked after themselves and left the community to look after itself. They fell back on the nearer loyalties of their immediate associates.

Your 'pal' at any rate was close at hand. If he 'let you down', you had a fair chance to 'get at' him. Little gang-nuclei came into existence, therefore, wherever unassimilated elements of the population were congested and humiliated or wherever intelligent men festered in unemployment and need.

In 1900 European society in particular was still nucleated about the family group in relation to a generally understood code of lawful behaviour. In 1950 its individuals were either nucleated into gangs, groups or societies or dissolved into crowds and the influence and pretence of any universally valid standard of good conduct had disappeared.

Robbery is the first great division in the catalogue of anti-social offences. Every efficient government in the past reserved to itself the sole right of dispossession, and every intelligent government exercised that right with extreme discretion. In the past of unregulated private ownership the filching of portable objects and raids upon unguarded possessions were always going on. In Great Britain, in which country the highest levels of social order were attained during the First Age of General Prosperity, stealing (with which we may include various forms of embezzlement and fraud) remained the chief offence upon the list. Almost all the others had become exceptional. But whenever there was a dip in the common prosperity, more active methods of robbery appeared to supplement the ordinary theft. The snatcher began to take his chance with bags and watches. The enterprise of the burglar increased. Then came the simple hold-up under threats, or robbery with assault. In a world of general confidence, unarmed and unaccompanied people were going about everywhere wearing valuable jewellery and carrying considerable sums of money. But that atmosphere of confidence could be rapidly chilled. Even in later-nineteenth-century Britain there were epidemics of robbery by single men or by men in couples, the 'garrotters' of the sixties, for example, who assaulted suddenly from behind and seized the watch and pocket-book. They would clap a pitch plaster over their victim's mouth. There were brief phases when the suburban regions even of London and Paris became unsafe, and at no time were any but the more central regions of some of the great American cities secure. This kind of thing increased notably everywhere after the World War.

There were manifest limits to this hold-up business. It was something that extinguished itself. There had to be a general feeling of practical security for that type of robbery to prosper. There had to be people to rob. Robbery from the person is an acute and not chronic disease of communities. So soon as the footpad became too prevalent people ceased to carry so many valuables, they shunned lonely or dark streets and roads, they went about in company and began to bear arms. The epidemic of hold-ups passed its maximum and declined.

The criminally disposed soon learnt the importance of association for the exploitation of new lines of effort. With a more alert and defensive and less solitary type of victim, the casual criminal developed into the planning criminal. In every country multiplying nuclei of crime began to work out the problems of that terroristic gang discipline which is imperative upon those who combine to defy the law. In Europe the intensifying tariff wars put an increasing premium upon the enterprise of the smuggler, and in smuggling enterprises men readily developed those furtive secret loyalties, those sub-laws of the underworld, which proved so readily applicable to more aggressive efforts. In America the repressive laws against alcohol had already created the necessary conditions for a similar morbid organisation of gang systems, which had become readily confluent with the older associations for political corruption and terrorism. As the economic breakdown proceeded throughout the thirties and forties of the twentieth century, ordinary social security diminished even more rapidly in America than in Europe. But everywhere a parallel dégringolade was going on. Now it would be the criminal forces in one country and now those in another which were leading in novel attack upon the law-abiding citizens of the decaying order.

The hold-up in force became bolder and more frequent. History repeated itself with variations. In the place of the highwayman of the seventeenth and eighteenth centuries came the motor-car bandit and the train-robber. Trains-de-luxe were successfully held up by armed bands, first of all in Eastern Europe and America and then very generally. These were operations involving the concerted action of a dozen men or more, who had to be sure of their 'get away' and with a market for their loot. Country houses and country clubs full of wealthy guests presently began to be attacked —the telephones cut and the whole place systematically

169

looted. Restaurants, gambling-clubs and other resorts of people with full pocket-books were also raided with increasing efficiency. Local banks and bank branches became insecure. Until the nineteen-thirties a town bank had a large open handsome office with swinging doors, low counters and glass partitions. Ten years later the face of the bank had changed: the clerks were protected by steel defences, they were armed with revolvers and they parleyed with the customer through small pigeonholes that could be promptly closed.

This change in the scale and quality of aggressive crime was reflected in public manners and display. The wearing of jewellery, gold watch-chains, expensive studs and suchlike challenges to poverty declined, costume became more 'buttoned up' and restrained. Hip-pocket weapons spread from America to Europe. Women's dress and ornaments, though if anything they improved in their artistic quality, diminished in intrinsic value. Everywhere there was a diminution of social ostentation. Houses with narrow exterior windows and well equipped with steel doors, locks, bolts and bars, were preferred to those candidly exposed to sunlight and exterior observation. The window displays of the town shops became more guarded.

The need for protection and the dread of conspicuousness affected automobile design. The common automobile of the middle twentieth century was a sullen-looking pugnacious beast. And its occupants were in harmony with it. Before the World War the spectacle of a broken-down vehicle or any such trouble by the wayside would induce almost any passing car to stop and offer assistance. Under the new conditions people feared a decoy. They would refuse to stop after twilight, and even in the daytime they sometimes hurried on, though injured or apparently injured people might be lying by the roadside.

Travel diminished very rapidly under such conditions. There is some difficulty about the statistics, but between 1928 and 1938 the number of pleasure travellers upon the roads and railways of continental Europe fell by something over, rather than under, eighty per cent. There were, of course, other causes at work besides the general insecurity of movement in producing this decline; there was a general impoverishment also which disposed people to stay at home. But the major factor was insecurity.

The roads were less and less frequented as they became unsafe. Many fell out of repair, and the old road-signs and petrol pumps, now dear to our school-museum collectors, vanished one by one from the landscape.

Improvements in robbery were only one group of the criminal developments in progress. A much more distressful aspect was the organisation of terroristic blackmail, at first directed against individuals and then against whole classes in the community. As people ceased to travel to be robbed, the robber had to pursue them to their homes. Here again American inventiveness and enterprise led the world. By imperceptible degrees the ordinary prosperous citizen found his life enmeshed in a tangle of threats and vague anxieties. Even during the prosperous period there had been an element of menace in the lives of the American well-to-do; their securities had never been quite secure and their positions never perfectly stable. But now over and above the ever increasing instability of possessions and income came the increasing need to buy off molestation. Breaking through the now inadequate protection of the police appeared silently and grimly and more and more openly the blackmailer, the kidnapper and the gang terrorist.

A particularly cruel form of attack upon unprotected private people was the threatening and kidnapping of young children. It had a minor grotesque side in the stealing and ransoming of pet animals. Many hundreds of children had been stolen, hidden away, and brought back for reward before the abduction and murder of the child of Colonel Lindbergh, a long-distance aviator very popular in America, called general attention to this increasing nuisance. Nothing effective, however, was done to control these practices, and in the bad years that followed 1930 kidnapping and the threat of kidnapping increased very greatly, and spread to

171

the old world. It was organised. Men and women were spirited away, intimidated by threats of torture, held captive. If the pursuit was pressed too hard they disappeared and were heard of no more. Assassinations multiplied. Bodies of men set themselves up almost without concealment under such names as Citizens' Protection Societies, or Civil Order Associations. The man who wanted to be left alone in peace, he and his household, was pressed to pay his tribute to the gang. Or he would not be left in peace. And even if his particular 'protectors' left him in peace, there might still be other gangs about for whom they disavowed responsibility and with whom he had to make a separate deal.

It was not merely the well-to-do who were worried and levied upon in this fashion. An increasing proportion of minor workers and traders found it necessary to pay a percentage of their gains or earnings to escape systematic persecution. 'Trouble' was the characteristic American word. 'You don't want to have trouble,' said the blackmailer, gently but insistently.

The new generation grew up into a world of secret compromises and underhand surrenders. The common man picked his way discreetly through a world of possible trouble. No one dared live who was not a member (and servant) of a Union of some kind. It was a return to very ancient conditions, conditions that had prevailed for ages in China, for instance, and in Sicily and Southern Italy. But it was a relapse from the freedom and confidence of the better days at the close of the nineteenth century. It was a contraction of everyday human happiness.

Kidnapping was not confined to kidnapping for ransom. There had always been a certain irrepressible trade in the beguiling and stealing of young persons for sexual prostitution, and this also increased again. Workers were kidnapped, and the intimidation of workers in factories became bolder and less formally legal. There was a great release of violence in personal quarrels, and in particular crimes of revenge multiplied. In a phase of dwindling confidence and

172

happiness, people of spirit no longer recoiled from the tragic ending of oppressive situations. They took the law into their own hands. They began to fight and kill, and they were no longer inevitably overtaken by the law.

The remaining rich, the financial adventurers who still appeared, the prominent political leaders, the transitory 'kings' of the underworld, all surrounded themselves with bodyguards. Types recalling the hired 'bravos' of the Italian cities of the later Middle Ages and the Samurai of the Japanese noblemen reappeared as the hefty private attendants of the wealthier Americans. After the economic slump had fairly set in the posse of needy retainers became a universal practice with all who could afford it. They protected the person and the home. They supplemented the police.

The transition from a protective to an aggressive bodyguard was inevitable. Leading American bootleggers were the chief offenders, but the example was contagious. 'Brawling' of retainers reappeared first in America, Germany and Ireland. These brawls were usually small street battles, or conflicts at race meetings and suchlike gatherings, or side issues to political meetings and processions. It was a courageous politician who would face an audience after 1938 unless he knew that his men were about him and posted at strategically important points in the meeting. And he would be wearing a mail undervest or suchlike protection of his more vital parts. There are hundreds of such garments in our museums.

No man, woman or child that 'mattered' went about 'unshadowed' after 1940. After the middle nineteenth century women had made great advances towards personal freedom. About 1912 a pretty girl in her teens might have taken a knapsack and marched off alone through the northern states of Europe or America in perfect safety, unmolested. All this freedom vanished during the age of insecurity. Women ceased to go about without an escort even in the towns. It was not until 2014 that there was any real return towards the former common liberties of the young and weak and

173

gentle. There was on the part of women, as the novels of the time reveal, a survival of social fear in human life, the fear of going alone, until the middle of the twenty-first century.

After 1945 a fresh aspect of insecurity appears in the records. There is mention of unsafe roadside hotels and a great increase not simply of streets, but of whole districts and villages where 'things happened', people disappeared and it was inadvisable for strangers to go. Some of these criminally infected areas did not recover their reputations for three quarters of a century. The *dangerous* big hotel with its secret lifts, passages, ambushes and sinister private rooms is still the delight of our popular romancers; it loses nothing in elaboration as it recedes into the past.

The psychology of the twentieth-century policeman has been made the subject of a whole group of historical studies. There was no connection in those days between the policeman and either the educational or medical services. This association which appears so inevitable to us to-day would have seemed insane to the organisers of the first police forces in the eighteenth and nineteenth centuries. The policeman, for them, was to be an animated barrier and signpost, capable of leaping into action at the sight of assault, petty larceny or unseemly behaviour. Beyond that very little initiative was expected from him. He took into custody people who were 'given in charge'. Above him were officers, usually of a different class and associated with the force was a group of criminal enquiry experts, who were quite capable of handling most of the offences against the law that prevailed in the era before the extensive introduction of rapid transit, power machinery and mass production. This pattern of police force worked fairly well up to the beginning of the twentieth century. Except in districts where sexual prostitution was rife it remained fairly honest. It maintained a fairly high level of liberty, security of property and social order for a century. Only when the control of morals or political intervention was thrust upon it did it prove unequal to the strain.

And then, as the greater community of the World-State began to struggle clumsily and painfully out of traditional forms, we see police control again outpaced by its task. It gives way. 'Why,' the student asks, 'was this police organisation unable to keep pace with the new stresses? Why were the ruling people of that time so incapable of fitting it to the new demands upon it?' We have already indicated the main lines of the answer. Just when the need for a fundamental refashioning of the police of the world was becoming urgent, came also, first that exacerbation of international hostilities, of 'secret service' and espionage to render any broad international handling of the problem impossible, and secondly that desperately foolish sacrifice of life to the creditor which seems to be the inevitable conclusion of any social system based on acquisition.

The Profit-Capitalist System was absolutely incapable of controlling the unemployment it had evoked and the belligerence it stimulated. It stagnated on its hoards. It fought against inflation and it fought against taxation. It died frothing economics at the mouth. It killed the schools on which public acquiescence rested. Impartially it restricted employment and the belief of the unemployed. Even on this plain issue of its police protection it economised. Impossible, it said, to plan a new police when we cannot even pay for the police we have.

And so the desperate fight of an essentially nineteenth-century pattern of police organisation, under-financed, inadequately equipped, divided up, controlled by small-scale, antiquated national or parochial authorities, in many cases rotten with corruption, against the monstrous forces of disorganisation released by the irregular hypertrophies to social development was added to the other conflicts of that distressful age.

In spite of a notable amount of corruption and actual descents into criminality, the general will of most of the police forces seems to have remained sound. Most but not all. Most of these organisations did keep up a fight for order even when they were in a process of dissolution. They did keep up their traditional war against crime. But their methods underwent a considerable degeneration, which was shared, and shared for the same reason, by the criminal law of the period. Police and prosecutor both felt that the dice were loaded against them, that they were battling against unfair odds. Their war against crime became a feud. It grew less and less like a serene control, and more and more like a gang conflict. They were working in an atmosphere in which witnesses were easily intimidated and local sympathy more often than not against the law. This led to an increasing unscrupulousness on their part in the tendering and treatment of evidence. In many cases (see Aubrey Wilkinson's *The Natural History of the Police Frame-up*, 1991) the police deliberately manufactured evidence against criminals they had good reason to believe guilty and perjured themselves unhesitatingly. Wilkinson declares that in the early twentieth century hundreds of thousands of wrongdoers were 'justly condemned on false evidence', and that they could have been condemned in no other way.

But the apologetics of Wilkinson for the police break down when he comes to the next aspect of their degeneration under stress. We have all read with horror of the use of torture in medieval practice and shuddered at the fact that there were even special machines and instruments in those days, the rack, the thumbscrew, the boot and so forth, for the infliction of pain. But there remains little doubt now that the police of the twentieth century, fighting with their backs to the wall against enormous odds, did go very far towards a revival of torture against those they believed to be social dangers. It is a difficult as well as an ugly task to disentangle this story now, but sufficient fact emerges to show us that in the general decay of behaviour that was going on, not merely casual blows and roughness of handling, but the systematic exhaustion, pestering, ill-treatment and actual torment of persons under arrest in order to extort confessions and incriminating statements became prevalent.

There is no real distinction in nature between the processes that led up to this chaotic nucleation of human beings about gangs and organisations for frankly criminal purposes and those which led to protective associations for the illegal maintenance of security and order and again to those much wider allegiances within the state such as the nationalist Sokols in the Austrian provinces that became Czecho-Slovakia, the Irish Republican organisations, the Ku Klux Klan in America, the multitudinous secret societies of India, China and Japan, the Communist Party which captured Russia, the Fascist who captured Italy, the Nazis who captured Germany, all of which pursued on bolder and bolder scales large intimidatory and revolutionary economic and political ends. All these were structurally great gangster systems. Instead of specific immediate blackmail they sought larger satisfactions; that is all the difference. Even when the organisation as a whole had large conceptions of its function, it was apt to degenerate locally into a mere boss or bully rule. All these forms of recrystallisation within the community, large and small, arose because of the inadaptability and want of vigour and co-operation in the formal governing, economically directive and educational systems. Because there was no foresight to ensure continuity in the growth of institutions, there were these unpremeditated and often morbid growths, expressive of the accumulating discomfort and discontent and of the need for a more intimate, energetic and fruitful form of human association.

It is paradoxical but true that the civilised human society of the later nineteenth and earlier twentieth centuries broke up because of the imperative need of human beings to live in active combination. It was pulled to pieces by its own new cohesions. Until there was a complete, satisfactory and vigorous World-State organisation potentially in being, the continuation of this breaking up and reassembling of social energy was inevitable. It was like the break-up of caterpillar organs in the cocoon to form the new structures of the imago.

Even the Modern State Fellowship itself, so far as many

177

of its nuclei were concerned, was at first of this nature, a coalescence of all these varied technicians who realised that employment would vanish, that everything they valued in life would vanish, with the spread of social disorder. They constituted protective and aggressive gangs with an un-exampled power of world-wide co-operation. Their con-fluence became the new world.

The demoralisation of the world's sea life, thanks to the surviving vestiges of naval power, was far less rapid and complete than the spread of disorder on the land. It was only after the series of naval mutinies towards the end of the last European war that the ancient practice of piracy was resumed. Even then ships could still be policed and a recalcitrant ship brought to book much more easily than the black streets of a town. One or two pleasure liners were boarded and held up in out-of-the-way ports in the thirties, but in no case did the assailants get away with their plunder. In 1933 the Chinese fleet had disintegrated into shipfuls of adventurers offering their services by wireless to the various governments who divided the country. But these stray warships did little mischief before they were bought, captured or sunk by the Japanese.

A Canadian pleasure liner, *The King of the Atlantic*, on one of the last holiday voyages to be made, was seized on the high seas by an armed gang in 1939, and an attempt was made to hold its passengers to ransom. They were all to be killed if the pursuit was pressed home. In the face, how-ever, of a combined attack by American sea and air forces, at that time still efficient though greatly in arrears with their pay, the hearts of the gangsters failed them and they surrendered ignominiously.

No ship of over 9,000 tons was ever captured by pirates. This relative maintenance of orderliness at sea was due to special conditions—the then recent discovery of radio communications, for example. It outlasted the practical cessation of shipbuilding in the forties and an immense shrinkage in the world's shipping.

Nor did new types of criminal appear in the air until after

178

the third European conflict, and then not overwhelmingly. Here again was a field of human activity, essentially simple and controllable. For a time indeed the aeroplane was the safest as well as the swiftest method of getting about the world. For some years after the practical cessation of general land travel the infrequent aviator still hummed across the sky, over dangerous city and deserted highroad, over ruined country houses and abandoned cultivations, recalling the memory of former disciplines and the promise of an orderly future.

There were fewer aeroplanes just as there were fewer ships, and, because of the general discouragement of enterprise, there was little change of type, yet the skies, like the high seas, remained practically outside the range of the general social débâcle until well past the middle of the century. The need for aerodromes, for repairing and fuelling, held the dwindling body of aviators together. Air outrages at the worst phase were still scattered and disconnected events. And it was in the air at last and along the air routes that the sword of a new order reappeared.

§ 4. *Changes in War Practice after the World War*

The science and practice of warfare during this Age of Frustration, having now no adequate directing and controlling forces over it, pursued, in its development, a preposterous and dreadful logic of its own.

In 1914, at the outbreak of the World War, military science had been a pretentious and backward lore. The War Offices, as we have told, had allowed the armament industry to put enormously outsize weapons into their

179

hands, but they had made none of the necessary mental adjustments needed to meet this change of scale. All the land commanders engaged in that struggle with scarcely an exception were still fighting clumsily according to the obsolete tradition of nineteenth-century warfare. They were still thinking in terms of frontal attack, outflanking, the break-through and so forth. We have told as briefly as we could the horrors of the ensuing harvest. The Admiralties, forewarned perhaps by their engineers, showed a livelier discretion and for the most part hid away their costly fleets from the disasters of combat in strongly defended harbours, and allowed them to emerge only on one or two wild occasions for battles so inconclusive that they were prolonged as controversies for years afterwards and remain undecided to this day. The submarine, the minefield, the aeroplane, the primitive 'tank', organised propaganda to weaken war will, tentative use of gas, and the replacement of many of the elder commanders as the war proceeded did something to modify land fighting, but to the very last, when the general collapse of 'morale' led to the armistice, the professional soldiers were clinging to the idea that nothing fundamental had happened to the methods of their ancient and honoured profession.

All this changed after the Peace of Versailles. A spirit of unrest entered into both the War Offices and Foreign Offices of the world. They were invaded by a consciousness of great changes none the less potent because it was belated and had accumulated. The younger generals who had been through the war could not put out of their minds memories of attacks from overhead, gas attacks, tank actions, and, above all, the loose ungentlemanly comments of temporary officers of practical ability and unmilitary habits of mind. These younger generals aged in their turn, and as they aged they succeeded to positions of authority. They came into power repeating perpetually : 'We must keep pace with the times.'

A phase of extreme innovation succeeded the conservatism of the older generation. Everywhere the War Offices stirred with novel conceptions of strange inventions, secret

180

novelties and furtive systematic research. Everywhere the obscure reports of spies and informants, carefully fostered by the armament dealers affected, stimulated this forced inventiveness.

It was realised that the old warfare had in fact perished in a state of lumpish hypertrophy in the trenches. It had indeed been a 'war to end war'—and the old war was done for. The new warfare had to replace it—and quickly. The Foreign Offices demanded it. They could not do without war of some sort. Sovereignty was war. The traditional state was an organisation against foreigners resting on the ultimate sanction of belligerence. They could imagine no other state of affairs, for to begin with that would have involved imagining themselves non-existent. The Thirties and Forties of the century teemed with furtive and grotesquely hideous researches to discover and develop the methods of the New Warfare. For the only alternative to further war was the abandonment of state sovereignty, and for that men's minds were altogether unprepared.

The changes in war method that went on between 1900 and 1950 C.E., with the possible exception of the introduction of firearms between the twelfth and sixteenth centuries, were far greater than anything that had ever happened since the earliest men hit and scuffled in their first rude group encounters. For endless ages the main conflict had been the 'battle', the encounter of bodies of men on foot or on horseback. The infantry had been the traditional backbone of the army, and (except when the Huns and Mongols refused to play according to the rules) the cavalry was secondary. Artillery was used only for 'preparation' before the attack. So fought Rameses, so Alexander, so Caesar, so Napoleon. The glorious victories during the romantic ages of human warfare all amounted to battles of practically the same pattern, to a great central battering with pikes, swords, bayonets, maces or suchlike implements, a swiping, pushing, punching, pelting, stabbing, poking and general clapperclawing amidst a shower of comparatively light missiles, that went on at longest for a few hours, and ended

181

in a break, a flight, a cavalry pursuit and a massacre. This 'open warfare' alternated, it is true, with long sieges, less sportsmanlike phases, in which the contending hosts refused battle and squatted unwholesomely in excavations and behind walls, annoying each other by raids and attempts to storm and break through, until hunger, pestilence, the decay of discipline under boredom, or the exasperation of the surrounding population broke up the party. Non-combatants suffered considerable temporary and incidental molestation during warfare; there was a certain amount of raping and looting, devastation to destroy supplies, pressed labour and spy-hunting on a scale which amounted in most cases to little more than an exacerbation of normal criminality. Wholesale devastation, such as the break-up of the irrigation of Mesopotamia by the Mongols, or the laying waste of Northumbria by William the Conqueror of England, was, when it occurred, a measure of policy rather than a war measure. War had to go on for many decades before it could produce such disorganisation as that of Asia Minor in the wars between Byzantium and Persia. The Islamic invasions were at first made additionally disagreeable by religious propaganda, but this was speedily replaced by discriminatory taxation. The long-distance campaigns of Roman, Hunnish and Mongol armies again spread various once localised infectious and contagious diseases very widely; but the total influence of the old warfare upon human destiny was enormously exaggerated by the nationalist historians of the old régime. It was of infinitely less importance than migration. The peasant life went on unchangingly, squalid and laborious, as it had been going on for the majority of human beings since agriculture began. The various 'Decisive Battles of the World' were high points in that fantasy of the pedants, the great 'drama of the empires', with which they befogged the human mind for so long during its gropings from the peasant state of life towards a sane and orderly way of living.

But with the Napoleonic wars the soldier began to invade and modify the texture of normal life as he had never done

182

before, by conscription, by unprecedented monetary levies, indemnities and taxes that dislocated economic processes; and conversely, quite uninvited by the soldier, as we have shown, the expanding forces of power industrialism and of mass manipulation through journalistic and other sorts of propaganda, invaded both the military field and the common life. War, which had been like the superficial ploughing of our ancestors, became a subsoil plough, an excavator that went deeper and deeper, that began presently to deflect underground springs and prepare extensive landslides.

The Generals of the World War were all in the position of inexperienced amateurs in charge of vast mechanisms beyond their power of control. War, which formerly had been fought on the flat along a 'front', suddenly reached through and over the contending armies, and allowed no one to stand out of it any more. The New Warfare, it was already being remarked by 1918, was a war of whole populations, from which all respect for the non-combatant was vanishing. People said this, and some few even tried to understand in detail what it meant. And now all over the world military gentlemen, many of them still adorned with spurs, epaulettes, froggings, buttons, stripes, ribbons, medals, residual scraps of armour and such like pretty glories of the good old times, set themselves most valiantly to work out the possibilities and methods of the New Warfare.

Courage was always the better part of the military tradition, and nothing could exceed the courage with which these men set themselves throughout this period to overtake the march of invention, to master engineering and engineers, chemistry and chemists, war correspondents and newspaper editors, biology, medicine and even finance, in their efforts to keep that ancient war idea, the idea of the battling sovereign state, alive. As we have seen, the schools stood loyally by them; they had the support of the armament industries, and, less wholeheartedly perhaps, the approval of the old religions and of the old royalties and loyalties. Their activities were profoundly stupid, but the grotesque horror of their achievements, the distress and

183

unhappiness of three generations of our race, are still recent enough to mask their ludicrous quality.

The literature of the military science of this period is a copious one, and perhaps the best survey of it all is Fuller-Metsch's *The Ideas of the New Warfare in the Middle Twentieth Century* (2001). Therein the writer sets himself to three enquiries: 'For what did they suppose they were going to fight?' 'How were they going to fight?' And, 'What did they consider would constitute a definitive end and winding-up of their fighting?'

The answer he gives is a composite one. No single individual seems to have grasped the New Warfare in its entirety. With a solemn pedantry, a pretentious modesty, each 'expert' dealt with his own department and left it to Fate to put the assembled parts together into a whole. But what the composite soldier of 1935 was contemplating rather foggily seems to have been very much as follows. He conceived the world as divided up among a number of governments of Powers. These were the sovereign states as the Treaty of Westphalia (1642) presented them. All these powers were competitive and passively or actively hostile. The intervals when the hostility was active were wars. The intervals of recuperation and preparation were peace. War was a cessation of a truce between the belligerents, a cessation arising out of an irreconcilable dispute or clash of interests and the objective then of each Power was to impose its Will upon its enemy. In the days before the twentieth century this imposition of Will was done more or less professionally by the governments and armies. One or other Power took the offensive, crossed its borders and marched on the enemy seat of government. After various operations and battles the capital would be captured or the invader driven back to his own, and a peace made and a treaty signed more or less in accordance with the Will of the victor. Boundaries would be adjusted in accordance with that Will, colonies transferred, indemnities arranged for; the victorious Power expanded and the defeated shrivelled. The people of the unsuccessful Power would be very much

184

ashamed of themselves. To the end of the nineteenth century this formula was observed.

But by the time of the World War much more than the disappearance of the 'front' and the increasing entanglement of the erstwhile non-combatants was happening to this procedure. The powers were losing their definite identities. The fine question of what constituted a responsible government capable of imposing a Will, or giving in to it, arose. In Russia, for example, was the new Communist régime responsible for the obligations of the Autocracy? Was Germany, were all the Germans, to be held responsible for Krupp–Kaiser militarism? Was a dummy Sultan in Constantinople, or Kemal Pasha in Angora, the proper authority to consent to the dismemberment of Turkey? Again, the United States of America had come gaily into the war and then declined effective participation in President Wilson's settlement. He had not, it seemed, been a plenipotentiary. Was that behaving as a Power should have?

Still further perplexities arose about the laws of war. If the front was abolished, if civilians were to be bombed from the air, what became of the right of professional soldiers to shoot *francs-tireurs* and destroy their homes? It was as if the arena of a football match were invaded by the spectators, who began kicking the ball about, chasing the referee and declining to keep any score as between the original sides in the game.

The military authority recoiled from these devastating riddles of the new age. Such issues, he decided, were not for him. There had always been sides in a war, and there must still be sides. It was for the politicians to define them. He fell back on his fundamental conception of a Power 'imposing its Will' upon another Power, but using now, in addition to the old invasion and march on the capital, the new methods of propaganda, blockades and attacks behind the front, and all the latest chemical and aerial devices to 'undermine the morale' of the enemy population and dispose its government to yield. In the end there must be a march, if only a concluding professional march, through the goal or capital of the losing side. He refused to entertain the inevitable problem of an enemy government not yielding but collapsing, and leaving no responsible successor. That was not his affair. Presumably in that case the war would continue indefinitely.

Nor was it his business to enter into the financial aspects of the matter, to estimate any ratio whatever between the costs of the New Warfare and the material advantages to be exacted when the Will of the conqueror was imposed. In that regard he was excessively modest. He could not be expected to think of everything. His business was to prepare the best and most thorough war possible, with all the latest improvements, and quite regardless of cost, for his Power. It was for his government to find out how to pay for and use the war he had prepared for it. Or to use it partially. War, just war itself, was the limit of his task.

Research for the latest improvements soon led the now almost morbidly progressive military mind to some horrifying discoveries. Some of the soldiers concerned were certainly badly scared by the realisation of what evils it was now possible to inflict in warfare. It leaked out in their speeches and books. But they kept on. They kept on partly because they had a stouthearted tradition and refused to be dismayed, but mainly no doubt for the same reason that the Christian priests and bishops who had lost their faith still stuck to their Churches—because it was the only job they could do. Throughout the three decades that followed the Congress of Versailles, thousands of highly intelligent men, specialist soldiers, air soldiers, engineering soldiers, chemical, medical soldiers and the like, a far ampler and more energetic personnel than that devoted to the solution of the much more urgent and important financial riddles of the time, were working out, with unstinted endowments and the acquiescence and approval of their prospective victims, patiently, skilfully, thoroughly, almost inconceivably, abominable novelties for the surprise and torture of human beings.

None of these experts seems to have been more than

186

mediocre; it was an age of mental and moral mediocrities: and even within the accepted limitation we have already noted, none of them seems to have worked out the New Warfare as a whole complete process. Groups of men working in secrecy, immune from outer criticism, naturally conspire not only against the foreigner but against each other, and most of the men in decisive positions were rather men skilled in securing appointments and promotion than inspired specialists. A certain lumbering quality in their devices ensued.

In Great Britain a group of these experts became exceedingly busy in what was called mechanical warfare. The British had first invented, and then made a great mess of, the tank in the World War, and they were a tenacious people. The authorities stuck to it belatedly but doggedly. In a time of deepening and ever bitterer parsimony their War Office spared no expense in this department. It was the last of all to feel the pinch. The funny land ironclads of all sizes these military 'inventors' produced, from a sort of armoured machine-gunner on caterpillar wheels up to very considerable mobile forts, are still among the queerest objects in the sheds of the vast war dumps which constitute the Aldershot Museum. They are fit peers for Admiral Fisher's equally belated oil Dreadnoughts.

The British dream of the next definitive war seems to have involved a torrent of this ironmongery tearing triumphantly across Europe. In some magic way (too laborious to think out) these armoured Wurms were to escape traps, gas poison belts, mines and gunfire. There were even 'tanks' that were intended to go under water, and some that could float. Hansen even declared (see *The Last War Preparations*, xxiv, 1076) that he had found (rejected) plans of tanks to fly and burrow. Most of these contrivances never went into action. That throws a flavour of genial absurdity over this particular collection that is sadly lacking from most war museums.

The British and the French experts, and presently the Germans, also worked very hard at the fighting aeroplane

—the British and Germans with the greatest success; the aerial torpedo, controllable at immense distances, was perfected almost simultaneously by the Italians and the Japanese. The French mind, for all its native brilliance, was hampered by its characteristic reluctance to scrap old plant for new. It was the German, American and Russian experts who went furthest with the possibilities of chemical attack. The disarmament of Germany necessarily forced its military authorities to concentrate on an arm that could be studied, experimented upon and prepared unknown to the outer world, and the Russians were forced to take up parallel enquiries because of their relative industrial poverty. The Germans had been first to use gas in the Great War, and they remained for a long time the war gas pioneers. But after the Great War much attention was given to this arm in America through the influence of the chemical industry. Biological warfare, that is to say the distribution of infectious diseases, was also extensively studied, America and the Central Europeans in this case leading the way.

Even before the Central European fighting in 1940 and the subsequent years, the distribution of various disease germs was no longer a merely theoretical possibility. Little containers, made to look like fountain pens, were already being manufactured. The caps could be removed to expose soluble ends, and then they could be dropped into reservoirs or running streams. Glass bombs also existed for use from aeroplanes, railway-train windows and so forth, which would break on hitting water. There are specimens in the Aldershot Museum. The enrolment and territorial organisation of medical men and trained assistants to inoculate threatened populations went on with increasing vigour after 1932.

But there was a certain hesitation about the use of disease germs. It is easy to distribute them but hard to limit their field of action, and if prisoners (military or civilian) were still to be taken and towns and territory occupied, a well-launched pestilence might conceivably recoil with deadly effect upon its users. Bacterial warfare seemed, even to the specialists who studied it, a very improbable method for any but an heroically vindictive population in the hour of defeat. Nevertheless, it was thought best to have it worked out. Except for the distribution of malignant influenza in Kan-su and Shensi by the Japanese during their efforts to tranquillise North China in 1936, 'without proceeding to extremities', its use was never officially admitted. Other alleged instances of its deliberate employment by responsible Powers had been shown by the researches of the Historical Bureau to have been due either to the unauthorised zeal of subordinates or to the activities of those religious fanatics who became so prevalent during the period of confusion after 1945. The sudden appearance of a vanished form of yellow fever in India in 1950, which did so much to diminish the population of that peninsula, has never been explained. It seems to have been a biological accident.

So far as method and invention went, what was called 'Gas Warfare' ran very parallel to bacterial warfare. Its beginning and end is now a closed chapter in the history of the human intelligence and will. It is surely one of the strangest. It set its stamp upon the clothing and urban architecture of the age. It ranks in horror with the story of judicial torture or the story of ritual cannibalism, but its inhumanity is more striking because of its nearness to our own times. Like those older instances, it brings home to us the supreme need for sound common general ideas to hold together human activities. It tells how thousands of clear and active minds, each indisputably sane, could, in an atmosphere obsessed by plausible false assumptions about patriotic duty and honour, co-operate to produce a combined result fantastically futile and cruel.

The people engaged in this business were, on the whole, exceptionally grave, industrious and alert-minded. Could they revisit the world to-day individually we should probably find them all respectable, companionable, intelligible persons. Yet in the aggregate they amounted to an organisation of dangerous lunatics. They inflicted dreadful deaths,

189

hideous sufferings or tormented lives upon, it is estimated about a million of their fellow creatures.

Most of the lethal substances prepared for gas warfare purposes have passed altogether out of general knowledge. They are either never manufactured now or they are produced upon rare occasions and under proper control for the purposes of physiological research. The old devices and appliances for their distribution seem nowadays like grotesque anticipations of many of the features of the large-scale agricultural and hygienic operations that are carried out to-day. The treatment of locust swarms by air attack, the spraying of the reafforested regions against various tree diseases, the regular cleansing and stimulation of our grain and root crops are all subsequent rationalisations of these practices of the Age of Frustration.

Faber, that Calvinistic optimist, with his doctrine that the bad is all to the good in this maddest of all conceivable worlds, thinks that all these big-scale methods were 'enormously stimulated' by the crazy inventiveness of the war period. But then he has also suggested that the aeroplane would not have come into general use for many years without war stimulation. We venture to think he carries his doctrine of the attainment of wisdom through imbecility too far. It is really only a modernisation of Charles Lamb's story of the invention of the roast pig. It had the touch of Rasputinism, this revival of the ancient heresy that one must sin *thoroughly* before one can be saved.

Much more after the gas-war pattern were the campaigns (2033 and 2035) against rats and mice that finally cleansed the world of the lurking poison of that medieval terror, bubonic plague, and the distributions of 'festivity gas' that were permitted in various regions in 2060. The countervailing use of benign-gases as a subsidiary to the suppression of the depressing cometary toxins of 2080 will also occur to the reader. The oxygenation of council chambers, factories, playing-fields and similar loci demanding special brightness and activity, and the use of Padanath Tagore's Lotus Gas in the Himalayan rest valleys, we may note, are also claimed by Faber as part of the legacy of gas warfare.

One or two of the offensive substances actually manufactured for war purposes are now utilised in relation to very special and specially protected processes in our industrial plants. The preparation of some of them is a major felony. They were a very various miscellany, for every chemical possibility was ransacked to find them. Very few of them were actually gases. Many were volatile liquids or even finely divided solids, which were to be sprayed or dusted over positions in enemy occupation. Dr. Gertrud Woker, in a paper on this subject contributed to an enquiry by the Inter-parliamentary Union in 1931, gave a useful summary of the existing state of knowledge at that time. In conjunction with various colleagues (*What would be the Character of a New War?* Historical Documents 937,205), she allows us to form an estimate of what was actually being contemplated by contemporary military experts. Except for one important exception, her list covers all the main types of poison gas substances that were actually prepared. This spate of investigation culminated about 1938. By that time the entire field had been explored. After that there were improvements but no major innovations.

After 1940 even military research was restricted by the increasing financial paralysis. In 1960 no plants capable of producing material for gas warfare on a sufficiently abundant scale were operating.

Of gases actually tried out in the World War itself, the chief seem to have been chlorine and various chlorine compounds (phosgene, Green Cross gas, chloropicrin and so forth). These attacked and destroyed the lung tissue. Chlorine was used by the Germans as early as April 1915, at Ypres, when 6,000 men were killed by it; it was soon abandoned, because it was so immediately irritating that its presence was detected at once, and precautionary measures could be taken. The other gases in this class got to work less frankly. Presently the victim began to cough. Then as the destruction of the bronchioles and alveoli of the lungs

191

went on, he retched and suffocated and coughed up blood and tissue. He died amidst his expectorations with a visage blue and bloated and blood-stained froth on his lips. If by good luck he survived, he survived with his lungs so injured that he easily fell a victim to tuberculosis or suchlike disease. Most of this group of gases had their own characteristic complications. One series, for instance, would attack the nervous system, causing wild excitement, terror, convulsions, screams and paralysis. Thousands of men had already died in agony from Green Cross gas during the World War, and the plans of some of these experts involved the massacre of whole populations in the same atrocious fashion. Green Cross gas was used, but not in sufficient strength to be very deadly, in the Polish bombing of Berlin in May 1940, and in a more concentrated form in the aerial torpedoes that were sent from Germany to Warsaw. It had been used also at Nankin in 1935 and in the Chinese reprisal at Osaka.

Yellow Cross gas, or mustard gas, was much more insidious and also more cruel and murderous. It was not really a gas; it was a volatile liquid. When cold, it spread unsuspected in a thin film over the ground, getting on to boots and clothing, being carried hither and thither. Slowly, as it vaporised, its presence was revealed. Discomfort came, a horrible suspicion, fear and then coughing and retching. It involved quite frightful and hopeless suffering. Steadily but surely it killed every living substance with which it came into contact; it burnt it, blistered it, rotted it away. One part of mustard gas in five million of air was sufficient to affect the lungs. It ate into the skin, inflamed the eyes; it turned the muscles into decaying tissue. It become a creeping disease of the body, enfeebling every function, choking, suffocating. It is doubtful if any of those affected by it were ever completely cured. Its maximum effect was rapid torture and death; its minimum prolonged misery and an abbreviated life. The gases used in the fighting in North China in 1934–37 and in the Chinese raids upon Japan were mostly of this group. And an evacuation of Berlin in 1946 was brought about by the threat of Yellow Cross bombs.

[They were actually dropped, but, either through accident or by the insubordination of the chemists employed by the Poles, they smashed ineffectively. It was one of the most striking instances of what appears to have been the pacifist sabotage that helped to end the formal warfare in Central Europe. Five of the chemical workers concerned were shot and seventeen given long sentences of imprisonment, but none of the records of their trial has survived.]

Allied rather than competing with these gases of the Green and Yellow Cross categories. Dr. Woker cites the Blue Cross group. These substances were essentially direct nervous irritants in the form of an almost impalpable dust. They could penetrate most of the gas masks then in use, and produced such pain, so violent a sneezing and nausea and such a loss of self-control that the victim would tear off his mask, so exposing himself to the Green or Yellow vapours with which Blue Cross was usually associated.

All these torments had been extensively inflicted already during the World War, but after its conclusion the secret activities of the various poison gas departments were sustained with great energy. It took them nearly twenty years even to open up the main possibilities of their speciality. One substance, which played a large part in the discussions of the time, was 'Lewisite', the discovery of a Professor Lewis of Chicago, which came too late for actual use before the end of 1918. This was one of a group of arsenical compounds. One part of it in ten millions of air was sufficient to put a man out of action. It was inodorous, tasteless; you only knew you had it when it began to work upon you. It blistered as much as mustard gas and produced a violent sickness.

Other war poisons followed upon this invention, still more deadly: merciful poisons that killed instantly, and cruel and creeping poisons that implacably rotted the brain. Some produced convulsions and a knotting up of the muscles a hundred times more violent than the once dreaded tetanus. There is a horrible suggestiveness in the description of the killing of a flock of goats for experimental purposes in these researches: 'All succumbed to the effect of the gas except three, *which dashed their brains out against the enclosure.*' And to assist these chemicals in their task of what Dr. Woker calls 'mass murder' there was a collateral research into incendiary substances and high explosives to shatter and burn any gas-attack shelter to which a frightened crowd might resort.

Dr. Woker's summary does not include Kovoet's invention of the Permanent Death Gas in 1934. Its composition is still a secret and its very complicated preparation a felony. This compound, although not absolutely permanent, decomposed with extreme slowness. It was in itself neither a gas nor a poison. It was a heavy, rather coarse-grained powder. It evaporated as camphor does, and as it evaporated it combined with oxygen to form a poison effective when diluted with fifty million times its volume of air. Its action was essentially of the Lewisite type. This was actually used in the first Polish War to cut off East Prussia. A zone of territory from a mile to three miles wide along the whole frontier was evacuated and dusted with Permanent Death Gas. East Prussia became a peninsula accessible only from Lithuania or by sea. In spite of the heaviness of the grains, the winds finally widened this band of death to about fifteen miles in width and carried its lethal influence into the suburbs of Danzig.

This murdered region was not re-entered, except by a few specially masked explorers, until after 1960, and then it was found to be littered with the remains not only of the human beings, cattle and dogs who had strayed into it, but with the skeletons and scraps of skin and feathers of millions of mice, rats, birds and suchlike small creatures. In some places they lay nearly a metre deep. *War Pictures* has two photographs of this strange deposit. Vegetation was not so completely destroyed; trees died and remained bare and pickled; some grasses suffered, but others of the ranker sort flourished, and great areas were covered by a carpet of dwarfed and stunted corn-cockles and elecampane set in

194

grey fluff.

A curious by-product of Permanent Death Gas is what is now known as the Sterilising Inhalation. This was first made by accident. A Chinese Vindication Society organised an air raid on Osaka and Tokio in 1935 and after the great Green Cross raid on Nankin in that year. It was intended to strike terror into the Japanese mind. Permanent Death Powder was to have been used, but because of the haste and danger of the preparations the Chinese had not tested it out, and here again, either by accident or design, things went wrong; the formula, it seems, had been falsified. Consequently, when the raid was made—all the machines employed were brought down on their way home—nothing ensued but a temporary fever accompanied by retching and purging.

There was much derision of the unfortunate aviators in Japan. It was only some months after that the Western World learnt that the medical services of both towns were reporting a complete cessation of early pregnancies. Not a litter of kittens or puppies had appeared for weeks, mares were no longer foaling nor cows in calf. Mice and rats vanished. The sterilisation in all cases was permanent. But birds were not affected for reasons that Crayford-Huxley has since made clear. The sparrows multiplied enormously and the hens still clucked triumphantly in these childless cities.

In some way the Chinese chemists had blundered upon one of those rare sub-radiant gases known as Pabst's Kinetogens, which affect the genes. A whole series of these are now known to biologists, chiefly through the work of Pabst and his assistant, and most of the more extraordinary flower sports and new aberrant animal types in our experimental gardens are due to their employment; but for a long time, until indeed Pabst took up the subject with an insight all his own, only the Sterilisation Inhalation was known. Most of the campaigns in the Forties of the twenty-first century against contagious rodents made an extensive use of this gas wherever regions could be isolated from human intrusion, and the day may not be distant when it will have important eugenic applications.

But the Japanese experience produced even a graver sensation throughout the world than the actual slaughter of the victims would have occasioned. The militarist class in Japan was as deeply sentimental as the Western equivalent in Europe, and as resolute that the common people should not only die but breed fresh battle fodder for their country. Until the patriots realised that the Chinese supply of this stuff was limited, they lived in horror. They saw themselves stripped bare of subject lives. They saw themselves extinct in the hour of victory. There was a great clamour about the world for the extensive application of this new find during the fiercer war years; there are proposals on record (*Hate Eugenics*, Historical Documents 5,752,890 and *seq.*) to apply it from the air to Palestine, Arabia, Ireland, the whole of China and the African Continent in part or as a whole. But mankind was saved from any such catastrophe by the fact that the first production of Sterilising Inhalation was essentially accidental. It had been prepared furtively, its makers were untraceable, and the proper formula was not worked out and made controllable until our insane world was well in the grip of the harsh humanity of the Air Dictatorship.

How all these hideous devices of the New Warfare were to be brought together to effect the definitive subjugation of the Will of a belligerent Power was apparently never thought out, or, if it was, the plans were kept so secret that now they have perished with their makers. After the millions had choked, after the cities were a stench of dead bodies—what then?

Perhaps the artistic interest of the business precluded such remote considerations. All we can disentangle now of this gas warfare, as its experts contemplated it, consists of projects of mere mischief and torture. They seem imbued with much the same wanton destructiveness as that displayed by some of the younger specimens among the Loando-Mobi chimpanzee hybrids.

Yet some of these plans are amazingly thorough up to a

certain point—up to the point when one asks, 'But *why*?' For instance, in the Marine War Museum in the Torcello Lagoon there are no fewer than half a dozen raider submarines built for four different great Powers, and all specially designed as long-distance bases for gas warfare. They carried no guns nor ordinary fighting equipment. They had practically unlimited cruising range, and within them from five to nine aeroplanes were packed with a formidable supply of gas bombs. One of them carried thirty long-range air torpedoes with all the necessary directional apparatus. There were four different types of gas mixture in the bombs, but they differed little in character and efficiency. The smallest of these raiders carried enough of such stuff to 'prepare' about eight hundred square miles of territory. Completely successful, it could have turned most of the London or New York of that time, after some clamour and running and writhing and choking, into a city full of distorted corpses. These vessels made London vulnerable from Japan, Tokio vulnerable from Dublin; they abolished the last corners of safety in the world.

These six sinister monsters gleam now in the great gallery side by side, their poison fangs drawn, their mission abandoned, the grim vestiges, the uncontrovertible evidence of one nightmare among the many nightmares of hate and evil that afflicted the human brain during the Age of Frustration. There they are. Men made them – as men made the instruments of torture during the previous dark ages. Even amidst the happy confidence of our present life it is well that we should remember that, given different conditions, men technically as sane as ourselves could design and make these things.

There is something revolting in these details. We have given enough for our purpose. History must not be made a feast of horror. From first to last gas warfare destroyed very painfully between one and one and a quarter million lives that might have been fruitful and happy. That much mischief was done. They suffered and they have gone. The gist of our story is that, after the humiliation and quicken-

197

ing of the military mind by the ineptitudes of the World War, belligerent science did not so much progress as lose itself in the multiplicity of its own inventions. It developed one frightful and monstrous contrivance after another, to dismay and torment mankind, to spread ill health and hate, to demoralise and destroy industrial life, to make whole countries uninhabitable and loosen every band that held men together in orderly societies, but it made no steps at all to any comprehensive and decisive conduct of war. With no plan for the future, with no vision of the world as a whole at all, these thousands of furtive specialists, these 'damned ingenious patriots', as Isaac Burtonshaw (1919–2003) called them, went on accumulating, here frightful explosives, there stores of disgusting disease germs, and there again stores of this or that fantastically murderous gas.

No comprehensive plan had held any of these centres of evil together into one premeditated whole, as, for instance, the military preparations of the Hohenzollern Empire were held together by a clear and deliberate scheme of conclusive warfare. Beneath the vulgar monarchist claptrap of the German effort of 1914 there was indeed a real scheme for the reorganisation and modernisation of civilisation about a Teutonic nucleus according to Teutonic ideals. It may have had its fatuous elements, but it was logical and complete. But war planning never recovered that completeness after 1914; never got back to the same logical foundations. After that belligerence lost its head. It still went on as everything else went on in those days—by inertia. But it had no longer any idea of what it was up to.

Yet over all the world these incoherent mines were prepared, and they might well have exploded, had their release been simultaneous, into such an outbreak of disorderly evil as staggers the contemporary imagination. It is conceivable that they might have destroyed mankind. It would have needed no change in the essential conditions but only a rearrangement of the determining accidents to have brought about that final catastrophe.

This menace of a chaos of disasters and aimless cruelties

198

hung over a disorganised and unprotected world for three-quarters of a century. It is what some historians call the Period of Maximum Insecurity, from 1935 to 1965. Here and there quite monstrous things occurred—at Nankin, Pekin, Osaka, Berlin, Warsaw, for instance; things terrible enough to hearten and steel the better elements in humanity for the achievement of that world peace towards which all these forces were urging it. Fortunately for mankind the two fundamental evils of traditionalism were just sufficient to neutralise each other during this long period of the incubation of the Modern State. The greed of the creditor balanced the greed of the armament dealer. As armaments grew more and more costly, the possible purchasers grew poorer and poorer. If economy starved and hampered many good things in human life, it did at least finally take all vigour and confidence out of the development of the New Warfare. The Chemical Armament industry followed the other typical institutions of the old order into the general social liquidation which wound up the bankruptcy of Private Profit Capitalism.

§ 5. *The Fading Vision of a World Pax: Japan Reverts to Warfare*

We have shown already how Parliamentary Democracy necessarily abolished real leaders in public affairs and substituted a strange type of pseudo-leader, men who were essentially *resultants,* who made nothing, created no forces, met no emergencies, but simply manoeuvred for position, prestige and the pettier rewards of power. They followed the collapse of the decaying order without an effort to arrest its decay. Why indeed should they have made an effort?

199

They were representatives of the popular will, and if there was no popular will ...

We have already considered the behaviour of this amazingly ineffective collection of men in face of the financial dislocation that was choking the economic life of the race. It is doubtful if a single one of them ever gave a month's continuous study to the plain realities of that situation. And in the face of the accumulating stresses created by the maladjustments of Versailles, this galaxy of humbugs to whom democracy had entrusted the direction of human affairs—humbugs unavoidably, for the system insisted upon it regardless of the best intentions—was equally enigmatical and impotent. Along the eastern frontiers of Italy and Germany the open sores festered. No one sought to heal them. In the Far East the conflict between Japan and China, failing a European protest, became frankly a formal war. Every world event cried louder than the last for collective action, and there was no collective action. The League of Nations appointed commissions of enquiry and produced often quite admirable analyses of hopeless situations.

No one knew how to arrest the grim development of the situation. The chiefs of states repeated the traditional gestures, as though these were all that could be expected of them. But the patterns of history served them no more. They found themselves like men who attempt to gesticulate and find their limbs have changed to cloud and rock.

Of all the 'Powers' of that time the behaviour of Japan was the most decisive. In 1931 an internal revolution in that country had put political power into the hands of a patriotic military group, diplomatically unscrupulous and grossly sentimental according to the distinctive Japanese tradition, and this coterie set itself now with extraordinary energy and an equally extraordinary lack of authentic vision to caricature the aggressive imperialism of the nineteenth-century Europeans. The mind of this ruling group was still intensely romantic, still obsessed by those ideas of national dominance and glory which had passed already so fatally over the intelligence of Christendom. Their military initiatives were quasi-Napoleonic, their diplomatic pretences and evasions modelled on the best European precedents. It was 'Japan's turn' now.

The investigation of just what these Japanese Imperialists imagined they were doing has greatly exercised our historical research department. But it is indeed only a special instance of the general riddle of what any 'Power', regarded as a mentality in itself, imagined it was doing in that age. Only a century and a half has passed since those Japanese columns were marching into one Chinese town after another, and to-day our psychologists confess themselves baffled by an enterprise that was manifestly undertaken by men like ourselves and yet had already assumed a quality of absolute insanity. Why did these very intelligent people behave in that fashion?

The clue lies in the extraordinary ease with which distasteful reality can be repressed by the human mind, and in the atmosphere of grotesque but flattering illusions in which these people were living. Just as in the West the bankers, economic experts, responsible statesmen, would not realise the complete smash to which their fiscal and financial methods were plainly heading until the smash had actually come, so these Japanese militarists could not see the inevitable consequences of their continental adventures. They could not see behind them a miserable peasantry breeding itself down to the basest subsistence; a miserable urban proletariat deteriorating physically and morally; they could not estimate the mutterings of revolt in all their sweated and driven industrial centres; they could not understand the protests of their own fine and growing intelligentsia.

Even the steady fall of the national credit abroad and the increasing economic stresses of the land aroused no misgivings of hallucination. Japan in her headlong pursuit of Western precedents was rapidly reproducing all the revolutionary conditions of the West. All that was lost upon her leaders. The one thing they could see clearly was that China was disorganised, that she was struggling with great difficulty to discover a new method of collective living to replace her ancient slack imperialism, and that by all the rules of the international game this was Japan's opportunity. They thought that, in very much the same way that the disorganisation of the Empire of the Great Mogul had laid India bare to the piratical enterprise of the Europeans and permitted the establishment of the unstable aimless Indian Empire of the British, so now Fate had invited them to an equally glorious opportunity, to a parallel Japanese domination of the most or all of Asia. Who could tell where their imperial adventure would end—or whether it would have an end? The mirage of limitless power and glory opened out before them, as it has opened out to all empire-builders since the world began.

They were reckoning without the New Warfare, reckoning without modern industralism, without the paradoxical self-destructiveness of Private Capitalist enterprise, without Russia, without America, without the superior mass, the traditional unity and mental obduracy of the Chinese population. They were thinking as a Pomeranian Junker or a British general from that 'hotbed of Imperialists', Ulster, might have thought before 1914. It was an archaic megalomania—that led to the killing of about three million combatants, an extreme social disintegration in China, and the final collapse of the Japanese monarchy.

In the special histories of this struggle, the student who needs or desires the knowledge may find the detailed particulars of the Japanese aggressions from 1931 onward which grew at last into the formal invasion of China proper; the tentative of Shanghai, the invasion of Manchuria and the establishment of the puppet kingdom of Manchukuo (1932), the attack on Shanhaikwan which led to the penetration of the Great Wall, the invasion of China Proper from the north and the march on Pekin. The operations up to that point were largely on the pattern of the old warfare as it had been practised up to 1914. The Chinese were poorly equipped and had little modern material; the Japanese found it unnecessary to make any excessively expensive efforts to attain their objectives.

All this earlier fighting went on to an accompaniment of protests from the quite powerless League of Nations of Geneva. A 'Lytton Report' prepared by a commission of enquiry is to be found in the Historical Documents Series (2,067,111). But counter-balancing these remonstrances were the ambiguous utterances of the British Foreign Office, the support of the French armament industry and its Press, the overt support of a great group of American banks and their newspapers. In view of these divisions, the Japanese militarists had every reason to disregard Western criticism altogether.

In 1935 the Japanese occupied Pekin and Tientsin. They set up a second puppet monarchy in Pekin. But they found very great difficulty in holding the country, particularly to the south and west of these centres. Manchuria, Inner Mongolia and Shansi remained seething with bandits and rebel bands, and the still unoccupied valley of the Yang-tsze-kiang remained fighting with an increasing unity under the leadership of the reorganised Kuomintang. In no part of China or Manchuria was it safe for a Japanese to go about alone, and a rigorous economic boycott, sustained by an omnipresent terrorism, continued. The Kuomintang was a directive association created by the great Chinese revolutionary Sun Yat Sen, and it had gone through various vicissitudes; it had a rough general resemblance to the Communist Party and the various European fascisms, and, like them, it sustained a core of conscious purpose throughout its community. It had no vital centre, no formal head; it was a thing of the mind, unquenchable by military operations. And under the stress of this resistance it had become violently patriotic and xenophobic.

In 1936 Japan already had more than a million and a half men scattered between the Manchurian frontier and Canton, where a third landing had been made, and still her hold upon China hardly extended beyond the range of her guns and the glitter of her bayonets. She had bombed Nankin twice on an extensive scale, Pekin before its surrender, and

Wuchang and Hankow, with Yellow Cross bombs. Hundreds of thousands of people had been slaughtered, but the great invertebrate body of China seemed able to endure such losses with a stoicism impossible in a more highly organised state. In return the 'Vindication of China' Society astonished the world by suddenly bombing and, through an error in the gas mixture, *sterilising* Osaka and Tokio.

No one knew of these Chinese air forces until they appeared in action. The machines had come from Sweden by way of Russia. But nearly every Western country was supplying contraband of war to the Chinese. Unaccountable hostile aeroplanes with untraceable bombs appeared in the sky and came humming over the sea to Japan. Then in 1935 a Japanese transport blew up and sank in the Gulf of Pe-chih-li. In 1936, three Japanese liners were destroyed by mines of unknown origin within fifty miles of port. War supplies of all sorts got into China from Soviet Russia in the north and from the French and British possessions in the south, and the help and sympathy of America became more and more manifest as the vast imperial ambitions of the Japanese leaders became unmistakable. Western feeling had at first been acutely divided between distrust of Japan and the desire to see China restored to order on capitalist lines and saved from Communism. But with every Japanese advance European and American feeling veered back towards China. Australia and New Zealand appealed to the Washington Government for a joint guarantee to supplement the Imperial tie in 1937. They were advocating a mutual guarantee of all the Europeanised regions of the Pacific. For a time it seemed as though the Western world might be guided to a sort of unity by the flares of Japan. But the unforgettable humiliations inflicted upon Central Europe after the war still rankled sufficiently to prevent that.

Even before the launching of the definitive conquest of China there had been considerable economic and social stress in Japan. The earlier successes, the easy capture of Pekin and the failure of an adequate Chinese army to materialise, had filled the island empire with patriotic enthusiasm and hope; the war was brought to a victorious conclusion three times, and each time it broke out again. No invader ever conquered Russia to the end, and no one ever completed the conquest of China. Always beyond the subjugated provinces appeared other provinces swarming with hostility. Szechwan and the south supplied inexhaustible support and supplies for the Kuomintang resistance. It seemed at last as though there could be no peace any more in China until the invaders fought their way through to Tibet.

War weariness descended upon Nippon. The peasants saw their sons marching off, never to return, and shortages of ordinary commodities deepened to famine. There was already vigorous 'Stop the War' agitation in Japan in 1935; there were continual strikes in Nagoya and hundreds of casualties, and afterwards there began a frantic dumping of accumulated goods abroad, to pay not merely for munitions but for such now vitally essential imports as Australian meat and Canadian and American corn. The war was starving the home fields of men and it was destroying the productivity of large areas of China. The social structure of Japan proved to be far too primitive to emulate the miracles of economy performed by the Germans during the World War. The confidence and credit of Japan sank steadily. Foreign loans became no longer possible even at such exorbitant rates as 14 or 15 per cent. And still there was no end in sight.

The Japanese militarists had gone too far to recede. Behind them they had a suffering population that might rapidly become vindictive, and about the arena of the struggle watched Russia, America and Europe. According to the best traditions of their culture, these national leaders resolved on a supreme military effort, a march in overwhelming force into the central province of Hupeh. Colossal preparations were made, and every able-bodied Japanese who was not already enrolled was called up. This was to be 'a blow at the heart'.

A convergent march from Nankin, Shantung and Canton was planned. This dispersal of the bases was justified by the necessity for living on the country as far as that remained possible. There were railways in existence from Canton and Shantung, but they were difficult to protect, and, apart from them, there was such an utter want of practicable roads that by the time the Japanese were in Hupeh a third of their forces were trailed out upon their lines of communication making roads, and the equipment of heavy guns and munitions they had been able to bring up was very little superior to that of the Chinese, who were still fighting with all the wealth of Szechwan at their backs and the almost overt sympathy of the West. The three great Japanese armies effected their junction in a loose ring round Wuchang—a ring that was for a time slowly drawn tighter and then ceased to contract. A deadlock ensued, a deadlock of mutual exhaustion. Neither up nor down the river was the closure of the ring complete. Throughout 1938, Japan waited for good news from the long crescents of trenches about Wuchang, and waited in vain. Pestilence broke out in July and defeated the utmost sanitary and medical efforts of the invaders. Then early in 1939 they began their retreat to Nankin, with transport disorganised, with mutiny growing, with all the country rising about them.

The horrors of that retreat have never been fully told. The three Japanese armies at their maximum strength had numbered well over two million of men; but probably about a million or less remained fit enough for the retreat. Famine was far more deadly with them than the Chinese guerillas; the exhausted wretches fell out along the line of march and waited stoically for the end; few prisoners were taken; the Chinese had no food even if they had had mercy to give quarter, and the fallen were left to perish in their own time. The broken remnant that assembled at Nankin did not greatly exceed a hundred thousand, and still smaller bodies from the lines of communication fought their way homeward to the north and south. The rest of these two million lay in the vast cemeteries of Puki and Ki-chow, or they had

206

been drowned in the floods, or their bodies were littered as they had dropped and crawled over the sad monotonous landscape of the Chinese hills. At Nankin the weary and dispirited survivors realised that Japan was now also at war with the United States and that Osaka and Nagoya were in the hands of Communist Committees.

For some weeks the Japanese army sprawled inactive in its former cantonments to the west of Nankin. Then it revolted, shot many of its officers, declared for the social revolution and fraternised with the Chinese Red Army which had marched in under its nose from Hangchow and taken control of the city proper.

The entry of the United States into the Eastern War, which did so much to complete the demoralisation of militarist Japan, was the climax of a prolonged wrangle about the supply of mines and submarines to the Chinese, that became more and more acute after the sinking of a Japanese transport in the gulf of Pe-chih-li.

It is only recently that the full history—which is also a very tedious and disputatious history—of the sea war against Japan has been worked out. Every contemporary record was falsified at the time; every event hidden completely or elaborately camouflaged. It is now fairly evident that not merely did private firms manufacture mines and build submarine minelayers but that the various European navies under the plea of economy sold out a large proportion of quite modern and valid under-sea craft for 'breaking up' to agents and dealers acting for South American intermediaries. The submarines, either intact or so 'broken up' that they could easily be reconstructed, went to various Peruvian and Chilian ports and thence found their way across the Pacific to the Philippine Islands. The Philippine Islands were quasi-independent, but the Manila declaration of President Roosevelt II in 1937 had practically extended to them the protection of the Monroe Doctrine and the Japanese had never had the surplus energy necessary to challenge this informal protectorate. Now these islands became the base for vexatious attacks upon their

207

overseas trade and sea communications.

The naval situation in the Pacific was a complicated one. To the east of the Philippines lie the Ladrones, a scattered group of volcanic islands, of which the largest, Guam, had been assigned to the United States of America by the Treaty of Versailles and was administered as a part of the American Navy, while the rest were held by Japan under a mandate. (The Powers previously in possession had been first Spain and, after 1899, Germany.) The Japanese were bound by treaty not to fortify their holdings, but as the situation grew tense they seem to have ignored this restriction, at least to the extent of establishing submarine bases. Now that the situation was growing tenser the state of affairs above and under water between the Ladrones, the Philippines and the Asiatic mainland became darker and more dangerous. There was a threatening concentration of the American Fleet between Guam and the Philippines to ensure the neutrality of the latter, a patrolling concentration of the Japanese along the Chinese coast, and an obscure activity of privateering submarines and ambiguous shipping, which smuggled munitions and supplies and raided weak points of the Japanese communications.

Above water a submarine, like any other ship, can fly a flag and claim the respect due to its nationality, but mines fly no flags, and under water a submarine may be able to recognise the coded signals of a co-national but has no means at all of distinguishing a neutral from an enemy. Mistakes and pseudo-mistakes were inevitable. Two American submarines disappeared in 1936. Then several Japanese submarines vanished from the Ladrone archipelago. Disputes that broke out in neutral cafés came to a murderous end in the depths. The American navy took matters into its own hands. By 1937 an informal naval war had developed in the Western Pacific.

Neither Power hurried on to an actual declaration of war. America, in spite of, or perhaps because of, the bold experimenting of Roosevelt II, was in a state of deepening economic and political disorder, and Japan was putting forth her utmost strength for that disastrous 'blow at the heart' in China. But many of the more conservative influences in the United States saw in a Pacific war a saving distraction of public attention and public energy. There was an agitation to re-annex the Philippines, and after the Japanese failure to hold Wuchang the drive towards open war became uncontrollable.

The particulars of the brief, destructive and indecisive naval war that followed need not occupy us here. The battle fleets met in the Western Pacific and separated after two days of gunfire and heavy losses. Ammunition gave out, it seems, on the Japanese side. At any rate they drew off in the twilight under a smoke-screen. The Americans claimed the victory because they were able to go on to Manila, while the Japanese withdrew to the protection of their minefields and submarines and were never able to emerge again for lack of material. Both Powers were now in a state of deepening domestic stress, and their war, in a technical sense, never ended. That is to say, there was no final treaty as between two Powers, because both had in effect collapsed. They fell apart. Social revolution swept the conflict off the stage.

[The student will be reminded, by this inconclusive termination, of the almost incessant, dreary and futile wars of Byzantine and Sassanid that devastated Asia Minor for three centuries and did not so much come to an end as suffer effacement from history by the sponge of Islam.]

The social disintegration of Japan, once it had begun, was very rapid. The great mass of the population, the peasants, had been scarcely affected by the process of Westernisation, and they lapsed very readily into the same unprogressive variant of Communism as their equivalents in Kwantung, Chekiang and Fukien had adopted. A small Westernised intelligentsia with many internal feuds and doctrinal disputes struggled, not very effectively, in the larger towns to turn this merely insurgent Communism into modern and constructive paths after the Moscow pattern. Fragmentation when it came was swift and thorough. Militarism de-

209

generated into brigandage and local feudalism. Here and there some scion of the old nobility reappeared with his attendant Samurai as a gangster boss.

In the space of a few years all Asia from the Pacific to Persia seemed to be sliding back to political and social chaos, to hand-to-mouth cultivation, destitution and endemic pestilence. For the greater part of India and most of Further India were also now drifting back to barbarism. There also the phrases and the insubordination, if not the spirit and methods, of Communism had captured vast multitudes who had remained completely unaffected by other European ideas. It was Communism without any Five Year Plan or indeed any conception of a plan. It was the class-war in its ultimate crudity. It killed moneylenders and tax-collectors with gusto and elaboration. It evolved strange religious fanaticisms, and it abandoned sanitation as 'boujawai', the accursed thing. The imperial power in India was not overthrown; rather it was stripped of effective prestige and receded to an immense distance. The princes remained formally 'loyal', though in some cases they tacitly annexed 'disturbed districts' adjacent to their proper dominions. Localities and local adventurers improvised a sort of social order at a low level and with a continually completer disregard of any central authority.

§ 6. *The Western Grip on Asia Relaxes*

The recession of the directive influence of the half-modernised European imperialisms in Asia went on steadily. Even as early as 1929 the spread of a peasant Communism similar to that which had obtained so strong a hold upon the popular imagination in China was causing grave alarm to the Indian Government. The seizure and trial of a group of British and Indian agitators at Meerut, and the extravagantly heavy sentences passed upon them in 1933, showed both the gravity of these fears and the unintelligent clumsiness with which the situation was being met.

For the British Empire there was to be no such decline and fall as happened to Rome. Instead it relaxed, as we shall now describe, to nothing.

Unhappily, before it relaxed in India it had, as in Ireland, a brief convulsive phrase of 'firmness'. . . .

[*Here several sheets from Raven's MS. appear to be missing.*]

§ 7. *The Modern State and Germany*

A question of primary importance in human history is this: Why were the lessons of the Great War, and the subsequent economic and social disorders, lessons which seem to us to-day to be as starkly plain as lessons could be—why were these lessons lost upon every one of the great communities of thought into which the world was divided? British thought, French thought, American thought, German, Russian, Italian thought, seem in our retrospect to ring the changes upon every conceivable sequence of prejudice and stupidity. Why was Wilson's start towards world unification not followed up? Why after 1932 was there no vigour to reconstruct the League of Nations, when all the world was crying for some central authority to unify money and economic life? Why did the Age of Frustration last so long? We have already noted some of the controlling causes, the mercenary Press, the vast anti-social private interests, the heavy weight of tradition, the reactionary quality of schoolmasters, the social disintegration due to economic demoralisation. But even these malignant influences, taken all together, do not seem sufficient for this blindness in the general intelligence of our race towards the obvious elements of its situation.

Behind all these conditions making for failure there was something else: there was an intrinsic weakness in the forces of reconstruction, there was a fundamental lack. *It was impossible for the world to get out of its difficulties because it had no definite complete idea of what it wanted to get out to.* It had ideas, yes, more than enough, but they were confused and often mutually contradictory ideas. A drowning man cannot save himself by swimming unless he has something solid to which he can swim. The deficiency was not moral nor material, it was intellectual. There was the will for salvation and the material for salvation, but there was no plan of salvation. The world had no definition of an objective. That had still to be made plain to it.

It will make this matter clearer if we consider the mental and emotional phases of one typical culture community of central importance at that time, the German. Stories similar in essence, if widely different in detail, could be given of the French, Anglo-Saxon, Russian and Spanish-speaking communities. The feature they had in common was this, a failure to realise that there could be no salvation now unless it was a comprehensive salvation. They were attempting to do severally and with a jostling competitiveness what could only be done with the utmost difficulty in unison. That meant for every one of them the paralysing influence of a war threat, extreme economic instability, incapacity for dealing with morbid financial conditions and a consequent state of mental 'worry' that made every move inaccurate and untimely.

It was only when we realise the sapping of that aggressive energy that had wellnigh Europeanised the whole world before the World War that we can understand the length of the Age of Frustration. Certain facts of fundamental importance to the continued health of our world community have to be stressed. Europe could not lead the world to unity when the world seemed dying to be led to unity, because Europe itself was profoundly disunited. The World War was merely the explosion of tensions that had been straining below the surface throughout the whole First Period of World Prosperity. Before the European peoples, who by 1920 amounted to a quarter of the whole human race, could resume the exploring, experimenting and civilising role they had played for two centuries, it was necessary that they should be purged of a chronic mental disease—a disease which had, it seemed, to rise to an acute phase and run its enfeebling and devastating course before it could be treated: the disease of hate.

Although each year in the Thirties saw the international tension in Europe increasing, it was only in 1940 that actual warfare broke out. All Europe was 'mined' for ten years before that time, but the very consciousness of that fact, if it did not hold back the drift towards war, increased the gravity of its onset. That ingenious contrivance of President Wilson's, the Polish Corridor, Poland's 'access to the sea', was the particular mine that exploded first. But it was only one of a series of accumulating detonations which were destined to blow the still creaking ineffective League of Nations, and indeed nearly every vestige of the unfortunate Treaty of Versailles, and its subordinate 'settlements', out of the way of human readjustment.

The mental phases of that great body of Europeans who used the German language summarise the world situation. The history of Europe from 1900 to 1950 could be told in a study of the German brain alone, its torment and the reactions it evoked in the peoples about it. It was a brain of outstanding vigour and crudity. It aroused admiration, envy and fear. Its achievements in material science were magnificent; its energy of industrial organisation was unparalleled. Its mathematical and psychological ineptitudes were redeemed by the Jewish intelligencies entangled in its meshes. Compared with the Anglo-Saxon brain its political thought was unsupple, and it had neither the extreme lucidity of the French intelligence, the boldness of the Italian, nor the poetic power of Spain and Russia. It had these conspicuous limitations. Its obstinate association with a stupidly arrogant monarchism and a woolly tangle of preposterous racial pretensions stood in the way of sympathetic co-operation with any other cultural system. It had failed conspicuously to assimilate the non-German subject populations involved in its political web. It had intensified the defensive nationalism of the French; its tactless challenge upon the sea had terrified and exasperated the British; it had roused even America to a wary disapproval and a final hostility. Russia it had never won, but then in the huge carcass of pre-revolutionary Russia there was very little to be won anyhow. (There was indeed no real national self-consciousness in Russia before the Soviet régime; there was only Dostoievsky and the Tsar.) Assertive ungraciousness had been the chief factor in Germany's isolation and the cause of its defeat in the World War.

Yet after defeat this afflicted German mentality, if only on account of a certain toughness and vigour it possessed, remained still the central reality and the central perplexity of the European system. War and disaster could not alter the fact that the backbone of Europe, the most skilled, industrious, teachable and intelligent block of its population, spoke and thought German. What might happen to it, what would happen to it, should have been the primary preoccupation of every intelligent statesman. For if Germany had gone right everything would have gone right. But there were no statesmen sufficiently intelligent to consider anything of the sort. Germany had had a phase of pride and megalomania. It had been immensely disillusioned, it had thrown off its glittering imperialist headship, it had accepted military defeat. It had even passed through a phase of humility. At first it did not hate conspicuously. Amidst great difficulties the new republic displayed creative cour-

214

age, moderation, a dawning sense of the significance of world politics.

Creative, forward-looking minds turned to Germany with an entirely pathetic hopefulness. 'Now we shall see what Germany can do,' they said. 'Be patient with Germany.' All the world scolded France for her inveterate distrust. Given courage and generosity abroad and leadership at home, this great mass of Teutonic brains might have taken up the task of the Modern State then, and fallen into co-operation with the rest of a disillusioned but renascent world. It might even have led in the work of reconstruction, and 1918 might have been the opening year of a phase of world renewal.

But that was not to be. The world had still to reap a harvest of disunion through sixty tragic years. At home leadership came to Germany too late. Stresemann mastered his lesson too slowly and died too soon. Brüning was betrayed by Hindenburg's mental decay. And abroad it seemed to the Germans that there was nothing but war-strained and vindictive enemies. They looked for friends and saw only Foreign Offices. We have told already how the role of only sinner in a world of outraged saints was thrust upon Germany by the Conference of Versailles. She was to be permanently enfeebled, restrained and humiliated. German babies yet unborn were expected to be born penitent about the war. They were to gasp for their first breath under the smacks of an unforgiving world.

How all the good effort in Germany was thwarted, how the nets of suspicion held her down, would make a long and intricate story. At last these losers of the World War became as violent and frantic as stifled creatures fighting for air. Only by a feat of imagination can we now put ourselves in their places. Everything seemed to be making for the strangulation of Central Europe. The young energetic men in the defeated countries were to be given no share in the rebuilding of their shattered world. That was to be reserved for the new generation of the conquerors. They were to live in an atmosphere of punishment, toiling, heavily taxed and outlawed from the advancement of civilisation to the very

215

end of their days. That they should recover prosperity or achieve great things would be an offence.

Naturally life so circumscribed was bitter and lapsed very easily towards vice, apathy or blind revolt. There is a remarkable novel in the Historical Documents Series (*Fabian*, by Erich Kastner, 1932) which renders the individual aspect of this phase of German life very vividly. Another novel almost equally vivid and illuminating is *Kleiner Mann, was nun?* by Hans Fallada, 1932.

These conditions of mind, this tied and stifled outlook upon life, were, it must be admitted, by no means confined to the German-speaking peoples. The intelligent and ambitious young Indian or Egyptian or Negro, the intelligent young man of any subordinated, handicapped and restrained people or class—and this covered perhaps two-thirds of the youth of our race in these days—participated in the same distress of a foreordained inferiority and futility. But the young German had recent memories of hope and pride and a greater fund of resentment and aggressive energy. He had no tradition of inferiority and subservient adjustment.

Unhappily no teachers or leaders arose to point him on to his legitimate role in the replacement of the current disorder by the Modern World-State. The Hohenzollern régime and the stresses of the war had stood in the way of his attaining anything like the cosmopolitanism of, say, the English and Americans. His new republicanism was superficial and half-hearted, and in the schools and universities the teachers and leaders of the old militarist régime were still living, active and malignant. The Press and all the organisations of instruction and suggestion stood out of the revolution and showed themselves only too eager and skilful in restoring a pre-war fierceness. The futility of the new Germany was their text. 'This is not German,' they insisted. 'Go back to the old Imperialism,' they said, 'and try again.' The spirit of the women about the new generation, mothers and sweethearts alike, was for the most part one of passionate indignation.

An acute contemporary observer, L. B. Namier, pointed out that it was almost a law in history that war-strained and defeated countries should relapse towards violent patriotism between twelve and fifteen years after the war in which they suffered concluded. He suggested that this was precisely the time when the children who, without any participation in the realities of warfare, had felt all the strain and bitterness of defeat and all the hatred of the enemy would have grown up to manhood. These children became the energetic stratum in the population by 1933.

It was at this phase in European history that the rise of Hitlerism occurred. Adolf Hitler, as the decisive product of Germany in labour, is one of the most incredible figures in the whole of history. He must have astonished even the teachers and writers who had evoked him. We can study his personal presence from a hundred different angles in Vol. 30,112 of the *Historical Portrait Gallery*, and it is that of an entirely commonplace man, void of dignity, void of fine quality. We can hear his voice, we can hear him persuading, exhorting and attempting to reason, from the numerous steel-tape records that were made of his speeches. It is a raucous, strained voice, talking violently but incoherently. It is the voice of a vulgar, limited, illiterate man, lashing himself to fierceness, shouting, threatening, beating his fists at the window, smashing the furniture about him, to escape from perplexity and despair. He was perfectly simple and honest in his quality. And that was perhaps the secret of his career. He gave vent to the German overstrain. He is the voice of Germany losing control.

He denounced foreigners, Jews, cosmopolitans, Communists, Republicans, owners of property and leaders in finance with raucous impartiality, and nothing is so pleasing to perplexed unhappy people as the denunciation of others. Not their fault, their troubles. They have been betrayed. To Fallada's question, 'Little Man, what now?' his answer was, 'Massacre Jews, expel foreigners, arm and get more arms, be German, utterly German, and increase and multiply.'

One has to remember that he never carried with him even

an absolute voting majority of the German public. But the people permitted him to seize power and shatter their republic, stifle public discussion and destroy their liberties. They had no energy to resist him. They had no conception left in their fagged and hope-starved brains of any finer role than that which his bawling nationalism, his violent campaign against Communists and imaginary Communistic plots, against Jews, speculators and Liberals, presented to them. The treason of the senile Hindenburg to the Republic that had trusted him, conduced inestimably to the adventurer's success.

Hitler's exploit in seizing Germany and turning it back towards reaction was modelled on Mussolini's precedent. But intellectually he was far inferior to that strange figure. He took all that was worst in the Fascist régime and never rose to the real constructive effort or the competent industry of his prototype. One little point that illustrates his general ignorance and essential feeblemindedness was the adoption of the Swastika, the running cross, as the emblem of his Nazis. This brisk, silly little sign is of very old origin, and, as we have noted in the earlier stages of this summary of history, its ornamental use was one of the associated characteristics of that type of Neolithic culture, that culture of brownish and dark-white warm-water peoples, from which the early civilisations sprang. It is hardly known in connexion with the so-called 'Nordic', or with the Negro peoples, and it is in no way expressive of an 'Aryan' culture. Old writers used to declare it was the 'symbol' of the sun, but it seems to have signified little beyond a certain cheerfulness. It took the place of an idea in the muddled heads of the Nazis and they treated it with immense solemnity and wore it on their banners, clothes, proclamations and wherever else they could. Arden Essenden, when it was revived in Europe during the struggle for the air control, called it the 'idiot's own trade mark', and it has certainly had a fatal attraction for many second-rate imaginative types.

So for a time, under a hubbub of young blackguards in

218

brown shirts and Swastika badges, Germany, just when her rather heavy but persistent and faithful mind would have been of primary value in mankind's struggle with the world problem, passed out of the intellectual commonweal of mankind. Her real mind went into exile, in America, in England, in Switzerland, in irony or in hiding. She missed her proper share in the unification of mankind in the twentieth century, just as she missed her share in the Europeanisation of the world in the eighteenth and nineteenth. At home this National Socialism sought destructively to construct, sought to restore her former scientific prestige and industrial efficiency by boasting, exhortation, intolerance, outrage and compulsion. It was a pitiful and tragic phase, the dementia of a great nation. The story of German life during this interval is a rowdy and unhappy story—a story of faction fights and street encounters, demonstrations and counter-demonstrations, of a complicating tyranny of blackmailing officials, and at last of an ill-managed and unsuccessful war, that belied the innate orderliness of the Teutonic peoples. There was a progressive increase of secret vice and furtive dishonesty, the outcome of hopelessness. The number of people killed or seriously injured in riots and civil conflicts in Germany, or murdered for political reasons, between 1932 and 1936 amounted to something over rather than under thirty thousand.

§ 8. A Note on Hatred

[*This section was in a detached fascicle, but its place seems to be here.—*ED.]

The student of history will find it almost impossible to understand the peculiar difficulties of political life as it was lived until about a hundred years ago, nor will he grasp the essential differences between what was called education in those days and the educational processes we are still developing to-day, unless he masters the broad facts about these systems of hatred that dominated the group relationships of mankind right up to the assertion of the Modern State. We have given the main particulars of the issue between the Germans and the Poles, but that is only one striking and historically important instance of a general condition. We could give fifty such chapters. Nearly everywhere populations were to be found steeped in and moved by mass hatreds of a volume and obduracy outside any contemporary human experience.

All these hatreds arose out of the same essential causes. Two or more population groups, each with its own special narrow and inadaptable culture and usually with a distinctive language or dialect, had been by the change of scale in human affairs jammed together or imposed one upon another. A sort of social dementia ensued. In the absence of a common idea of community, civilised motives gave place to instinctive hostilities and spasmodic impulses.

Wherever there were mingled populations these hates were found, and, except in the Basque country, Wales and Lapland, they were intense enough to be of primary political importance. South and east of Bohemia there

220

seemed no boundary to the realms of hate. The Magyar hated the Slav, the Slav the Italian, the Roumanian the Russian. Religious differences, the mischief of priests, cut up even racial solidarities; the Catholic Slav hated the Orthodox Slav and the Orthodox Greeks in Macedonia were hopelessly divided among themselves. Over all the ancient domain of the Sultan, through Persia, through India, hates extended. Islam was rent by two ancient hate systems. These mass hatreds were accepted in a kind of despair by even the wisest. They defied the policies of statesmen absolutely. They were supposed to be beyond human control.

It is extraordinary how recent is the intelligent mitigation and suppression of hatred. Our ancestors did not envisage this as a controllable mental disease. They did not know that it was possible to get through life without hatred, just as they did not know that the coughs and colds that afflicted them and most of the phenomena of senility were avoidable.

But it is amazing to think how submissively human beings allowed their lives to be spoilt by controllable things—until almost within living memory. It was not only against hate and envy that they made no effort. They left their poor nerves bare and unprotected from an endless persecution by man-made afflictions. Up to 2010 they lived in towns that were crazy with noise; there was practically no control of offensive sounds, and the visual clamour of advertisements died out only in the needy decades that preceded the Air Dictatorship. But then it was still hardly more than a century that there had been sufficient light upon the towns and highways to drive away the blackness of night and overcast weather. In northern climates in the winter before the twentieth century people lived between the nocturnal dark and a dismal grey half-light which they called daylight, not seeing the sun often for weeks together.

And before the nineteenth century it is clear to anyone who can read between the lines that mankind *stank*. One has only to study the layout and drainage of their houses and towns, their accommodation for washing, their exiguous wardrobes, the absence of proper laundry organisation and of destructors for outworn objects, to realise that only usage saved them from a perpetual disgust and nausea. No wonder that, quite apart from their bad food and loathsome cooking, they coughed, spat, ached, went deaf and blind and feeble, in a continual alternation of lassitude and mutual irritation.

These conditions of life have gone one after another and almost imperceptibly. Few of us realise how different it was to be a human being only a few hundred years ago. It is only when we take our imaginations with us back into the past that we realise how evil to nose, eye, ear and soul the congregation of human beings could be. And necessarily, inevitably, because of the ill-interpreted protests of body and mind against this mode of existence, they hated—almost at haphazard. We have in Swift's *Gulliver's Travels* (1726) the cry of one man of exceptional intelligence and sensibility who discovered himself imprisoned as it were in the life of the eighteenth century and could find neither outlet nor opiate. The reek of the kennels of a medieval town was nothing to the stench of hatred in the popular Press of the twentieth century. The ordinary newspaper of that time was not so much a news sheet as a poison rag. Every morning the common man took in fresh suggestions of suspicion and resentment and gratified his spite with bad news and malicious gossip.

Hatred, we know, is a morbid, infectious and preventable relapse to which the mammalian cerebrum, and particularly the cerebrum of the social types, is prone. It is a loss of rational control. It is caused normally by small repeated irritations of the cerebral cortex. The contagion may occur at any phase before or after maturity, and acute attacks predispose the brain for recurrence and may run together at last into a chronic condition of vindictive disapproval.

Once hatred has established itself to that extent it seems to be ineradicable. The patient seeks, often with the greatest ingenuity, occasion for offence, and finds a profound satisfaction in the nursing of resentment and the search for reprisals and revenges. He has what he calls his 'proper pride'. He disapproves of his fellow creatures and grudges them happiness. Our current education is framed very largely to avert and anticipate this facile contagion, but the Press of that time subsisted by its dissemination, in the interests of reactionary forces. We are as sedulous now for cleanliness and ventilation in our mental as in our physical atmosphere. The contrast between a contemporary crowd and the crowds depicted by Hogarth or Raphael is not simply in the well-clad, well-grown, well-nourished and well-exercised bodies, the absence of rags and cripples, but in the candid interested faces that replace the introverted, suspicious and guarded expressions of those unhappy times. It is only in the light of this universal malaria that human history can be made comprehensible.

And now this great German mind stretching across the centre of Europe in seventy million brains was incapable of autotherapy, and let its sickness have its way with it. It would not recognise that it suffered from anything but a noble resentment. Least of all peoples was it able to entertain those ideas of a world-wide co-operation, of the World-State, which were still seeking their proper form and instrument. It was a deeper hate altogether than the fear-begotten hate of the French. In both these antagonised countries cosmopolitan sanity went begging, but most so in Germany.

The fluctuations in German hatred during the Thirties were curiously affected by subconscious currents of discretion. Though Germany was fiercely belligerent in spirit, her armament still lagged behind that of her neighbours; her Hitlerites snarled and threatened, but rather against Poland than France, and when the tension became too great it found relief by outrages upon Communists, Pacificists and intellectuals and by an exacerbated persecution of those whipping-boys of the Western civilisation, the Jews. From the accession of Hitler to the chancellorship of the Reich in 1933 onward, not only looting and massacre, but legalised outrage became an ever present menace in the life of the German Jew.

Faber speaks in his studies of political psychology of the

'hate map' of the world. The intensity of the colouring of such a map would vary widely. The English-speaking states (except for Ireland, that erstwhile 'island of ever-green malice', which is now the most delightful and welcoming of summer resorts) and the Spanish-speaking communities felt hate far less intensely than the peoples of the continental European patchwork. They were less congested, they were free from acute alien interference, they had more space to move about in and the infection was not so virulent. For two decades Spain and Spanish South America (after the Peruvian Settlement) sustained indeed a more liberal and creative mentality than any other region of the world. The Spanish contribution, beginning with Unamuno and Ortega Y. Gasset and going onward through a long list of great names, was of increasing importance in the building up of the Modern World-State.

Russia, we may note, was never so constructive mentally as Spain. She had not now the same wealth of freely thinking and writing men. She had no surplus of mental energy to philosophise. She ecstasised, prophesied or dogmatised. Such brain discipline as she had was used up in her sprawling technical efforts. But she again was not a malignant country. Young Russia was taught to hate indeed, but to hate a dissolving enemy, the Wicked Imperialist. Even in that hate there was an element of humorous caricature. When in due course the Wicked Imperialist faded away to the quality of a nursery Ogre, he took with him most of the hatred out of Russia. Hate, except in brief vivid spurts, does not seem congenial to the Russian temperament.

Few people in 1940 realised that the essential political trouble in the world, as distinguished from its monetary malaise, was this endemic disease, and still fewer had the boldness of mind even to think of the drastic cleansing and destruction of infected social institutions and economic interests and accumulations that was needed if the disease was ever to be stamped out. Meanwhile along the tangled frontiers of Central and Eastern Europe the sores festered and the inflammation increased.

Among the more frequent methods of releasing hatred in the more troubled communities were aggressive demonstrations inviting or involving violence, attacks on representative buildings, such as embassies and consulates, the defilement of flags, statues and other symbols (in India the slaughter of sacred or forbidden animals such as cows or pigs in holy places), quarrels picked in cafés and restaurants, beatings-up, assassinations, the throwing of bombs and crackers into parties and gatherings of the objectionable nationality, or into law courts, religious buildings and other unsuitable places for an explosion, firing at sentinels and across boundaries. Along the Adriatic coast it would appear there was an exceptionally strong disposition to insult the characteristic Italian respect for statues and pictures.

This was of recent origin. At the Congress of Versailles Italy had been bilked by her French and British allies of a considerable amount of the Dalmatian coast line—to which indeed neither she nor they had any right, but which nevertheless had been promised to her in the secret engagements that had brought her into the World War. Her patriots had never ceased to resent this broken promise, nor the Yugo-Slav peoples, who held the coveted districts, to fear a forcible annexation. There had been much propaganda about the dispute. One prominent argument of the Italian side was that the Republic of Venice (of which Rome was the natural heir) had formerly dominated this coast, and, in proof of this, appeal was made to the public buildings in the towns of the disputed regions, which everywhere bore the insignia of their Italian founders and particularly the distinctive lion of Venice. For that was the Fascist fantasy: wherever the Venetian lion had made its lair or the Roman eagles cast their shadows, from Hadrian's Wall in England to Mesopotamia, the Fascist claimed to rule.

This contention, though taken calmly enough by the English, French, Spanish, Turks and other emancipated peoples, was bitterly resented by the populations more immediately threatened, and particularly did it arouse resentment and hatred along the Dalmatian coast. For the young and excitable Slav, those sculptured lions and archaic eagles, those antique vestiges, were robbed of their artistic and historical charm; they took on an arrogant contemporary quality and seemed to demand an answer to their challenge. His response was to deface or mutilate them.

Already in 1932 there were bitter recriminations between Rome and Belgrade on this score, and in 1935 and again in 1937 fresh trouble arose. The later occasions were not simply matters of chipping and breaking. These heraldic and highly symbolic animals were now painted, and painted in such a manner as to bring them into grave contempt. And the outrages were not confined to heraldic animals. Portraits and images of Mussolini were also adorned all too often with pencilled moustaches, formidable whiskers, a red nose and other perversions of his vigorous personality.

Such vexatious modes of expression were in constant evidence in all the inflamed areas. To us they seem trivial, imbecile, preposterous, but then they were steeped in tragic possibility.

The reader must picture for himself, if he can, how things went in the brain of some youngster growing to manhood in one of these hate regions, the constant irritation of restrictions, the constant urge to do some vivid expressive thing, the bitter, unconsoling mockery against the oppressor and at last the pitiful conspiracy, the still more pitiful insult. He must think of the poor excitement of getting the paint-pot and the ladder, of watching the receding police patrol, the tremulous triumph of smearing the hated object. That perhaps was the poor crown of life for that particular brain. Then the alarm, the conflict, the flight, a shot, a wound, straw and filth in a prison cell, the beatings and the formal punishment, the intensified resolve to carry on the resistance. There was nothing to think of then but the next outrage, the next riot. So very often the story went on to wounds and death, the body crumpled up on a street pavement and trampled under foot or put against a wall to be shot, and then the rotting away and dispersal of that particular human brain with all the gifts and powers it possessed. That was all that life could be for hundreds of thousands of those hate-drenched brains. For that they came into being, like flowers that open in a rain of filth.

A Natural History of Cruelty has recently been published by Otto Jaspers (2085–), a lineal descendant of that Professor Jaspers of Heidelberg University under whom De Windt studied and to whose *Die geistiger Situation der Gegenwart* De Windt was greatly indebted. Cruelty in the twentieth century is treated in considerable detail, and it makes very terrible reading indeed. Happily it is not considered a necessary part of a general education to probe under those dark processes of the human mind which made the infliction of horrible pain and injuries a relief to otherwise intolerable mental distresses. The psychologist, however, must acquaint himself with all those facts; he cannot fully understand our intricate minds without them, and the practical disappearance of deliberate cruelty from our world to-day makes the horror literature of the World War and World Slump periods a mine of essential material for his investigations. One or two glimpses we have given the student. If he has any imagination he will be able to expand those hints for himself into an infinitude of mutilations, tortures and wanton violence.

The older psychologists were disposed to classify cruelty as a form of sexual aberration—in ordinary speech we still use their old word Sadistic—but this attribution is no longer respected by contemporary authorities. Cruelty goes far beyond the sexual field. Just as hate is now understood to be a combative fear compound, the stiffening up of a faltering challenge, which may become infectious, so cruelty is regarded as a natural development of effort against resistance, so soon as the apprehension of frustration exceeds a certain limit. It is a transformation of our attempt to subdue something, usually a living thing, to our will, under the exasperation of actual or anticipated obduracy.

This interpretation makes it plain why the breakdown of the private capital economic and political system and the world-wide uncertainty, dismay and want which ensued was followed by wave after wave of unprecedented cruelty. In 1900, a visitor from another sphere might reasonably have decided that man, as one met him in Europe or America, was a kindly, merciful and generous creature. In 1940 he might have decided, with an equal show of justice, that this creature was diabolically malignant. And yet it was the same creature, under different conditions of stress.

There were many thousands of suicides between 1930 and 1940—suicides of sensitive men and women, who could endure the dreadful baseness and cruelty of life no longer. Yet in the records of the reviving world of 1980 there is scarcely a mention of atrocious conduct towards human beings or animals. It was not a change of nature; it was a change of phase. Millions of people who had actually killed, massacred, tortured, were still alive—and they were behaving now quite reasonably and well. Most of them had forgotten their own deeds more or less completely. Hope had returned to human life. The frantic years were past.

§ 9. *The Last War Cyclone*, 1940–50

The drift to war in Europe became more powerful with the elimination of Japan and the United States from the possibility of intervention, and with the deepening preoccupation of Britain with Indian disorder and with the Black Revolt in South Africa. The last restraints upon continental hatreds had gone. The issues simplified.

War came at last in 1940. The particular incident that led to actual warfare in Europe was due to a Polish commercial traveller, a Pole of Jewish origin, who was so ill-advised as to have trouble with an ill-fitting dental plate during the halt of his train in Danzig. He seems to have got his plate jammed in such a fashion that he had to open his mouth wide and use both hands to struggle with it, and out of deference to his fellow passengers he turned his face to the window during these efforts at readjustment. He was a black-bearded man with a long and prominent nose, and no doubt the effect of his contortions was unpleasing. Little did he realise that his clumsy hands were to release the dogs of war from the Pyrenees to Siberia.

The primary irritant seems to have been either an orange-pip or a small fragment of walnut.

Unhappily, a young Nazi was standing on the platform outside and construed the unfortunate man's facial disarrangement into a hostile comment upon his uniform. For many of these youths were of an extreme innate sensibility. The flames of patriotic indignation shot up in his heart. He called up three fellow guards and two policemen—for, like the Italian Fascisti, these young heroes rarely acted alone— and boarded the train in a swift and exemplary mood. There was a furious altercation, rendered more difficult by the facts that the offending Pole knew little or no German and was still in effect gagged. Two fellow travellers, however, came to his help, others became involved, vociferation gave place to pushing and punching, and the Nazis, outnumbered were put off the train.

Whereupon the young man who had started all the trouble, exasperated, heated and dishevelled, and seeing that now altogether intolerable Jew still making unsatisfactory passes with his hands and face at the window, drew a revolver and shot him dead. Other weapons flashed into action, and the miniature battle was brought to an end by the engine-driver drawing his train out of the station. The matter was complicated politically by the fact that the exact status of the Danzig police was still in dispute and that the Nazis had no legal authority upon the Danzig platform.

By itself this distressing incident might have been arranged without the outbreak of a European war. The moribund League of Nations might have been invoked or even the mummified Hague Tribunal galvanised into activity; either institution was still fully capable of dealing with, let us say, a Polish dentist who might have been treated as the culpable party, traced, punished and made the scapegoat of Europe. But that would have needed a certain good will on the part of the Powers directly involved, and at that time no such good will was forthcoming.

For eight years now the German mind had been working up for a fight over the Corridor, and the rearmament of Germany, overt and secret, had been going on. Both France and Poland had been watching the military recovery of Germany with ever-deepening apprehension, and the military authorities of both countries were urgent that a blow should be struck while they were still disproportionately stronger. Time after time it seemed that the crisis had come, and time after time nothing more than a stock-exchange tornado had occurred. Now the last reasons for patience had disappeared. The tension had risen to a point at which disaster seemed like relief and Europe was free to tear itself to fragments.

Such a situation was the inevitable climax to every 'armed peace' in the old belligerent world. At some point there was an irresistible logic in 'Strike now before they get too strong'. That had been in underlying motive of primary force in the British readiness to fight in 1914. They were eager to strike before the ever-growing German fleet equalled their own. So they ended an intolerable tension. The Germans had 'asked for it', they said. 'Better now than to-morrow.'

Now again Germany had 'asked for it' and Poland was leaping to the occasion. The War Offices pressed their bell buttons. The printing machines of Paris, London and New York were still busy with various misstatements about the murdered commercial traveller, while the Polish and German air patrols were in conflict all along the fatal boundary. That dental plate apparently began to feel uncomfortable about one o'clock in the afternoon of Friday, January

5th 1940. On Saturday, about three o'clock in the afternoon, Michael Koreniovsky, the Polish ace, after a brilliant fight with three antagonists, fell flaming out of the sky into the crowded Langgasse of Danzig and set fire to the Rathaus.

The first Polish air raid on Berlin and the unresisted 'demonstration flight' of two hundred French air squadrons in formation over Bavaria and West Prussia followed. The Germans seem to have been taken completely by surprise by this display of immense and immediate preparedness. They had not thought it of the French. But they had the quickness of apprehension to decline an air battle against odds, and the French flew home again. The fighting on the Polish–German frontier continued.

The authorities in Paris were uncertain whether they were disappointed or relieved by the non-resistance of their old enemies. A smashing air victory over Germany would have been very satisfactory and conclusive, but these aeroplanes were also wanted at home to cow the ever-increasing domestic discontent. An indecisive battle—and that was always possible in the air—might have produced serious internal stresses.

For a week of years from the resumption of armament by Germany in 1933, the diplomatic centres of the world had been watching the steady onset of this conflict and had been doing nothing to avert it. Now London, Washington, Madrid and Geneva became hysterically active. There was a mighty running to and fro of ambassadors and foreign ministers. 'Delay,' said Geneva; though there had already been twenty years of delay.

'Localise the conflict' was a phrase that leapt into vivid prominence. It found favour not only in the neutral countries, but in Paris and Berlin. In effect 'localise the conflict' meant this: it meant that Paris should scrap her engagements to Poland and leave the Poles to make what sort of arrangements they could between Germany and Russia. For Russia now, by an enigmatical silence combined with a prompt mobilisation of the Red Army, became almost immediately an important piece in the developing international game.

And Paris had seen very excellent reasons for not pushing a conflict with Berlin to extremities. The first Frenchman to be killed in the New Warfare had been killed already. And he had been killed in the Maritime Alps, shot by the bullet of an Italian patrol.

On Sunday night, January the 7th, while the Polish aeroplanes were dropping gas bombs on Berlin, the Italians were administering the same treatment to Belgrade. At the same time an incidental note had been dispatched from Rome to all the Powers giving Italy's reasons for this decisive blow. It seemed that between Friday evening and Sunday morning there had been a violent recrudescence of Yugo-Slav irreverence. The Fascist agents who had to supply the material for grievance and indignation had in fact overdone their task to the pitch of caricature. On Saturday the entire Italian population found itself roused from its normal preoccupation with its daily budget by the terrible intelligence of Mussolini everywhere made bibulous and ophthalmious with red paint, of Venetian lions coloured as indelicately as baboons and of shamefully overdecorated Roman eagles. Eloquent and dishevelled young Fascists, often in tears, protested at every street corner against these intolerable indignities and called for war. The cup of Yugo-Slav iniquity was full. It was only in later years that astounded students, tracing these outrages to their sources, realised how excessively that cup had been filled to justify the Fascist invasion.

Once the Polish and Italian forces had crossed their boundaries the other states of Eastern Europe did not wait even to produce an insult before launching their offensives. The whole crazy patchwork of Versailles dissolved into fighting—the joyless, frantic fighting of people full of hate and fear, led blindly to no ends that anyone could foresee. For two straining years the theory of localising the conflict held Russia and France out of the fight. A 'formula' was found by which France undertook not to intervene on the side of her erstwhile allies, on the understanding that Russia

232

by way of compensation also refrained from any action against them. Moreover, the trade in munitions was to be carried on 'impartially'. It was a flimsy formula to justify a diplomatic default, but it kept warfare away from the Western front of Germany for two distressful years. The persistent shooting by Italians over the French boundary was difficult to explain away, and indeed it was not so much explained away as quietly disregarded. The air fleets of France paraded at intervals, to the increasing irritation of all her immediate neighbours, but on the whole as a restraining influence. The demonstration chilled the foreigner and assuaged the hotheads at home.

From the outset there was far less enthusiasm for this 'localised' European war of 1940 than had been displayed by the populations of the belligerent countries in 1914. What enthusiasm was displayed was confined to the inexperienced young of the middle and upper classes, the youth of the Fascisti, Nazi, 'public schoolboy' and scoutmaster type. They went about, shouting and urgent, in a heavy, sullen and apprehensive atmosphere. No nation 'leapt to arms'. The common soldiers deserted and 'fell out' incessantly, and these shirkers were difficult to punish, since the 'deserter mentality' was so widespread, more particularly in the peasant armies of Eastern Europe, that it was impossible to shoot offenders. One Posen battalion went into battle near Lodz with thirty-nine officers and fifty-seven men.

From the first 'economies' marched with the troops. From the first there was a threadbare needy quality about the struggle. General orders insisted upon 'a restrained use of ammunition'.

The actual fighting was, however, on a much higher level, mechanically and scientifically, than the Japanese war in China. The military authorities had good roads, automobiles, camions, railways, rolling stock, electrical material, guns of all sorts and great air forces available. Behind the fronts were chemical and other munition factories in good working order. If there were no longer infantry battles there were some brilliant conflicts of technicians. The prompt cutting off of East Prussia from any help from main Germany by the Permanent Death Gas was an operation far above the technical level of any Eastern operations. It was strategically silly but technically very successful.

The first offensive against Berlin was also planned with modern equipment and the maximum of contemporary military science. It was to be another 'blow at the heart', and the Polish general staff relied upon it as firmly as the Germans in 1914 had relied upon their march on Paris. Unfortunately for the Poles, it had been necessary to consult a number of 'experts' in preparing this advance; there were leakages through France, through the Czech and Swedish munition makers, through Russia, and through domestic treason and the broad outline of the plan was as well known and understood in Berlin as it was in Warsaw. The great gas raid on Berlin was indeed terrifying and devastating, but the rush of tanks, great caterpillar guns and troops in motor transport was held and checked within sixty miles of the German capital by an ingenious system of poison-gas barriers—chiefly Lewisite and Blue Cross— wired mines and 'slime pits' of a novel type in the roads and open fields. A cavalry raid to the north between Berlin and the sea failed disastrously amidst wire, gas and machine-guns; nearly forty thousand men were killed, wounded or taken prisoner. Moreover, there had been mistakes in the manufacture of the gas masks worn by the Polish troops, and several brigades gave way to the persuasion that they had been sold and betrayed. The main Polish masses never came into actual contact with the German troops, and only their great numerical superiority in aeroplanes saved their repulse from becoming a rout.

The Polish armies rallied and, according to the secondary plan prepared for any such failure, extended themselves and dug themselves in along a line between Stettin and the Bohemian frontier. Behind the barrier they began a systematic reduction of Silesia. Every night an air battle raged over both Berlin and Warsaw. It was often an indecisive battle. The Poles had the numerical superiority, but the German machines were more efficient and better handled. But the Poles had far more of the new aerial torpedoes—which could go to an assigned spot two hundred miles away, drop a large bomb and return—than their adversaries.

Bohemia, like France, had mobilised but did not immediately enter the war. The Czecho-Slovak armies remained in their mountain quadrilateral or lined out along the Hungarian front, awaiting the next turn in the game. Austria also remained excited but neutral.

The Southern war opened brilliantly for the Italians, and for some weeks it went on without any formal connexion with the Polish conflict. Bulgaria, Albania and Hungary also declared war upon Yugo-Slavia, the Italian air forces 'darkened the sky', and few of the towns in Croatia and Serbia escaped an aerial bombardment. The Italian fleet set itself to capture the ports and islands of Dalmatia. But the advance of the Italian troops into the hills of Slavonia and Croatia was not as rapid as had been expected. Six weeks passed before they were able to fight their way to Zagreb.

The country was a difficult one, ill adapted to the use of gas or mechanism; there was no central point at which a decisive blow could be struck; and the population had a long tradition of mountain warfare. It did not affect these sturdy peasants whether the townsmen were bombed or not. They never gave battle; they never exposed themselves in masses, but their bullets flew by day and night into the Italian encampments. The defenders went to and fro between their fields and the front. Munitions poured in for them through Roumania, which, with a big Red Army on its Bessarabian frontier and its own peasants recalcitrant, remained also ambiguously, dangerously and yet for a time profitably, out of the struggle. The Hungarians crossed the Yugo-Slav frontier and threatened Belgrade, but the mass of their forces faced towards Czecho-Slovakia and awaited further events.

A curious pause in the fighting occurred at the end of the

year. The frantic efforts of Prague, London and Paris to call a halt were temporarily successful. The invaders of Germany and Yugo-Slavia remained upon enemy territory, but neutral zones were improvised and there was a cessation of hostilities. An eleventh-hour attempt was made to stop the war by negotiation and keep the two conflicts from coalescence. There were weeks during which this seemed possible. Both Germany and Poland were of two minds about continuing the war now that the Polish advance was held; and Italy hoped to be left in possession of Dalmatia without an irksome campaign of further conquest. It was as if the spirit of civilisation had once more come near to awakening from its hallucinations and had asked, 'Why on earth is this happening to us?'

The British Cabinet thought the occasion opportune for a conference at Vevey to revise the Treaty of Versailles 'finally'. The pacific speeches of Duff-Cooper, Hore-Belisha, Ellen Wilkinson and Randolph Churchill echoed throughout Europe and were brilliantly supported by Benito Caruso and Corliss Lamont in America. The Pope, the Archbishop of Canterbury, the Nonconformist Churches, the President of the Swiss Republic and the able and venerable President Benes swelled the chorus of remonstrance. France, which had been growing steadily more pacificist after her social conflicts in 1934–35, found able spokesmen in Louchère and Chavanne. Once again we are reminded of the impulses of Henry Ford and Wilson. Once again the concept of a World Pax flickered in the human imagination and vanished. This time it was a fuller, more explicit and more unanimous chorus than that which had cried aloud in 1916–17. Yet at the time it was hardly more effective. Vevey prolonged the truce throughout 1941 until June, but it could settle nothing. The military authorities, having had a breathing-time, became impatient. With a mutually destructive malice the fighting was resumed 'before the harvest could be gathered'.

Vevey failed because the constructive conception of the Modern State had no representative there. It was just another gathering of national diplomatists who professed to seek peace, and yet who set about the business with all those antiquated assumptions of sovereignty that were bound to lead to a revival of the conflict. The fantasy of some 'balance of power' was as near as they ever came to a peace idea. Such a balance was bound to sway from year to year and from day to day. Whatever the common people and men of intelligence were thinking, the experts now wanted to see the war fought to a finish. 'The Germans hadn't been beaten enough' was all too acceptable to the munition dealers and the Press in France and Scandinavia. 'The Italians had their hands full in Yugo-Slavia.'

The British and Americans, who hoped to keep out of the conflict to the end, had experienced an exhilarating revival of exports and found their bills against the belligerents mounting very hopefully. Once more Tyneside echoed to hammering; steel, iron and chemical shares boomed and the iron and steel industry, like some mangy, toothless old tiger, roused itself for the only quarry it had now the vigour to pursue—man-eating. It had long ceased to dream of new liners or bridges or railways or steel-framed houses. But it could still make guns and kill. It could not look far enough ahead to reckon whether at last there would be any meat on the man's bones. The only countries that really wanted peace, enduring peace, were Czecho-Slovakia and Austria, which stretched out between the two combatant systems and had possible enemy frontiers on every hand. The human will for peace as it found expression at Vevey was still a tangled and ineffective will.

The fighting revived almost simultaneously in the Polish Ukraine, where peasants had revolted and were evidently fighting with Soviet officers and equipment, and in a vigorous surprise attack upon the Polish lines to free the German soil from the invader. The Germans had been working night and day during the truce to equalise conditions in the air; they produced new and swifter aeroplanes and a particularly effective machine-gun, and for some weeks there was such aerial fighting as was never seen before or since.

Gradually the Germans established a sufficient ascendancy to bring their bombers and gas into play. Lodz and Warsaw were terrorised and the civilian population evacuated and the Polish line broken so as to restore communications with Silesia. And then the conflict broadened. Lithuania, evidently with Russian encouragement, seized her old city of Wilna, and Austria linked the Northern and the Southern struggle by entering both wars as the ally of Germany and Italy. Germany declared her final union with Austria. Very swiftly now the remaining European states followed one another into the cauldron. Hungary attacked Eastern Czecho-Slovakia without a declaration of war 'to restore her legitimate boundaries', and brought the army frameworks of Roumania into the field against her. Thereupon Russia announced the impossibility of maintaining her understanding with France in the face of these events, and the Red Army advanced on Lemberg. Macedonia was already a seething mass of fighting, village against village; Bulgaria entered the 'South Slav' alliance and assailed Albania, and Greece seized Rhodes, which had been up to that time held by Italy.

So France saw her ancient policy of 'security', of setting state to balance state and allying herself with a countervailing state at the back of every antagonistic neighbour, work out to its necessary conclusion. Gladly would her business men and her peoples now have rested behind her immensely fortified frontiers and shared the profits of neutrality and munition-selling with the British and Americans, but her engagements were too binding. After one last ambiguous attempt on the part of London, Washington and Geneva to avert the disaster, France declared war against Central European alliance in 1943.

On the face of it the new war resembled the World War of 1914–18. It seemed to be an attempt to reverse or confirm the Versailles settlement. It had an air of being the same sort of siege of Central Europe. But now Italy was in close alliance with the Teutonic powers; Belgium, in a state of extreme industrial distress, was out of the war; Britain stood aloof; and in the place of her former Allies France had to help—rather than be helped—by the band of states from the Corridor to the Black Sea and the Balkans which the Quai d'Orsay had toiled so painfully to knit into an anti-German alliance.

Russia, however, was a doubtful ally of the Central Powers; she was not operating in concert with them; she was simply supporting the new Soviet republics in Eastern Poland and Bessarabia. There the Red Army halted. The old enthusiasm for a World Revolution had faded out of the Russian imagination. Marxism had become so Russianised that it feared now to take in too large a contingent of Western adherents. The Kremlin was content to consolidate the kindred Slav Soviets and then rest. Japan and China and the American continent remained out of the mêlée, concentrated on their own social difficulties.

It would be possible for a superficial student to regard all this merely as a rearrangement of the familiar counters of sovereign state politics. But in reality the forces in collision were profoundly different. France, in spite of her internal social stresses, was still a capitalist community of the nineteenth-century type, with democratic parliamentary forms and irresponsible finance and industrialism. Save for the teaching of a sentimental patriotism, her young people were mentally unorganised. Her allies were peasant states with governments of the royal or parliamentary form, and, if anything, more old-fashioned. But the Central Powers were all of the new Fascist pattern, more closely knit in its structure and dominated by an organisation of the younger spirits, which claimed to be an élite.

Except for the fundamentally important fact that these Fascisti were intensely nationalist, this control by a self-appointed, self-disciplined élite was a distinct step towards our Modern State organisation. These various Fascisti were destined to destroy their own states and disappear because of their essentially shallow and sentimental mentality, their inability to get outside nationalist traditions and coalesce; there is no direct continuity between them and our modern

239

educational and administrative system; but there was nothing like them in the World War of 1914–18 anywhere, and they are noteworthy, as the Russian Communist Party (in spite of its proletarian formula) is noteworthy, for their partial but very real advance on democratic institutions. Amidst the chaos, that organised 'devotion of the young' on which our modern community rests was clearly foreshadowed in these Central European states. The idea of disciplined personal participation in human government was being driven into the mentality of the new generation.

Until something more convincing appeared, it had to crystallise, disastrously enough, about such strange nuclei as the theatrical Mussolini and the hysterical Hitler. It had to be patriotic because that was the only form in which the State then presented itself. But after these first crystallisations had been shattered and dissolved in the war disasters that now ensued, the idea was still there, this idea of banded co-operation ready to be directed to greater ends. Youth had ceased to be irresponsible in all the Fascist countries.

Not only were these new wars unlike their predecessors in the fact that they were not, so far as the Central Powers were concerned, wars of the democratic masses, but also they were quite unprecedented in the range and quality of the fighting. We have already indicated some of the main differences between the New Warfare and the Old. These now became accentuated by the extraordinary way in which the boundaries of the battling states interdigitated. In the first spurt of conflict there was indeed a 'front' between Poland and Germany; but after 1943 there was no front, no main objective and no central idea to the storming destruction that spread over Europe.

The Poles tried to draw a line of Permanent Death Gas across East Brandenburg before their withdrawal to Posen, but their collapse came too swiftly, and they were able only to poison three small areas of no strategic importance. After 1943 the war became mainly a war in the air, with an increasing use of gas and landing raids, raids rather than invasions, to seize, organise and hold advantageous posi-

240

tions. A bitter and intense naval struggle went on in the Mediterranean to cut off reinforcements and supplies between North Africa and France, but there was little molestation of the Atlantic traffic of France.

There was never an Aerial Trafalgar, never an Air Ecnomus. War in three dimensions does not afford those channels, straits, narrow seas, passes, main roads, by which an inferior force may be brought to a decisive battle, and indeed to this day it is uncertain which side was absolutely predominant in the air. It was a war of raids and reprisals, and no large decisive operations were attempted. A big German infantry push into Posen was held by gas and slimes, and a French invasion of Italy got no further than Turin.

The complete exhaustion of the adversary, materially and morally, became the only possible road to any sort of victory. Once more the tormented populations were urged to sustain a 'war of attrition'. 'It is the man who holds out half an hour longer than the other who wins' was translated into every European language. The attacks on social order increased in malignancy as the impossibility of any military decision became manifest. Crops and forests were deliberately fired, embankments smashed, low-lying regions flooded, gas and water supplies destroyed. The aviators would start off to look for a crowd and bomb it. It became as cruel as the fighting of ferrets.

There was still, in spite of a decade of financial dislocation and industrial depression, a vast amount of mechanical material in Europe; everywhere there were factories strongly protected against air attack and skilfully camouflaged. Moreover, all the chief belligerents had sufficiently open frontiers for the importation of material, so long as anything compact and valuable could be wrung out of their nationals by tax or levy, to pay for such supplies. The goods crossed the frontier at night; the cargoes were piloted into unlit harbours. Every able-bodied adult not actually in the fighting forces was pressed to work at excavations for bomb shelters and the reconstruction of buildings against gas and high explosive. Much of this also was night work. Recalcitrance and shirking were punished by a deprivation of rations. There is a grim picture by Eglon Callet called 'Security at last', of which the reader may have seen reproductions. A chain gang of emaciated and ragged Frenchmen is working under the lash in a tunnel. In the foreground one who has fainted is being given a stimulant; another, past help, dies untended.

In comparison with the abundant literature of personal experiences in the World War, at least so far as the Western front was concerned, there are remarkably few records either of combatant or non-combatant adventures during the Fighting Forties. The big air raids seem to have been altogether horrible. They were much more dreadful than the air raids of the World War. They began with a nightmare of warning maroons, sirens, hooters and the shrill whistles of cyclist scouts, then swarms of frantic people running to and fro, all pride and dignity gone, seeking the nearest shelter and aid, and they ended for most of their victims in an extremity of physical suffering.

We have already given some intimation of the nature of those torture deaths. In nearly every case the organisation of refugees and gas masks broke down. In many cases there had never been a real provision, but only sham visors and sham bomb-proof buildings to allay 'premature' panic and 'keep up the popular morale'. None of these great raids was ever reported in the newspapers that still struggled on into the war years. Even in America the publication of any detail was treated as 'pacificist propaganda against recruiting'.

There is a descriptive letter from Berlin after an air raid, undated and signed 'Sinclair', which is believed by most competent critics to have been written by Sinclair Lewis the novelist (1885–1990). One passage may be quoted:

'We went down Unter den Linden and along the Sieges Allee, and the bodies of people were lying everywhere, men, women and children, not scattered evenly, but bunched together very curiously in heaps, as though their last effort

242

had been to climb on to each other for help. This attempt to get close up to someone seems to be characteristic of death by this particular gas. Something must happen in the mind. Everyone was crumpled up in the same fashion and nearly all had vomited blood. The stench was dreadful, although all this multitude had been alive twenty-four hours ago. The body corrupts at once. The archway into the park was almost impassable....'

So we get one glimpse of how peaceful town-bred people might die a century and a half ago.

The individual stories of the actual fighting in that last warfare are no more ample than the non-combatant descriptions. There was little inducement for anyone to write about it in the subsequent decades; there was not the same high proportion of literate men as there was in the Western armies during the Great War; there was a less artless interest in what was happening and more running away, desertion, apathy, drunkenness, raping, plundering and malignant cruelty, which are not things of which men leave records. The whole world was less sensitive than it had been thirty years before; if it suffered more grossly it suffered less acutely. In 1914–15 many of the British and German rankers kept diaries from day to day. This shows a sense of personality and a receptiveness to events quite outside the sullen fatalism, shot with gleams of primitive exaltation of fury, which seems to have been the prevalent state of mind in the armies of the Forties.

In the Historical Documents Series there is a diary of a Japanese officer who was killed in the retreat from Wuchang. Failing any European material of the same kind, it may perhaps be quoted here to show how it felt to fight in the last wars of all. It is not, however, a very vivid document. He was an intellectual, a socialist and a strong believer in the League of Nations, and his record is mainly a series of hostile criticisms in cipher of the superior command. But in the latter half these dissertations die out. The diary becomes a broken record of what he found to eat and drink and how he fought against influenza and dysentery. He seems to have had a company of men with him; he notes twice when he contrived a haul of food for them, and he jots down names as they are killed or missing. There are also figures that may be a note of his diminishing ammunition. He was already badly starved when he was killed. As he weakened he seems to have found his rather complicated cipher too difficult to use, and he lapsed first into bad English and then into plain Japanese. The very last item is an unfinished poem, a fragment in the old style, which might be rendered as follows:

> *Almond blossom in the spring sunshine,*
> *Fuji-Yama gracious lady,*
> *Island treasure home of lovely things,*
> *Shall I never see you again? . . .*

Something, death perhaps, prevented the completion of his naïve verses. He and his detachment were probably overtaken and done to death near Kai-feng.

In none of these later war memoirs is there anything to recall that queer quality of the 1914–18 stories, of men who felt they were going out from absolutely sure and stable homes and cities, to which with reasonable good fortune they would return—and live happily ever afterwards. The mood then was often extraordinarily brave and tender. The men of this later cycle of wars felt that there would be no such home-coming. They knew that they went out to misery and left misery in active possession at home. Their war was not an expedition; it was a change for ever. The memoirs of the airmen who did so much destruction are amazingly empty. They note fights, but quite flatly. 'Put down two Polaks', for example; 'a close shave'; but they do not seem to have had an inkling of the effect of the bombs they dropped upon the living flesh below. Many of these young men survived to become Modern State aviators and to serve the Air and Sea Control after 1965. But though some wrote well of their later experiences, none of them has left any useful documents for the history of the war time. The historian turns to his dates, maps and totals again from this meagre salvage of the hopes, fears, dreads, curiosities and agonies of the millions who went through that age of cruel disaster, doubtful whether he is sorry or thankful that most of that welter of feeling and suffering has vanished now as completely as though it had never been.

After 1945 the signs of exhaustion multiplied. Such despair had come to the souls of men that even defensive energy failed. They lay starving in their beds and hovels and let the bombs fall about them. But a whiff of gas could still cause a panic, a headlong rush of tormented people coughing and spitting through the streets to the shelter pits. Influenza with its peculiar intensity of mental depression came again repeatedly after 1942, and in 1945 came cholera. These epidemics, though they seemed grave enough at the time, were the mere first scouts of that great 'Raid of the Germs' which was in preparation for disunited humanity. It was as if they were testing the defensive organisation of mankind.

Except for air warfare, Britain and the North European neutrals were suffering almost as acutely as if they were actually at war. They had poured munitions into Europe and reaped a harvest of bad debts. After the first economic exhilaration due to this spate of employment, the exports of Great Britain, which had once been the pioneer of free world trade and cosmopolitan thought, dwindled to insignificance; the erstwhile creditor of the world could not collect such debts as were still due to her, and could not pay therefore for the food supply of her dwindling but still excessive population. Her former sanitation had rotted to filthiness under a régime of relentless saving. Housing in that disagreeable climate passed from congestion to horror. The first cholera epidemic found her in the throes not only of famine but of civil disorder, controlled and suppressed by her highly mechanised army and by the still very powerful habits of orderliness and subordination in her people. Never, since the Black Death of the fifteenth century, had the British

Isles known such a pestilence. They had believed the days of pestilence were past for ever. And yet that cholera was only the precursor of the still more terrible experiences that were to follow it in the subsequent decade.

Slowly but surely the spirit of protest and mutiny spread through Europe. That growing despairful insubordination that had done so much to bring about the winding up of the World War in 1918 reappeared in new forms. But because now war was no longer primarily an infantryman's business, mass mutiny, such as had crippled the French offensives after 1917, taken Russia out of the war, and led to the final German collapse, had not now the same disabling effect. There were not the same big aggregations of men under exasperating discipline and in touch with 'subversive' suggestions. Power had passed over to the specialised forces— to the aviators and war technicians. By the use of small bombs, machine-guns and the milder gases they could 'handle' and disperse mass meetings and 'tranquillise' insurgent districts in a manner that would have been inconceivable to the street-barricade revolutionaries of the later eighteenth century.

Even strikes in the munition factories were no longer so effective as they had been, because even there the increased efficiency of power production had ousted the comparatively unskilled worker in his multitudes. For the same reason the propaganda of insurrectionary class-war Communism, though it now dominated the thought of nine-tenths of the European peasants and workers, found unexpected obstacles in its attempts to seize control of affairs. It could not repeat the Russian social revolution because the new conditions were entirely different. The Bolshevik success had been possible only through the backwardness of Russia and the absence of a technically educated social stratum. The unrest and insubordination of the common people in Central and Western Europe could and did produce immense passive resistances and local revolutionary movements, but it found opposed to it a whole system of aviators, mechanics, technicians, scientific workers and so forth who had learnt from

246

Red Russia what sort of direction and planning to expect from a proletariat led by party politicians. Whatever they thought about their own governments—and already they were beginning to think in a very fresh and vigorous fashion about them—it was not towards democratic Communism that the minds of the scientific and technical workers were turning.

Nevertheless, with the help of organisers from Russia, the protest of humanity against the prolongation of the New Warfare took for a time the form of Communist risings. In 1947, in Marseilles, St. Etienne, Paris, Barcelona, Milan, Naples, Hamburg, Lodz and Glasgow there were mutinies of troops under arms and risings sufficiently formidable to sustain provisional soviets for periods varying from a week to several months. The Hamburg and Glasgow soviets were the best organised and held out longest, collapsing only after considerable bloodshed. Almost everywhere there were minor incidents of the same character. And the formal suspension of the war by the responsible governments concerned was certainly due more than anything else to their terror of a general social revolt. As the material organisation of the system was shattered, as the behaviour of the technicians became uncertain, the threatening visage of the class-vindictive proletarian drew nearer and nearer to the face of the stockbroker, the war-monger, the banker, the traditional ruler.

It took nearly three years to end the last war. The conference of London in 1947 did its best to work out a stable settlement of Europe on the lines of the Versailles Treaty, but the politicians and diplomatists were still incapable of the frankness and generosity needed. Face-saving was so much more important than life-saving to these creatures that they actually allowed the now pointless hostilities to be renewed in 1948.

In the spring of 1949, however, at Prague, President Benes achieved what had seemed to be the impossible, and brought the fighting to an end. He did this by inventing a phrase and suggesting, instead of a treaty, a 'Suspension of

Hostilities'. Each Power was to remain in possession of the territory it occupied, and there was to be no further fighting pending the assembly of an unspecified Conference to be organised later. Influenza, cholera and at last maculated fever, the progressive enfeeblement of economic life and new developments of human relationship prevented that onference from ever meeting. The Benes Suspension of Hostilities became a permanent suspension. It endures to this day.

§ 10. *The Raid of the Germs.*

That same dearth of detailed description which takes the colour out of the history of the last wars becomes even more apparent in the records of the epidemics that made any resumption of that warfare impossible. Diaries, letters and descriptive writing were out of fashion; there were other things to do and no surplus energy in the brain. It is as if the micro-organisms had taken a leaf out of the book of the Foreign Offices and found in mankind's confusion an opportunity for restoring the long-lost empire of the germs.

The attack began in the best style without a declaration of war. The first line of advance consisted of a variety of influenzas, impoverishing fevers, that were highly infectious and impossible to control under war conditions. The depleted strength of the belligerent populations, a depletion due to their reduced and disorganised nourishment and the collapse of their sanitary services, gave these infections full scope; they killed some millions and diminished the already lowered vitality of the great populations still further. That lowering of the general vitality was far more important

248

than the actual mortality. Cholera and bubonic plague followed, and then, five years and more later, when the worst seemed to have passed, came the culminating attack by maculated fever.

This obscure disease, hitherto known only as a disease of captive baboons, seems to have undergone some abrupt adaptation to the kindred habitat of the human body; possibly there was some intermediate host which prepared the bacilli for their attack on mankind. Or it may be that the preceding epidemics had changed some hitherto defensive element in human blood. We are still quite in the dark upon these points because at that time there were no doctors or biologists with the leisure to record observations, even had they had time to make them, and scientific publications had ceased to appear anywhere.

The disease appeared first in the vicinity of the London Zoological Gardens and spread thence with incredible rapidity. It discoloured the face and skin, produced a violent fever, cutaneous irritation and extreme mental distress, causing an uncontrollable desire to wander. Then the bodily energy vanished in collapse and the victim lay down and died. The fever was not simply infectious through water, but transmitted by the almost impalpable scabs scratched off by the sufferer. Wind, water and the demented sick carried it everywhere. About half humanity was vulnerable, and so far as we know now all who were vulnerable took it, and all who took it died.

So the world's malaise culminated in the terrible eighteen months between May 1955 and November 1956, at which latter date Nature with a pitiless but antiseptic winter came to the rescue of the human remnant. No effectual cure was ever devised for this fever and no helpful palliative. It swept the whole world and vanished as enigmatically as it came. It is still a riddle for pathologists. It no longer affects even the surviving baboon population, so that investigators can make no cultures, nor attempt any experiments. There is no material. It came, it destroyed and it seems to have at last committed suicide with some unknown anti-body of its

249

production. Or the real disease, as Mackensen believes, may have been not the maculated fever at all, but the state of vulnerability to its infection. That vulnerability had spread unsuspected throughout the world, he thinks, in the Warring Forties. The actual pestilence was not the disease but the harvest of a weakness already prepared.

History is like the individual memory in this, that it tends to obliterate disagreeable experiences. One of the most nonsensical things that was ever said was that a country is happy that has no history. On the contrary, it is only the really secure and prosperous phases that have left anything like sufficient material for historical reconstruction. We know of the pleasant social life of all the centuries of abundance in Egypt; we know the greatness and conquests of Assyria; the court-life of Ajanta and Central Asia is pictured for us to share; but the days of military disaster leave nothing but a band of ashes, and the years of pestilence merely break the continuities of the record. There is a good account of the Plague of London (1665) written by Defoe (1659–1731), and the unwary reader has to be warned that that account was compiled and fabricated many years after the event by an ingenious writer who was not even an eye-witness. There is a painting by Raphael of the plague in Rome which is similarly reminiscent. Most of the great plagues of history took their dead and departed unportrayed. What concerns history is the subsequent social and economic dislocation. On that Clio becomes copious again. What goes on again matters to her, but what is dead is dead.

The flowering prosperity of the nineteenth and early twentieth centuries has left us an almost uncontrollable mass of record about people who knew nothing except by hearsay of the more frightful experiences of mankind. We have novels, letters, diaries, memoirs, pictures, photographs and so on by the million. But there survives hardly a letter, no pictures and not a book or newspaper to throw light on those years 1955 and 1956, little more than a century and a third ago, which were certainly the most terrible through which our race ever passed. What was written at the time was destroyed as infectious. Afterwards it was left for a new generation of Defoes and Stephen Cranes to contrive a picture.

The descriptions of Cable, Nath Dass, Bodesco and Martini seem to be fairly justifiable, and to these fictions the reader is referred. They ring the changes upon not only villages but towns and cities with none but dead men and women in them; people lying unburied and gnawed by packs of hungry dogs and solitary cats; in India the tigers and in Africa the lions came into the desolate streets, and in Brazil the dead population of whole districts was eaten chiefly by wild hog, which multiplied excessively. Rats swarmed, and with an unwonted boldness threatened even the immune.

One terror which is never omitted is the wandering of the infected. Nothing would induce them to remain in bed or hospital; nothing could keep them from entering towns and houses that were as yet immune. Thousands of these dying wanderers were shot by terror-stricken people whom they approached. That dreadful necessity horrifies us to-day as much as that other grim act of self-protection; the survivors in the boats of the big steamship *Titanic* which struck an iceberg in 1912 beating at the knuckles of the drowning men and women who clung to the sides and threatened to swamp them. For a while, under such desperate and revealing stresses, men ceased to obey the impulses of a social animal. Those of the population who resisted the infection—and with maculated fever the alternatives were immunity or death—gave way to a sort of despair and hatred against the filthy suffering around them. Only a few men with medical, military, priestly or police training seem to have made head against the disaster and tried to maintain a sort of order. Many plundered. On the whole, so far as the evidence can be sifted, women behaved better than men, but some few women who joined the looters were terrible.

This nightmare came and passed.

In January 1957 people were walking about in the deserted towns, breaking into empty houses, returning to aban-

251

doned homes, exploring back streets littered with gnawed bones or full-clad skeletons, and they were still unable to realise that the wrath of Nature was over and life still before them.

Maculated fever had put gas warfare in its place. It had halved the population of the world.

§ 11. *Europe in* 1960

The more advanced student of history finds it necessary to work out in detail the local variations of the process by which the great patchwork of empires and nationalist states set up during the Age of European Predominance lost its defining lines, lost its contrasted cultures and its elaborated traditions, and ceased to divide the allegiance and devotion of men of good will. It was still standing—a hollow shell in 1933; in 1966 it had gone. It crumpled up, it broke down; its forms melted together and disappeared.

For the purposes of general education, the intricate interplay of personalities and accidents in this world débâcle can be passed over, as we pass over the details of the Great War or of Napoleon's various military campaigns, and as Gibbon, the author of the *Decline and Fall of the Roman Empire* (published between 1776 and 1778) passed over a thousand years of Byzantine court life. Nowadays that sort of history has become a mine for those admirable biographical studies which are ousting the old romantic novel from the entertainment of our leisure so soon as our imaginations have passed beyond the purely romantic stage. All that is needed for our present purpose is some understanding of the broader forces that were operating through this lush jungle of human reactions.

The tempo of human affairs increases continually, and the main difference between the decline and fall of the Roman system and the decline and fall of the world rule of private-profit capitalism in the twentieth century lies in the far more rapid onset and development of the later collapse. A second important difference is the much livelier understanding of what was happening on the part of the masses involved. Each of these two great depressions in the record of human well-being was primarily a monetary breakdown, due to the casual development of financial and proprietary law and practice without any reference to a comprehensive well-being, and to the lag in political and educational adaptation which left the whole system at last completely without guidance. But while the former débâcle went on to the pace of the horse on the paved road and of the written and spoken word, the phases of the new downfall flashed about the globe instantaneously and evoked a body of thought and reaction out of all comparison greater than the Roman precedent. So we see only a much compressed and abbreviated parallelism. From the demoralisation of the deflated Roman Empire by the great plagues at the end of the second century of the Christian era, to the reappearance of commerce, industry, art and politeness in the cities of the thirteenth and fourteenth centuries, was well over a thousand nerveless years; from the invasion of Belgium by the Germans in 1914 to the return of general material prosperity under the Air Dictatorship after 2010 was roughly a century.

The mental process, if for this reason alone, was much more continuous. It got to it conclusions while still in contact with its premises. The first world collapse was spread over a number of generations, each one oblivious of the experiences of its predecessor, but the larger and swifter part of the second world collapse fell well within the compass of a single long life. People who could remember the plentiful and relatively stable times between 1924 and 1928 as young men and women were still only at the riper end of middle age in 1960. Many who were children at the onset of the Hoover Slump were taking an active part in affairs in the days of the first international police, the Police of the Air and Sea Ways. It was possible to grasp what was happening as one whole. It is doubtful if any Roman citizen under the Empire ever grasped what was happening.

Nevertheless in each case there was a parallel obliteration of old of the second century of the Christian era, to the re-appearance of time-honoured traditions, the lapsing of debts and obligations, the disappearance of religious and educational organisations, the impoverishment of favoured and privileged classes, the recrudescence of lawlessness, the cleansing disillusionment. Each was the effectual liquidation of a bankrupt civilisation preparatory to a drastic reconstruction.

We will now take a sort of rough cross-section of the world at about the date of 1960 c.e., and consider the condition of the main masses of the world's population and the great forces at work among them. In the light of subsequent events we can realise that there was already a very considerable convergence of conditions going on throughout the middle decades of the century. But it may be doubted whether that was evident at the time. The goal towards which the fundamental bionomic forces were driving was everywhere the same, but the particulars varied widely with the geographical, ethnic and traditional circumstances, and their immediate interpretations were even more diverse.

We have viewed the events of the Era of European Pre-dominance as the outcome of an uncontrolled irregularity in growth, of economic hypertrophy in a phase of political and cultural atrophy. An immense increase in the energy of human society had occurred which had relieved itself partly in a great multiplication of the human population (Europe from 180 to 420 millions between 1800 and 1914, says Werner Sombart, in spite of a great emigration), partly in a monstrous exaggeration of warfare, and less considerably in an increased fullness and speed of the individual life.

254

But, as we have related, the forces of conservatism and functional resistance embodied in the creditor and legal systems were presently able to give pause to the release of fresh energy. For the second time in human experience the inadaptable quality of the financial and proprietary organisation produced a strangulation and an arrest.

The money and credit organisation of the prosperity of the nineteenth century differed in many respects from, and was more elaborate than, the Roman, but its life history was essentially the same. It wound itself up in the same fashion. First came a vast expansion and increase of private fortunes and then destructive taxation. So far history repeated itself. The European system, like the Roman system before it, impoverished itself finally by the violent expenditure of its vast windfall of energy. It repeated the same blind story of wastage, but with the unprecedented headlong facilities science afforded it. It ran through its available fortune and was helplessly in debt in a few decades. The height of its expenditure was between 1914 and 1950. Thereafter the pace was less catastrophic.

Regarded even as destruction, the New Warfare proved in the end to be a failure. It went to pieces when it was attempted. It did not kill as it might have killed—which is why the reader is alive to read this history. The actual battles of the European wars in the Forties—the purely military operations, that is to say—in all their ramifications cost mankind hardly a quarter of the battle slaughters of 1914–18. And yet they mark the highest level of scientific fighting ever attained by mankind. The Asiatic troubles had been more destructive because they were nearer the barbaric level, but even there actual deaths in warfare are estimated as under nine million. Of these, nearly five million are to be ascribed to the final offensive of Japan in 1938, the deadlock in Central China, the desperate fighting with the Kuomintang levies west of Hankow and the subsequent retreat.

Man had fallen as short as all that of the magnificent horrors he had anticipated. He had failed to raise war to its

255

ultimate mechanical level. The social and political dislocation following upon these two main struggles was indeed
proportionately far greater than the disorder of 1917–19, but
warfare was its prelude rather than its cause. This New Warfare, which the prophets had said would end in a scientific
massacre of mankind, passed insensibly into a squalor of
political fiascos, unpayable debts, unsubscribed loans,
scrapped machinery, insurrection, guerilla and bandit conflicts, universal hunger and the great pestilences. Gas warfare and air war faded out of the foreground or human
experience, dwarfed and overwhelmed by the more primitive realities of panic, famine and fever. The ultimate victor
in the middle twentieth century was the germ of maculated
fever. The main causes in the fall of the world's population
from about two thousand million in 1930 to a little under
half that total in 1960 were diseases or simple starvation,
arising directly from the complete economic collapse. Where
war slew its millions in a few great massacres, pestilence
slew its hundreds of millions in a pitiless pursuit that went
on by day and night for two terrific years.

As Imhoff has said, there is no single European history
of these Famished and Pestilential Fifties which followed so
swiftly on the war years; there are ten million histories. The
various governments created by the Treaty of Versailles
were for the most part still legally in existence throughout
this age, but with the monetary cessation they had become
so faded and ineffective that they had ceased to have any
great influence on everyday life. Some, like the British and
the French, limited their activities to efforts—generally quite
futile efforts, at tax-collecting; they went on finally in a
way which will remind the student of the old tribute-levying
Empires before the Hellena-Latin period. They interfered
spasmodically with local affairs, but for the most part they
let them drift. They ignored or compromised with active
resistance. The British government was still, it seems, paying
arrears upon its various loans, in 1952, to such stock-
holders as it was able to trace. The records are obscure; the
payments seem to have been made in a special paper

currency without real purchasing power. Other governments, like the Italian and Spanish, carried on as real administrative bodies within restricted areas. Rome, for instance, remained in fairly effective control of the triangle marked out by Genoa, Florence and the Mediterranean Coast, and Barcelona and Madrid kept order throughout most of the Peninsula except the Sovietised Spanish Riviera, Portugal and Andalusia.

The process in America was roughly parallel. Detachment was easier so soon as the bankrupt railways ceased to operate there, because the distances between population centres were greater and the capacity of the people for local autonomy much greater. They were still not a century from pioneering. The railways never resumed after the pestilence. The authority of the Federal Government of the United States shrank to Washington, very much as the Eastern Empire shrank to Byzantium, but Washington had none of the vitality of Byzantium, and it was already a merely historical capital long before the revival of tourism towards 2000. Germany as a unity did not survive the Polish wars, and Berlin dwindled rapidly to the status of a group of villages amidst the ruins of the Polish aerial bombardments.

The practical effacement of these bankrupt political systems in a few years, the equally rapid drying up of general transport and communications, the crescendo of the monetary breakdown, the speedy degeneration of military organisations, threw back the tasks of social order upon such local and regional leading as still existed. They found themselves astonishingly called upon. In Europe, as all over the world throughout this extraordinary decade, towns, cities, rural districts, discovered themselves obliged to 'carry on' by themselves. The plague only drove home that imperative need. The municipal authorities organised such health services as they could against the infection, or gave way to emergency bodies that took things out of their hands. When the plague disappeared, they were like shipwrecked sailors on a strange island; they had to reconstitute their shrunken economic life. They used old authority for new

257

needs and old terms for new things. Here it would be an energetic leader who called himself the Mayor or the Duke, here a resolute little band, self-styled the Town Council or the Citizens' Union. Here 'advanced' terminology prevailed, and it was a 'Soviet of Workers' which took control. In effect the latter would be very similar to a Citizens' Union. Its chief distinction was its consciousness of being in a new social phase.

There was the most extraordinary variation in the political structure of this phase of dislocation, and a flat contradiction between the actual and the 'legal' controls. Across South Germany, Poland and North France, the prevalent impression was one of social revolution, and soviets were in fashion. But they were very different in character from the original local Russian soviets. It was possible to find a Communist district referring itself vaguely to Moscow, lying side by side with another that was under the control of its former owners and employers and professed to be, and often was, still in communication with the national government in the capital. An uneasy truce would be maintained between these theoretically antagonistic systems. Deputations would go for authority in various disputes—arrears of taxes in hand—to Westminster, Paris or Rome, very much as the barbarian chiefs of the Early Medieval period would upon due occasion refer to Byzantium or Rome. Local conflicts and revolutions were constantly occurring. They were recognised at the capitals only as local riots and municipal readjustments.

Scattered through this disarticulating Europe were the vestiges of the old militarism, broken fragments of unpaid armies with irreplaceable weapons and a dwindling supply of ammunition. They consisted of the officers who were soldiers by profession, and the levies who had not been disbanded or who had refused to be disbanded because there was no employment for them outside the ranks. These men had their officers very much under control because of the great facilities for desertion. In some cases these shrivelled military forces were in contact with the capital and the old legal government, and conducted, or attempted to conduct, tax requisitions and suchlike surviving functions of the old order; in other instances they became frankly brigand forces, though often with high-sounding titles, Public Order Guards or Emergency Army. Most merged with the local police of aggressive Mayors or councils. Small wars of conquest went on in the early Sixties. Old empires and sovereign states reappeared, in duplicate or triplicate, and vanished or became something else. After 1960 there were even quasimilitary forces levying contributions, keeping a sort of order and professing to be Modern State nuclei. They would occupy the old barracks and accommodation of garrison towns.

In the Forties these soldiers had been raw recruits. In the following decades those who remained in their old formations became formidable middle-aged rascals in patched and shabby and supplemented uniforms. Some of the commandants had gained control of local aerodromes and local munition factories, but everywhere the military found themselves more and more out of sympathy with the technical workers they needed to make these acquisitions effective. They degenerated to the level of the nineteenth-century infantry and were at last glad to get even a few thousand roughly made cartridges to replenish their supply.

Under the necessity of doing things for themselves, people did things for themselves that they had left to the central government for a century. Even during the World War, and in the year or so of stress that followed it, various French Chambers of Commerce had supplemented the deficiency in small change by local token coinages. Now this practice reappeared widely. To-day our museums contain hundreds of thousands of specimens of these improvised European coins of lead, nickel, tin and all sorts of alloys, *jetons* or checks of wood, and tons of signed, printed paper notes, useful in the local market, acceptable for rents and local taxes, but of no avail at all at a distance of a few score miles. The local bank manager as often as not would improvise a local credit in co-operation with the local solicitor; the doctors

259

would contrive a way of getting along without the Home Office. There were still printers' establishments in most centres of population, and for some years local periodicals, often of considerable originality, appearing weekly or monthly and printed on the roughest and most variable paper, supplied all that remained alive of the European Press. But their foreign news amounted to little more than rumour. The great Press agencies were bankrupt and dead; the telegraph organisation was out of gear.

Save in a few exceptional centres, the diffusion of news by radio died out completely. The manufacture of receiving sets was entirely disorganised. From 1960 to 1970 the 'ether' for all except the special purposes of air transport was still. There is a long and interesting study in the Historical Record Series of the vicissitudes of posts, tele-graphs and telephones between 1950 and 1980. There seem to have been extraordinary survivals. Apparently London, Paris and Rome were in telephonic communication almost without a break, and the news of the great London land-slide was telephoned to Madrid and thence radioed to Buenos Aires in 1968. But that may have been a revival connected with the new Air and Sea Control.

The disappearance not only of radio sets but of an enormous variety of small conveniences and appliances was extraordinarily rapid after the collapse of world trade. Photography, for instance, was wiped out almost at once. The bicycle became rare, and the old pneumatic tyre was replaced by a thin solid one often very badly adulterated 'remade' rubber. Electric lighting flickered out and vanished for want of the proper material for filaments. All electrical material deteriorated, and tramway systems either fell into complete disuse or returned to horse traction.

Ordinary life had been lowering its standards bit by bit from the World War onward. First one thing went and then another. Neither in the British nor the French provinces did the housing of the common people recover from the cessation of building during the actual warfare. Except in places like Berlin or Vienna where there had been a vigorous outbreak of post-war building which provided accommodation in excess for the shrunken population, the mass of Europeans were even more congested and dirty in their domestic accommodation than they had been before the conflict, though indeed they never sank to the immemorial squalor and poverty of the Chinese and Indian towns. Cleanliness diminished at such a pace as to be noted even by the newspapers after 1933. There are constant complaints of the dirtiness of the streets and the bad repair of the roads, and regretful comparisons with the trim orderliness of twenty years before.

Clothing declined with housing. The clothing trade shrank steadily per head of population for nearly forty years. The city crowds, in spite of the more and more abundant uniforms (until 1950), lost nearly all their former brightness and élan. People patched up their old clothing for want of new, and rags became increasingly common. The supply of boots was very restricted. The mass production of boots had been commandeered at the outbreak of the war and was never turned back to commercial use because of the complete financial ruin that ensued. But the old-fashioned shoemakers had been driven off the face of Europe long before by this mass production, and so throughout the Famished Fifties the Europeans were very painfully shod. Spain had the best boots and France and Britain took to sandals—and chilblains. A certain manufacture of footwear went on in some centre in Bohemia, now untraceable, and next to Spain ranked Central Europe in the order of shoe welfare. There was an extreme scarcity of hats everywhere.

There was also a universal decline in the little comforts and accessories of life to which the world had grown accustomed. Except in a few favoured regions where it was actually grown, tobacco disappeared. The mass production of cigarettes died out, and those who smoked, smoked pipes of substitute. Real tea became a great rarity, and sugar was scarce. Dietetic diseases and diseases of under-nutrition increased.

During the strain and effort of the Great War most of the

Europeans had already learnt something of contrivance and makeshift. Now they were to have a decade of domestic management under difficulties. The Germans were already familiar with the word Ersatz; there was much technical knowledge and ability diffused among them; and it is indisputable that they contrived to keep much nearer comfort than the rest of the world during these dismal years. They devised substitute leather, substitute cotton, substitute coffee and tea, substitute tobacco, substitute quinine and opium and a very respectable list of other substitute drugs.

At the other extreme were the shiftless Irish. Until the return of production their physical misery was very great indeed. One observer doubted if there were a million yards of new cloth produced in that country between 1950 and 1960. 'They live,' he reported, 'on buttermilk, potatoes, whisky and political excitement. They have contrived garments of woven straw, often very picturesquely dyed, which they call Early Erse and of which they boast inordinately, and they warm themselves by means of fires of peat and dung and a great warmth of mutual invective.' This sounds quite barbaric. Yet it is this period that we owe the graceful—though, according to a recent Historical Documents report, rather rickety—Church of the Atonement, built on the site of the Dublin Royal College of Science after that had been suppressed by the Censorship of 1939 for 'teaching biology in a manner tending to disintegrate the Holy Trinity'.

The student must be more or less familiar with the representations of this period in that useful compilation *Historical Scenes in a Hundred Volumes*, and he has probably read a number of romances and stories of this time. Actual photographs are least abundant in the later fifties and early sixties. There were still plenty of cameras in the world, but the supply of films seems to have died out after 1955, and there are hardly any but slow wet-plate exposures after that time for nearly ten years. We get only a few scores of such animated snapshots as were abundant during the preceding decades, and there are no European cinematograph films at all. Neither was there much sketching except of single figures, and so the editors have had to supplement their material by very carefully studied drawings and photographed restorations made at a later date.

There are six interesting snapshots of scenes in Lyons in 1959. Someone seems to have found a spool of film and been able to develop it. One shows the big central square, the Place Bellecour as it was called, on a market day. Earlier pictures show a big bronze equestrian figure of Louis XIV, but this had already disappeared, probably it had been melted for its metal; and the windows of some of the big buildings, formerly hotels, and hospitals, in the background have the empty frameless look of gutted houses. But the scene is quite a busy one. It was probably the monthly market, and there is a considerable amount of cattle, numerous horses being traded, hurdled sheep, many goats and a row of pig-pens. The people are mostly peasants wearing straw hats and either very old coats or in some cases shawls wrapped about them. Townspeople are still wearing the clothing of the Thirties, shabby and patched, and there are three market officials or magistrates in the old-world top hat. In the foreground a bearded man leads a couple of oxen harnessed to a small 'runabout' car in which a corpulent woman sits in front with a crate of ducklings while behind is a netted calf. The lady smiles broadly at the camera, unaware that she is smiling at posterity.

Another of these snapshots shows a bowls competition in the deserted railway station. It is clearly a festive occasion, and several games are in progress. The rails have disappeared from the tracks, which have been levelled for the game, and the ponies and mules of the players are tethered on the platform in a long line. The doors of the various bureaus have been taken away, but the inscriptions *Chef de Gare, Salle d'Attente, Restaurant*, are still faintly visible. There are two long tables on one of the middle platforms on which simple refreshments are being served. A third picture shows a crowd staring at the ruins of a row of houses which have just collapsed down a steep slope in what is apparently the district known as Fourvière. Here two bearded men in the unmistakable uniform of the old Alpini are keeping order. We know as a matter of fact that the Lyons municipality at that time had three regiments of these soldiers quartered in barracks. They are wearing sandals supplemented by cloth strips that are twisted round their legs, and their cloaks are in good condition.

Three others of these photographs give us a glimpse of the state of affairs in a disused silk factory. Up to the time of the economic collapse, the silk manufactured at Lyons was still largely that produced by the silkworm, but the supply of raw material seems to have died out more or less completely in the Rhône valley, and the shrinkage of trade and then the war diminished the importation of the reeled-up thread. But silk was needed in the manufacture of shells, and probably there were special efforts to maintain the supply up to the last. This particular establishment seems to have been carrying on a diminished output until the Lyons commune in 1951. Then no doubt it was abruptly abandoned. One photograph shows a great heap of paper litter among weaving-machines and a number of petrol cans. Apparently there was an attempt to fire the place. Another gives a vista of winding-machines shrouded in spiders' webs and fine dust. In a third a wild cat crouches among the spindles of a spinning-machine and spits at the unwanted intruder. The machinery has all the complicated clumsiness characteristic of twentieth-century mechanism. Apparently a window of some sort was opened or a blind drawn back to make this particular photograph, for the picture is blurred with a multitude of whirling moths, most of them out of focus, evidently just stirred up.

These particular pictures are valuable because of their authenticity. There are also two contemporary dry-plate pictures of the Café Royal, the big restaurant of the Grand Hotel of Stockholm, deserted and still intact. They are oddly suggestive of two pictures of the ruins of the Baths of Caracalla in Rome as they appeared a hundred years earlier. And there is also a photograph of the remains of the old dining-room of the Hotel Métropole at Brighton in England before it was undermined and fell into the sea. But all the rest of the pictures given in *Historical Scenes* between 1955 and 1963 are arranged pictures. The Transport organisation was running scores of aeroplanes and radio communications were restored long before the complex manufacture of photographic apparatus and material was set going again.

There are some very interesting restorations of conditions in London showing the empty streets and the vacant tumbledown warehouses of the city after the pestilence. The pictures of the corridors of the hotels in the Strand turned into hospital wards are very impressive. So too is the sketch of a great fight between the cow-keepers and the potato-growers for the possession of Hyde Park and Kensington Gardens in which three hundred people were killed. The dreadful pictures of the bodies of plague victims floating down the Thames and accumulating in the Pool of London, however, are now said to be exaggerated.

We try in the midst of our present securities to imagine the phases of anxiety, loss, incredulity and reluctant acquiescence through which the minds of hundreds of millions of Europeans passed, day by day, from the general comfort of the Twenties, through the shocks, fear, horror, rage and excitement of the war cycle, into this phase of universal impotence and destitution. The poor perhaps had a less vivid apprehension of disaster than the rich. Even in the days of General Prosperity, as it is called, they had at the best what we should consider very dull, drab, irksome lives. Even though they mostly ate sufficiently, they ate badly, and there was never a stage of universal decent housing at any time for them. They went from bad to worse. They passed from toil to unemployment and lethargy. But the middling sort passed from good to bad, from something one might almost consider tolerable living to the hopeless neediness of the masses.

A class that went through great unhappiness everywhere during this period was the class of elderly and 'retired' persons and persons of 'independent means' (and no responsibilities) which had expanded so enormously during the First Age of General Prosperity. This superfluity of prosperous humanity had spread itself out very pleasantly over the world, oblivious of the exertions that sustained social discipline and ensured its security. Insensibly it had taken the place of the old administative and directive noblesse and country gentry. The investment system during its period of steady efficiency had relieved this social stratum of every bother. There were great areas of agreeable country, residential districts, given up to this 'well-off' society, to its gardens, which were often delightful, its golf-courses, race-courses, mountain sport centres, parks, country clubs, plages and hotels. It wilted a little during the World War, but revived again very hopefully in the decade of hectic and uncertain expansion that followed. Then, as the Great Slump developed its grim phases, this life of leisure passed away.

The Phase of Economy is really a misnomer. There was really no economy; there was strangulation and inaction through a cessation of expenditure. Nobody—unless it was a dexterous speculator on a falling market—grew richer, or even relatively richer. The only profits appeared in bank balance sheets. As the malady of arrest spread, traffics declined, enterprise died out, borrowing states and corporations suspended payments, and these children of good fortune, these well-off people, found themselves confronted at the same time by a suspension of payments and more and more urgent charitable appeals. Their bankers and solicitors informed them that first this trusted prop and then that was in arrears or in default. The waters of repudiation rose, submerging security after security. If they sold out and hoarded, some fluctuation in exchange might still engulf great fractions of their capital. 'Whatever else may be falling off, sleepness nights are on the increase,' a financial paper remarked in 1933. The head full of self-reproach that tossed on the crumpled pillow in the villa marked time with the fretting of the unemployed who worried in the stuffy cold of the slum.

266

We have the *Diary of Titus Cobbett,* who rode on a bicycle from Rome and along the Riviera to Bordeaux in 1958. He had begun life as an art dealer, and had served the British Inland Revenue for some years as a valuer of furniture, pictures and the like. His tour seems to have been a journey of curiosity. He complains bitterly of the difficulty of changing money between Genoa and Bordeaux. He seems to have had some obscure diplomatic or consular function, but of that he is too discreet to speak. Perhaps he was sent to make a report, but if so there is no record of his instructions.

His description of that smitten coast is still very interesting reading. He had, as a young man with good connections, known Monte Carlo well in the twenties, and the places he visited were often those at which he had stayed as a guest. He records the abandonment of hundreds of lovely châteaux, locked-up, unsaleable, abandoned, in the keeping perhaps of some old domestic, or frankly looted by the people of the district, once delightful gardens whose upkeep had become impossible, blind tangles of roses, oleanders, pomegranates, oranges, cypresses, palm trees, agaves, cacti and weeds; unremunerative hotels allowed to fall into ruins, broken-down water-conduits washing away the roads, bungalows taken over by the peasants. Something of the same swift desolation must have come upon the Campagna and the villadom of the Bay of Naples during the ebb of Roman vitality, but this had been a swifter decline. The roads, he says, were very variable, but a great number of the road signs and roadside advertisements were still making their mute appeal to a vanished traffic. As he rode alone wondering whether he would find a reasonably clean and hospitable shelter for the night, he read, he says, picked out in metallic knobs that answered brightly to his oil lamp:

H TEL S LEN ID
CU SINE RENOM
T T LE C NFOR M RNE

267

Whither had host and guests departed? Where were the owners and tenants of these villas and gardens; the bright clientèle of the pleasure resorts? Many of them no doubt were already dead, for the Riviera owners had been mostly middle-aged and oldish people. The rest were back in their own countries leading impoverished lives, full of tiresome reminiscences, lost in the universal indigence.

Cobbett visited the ruins of the old Casino at Monte Carlo, and the younger Sports Club. The ceiling of the American Bar had fallen in a few days before his visit. 'They looked small,' he says. 'When I was young they had seemed tremendous places.'

The celebrated garden in which suicidal gamblers used to put an end to their troubles was overgrown with mesembryanthemum.

Yet there was one exception to this general decadence, and our observer stresses the significance of that. Air traffic was still going on. Between Rome and Marseilles he notes very precisely that he saw thirteen aeroplanes going east or west, besides two that he heard before he got up in the morning. 'I doubt if I should have seen so many twenty-five years ago,' he writes, and goes on to enlarge, very illuminatingly, on the revival of trade and the possible revival of order these throbbing mechanisms portended. At Nice and at Marseilles he noted there was shipping—'not mere fishing boats but ships of a thousand tons or more'; and at Nice they were building a bigger ship—he estimated it as a three-thousand tonner. We have no other records of shipbuilding between 1947 and 1962. Long before 1940 the building of very big ships had ceased to be a 'paying proposition' and it is fairly certain that no sea-going ships whatever, big or little, were built anywhere in the world in the early fifties. Year by year the transport system of the bankrupt planet had been sinking into disuse. It is only nowadays that our historical students are attempting to work out statistical charts of that swift decadence.

Cobbett also notes with surprise and hope a stretch of railway (operated by lever trolleys and a petrol engine or so) between the port of Marseilles and some inland quarries. He was clearly under the impression that no railways were operating in the world any longer. So soon as the traffic had sunken to a level below the possibility of paying subsistence wages, maintaining the permanent way and meeting running expenses, it had been impossible even for speculative buyers to handle these once valuable properties. They had become old junk on the landscape, tracks of torn and rusty rails smothered in agaves and wild flowers. He mentions the beauty of the viaducts of the old Sud de France, and tells how he bicycled along the footworn side-path of the Paris–Lyon Méditerranée in preference to the road. The peasants had used the derelict railway as a convenient iron-mine, and few rails remained. Most of the sleepers had been used for fuel.

At Fréjus there was an aerodrome, and here he describes a very illuminating conversation with a Spanish-American aviator who had served first with the Poles, then with the Germans and finally with the French during the warfare. Cobbett was impressed by the evident revival of trade, and surprised to find rubber, spices, mercury and block-tin among the commodities coming by air from the East, while clocks, watches, compasses, knives, needles, buttons, hardened glass and the like were going back in exchange. Most of the trade was barter, and the profits were so considerable that there seemed every reason to expect a steady expansion of the service.

He seems to have learnt for the first time of the developing combination of air-merchants, who were mostly aviators surviving from the war. They had already organised a loose world union, it seems, and were keeping the airways and air lights in order.

Cobbett remarked on the shipping revival he had noted.

'We shall have to watch that,' said the aviator significantly.

'You take passengers?'

'When they can pay a passage.'

'But this is civilisation coming back!' cried Cobbett.

'Don't believe it! It's a new civilisation beginning.'

And he seems to have opened Cobbett's eyes for the first time to some of the ideas that were already taking shape in such brains as his. 'World Empire?' he said. 'That's an old idea? The men who hold the air and the transport hold the world. What do we want with empires and that stuff any more?'

Cobbett was greatly impressed by this conversation. He went on across France to Bordeaux, where it seems some sort of money awaited him, thinking this over and jotting down his thoughts. He makes one sound and interesting parallel between this new World Transport Organisation and those Hansa Merchants who played such an important role in the revival of civilisation about the Baltic and North Europe generally after the Roman collapse. 'After all,' reflects Cobbett, 'we have never given organised transport and trading its proper importance in history.'

At Bordeaux he sold his bicycle and was able to get a passage in an aeroplane to Le Bourget (an aerodrome of old origin near the ruins of Paris) and thence to fly to Hendon. His 'plane landed at Le Mans for an exchange of goods. His delight to escape from the rough roads he had been riding is infectious.

He describes the recovery of the devastated French forests in the form of scrub, and he peered down at the little peasants' clearings that were appearing in groups and patches round the old towns. He sees the aviators and mechanics at the aerodromes with new eyes, and he learns from them of the way in which World Transport was picking up and reinstating metallurgical and electrical works. He has an eye for the beauty of Le Mans Cathedral, which he had seen and admired in his student days, and which he rejoices to find intact, and he describes that early monument to the pioneers of aviation in the Place below which still survives. Amiens Cathedral was also uninjured at that time.

His diary ends on a melancholy note. Apparently he had not visited England for some years, and he is shocked by the ruinous desolation of the outer suburbs of London.

Plainly he had lived in and loved London as a boy. A part of Hyde Park, in spite of the opposition of the squatter cultivators, had been converted into an aerodrome, but he found the rebuilding of the central region haphazard and unpleasing. He objects to the crowding of heavy buildings, with their vast anti-aircraft carapaces of cement, at the centre, due to the decay of suburban traffic facilities. It looked, he says, like a cluster of 'diseased' mushrooms. 'When shall we English learn to plan?' he asks, and then with an odd prophetic gleam he doubts whether the northern slope of the Thames depression, so ill drained and so soft in its subsoil, can carry this lumpish mass of unsound new buildings to which the life of the old city was shrinking.

Only ten years later his fears were to be justified. The bed of the Thames buckled up and the whole of the Strand, Fleet Street, Cornhill and, most regrettable of all, the beautiful St. Paul's Cathedral of Sir Christopher Wren, so familiar to us in the pictures and photographs of that age, collapsed in ruin and perished in flame. The reader who has pored over *Historical Scenes in a Hundred Volumes*—and what child has not?—will remember the peculiar appearance of the old Waterloo Bridge, crumpled up to a pent-house shape, and the grotesque obliquity of the Egyptian obelisk, once known as Cleopatra's Needle, that venerable slab of hieroglyphics, cracked and splintered by air-raid shrapnel, which slanted incredibly for some years before it fell into the banked-up water of the Lambeth–Chelsea lake.

§ 12. *America in Liquidation*

The preceding sections have given a general view of the course of history in the Old World during the middle decades of the twentieth century. Even in Europe certain regions, as we have noted, stand rather aloof from the essential drama, following a line of development of their own, less tragic and intense than that of the leading Powers. Spain, for example, the new Spain that was born in 1931, has the role of an onlooker, an onlooker much preoccupied with his own affairs. Still more noticeable is the non-participation of both Latin- and English-speaking America in those passionate and violent happenings. They suffered parallel economic, political and social stresses, but within their own limits. After the financial storms of the early Thirties, the shocks that came to them from the European troubles affected them less and less. They took up their particular aspect of the decline and fall of private capitalism and worked it out in their own way.

Yet the fact that they did share in that decline and fall brings out very clearly a fact that was sometimes disputed in the past: *the immediate causes of the world collapse in the twentieth century were first monetary inadaptability, secondly the disorganisation of society through increased productivity and thirdly the great pestilence.* War was not a direct cause. The everyday life of man is economic, not belligerent, and it was strangled by the creditor. Had the world been already one state in 1900, and had it still been an economy of private accumulation with a deflating currency, it would have collapsed in very much the same fashion that it did collapse. Had it been cut up into a hundred belligerent states at that time, but with a monetary

272

system that restrained the creditor and allowed industrial development without limit, it might have released sufficient energy to have gone on with its wars for another century or so before it reached the goal of mutual extermination. The monetary collapse was the most immediate factor in the world's disorganisation, enfeeblement and famine. Without it man might have pursued a far longer and more strenuous career to massacre and suffocation. On the whole it was perhaps well for him that progress tumbled over finance in the nineteen-thirties.

The futility of all the early anti-war movements becomes understandable only when we grasp the essential importance of a sane monetary nexus. On this we have insisted throughout, we have elucidated the connexion of the creditor and traditional antagonisms from half a dozen angles, and nothing could emphasise and drive home the lesson more than the parallelism of the American and Old-World experiences.

From the days of their first political separation from the European system the American communities had gone through their own series of developmental phases, independent of and out of rhythm with the course of events in the Old World. Independent—and yet not completely independent, because they were upon the same planet. Throughout the nineteenth century the American mind, in north and south alike, was saturated with the idea of *isolation*. It was taught in the schools, in the Press, in every political utterance of a general import, that the New World was indeed a new world, an escape from the tyranny of ancient traditions to peace, liberty, opportunity and a fresh life for mankind. It had to avoid all 'entangling alliances' with Old-World states and policies, forget the inveterate quarrels and hatreds of Europe even at the price of forgetting kinship and breaking with a common culture, and work out and set the example of a more generous way of living. From the days of George Washington to the days of Woodrow Wilson, in spite of the Civil War and much grave economic trouble, the American mind never abandoned its belief in its own

273

exemplary quality and its conception that towards the rest of the world its attitude must be missionary and philanthropic. It realised that it knew many things very simply, but it had no doubt it knew better.

Throughout the nineteenth century both America and Europe expanded enormously, economically, biologically. America was profoundly impressed by her own growth and disposed to disregard the equal pace of European progress. Assisted by a tremendous immigration from Europe, the population of the United States increased by about 80 millions in a hundred years. But in spite of that tremendous emigration, Europe during that period added 240 millions to her multitudes. The American cherished a delusion that he had 'got on' relatively to Europe. His life had in fact expanded, concurrently with the European's, and through the working of ideas and inventions and the importation of human energy from the older centres. In his unimpeded continent the different elements in the expansion increased at rates that did not correspond with the European process. He was living in a similar progressive system, but he was more and more out of phase with transatlantic developments.

And throughout that century inventions in transport and communications were 'abolishing distance' and bringing points that had formerly been months apart into a few hours' or a few moments' distance from one another.

The resulting alternations of intimacy and remoteness across the Atlantic constitute one of the outstanding aspects of twentieth-century history. It is like two great and growing tops that spin side by side. They approach, they touch and clash, they wobble and fly apart. Or it is like two complexes of machinery, destined ultimately to combine into one world mechanism, whose spinning wheels attempt to mesh and fail to mesh and jar with a great shower of sparks and splinters and separate again. From the end of the nineteenth century onward the unifying forces of life were tending to gear America with Europe. By the middle of the twentieth century any observer might have been forgiven the conclusion that the intergearing had failed.

We have already given great prominence in this history to the figures of Henry Ford, Woodrow Wilson, and the second Roosevelt, Franklin Roosevelt. We have told of the magnificent advance upon Europe and the subsequent recoil of America within and about them. A brief but competent contemporary book by an American publicist, Frank H. Simonds, *Can America stay at Home?* (1933) surveys the question of isolation very illuminatingly as it appeared in the opening years of the great economic slump which closed down for good and all the wild freedoms of Acquisitive Private Capitalism. He shows how the phases of approach and repulsion succeeded one another from the first imperialist enterprises of Roosevelt I (Theodore Roosevelt, 1901–09) onward; how impossible it seemed for America either to keep out of Old-World affairs or to mingle frankly in them. It expressed its virtuous opinions and would not back them. It insisted upon moral judgments and would not take responsibility. In European eyes, to quote Simond's new historical phrase, 'American concern for peace appeared a transparent endeavour to combine the mission of John the Baptist with the method of Pontius Pilate'. The explanation lay in just that mixture of liberal modernity and naïve crudity in the American intelligence on which we have laid stress.

From its beginning the American Republic was a break with history, a new thing, far newer, having regard to its period, than the Soviet Republic of Lenin, and from its beginning it was failing to go on with its newness, failing to develop and intensify its ideas. It evolved a body of higher schools and cultivated men to think itself out only after more than a century of independence; in the interim it left its mass education to underpaid teachers and repetitive women. It grew bodily, immensely and for more than a century it lived on imported brain-food. The result was this rawness, this immense sense of its mission and this want of any subtlety or vigour in its conduct. Wilson's foolish preachments and arrangements, so foolish and yet so saturated with the wisdom of world peace, were perhaps the highest expression of the American mind of his time.

The American mind even in the nineteenth century was not an ignorant mind; it was an immensely uneducated mind. If it was clumsy, it was also free. Its religious 're-vivalism' was exactly parallel to its political fluctuations. We find in the stories and studies of authentic American life such features as camp-meetings and organised emotional campaigns for repentance and conversion. We think of firelit scenes, of harsh preaching and lusty chanting. These waves of popular feeling, these gatherings, often in the woods, with their hymn-singing, their exhortation, their shouts of penitence and exultant belief, the mindless exalta-tion and the subsequent mindless deflation of American spiritual life, were precisely reflected in these booms and slumps of the American world mission. Only with the shock of world economic disaster did the real social and political thinking of America rise to its full vigour. The retreat of the United States from the imbroglio of European affairs as the great depression intensified was marked by a new, more vigorous determination to grip the essentials of social life.

And certainly there was everything to stimulate thought in the internal situation. The dégringolade was at first more rapid even than in Europe. The industrial edifice had been reared to giddier heights of mass production and fell more heavily. In 1928 the United States of America still believed itself the most prosperous country in the world; in 1933 its unemployed were more hopeless and formidable than those of any other continent. But they made no organised effort of revolt; they had no revolutionary formula to bring them together. They revolted as individuals and gangs and be-came criminals. Society was not overthrown, but it crumbled rapidly to dust and disorder. The crime wave, the financial stress, the frantic efforts to economise and all the consequent strangulation of popular education and the dissolution of confidence, order and intercommunication—that sequence which we have already traced in general terms manifested itself most severely and typically in this vast, comparatively

276

unhistorical area. Roosevelt II struggled gallantly, but he came too late to stop the rot.

In America as in Europe a phase of fragmentation set in. It was not a smash to which one can give a definite date, but every day there was something happening in the direction of dissolution. In America as in Europe State governments became insolvent phantoms making feebler and feebler efforts to collect taxes, and the Federal authority in Washington faded away, if not as completely as the League of Nations in Europe, at any rate in a comparable manner. We have the same phenomena of municipalities becoming autonomous, and provisional controls, Citizens' Unions, Law and Order Societies, Workers' Protection Associations and plain Workers' Soviets (in New Mexico and Arizona) springing into activity here, there and everywhere. In the Blue Mountains and on the Pacific coast small republics had already isolated themselves in 1945 and were carrying out a strange blend of Methodism, 'Technocracy' and the Douglas Plan, and Utah had become a practically autonomous Single-Tax State and had restored Mormonism of the original type as the State religion. But there had been no formal secession from the Federal Union anywhere.

There is in the Records a description of Washington in the year 1958, by a former attaché of the British Embassy there. (All the Ambassadors of the British Empire had been replaced by 'consolidated consuls' in 1946.) He describes a visit to the White House, where he was entertained at lunch by President Benito Caruso. The President was carrying on although his term had expired because his successor elect had disappeared on his way to the capital in the Allegheny Mountains. There had been considerable confusion about the last election, and two Secession Presidents who were disputing possession of the State of New York after a conflict over the Yonkers Ballot Boxes had cut off communications with New England altogether.

The President received his visitor very cordially and asked many very sympathetic and intelligent questions about the European situation. He spoke very hopefully of the American outlook. The 'return to Normalcy', he said, was at last in sight. There had been a restoration of the steamboat traffic on the Mississippi, and cotton was going through to the north again in spite of the political unrest. A hundred and forty automobiles had been sent to South America alone in the year 1956–57 in the place of only seventy-two for the previous year. The new quinine–coffee barter system was working well. He looked forward now to a steady upward movement in business affairs. The Hoover Slump had, he admitted, lasted much longer and had gone much lower than had been expected, and it had tried the people to the utmost, but they had faced their trials in a manner worthy of the fathers of the republic. He concluded with the compliments usual then between the two great divisions of the English-speaking peoples.

The lunch was plain but ample. There was excellent pork and a variety of vegetables which the President with genuine democratic frankness boasted he had raised himself with the help of his Negro 'secretariat' in pig-pens and garden at the back of the White House. The duties of the secretariat seem to have been in the household rather than the office. They had been appointed for abstruse political reasons, and several of them were unable to read. Mrs. Caruso, a very pleasant lady of Irish extraction, was disposed to dwell on the difficulties of housekeeping in Washington in view of the increasing unpunctuality in the collection of the Federal revenue, but the President checked her, evidently considering these domestic matters a reflection upon the solvency of the nation.

At that time only about a third of the States were actually represented by Congressmen in the Assembly. The rest had found it either too expensive or unnecessary to send delegates. A member was in possession of the house, a tattered individual, reciting some lengthy grievance; there were no reporters visible, and nobody was listening to him. Apparently this man was trying to 'talk out' some legislative proposal, but the visitor could not find anyone who could explain the situation precisely.

278

The visitor dined on the following day with the eloquent, vital and venerable Senator Borah from Idaho (1865–1970). He was in excellent form, and talked throughout the meal. Indeed, he talked so ably that his visitor was unable to ask him several questions previously prepared for him. He too was extremely hopeful for his country. He admitted that there had been a marked decline in the grosser welfare of America during his lifetime. He would not quarrel with statistics. In tons of coal and steel, in miles of railway run, in the mass production of motor-cars and commodities generally, it was possible to institute unfavourable comparisons with the past. 'But man does not live by bread alone,' said America's Grand Old Man. 'Let us look a little nearer the heart of things.'

That heart, it seemed, had never been sounder. The pestilence, like everything that came from God, had been 'wholesome'. The standard of life was, he maintained, higher than it ever had been, having regard to the nobler aspects of things. Fewer bathrooms there might be, at least in working order, but there was far more purity of mind. In his younger days there had been a lamentable lapse into luxurious indulgence and carelessness on the part of the free people of the States, but all that was past. America was nearer now to the old Colonial simplicity, honesty and purity than she had ever been.

A little inconsecutively the Senator went on to denounce the dishonesty of Europe and the disingenuousness of European and particularly of British diplomacy. He seemed for a time to be repeating long-remembered speeches and to have forgotten how completely British diplomacy had lapsed. He had apparently heard the word 'attaché' before he began to talk, and that had sent his mind back to old times. He returned to the present situation. The United States, he insisted, had gone through far blacker phases in its early history. A hundred and fifty-four years ago Washington had been burnt by a victorious British army. Nothing of the sort had occurred during the present depression—if it could be spoken of as a depression. Even at the darkest hour in this great Hoover Slump nobody had ever thought of burning Washington.

Later on this same traveller visited the University of Chicago, Columbia University, Harvard and a number of other centres of intellectual activity. His comments are shrewd and intelligent, and fall in very conveniently with our examination of the mental reactions that even then were rapidly producing a new and more sinewy American consciousness amidst the ruins of its ancient laxity.

These institutions were naturally in a most varied state of adjustment to the new conditions. Not all were progressive. Harvard reminded him of what he had read of the ancient lamaseries of Tibet. There was practically no paper to be got for note-taking or exercises, and the teaching was entirely oral and the learning done by heart. The libraries were closely guarded against depredations, and the more important books were only to be inspected in locked glass cases. A page was turned daily. The teachers varied in prestige with the number of their following. They either sat in class-rooms and under trees and lectured, or they went for long walks discoursing as they went to a rabble of disciples. They varied not only in prestige but physical well-being, because it was the role of these students to cultivate food for their masters and themselves in the college grounds and produce woven clothing and sandals in the Technical and Art Buildings. Some literary production was going on. The more gifted students wrote verses on slates, and these, if they were sufficiently esteemed by the teaching staff, were written up on the walls or ceilings of the building. The atmosphere was one of archaic simplicity and studied leisure. The visitor was entertained by President Eliot, a tall distinguished-looking elderly man in a toga, who had inherited his position from his grandfather. There was a large open fire in the room, which was lit by tallow candles which two under-graduates continually snuffed. The President talked very beautifully over his simple soup, his choice Maryland claret and a cornucopia of fruit and nuts, and the conversation went on until a late hour.

The impression of Nicholson, the visitor, was one of an elegant impracticability. The simple graciousness of the life he could not deny, but it seemed to him also profoundly futile. He seems, however, to have concealed this opinion from the President and allowed him to talk unchallenged of how Harvard had achieved the ultimate purification and refinement of the Anglican culture, the blend of classicism and refined Christianity, with a graceful monarchist devotion.

'There is a King here?' asked the visitor.

'Not actually a King,' said the President regretfully. 'We have decided that the Declaration of Independence is inoperative, but we have been unable to locate the legitimate King of England, and so there has been no personal confirmation of our attitude. But we have an attitude of loyalty. We cherish that.'

The chief subjects of study seem to have been the Ptolemaic cosmogony, the Homeric poems, the authentic plays of Shakespeare and theology. The scanty leisure of the students did not admit of a very high standard of gymnastics, and they seem to have abandoned those typical American college sports of baseball and football altogether. The President spoke of these games as 'late innovations'. One chief out-of-door employment seems to have been wood-cutting and felling.

This glimpse of graceful and idealistic pedantry is interesting because it left so few traces for later times. It depended very much on the personality of the President himself, and after his death at an advanced age, and the hard winters of 1981 and 1983, this ancient foundation seems to have been completely deserted and allowed to fall into ruin.

Both Columbia University and Chicago were in violent contrast to Harvard. Here the influence of the new De Windt school of thought was very evident, and the traditions of Dewey, Robinson, the Elmer Barnes couple, Raymond Fosdick, Beard and their associates were still alive. Although New York City was already abandoned and dangerous because of the instability of its huge skyscrapers, there was still considerable trading on the Hudson River and some manufacturing activity. The great iron bridges were still quite practicable for pack horses and mules, and, affording as they did a North and South line of communication of quite primary value, they gave the place a unique commerical importance. The industrial workers there and in Chicago were in close contact with the college staffs and they were working with very great energy at what they called 'The General Problem of Recovery'.

'They don't,' writes Nicholson, 'admit that civilisation has broken down. They talk here just as they did in Washington, of the Hoover Slump. I never met people so confident that somehow and in some fashion things will pick up again. There is nothing like this at home. One night there was a tremendous crash and an earthquake. A huge pile called "Radio City" had collapsed in the night. In the bright keen morning I went out to the Pantheon, and there a crowd of people was watching the clouds of dust that were still rising, and listening to the occasional concussions that marked minor fallings-in. Were they in the least down-hearted? Not at all. "There's a bit more liquidation," said a man near me. "We have to get these things off our hands somehow." '

Nicholson gives a fairly full account of the curricula of both Columbia and Chicago. He is greatly struck by the equipment of the scientific laboratories and the relative importance of experimental work. 'I felt almost as though I was back in 1930,' he says, 'when I visited the Rockefeller chemical laboratory.' But still more was he struck by the advanced state of the sociological work. 'They are producing a sort of lawyers who are not litigators,' he writes. 'I think the new law stuff they are doing here is the most interesting thing about the place. It isn't what my father would have recognised as law at all. It's the physiology and pathology of society and social therapeutics arising therefrom. There are one or two men here, Hooper Hamilton and Rin Kay for instance, whose talk is a liberal education. They won't hear any of the rot we deal out at home about the Sunset of Mankind.'

That was his key observation, so to speak. But it is interesting to note that the reduction of Basic English to practicable use was also being made. Spanish and English were already on their way to become the interchangeable languages they remained throughout all the earlier twenty-first century. The teaching of French had fallen off very greatly, and the old classical studies (Greek and Latin), to judge by his complete silence about them, had been completely abandoned.

Our tourist flew from Chicago to the Ford Aerodrome at Dearborn, saw the ruins of the main factories and the reconstructed settlement, and spent some days with the Technological School there and in the still very imperfectly arranged Museum of American Life. It was startling to see some scores of square miles of closely cultivated land round the open space of the Aerodrome and to learn that an old Ford idea of dividing the time of the staff between agricultural production and mechanical work was still in effective operation. There were associated textile and boot factories in Detroit. There was still an output of some thousand-odd automobiles a year and a 'few hundred' (!) aeroplanes. And there was a small but healthy radio department.

'We keep in touch,' said the Director. 'We don't interfere with people, and we are not interfered with. We are running all that is left of the distance letter post. . . . Yes, Canada and Mexico as well. Nobody bothers us now about the boundaries, and we don't bother. When trade was at its worst we sat tight, cultivated our farms and did experiments.'

The Henry Ford, that 'great original' whose adventure of the Peace Ship has been chosen to mark a turning-point in our history, had long since played out his part, but the Director mentioned in these papers seems to have been his son Edsel, carrying on the initiatives of his finely simple-minded parent.

That the place was able to 'sit tight and carry on' was no

283

empty boast. The visitor from a slovenly world dwells on the 'tidiness' of everything. The Edison workshop was still in the original state as it had been re-erected by Henry Ford; there or in the Museum Nicholson was shown the first phonograph and the first telephone ever made, and the earliest experimental automobiles and aeroplanes.

'It is as recent as that,' he tells us he said. 'In the lifetime of ourselves and our fathers we have seen the beginning, the triumph and the collapse of the greatest civilisation that the world has ever seen. We have spanned the whole history of mechanical mass production.'

'Not a bit of it,' said the Director. 'It's hardly begun.'

There followed a long conversation the gist of which the visitor seems to have written down immediately in dialogue form. Its interest for the student of history lies in the fact that here again we have evidence of the way in which amidst the world-wide collapse into misery, disorder and incoherent peasant life the vitality of the mechanical transport system was manifesting itself. We can put the talk of the Dearborn director side by side with that of the European aviator reported by Titus Cobbett. There is the same realisation of the final death of the old order. 'All that king business and congress business is as dead as mutton,' said the Dearborn director. 'And the banking business is deader.'

'And what is coming?' asked the visitor.

'*That*,' said the director, and pointed to a mounting aeroplane inaudible and almost invisible in the blue.

BOOK THE THIRD

THE WORLD RENASCENCE: THE BIRTH OF THE MODERN STATE

THE WORLD RENASCENCE: THE BIRTH OF THE MODERN STATE

§ 1. *The Plan of the Modern State is Worked Out*

In the preceding chapters the culmination, the dislocation and the collapse of the private capitalist civilisation has been told. It has been a chronicle of disaster, wherein particular miseries, the torment and frustration of thousands of millions, are more than overshadowed by its appalling general aimlessness. We have seen the urge towards unity and order, appearing and being frustrated, reappearing and again being defeated. At last it reappeared—and won. The problem had been solved.

The world was not able to unify before 1950 for a very simple reason: there was no comprehensive plan upon which it could unify; it was able to unify within another half-century because by that time the entire problem had been stated, the conditions of its solution were known, and a social class directly interested in the matter had differentiated out to achieve it. From a vague aspiration the Modern World-State became a definite and so a realisable plan.

It was no great moral impulse turned mankind from its drift towards chaos. It was an intellectual recovery. Essentially what happened was this: social and political science overtook the march of catastrophe.

Obscure but persistent workers in these decades of disaster pieced together the puzzle bit by bit. There is a fantastic disproportion between the scale of the labourers and the immense consequences they released. The psychology of association, group psychology, was a side of social biology that had been disregarded almost entirely before the time of which we are writing. People had still only the vaguest ideas about the origins and working processes of the social structure in and by which they lived. They accepted the most arbitrary and simple explanations of their accumulated net of relationships, and were oblivious even to fundamental changes in that net. Wild hopes, delusions and catastrophes ensued inevitably.

If you had interrogated an ordinary European of the year 1925 about the motives of his political activities and associations and his general social behaviour, he would probably have betrayed a feeling that your enquiry was slightly indelicate, and if you overcame that objection, he would have talked either some nonsense about the family as the nucleus of social organisation, a sort of expansion of brothers and cousins, kith and kin to the monarch, the Sire of the whole system, or he would have gone off in an entirely different direction and treated you to a crude version of Rousseau's Social Contract in which he and the other fellows had combined under agreed upon rules for mutual defence and aid. The betting would have been quite even as to which of these flatly contradictory explanations he would have given.

He would have said nothing about religious ties in 1925, though fifty years earlier he might have based his whole description on the Divine Will. He would have betrayed no lucid apprehension of the part played by the money nexus in gearing relationships; he would have been as unconscious as his Roman predecessor of the primary social importance of properly adjusted money. He would have thought it was just stuff you earned and handed out and got things for, and he might have added rather irrelevantly that it was 'the root of all evil'. He would certainly have referred to the family idea when his patriotism was touched upon, if not before, to justify that tangle of hates, fears and consequent and subordinate loyalties; he would have talked of 'mother country' or 'fatherland'. If he practised any craft or skill, he might not have had his mind organised in

288

relation to his profession or trade union, but there would be no measure between that and his patriotism, either might override the other, and either might give way before some superstitious or sexual complex in his make-up.

Incidentally he would have revealed extensive envy systems and social suspicion and distrust systems, growing up at every weak point like casual fungi. Everything would be flavoured more or less with the chronic endemic everywhere. And all these disconnected associations from which flowed his judgments and impulses he would have regarded as natural—as natural as the shape of his ears; he would have been blankly unconscious that the education of school and circumstances had had anything to do with his accumulation.

On millions of minds equipped in this fragmentary fashion, uninformed or misinformed and with no internal connectedness, the institutions of the world were floating right up to the middle of the twentieth century. Tossing at last, rather than merely floating. Men called themselves individualist or socialist, and they had not the beginnings of an idea how the individual was and might be related to society; they were nationalist and patriotic, and none of them could tell what a nation was. It was only when these institutions began to batter against each other, and leak and heel over, and show every disposition to go down altogether, that even intelligent men began to realise how haphazard, sentimental and insincere were their answers to the all-important questions: 'What holds us together and sustains our co-operations?'

This prevalent superficiality and ignorance about socialising forces was the necessary reflection of a backwardness and want of vigour in academic circles and the intellectual world. The common man, busied about his petty concerns, did not know or think about collective affairs, because at the time there existed no knowledge or ordered thought in an assimilable form to reach down and stimulate his mind. The social body was mentally embryonic from the top downward. That it was possible to demonstrate a complete system of social reactions, and to state the necessary idea of the Modern State in convincing and practically applicable terms, had still to penetrate to the minds not merely of the politicians and statesmen, but of the psychologists, historians and so-called 'economists' of the time.

In 1932 Group Psychology was at about the same level of development as was physical science in the days of the Marquess of Worcester's *Century of Inventions* (1663). It was still in that vague inconclusive phase of 'throwing out' ideas. It was no more capable of producing world order than the physical science of 1663 could have produced an aeroplan or a steam turbine. The ordinary man seeking guidance in the dismay of the Great Slump (see Emil Desaguliers' *Ideas in Chaos and Society Collapse*, 2017) was confronted with a sort of intellectual rummage sale. He had believed that somewhere somebody knew; he discovered that nobody had ever yet bothered to know. A dozen eminent authorities with the utmost mutual civility were giving him every possible and impossible counsel in his difficulties, suavely but flatly contradicting each other. They were able to do so because they were all floating on independent, arbitrary first assumptions without any structural reference to the primary facts of human ecology.

Nevertheless certain primary matters were being rapidly analysed at that time. The general understanding of money, for example, was increasing rapidly. Desaguliers notes about a hundred and eighty names, including the too-little-honoured name of that choleric but interesting amateur, Major C. H. Douglas (*Works* in the Historical Documents, Economic Section B. 178,200), who were engaged in clearing away the conception of a metallic standard as a monetary basis. They were making it plain that the only possible money for a progressive world must keep pace with the continually increasing real wealth of that world. They were getting this into the general consciousness as a matter of primary importance.

But they were proposing the most diverse methods of realising this conception. The 'Douglas Plan' appealed to the general social credit, but was limited by the narrow political outlook of the worthy Major. who could imagine bankers abolished but not boundaries. In America an interesting movement known as 'Technocracy' was attracting attention. Essentially that was a soundly scientific effort to restate economics on a purely physical basis. But it was exploited in a journalistic fashion and presented to a remarkable receptive public as a cut-and-dried scheme for a new social order in which social and economic life was to be treated as an energy system controlled by 'experts'. The explicit repudiation of democratic control by the Technologists at that date is very notable. The unit of energy was to be the basis of a new currency. So every power station became a mint and every waterfall a potential 'goldmine', and the money and the energy in human affairs remained practically in step. Another important school, represented by such economists as Irving Fisher and J. M. Keynes, was winning an increased adherence to the idea of a price index controlling the issue of currency.

It was a phase of disconnected mental fermentation. Many of those who were most lucid about monetary processes were, like Douglas and Keynes, still in blinkers about national and imperial boundaries; they wanted to shut off some existing political systems by all sorts of artificial barriers and restraints from the world at large, in order to develop their peculiar system within its confines. They disregarded the increasing flimsiness of the traditional political structure altogether. They were in too much of a hurry with their particular panacea to trouble about that. And if the money reformers were not as a rule cosmopolitans, the cosmopolitans were equally impatient with the money reformers and blind to the primary importance of money.

A third class of intelligences stressed the urgent necessity for great public enterprise to correct the paradoxical increase of unemployment consequent upon the increase of productivity that had taken the shiftless world by surprise. That was an independent maladjustment. But thinkers of this school were apt to disregard the importance of monetary rectification. As to who was to control the more complicated methods of mutual service proposed, the world money and the world socialism and so forth, there was an even greater diversity of outlook and an even greater conflict of mental limitations. As Desaguliers says in his summary: 'People could not get out of the sinking social vessels in which they found themselves for the simple reason that nothing but the imperfectly assembled phantom of a salvage ship was yet in sight, a large rudderless, powerless promise, so to speak, standing by.'

Only very knowledgeable people could have foretold then how nearly this phase of throwing out bright but disconnected ideas was drawing to its end, and how rapidly the consolidation of social and educational science into an applicable form was to go forward, once it had begun. The rush of correlated social discoveries and inventions to the rescue of mankind, when at last it was fairly started, was even more rapid and remarkable than the release of steam and electrical energy in the nineteenth century. It went on under difficulties. Perhaps it was quickened and purified by those very difficulties.

Gustave De Windt's great work, *Social Nucleation* (1942), was the first exhaustive study of the psychological laws underlying team play and *esprit de corps*, disciplines of criminal gangs, spirit of factory groups, crews, regiments, political parties, churches, professionalisms, aristocracies, patriotisms, class consciousness, organised research and constructive co-operation generally. It did for the first time correlate effectively the increasing understanding of individual psychology, with new educational methods and new concepts of political life. In spite of its unattractive title and a certain wearisomeness in the exposition, his book became a definite backbone for the constructive effort of the new time.

De Windt worked under all the handicap of the intellectual worker in that uncomfortable time. Much of his writing, like that of Marx and Lenin, was done in the British Museum in London, but he was expelled from England during a phase of xenophobia in 1939, and he was not allowed to return from Holland to his 'beloved Bloomsbury' until 1941. He was slightly gassed during the ninth Polish air raid on Berlin, and this no doubt accelerated his death in Bloomsbury, the tuberculous London slum in which his book was completed.

Much has been done since to elaborate and correct the broad generalisations he established. But his name stands with those of Plato, Galileo, Newton, Darwin and Robert Owen as marking a real step forward in the expression and expansion of human ideas. Such men are all in their various dimensions something more than themselves, like stones that have become surveyor's datum marks. After 1950 De Windt's doctrines and formulae spread with great rapidity, in spite of the disturbed state of the world—assisted and enforced indeed by the disturbed state of the world.

Few people read De Windt nowadays, just as few people read Plato or Bacon or Charles Darwin or Adam Smith or Karl Marx, but what he thought has been built into the general outlook of mankind. What he established is now platitude, but in his time very much of what he had to say would still have seemed heresy and fantasy, if it had not been for the patient massiveness, the Darwinesque patience, with which he built up his points.

The most important features of his teaching were, first, that he insisted with an irrefutable rigidity upon the entirely artificial nature of the content of the social side of a human being. Men are born but citizens are made. A child takes to itself what is brought to it. It accepts example, usage, tradition and general ideas. All the forms of its social reactions and most of its emotional interpretations are provided by its education.

'Obviously,' the reader will say. But it is essential to the understanding of history to realise that before De Windt's time this was not obvious. Moral values, bias and prejudice, hatreds and so forth were supposed to come 'by nature'. And consequently the generation about him had grown up in a clotted mass of outworn explanations, metaphors, mytholo-

293

gies and misleading incentives, and the misshapen minds reflected and condoned the misshapen social order. His role in intellectual history is primarily that of a strong arm sweeping a terrible litter of encumbrance aside, and replacing it by a clearly defined structure. He restored again to credibility what Plato had first asserted: that, however difficult, it was possible to begin again at the beginning with uninfected minds. And having cleared his ground in this way he proceeded to build up the imperatives of that sane progressive education and life for mankind which now opens out about us.

He brought home clearly to the general intelligence firstly that the monetary method of relationship was essential to any complex productive society, since it was the only device that could give personal choice and freedom in return for service. It liberated economic relationships. But money was not a thing in itself, it was a means to an end, and its treatment was to be judged entirely by its attainment of that end. It had indeed grown out of a barterable commodity, a thing in itself, silver or gold or the like, but it had ceased to be this, and it was the difficulties in the transition of money from the former to the latter status that he had released those diseases of the economic system which had in succession first destroyed the Roman imperialism and then the European sovereign states. A completely abstract money, a money as abstract and free from association with any material substances as weight or measure, had to be contrived for mankind. Human society could not be saved from chaos without it. It had to be of worldwide validity; its tokens and notes had to be issued to maintain a practically invariable price index, and it had to be protected by the most stringent laws against any form of profit-making manipulation. He demonstrated that not merely forgery, but every form of gambling and speculation had to be made major offences under a criminal code. He showed that usury was unnecessary. He unravelled the old entanglements by which new production had hitherto been saddled with permanent debts for its promotion and experiments. He made profit-making banking, that Old Man of the Sea, get off the back of enterprise. He eliminated every excuse for its profits. Banking was a public function. The distribution of credit was a vital part of government.

The New Banking of the twenty-first century grew up along the lines he established for it. To-day it is our system of public bookkeeping, a part of our state statistical organisation, a clearing-house of obligations and a monetary record of the accumulating surplus of racial energy, which the world-controls apportion to our ever expanding enterprises. It is entirely public and entirely gratuitous. It is hard to realise that it was ever allowed to be a source of private and secret profit. We register a man's earnings and spending as we register births and deaths. Our money is fundamentally a check on these publicly kept private accounts.

But this desideratum of a sufficiency of invariable money was only a 'foundation need', a quantitative basis for the establishment of vital relationships, or, in De Windt's terminology, for 'social nucleation'. So soon as money was put in order it ceased to be necessary to trouble about money, just as it is needless to think about light and air in a properly lit and ventilated room.

For a couple of centuries before De Windt, the family, which had been the common social cellule throughout the whole agricultural age of mankind, had been losing its distinctness, had been dissolving into larger systems of relationship, more especially in the Northern and Western communities. It had been losing its economic, its mental and its emotional autonomy at the same time. In the nineteenth century this dissolution of the family had gone on very rapidly indeed. The domestication of women, and their concentration upon children and the home, had diminished greatly.

By general sentiment, the instinctive factor in family unification had always been overrated. In effect, that instinctive bond dissolves long before the children are thirteen or fourteen. After that age the binding force of parent to child and vice versa is not instinct, but affection, con-

295

venience, habit and tradition. And that convenience, usage and tradition had dwindled. Put to the test of exterior attractions, family solidarity had weakened not only in the West, but also, as Asia had been Westernised, in Turkey, India, China and Japan. This was so essentially, even more than apparently. The family home remained generally as a meeting-place and common domicile for parents and children, but it ceased to be a vehicle of tradition, it ceased to train and discipline. It ceased to do so for the simple reason that these functions were now discharged with far more emphasis, if with less intensity, by exterior agencies. Citizens were begotten in the home but they were no longer *made* in the home.

De Windt drew a vivid contrast between the home life of a Central European family in the late eighteenth century, with the father reading the Bible to his assembled offspring, conducting daily prayer, watching over, reproving and chastising his sons and daughters up to the age of sixteen or seventeen and even controlling their marriage, and the loosely associated family structure in the early twentieth century.

This structural dissolution was universally recognised long before the time of De Windt, but it was left for him to emphasise the need for a planned 'renucleation' in the social magma that arose out of this dissolution. The popular school, the experiences and associations of industrialised production, the daily paper and so forth, had knocked the strength out of the mental and moral education of the home and put nothing in its place. The sapping forces had not, in their turn, been converted into 'organic forces'. In default of these, minds were lapsing towards crude and base self-seeking and entirely individualistic aims.

These contemporary emotional suggestions and haphazard ideologies were not good enough, he preached, to make a human being a tolerable social unit. Social tissue was not to be made and co-ordinated on such lines. The stars in their courses were pointing our race towards the organised world community, the Modern State, and if ever that goal was to be attained, if the reorganisation of the species was not to collapse, degenerate and perish by the wayside, then the individual mind throughout the world had to be educated, had to be disciplined and equipped, definitely and sufficiently to this end. That would not come by nature. The social side of the individual had to be oriented deliberately. 'Society is an educational product.'

For the race to get to this Modern State as a whole it had to get there as so many hundreds of millions of human beings, all individually aware of that as the general objective at which their lives aimed. The Modern State could not arrive as an empty form with all humanity left behind it. Every teacher, every writer, every talker, every two friends who talked together constituted a potential nucleus in a renascent social system. These nuclei had to be organised. Their existence had to be realised, and they had to be brought into effective co-operation.

It is hard nowadays to realise that once upon a time such commonplaces as these were not commonplaces, and that in the very days when De Windt was writing, multitudes of well-meaning people were attempting to assemble 'movements, for social reconstruction and world revolution out of the raw, unprepared miscellany of the contemporary crowd. It was with extreme reluctance that impatient reformers turned their minds from impossible *coups d'état* and pronunciamentos strikes against war and booby millennia, to this necessary systematic preliminary renucleation of the world. The immediate task seemed too narrow and intense for them and its objective too high and remote. 'It is no good asking people what they want,' wrote De Windt. 'That is the error of democracy. You have first to think out what they ought to want if society is to be saved. Then you have to tell them what they want and see that they get it.'

And further, he urged, if you cannot start nucleation everywhere, then at least you can start it close at hand. 'Get the nuclei going. Be yourself a nucleus.' From the beginning of life, nuclei have begotten nuclei. The Modern State, which had to be evoked everywhere, could be begun anywhere.

Another point that was new in this time, so far as Western civilisation went, was his insistence upon the greater importance of adolescent education and his denial of the primary right of the parent to shape his offspring according to his fancy. The 'renucleation' of society had to be complete. The 'nuclei' which were ultimately to become the sole educational and disciplinary units of a new-born society would be in the first place, and usually, intensive study circles and associations for moral and physical training. Their social and political activities were to be secondary exercises, subordinated to a primary mental, moral and bodily training. He searched the social disorder about him for favourable conditions for the pioneer nucleations. He looked to factories, laboratories, technical schools, public services, hospital staffs, to banded men and women of all sorts, for the material for his nucleation. He insisted that the impulse to build up a social order was instinctive. Wherever there was social confusion the crude efforts to get together into a new directive order appeared.

He pointed to the Sokols, Nazis, Fascists, Communist Party members, Kuomintang members of his time, as the first primitive intimations of the greater organisation that was coming. They had the spirit of an élite class, although they wasted it more or less upon the loyalties and prejudices of the past. People are not leading these young men, he argued; 'they are taking advantage of the instinctive needs of these young men. Try to realise what it is they are—however blindly—seeking.'

Like St. Paul, the founder of Christianity, speaking to the Athenians—he quotes the passage—he said: 'That Unknown God, whom ignorantly ye worship, him declare I unto you.' He was declaring the as yet unknown Modern State.

Intensively De Windt's teaching was a theory of education; extensively it was the assertion of the Modern State. These were inseparable aspects of the same thing. 'A community is an education in action,' he declared. And with a complete continuity he carried up his scheme of social structure

298

through every variety of productive organisation, control and enterprise. Men were to 'fall in and serve this end'.

Borrowing a word from Ortega Y. Gasset, but going boldly beyond that original thinker, he declared that 'plentitude' of life was now only to be attained by living in relation to the Modern State. All other living was 'waste, discontent and sorrow'. It was becoming impossible to retain self-respect, to be happy within oneself, unless one was 'all in' upon that one sound objective. The old loyalties, to flag, to nation, to class, were outworn and discredited. They had become unreal. They did not call out all that was in a man, because now we saw their limitations. They could no longer keep up the 'happy turgidity' of life. They could not be served 'with a sure and untroubled soul'. They would certainly leave a man in the end 'deflated, collapsed into an aimless self'. In the past men could live and live fully within their patriotisms and their business enterprises, because they knew no better. But now they knew better.

Finally De Windt set himself diametrically against one of the dirtiest concepts of Parliament Democracy, a concept that still had enormous influence in this time, and that was the idea of the 'Opposition'. 'Criticise,' he wrote, 'yes, but do not obstruct.' If a directive organisation is fundamentally bad, he taught, break it and throw it away, but rid your minds altogether of a conception of see-saw and give and take as a proper method in human affairs. The Parliamentry gang Governments, that were then in their last stage of ineptitude, were rotten with the perpetual amendment and weakening of measures, with an endless blocking and barring of projects, with enfeebling bargains and blackmailing concessions. Against every directive body, every party in power, sat another devoting itself to misrepresenting, thwarting, delaying and spoiling, often for no reason or for the flimsiest reasons, merely for the sake of misrepresenting, thwarting, delaying and spoiling, what the governing body was attempting to do, in the hope of degrading affairs to such a pitch of futility as to provoke a change of government that would bring the oposition into power. The opportunities of profit and advancement afforded in such mental atmosphere to a disingenuous careerist were endless.

All this tangle of ideas had to be swept aside. 'About most affairs there can be no two respectable and antagonistic opinions,' said De Windt. 'It is nonsense to pretend there can be. There is one sole right way and there are endless wrong ways of doing things. A government is trying to go the right way or it is criminal. Sabotage must cease. It has always been one of the ugliest vices of advanced movements. It is a fundamental social vice.'

His discussion of the difference between Criticism and Opposition is one of those classics that few people read. It is a pity, because it is a very good specimen of twentieth-century English prose. The right to criticise and the duty of well-wrought criticism are fundamental to modern citizenship. He considered how that right and duty had been ignored by the shallow mentality of Italian Fascism and how fatally they had been entangled with the suppression of malignancy in Russia. He analysed the reckless irresponsibility of censorship in the Western communities. There was no law anywhere to restrain conspiracies, on the part of religious, political or business bodies, for the suppression of publications. His warnings against the suppression of opinion were not so immediately effective as his general revolutionary project. Many people did not realise what he was driving at. In practice the conflict of world order with the opposition spirit, during the struggle to maintain the Air Dictatorship, was to lapse again and again into the suppression of honest criticism. In practice it was found that criticism and suggestion passed by insensible degrees into incitement and insurrectionary propaganda.

This clear-cut revolutionary scheme of De Windt's was vividly new and tonic to the energetic young men of the middle twentieth century. We summarise here its main constructive conceptions in spite of its present platitudinousness. It is unnecessary to tell in any detail his far-sighted schemes to link his nuclei into a world propaganda, because by insensible degrees that organisation has grown into the education system of our world to-day. This history and indeed every text-book in use in the world could well be dedicated to him. And his complex and very detailed anticipations of the process of a world revolution need not detain us here (his Book V, *The New World in the Body of the Old*, contains most of this), because we can now tell of that vast reconstruction itself.

In some respects he was remarkably prescient, in others he estimated human reactions inaccurately and even incorrectly. The reconstruction of human affairs involved some very rough work from which he would have recoiled. None the less he put all the main structural factors in the establishment of the Modern State so plainly and convincingly before his fellow-men that soon thousands and presently millions were living for that vision, were bringing it out of thought into reality. He made it seem so like destiny that it became destiny.

For some years his views spread very slowly. An increasing number of people knew about them, but at first very few made serious efforts to realise them. One man after another would say, 'But this is right!' and then, 'But this is impossible!' De Windt was dead before his school of thought became a power in the world. Like Karl Marx, he was never to know of the harvest he had sown.

In our description of the failure of the League of Nations we have noted how foredoomed that experiment was, because nowhere among either the influential men of the time nor among the masses was there any sense of the necessity and the necessary form of a new world order. The statesmen, diplomatists and politicians of the time impress us as almost incredibly blind to things that are as plain as daylight to us now, and it is hard for us to believe that the blindness was not wilful. It was not. They could not see it. We read their speeches at conference after conference until their voices die away at last in the rising tide of disaster, and we almost cry out as we read: 'You idiots! Wasn't world control there just under your noses? And was anything else but disaster possible?'

The answer is that it was not precisely under their noses. Slowly, laboriously, with perpetual repetitions and slight variations, the Obvious had to be got into and spread and diffused in the human mind. It is De Windt's peculiar claim to human gratitude, not that he discovered anything fresh, but that he so built up and fortified the Obvious that not the most subtle and disingenuous mind, nor the biggest fool who ever sentimentalised and spouted, could escape honestly from its inexorable imperatives.

§ 2. Thought and Action: the New Model of Revolution

It is a wholesome check upon individual pride that no single man and indeed no single type of man is able both to conceive and carry through the simplest of our social operations. Even the man who cultivates the earth and grows food cannot make the productive implements he uses or select the seeds and plants that yield him increase. Defoe's queer story of Robinson Crusoe is an impossibly hopeful estimate of what a single man, with only a little flotsam and jetsam from the outer world, and in unusually benign climatic conditions, could on a desert island contrive to do for his own comfort and security. Still more does this interdependence of men and different types apply to the complex processes that now, in this Age of Maximum Insecurity, were demanded, if the new generation was to escape from the economic and institutional wreckage amidst which it found itself, and create the social order in which we live to-day.

First came the intellectuals, men living aloof from responsibility, men often devoid of the qualities of leadership and practical organisation. Like De Windt they planned everything and achieved no more than a plan. Such men are primarily necessary in the human adventure, because they build up a sound diagnosis of events; they reveal more and more clearly and imperatively the course that lies before the race and in that task their lives are spent and justified. Then it is that the intelligent executive type, capable of concentration upon a complex idea once it is grasped, and resisting discursiveness as a drag on efficiency, comes into action. Their imaginative limitation is a necessary virtue for the task they have to do. No man can administer a province successfully if he is always wandering beyond its frontiers. The rather unimaginative forcible type is the necessary executive of a revolution, and the benefit of a revolution is entirely dependent upon the soundness of the ideology with which he has been loaded.

Because of this necessity for complementary types of revolutionary, history does not produce any modern equivalents to the legendary figures of Solon, Moses or Confucius in its story of the coming of the Modern State. De Windt was not so much a creator as a summariser, a concentrator, a lens that gathered to a burning focus the accumulating mental illumination of his day.

The light of understanding that lit the fires of this last revolution came from no single brain. It came from ten thousand active and devoted minds, acting and reacting upon one another, without order or precedence; it was like the growth of physical and biological science that preceded it, something that happened as a whole, something that happened not in any single consciousness but in the consciousness of the race.

We have already noted how far back the first germination of the World-State idea can be traced; we have shown how the forces of economic life drove towards it in the nineteenth century. We have displayed it working as a quasi-instinctive aspiration in the brains of Henry Ford and

303

Woodrow Wilson. With De Windt's *Social Nucleation* we see it made concrete, with all its essential structures projected and all its necessary conditions laid down, a practicable proposal. The World-State has ceased to be a cloudy aspiration and it has become a plan. Forceful men could adopt it.

A distinct change in the quality of those who were promoting the movement for the Modern State became very evident even before the War Cycle of the Forties. It was now sufficiently 'thought out' for men of resolute character to incorporate it in their personal lives. It was passing over from the reflective to the energetic types. Its earliest propagandists had been largely reflective and practically ineffective individuals; a miscellany of pacificists whose dread and detestation of war was overwhelming and who had the intelligence to realise that war can only be avoided by establishing a World Pax; a number of writers, 'pure' scientific workers, young sociologists, economists and the like and 'intellectuals' from the working class movement. Now a multitude of engineers, architects, skilled foremen and industrial organisers, technicians of all sorts, business men and captains of industry, were also beginning to 'talk Modern State' and put in an increasing proportion of their time and attention to its advocacy.

The transition is easily explicable. The increasing social disorder was driving men of the vigorous practical type out of satisfactory employment. During the First Age of Prosperity, and during the false recovery after the World War, such men had been able to find ample work agreeable to their temperaments in the immense industrial developments of the time. They had organised great businesses, vast production; they had exploited the incessant stream of inventions; they had opened up the natural resources of hitherto backward regions. They had carried production far beyond the consuming power of human society. So long as all this enterprise could go on, it did not seem necessary to them to trouble about the political and monetary methods of their world. Now and then some of them showed a cer-

304

tain restiveness at the banking network; our typical original-minded industrial Henry Ford, for instance, had two vigorous tussles with the bankers during his career; but generally the phenomena of political and financial strangulation only began to compel their serious attention after the great Hoover Slump (the Thirty Year Slump) was well under way.

Then they began to think, talk and write about the social order with the energy or men accustomed to handle large affairs and work for immediate tangible results. The vast experiment of Soviet Russia aroused their technical jealousy and a sort of envious impatience both at its opportunities and its incapacities. And the young men coming on from the abundant technical schools of the time, stirred by the books and talk and omnipresent hopes and memories of the immediate past, and looking for adventure and achievement in material enterprise, realised very rapidly that the lights of opportunity upon their paths were being turned down in a manner at once mysterious and exasperating.

The revolutionary movement in the nineteenth century had seemed to such men a tiresomeness of slacking workers, aided and abetted by critics like Ruskin, artists like William Morris, playwrights like Bernard Shaw and suchlike impracticable and unconvincing people. It was associated in their minds with sham Gothic, yellow-green draperies, long hair, anti-vivisection and vegetarianism. There was scarcely a man of scientific or technical eminence on the revolutionary side before 1900. But by the third decade of the twentieth century two-thirds of the technicians, scientific workers and able business organisers were talking active revolution. It was no longer to be class insurrection of hands; it was to be a revolt of the competent. Their minds were feeling round for ideas. They found in such books as De Windt's exactly what they wanted. They began to set about the evocation of the Modern World-State in no uncertain fashion.

A revolution in revolutionary ideas had occurred. The

protean spirit of Revolution had cut its hair, put on blue overalls, made blue prints for itself, created a New Model and settled down to work in a systematic fashion.

§ 3. *The Technical Revolutionary*

The existence of this large number of scientific and technical workers in the Western communities and their rapid and lively apprehension of the breakdown about them is one of the profoundest differences between the second and the first Decline and Fall.

We find no real equivalent at all to them in the Roman story. There were great numbers of artisans without any science, steeped in tradition; and quite out of touch with these artisans there were a few small groups of ineffective philosophers whose speculations were finally swamped by the synthesis of Christianity. Artisan and philosopher were in different worlds. The philosopher had left it on record that he despised the artisan. Probably the artisan despised the philosopher in equal measure so far as he knew about him; but he has not left it on record. Neither artisan nor philosopher seems to have had any awareness of the broad social forces that were destroying the common security in which he went about his affairs, and turning the Empire into a battling ground for barbarian adventurers.

It is doubtful if at any time the imperial court or the imperial civil service had any real conception of any sustained decline. Nineteenth- and twentieth-century historians, as Oglivy and Freud point out in their *Roman History* (2003 and revised by Pan Chow Liang 2047), were all too apt to imagine an up-to-date intelligence for such emperors as

306

Julius Caesar, Octavius, Marcus Aurelius or Domitian. They represented them as scheming and planning on almost modern lines. But there is no proof of any such awareness in the Latin record. One large element in that old Roman world that would surely have displayed some sense of the needs of the time, if anywhere there had been that sense, was the universally present building industry. It did hold on in a way throughout the decline and fall, but consciously it did nothing politically.

Students are still working out the preservation and continuation of the art and mystery of the masons into the Middle Ages. There was a great loss of knowledge but also a real survival. The medieval free-masons who built those flimsy but often quite beautiful Gothic cathedrals it is now such a task to conserve carried on a tradition that had never really broken with that of the pyramid-builders. But they had no sense of politics. They had a tradition of protective guild association similar to the Trade Unions of the Capitalist age, they interfered in local affairs in order to make jobs for themselves, but there is no sign that at any time they concerned themselves with the order and stability of the community as a whole. Their horizons were below that level of intelligence.

Now the skilled and directive men of the collapsing order of the twentieth century were of an altogether livelier quality. Their training was not traditional but progressive, far more progressive than that of any other class. They were inured to fundamental changes in scope, method and material. They ceased to be acquiescent in the political and financial life about them directly they found their activities seriously impeded. Simultaneously with the outbreak of that very expressive and significant word 'Technocracy' in the world's Press (1932–33) we find, for instance, a Professor of Engineering, Professor Miles Walker, at a meeting of the British Association for the Advancement of Science, boldly arraigning the whole contemporary order by the standards of engineering efficiency. Everywhere in that decadence, amidst that twilight of social order, engineers, industrialists and professors of physical science were writing and talking constructive policies. They were invading politics. We have already noted the name of Professor Soddy as one of the earlier men of science who ceased to 'mind his own business', and took up business psychology.

At first these technicians and business men were talking at large. They did not immediately set about doing things; they still assumed that the politicians and monetary authorities were specialists with sound and thorough knowledge in their own departments, as capable of invention and adaption as themselves; so that they did no more than clamour for decisive action—not realising that the very conditions under which bankers and politicians lived made them incapable of varying their methods in any fundamental fashion. But this grew plain as disaster followed disaster. A new type had to assume authority if new methods were to be given a fair chance. New methods of government must oust the old. An increasing proportion of the younger men, abandoning all ideas of loyalty to or co-operation with the old administrative institutions, and with an ever clearer consciousness of their objective, set themselves to organise nuclei after the De Windt pattern and to link these up with other nuclei.

The movement spread from workshop to workshop and from laboratory to laboratory with increasing rapidity all over the world. Al Haran estimated that already in 1960 seven-eighths of the aviators were Modern State men, and most of the others he says were 'at least infected with these same ideas'. Such infection went far and deep.

Wherever there was little or no repression the development of this movement to salvage civilisation went on openly. But to begin with it encountered some very serious antagonisms. The military element had always been disposed to regard the man of science and the technician as a gifted sort of inferior. The soldier in his panoply ordered them to do their tricks, and they did their tricks. That was the idea. The behaviour of both types during the World War did much to confirm this assumption of their docility.

The Peace of Versailles came before there was any serious disillusionment. The nineteenth-century scientific man had been a very lopsided man; often he had proved himself a poor conventional snob outside his particular investigations.

'The sciences,' as Simon Azar remarked, 'came before Science'; the scientific outlook was a late result and not a primary cause of the systematic pursuit of knowledge. It was a discovery and not a starting-point. Science taught the men who served it, and the pupil learnt more than the teacher knew. There was and is an incessant conflict in the scientific world between achievement and fresh enquiry, and in the nineteenth and early twentieth centuries it was acute. The older men suspected younger men with broader ideas and hindered their advancement. They wanted them all to work in specialist blinkers. But after the World War the world of pure and applied science found itself obliged to think about things in general, and, as the Great Slump went on without surcease, it thought hard. The technicians, because of their closer approach to business and practical affairs generally, were considerably in advance of the 'pure' scientific investigators in this application of constructive habits of thoughts to political and social organisation.

Even during the Chinese warfare there were intimations that chemists, engineers and doctors might have different ideas from the military. After the Tokio sterilisation fiasco, and still more so after the failure of the eleventh gas offensive upon Wuchang to produce adequate results, the Japanese military authorities began to enquire into the possibility of 'expert sabotage', and their enquiries had a certain repercussion upon the relations of 'scientific' military men to real scientific and technical experts in Europe. There was an attempt to distinguish between experts who were 'loyal' and experts who were 'subversive'. More often than not it was the latter who were the brilliant and inventive men. Uncritical loyalty was found to go with a certain general dullness. The authorities found themselves in a dilemma between men who could not do what was wanted of them and men who would not.

A campaign against pacificist, disturbing and revolutionary ideas had been gathering force during the thirties. It became a confused and tiresome persecution in the later forties. But it was ineffective because it was incoherent. Attempts to weed the staffs and students of technical schools and to reduce the teaching profession to docility failed, because there seemed to be no way of distinguishing what was essential science from what was treasonable thought. The attempt to destroy freedom in one part of a man's brain while leaving other parts to move freely and creatively was doomed to failure from the outset.

§ 4. *Prophets, Pioneers, Fanatics and Murdered Men*

History, especially general history, is prone to deal too much with masses and outlines. We write that 'all Germany' resented an insult, or the 'hopes of Asia' fell. But the living facts of history are changes in thought, emotion and reaction in the minds of thousands of millions of lives.

In the preceding sections we have spoken in general terms of 'concepts of combination' developing; of ideologies dissolving and giving place to other ideologies like clouds that gather and melt and pass across the mental skies of mankind. In the books before those sections we traced the growing awareness of a possible World-State in the thoughts of men throughout two thousand years of slow awakening. But the presentation is incomplete until we have turned our attention, for a chapter at least, from the broad sweep of opinion and the changing determination of the collective will to the texture of individual experiences, the brain storms, the tormented granules, which shaped out these massive structural developments.

One must draw upon the naïve materials of one's own childhood to conceive, however remotely, the states of mind of those rare spirits who looked first towards human brotherhood. One must consider the life of some animal, one's dog, one's cheetah or one's pony, to realise the bounded, definite existence of a human being in the early civilisations. The human life then was just as set in its surroundings as any animal's. There was the town, the river, the cultivations, the distant hills, the temple, near friends and strange distant enemies constituting a complete and satisfying *all*. The gods were credible and responsible, taking all ultimate responsibility off your shoulders; the animals had souls like yourself, as understandable as yourself, and the darkness and shadows were haunted by spirits. In that sort of setting innumerable generations lived and loved and hated and died. Everything was made familiar and understandable by the trick of personification. You brought the stranger into your family; you made it a member of your group. Earth was a mother and the sun a great father of glory marching across the sky.

It is a marvellous intricate history to trace how the human mind began to doubt, to pry and question, to penetrate the curtains of assurance and fancied security that enclosed it. Perhaps it was rather torn out of its confidence than that it fretted its way out by any urgency of its own.

The Hebrew Bible, which Christianity preserved for us, is a precious record of uneasy souls amidst the limited conditions of these ages before mechanism or travel or logical analysis. It tells how man came out of the Eden of unquestioning acceptance and found perplexity. It gives us intimate glimpses of states of mind that were typical of what went on in hundreds of thousands of struggling brains. They were beginning to note thorns and weeds, toil and the insecurity of life. They made great efforts to explain their growing sense that all was not right with the world. They had to dramatise the story. They had as yet only 'personification' as a means of apprehending relations and causes. They had no way of getting hold of a general idea except by imagining it as a person. Strange thoughts frightened them. They seemed exterior to them. They dared not even say, 'I think'; they had to say, 'I heard a voice', or the 'Word of the Lord came to me'. Enormous effort therefore was needed to pass from the thought of a patriarchal tribal God to a mightier over-riding God. Men did not unite communities; they identified their Gods. Monotheism was the first form of the World-State in men's minds.

What a desperate deed it was for some inwardly terrified man to lift up his voice against the local elders and the local idol, proclaiming, 'There is no God but God'! The reactions of his fellows, living still within the framework of accepted beliefs, to this attempt to break out to wide relations, were scorn, amusement, irritation, dislike or horror and super-stitious fear. We have the story of Mohammed recorded, and of his fight with the gods of Mecca, but that was a late and sophisticated instance of something that happened in in-numerable times and places; the challenge of the man 'inspired' by his new idea to the social mental nest out of which he was breaking.

Men who saw the light and spoke were only one species of a larger genus of human beings whose minds worked differently from the common man's or were simply more feverishly active. The others were eccentrics or downright madmen. One sort was hardly to be told from another, for both were sayers of incredible things.

The beginning of written record in the millennium before Christ shows a long tradition already established for the treatment of these odd, disturbing exceptions. So far as we can peer into the past we find the tranquillity of the every-day community broken by these troubled troublesome in-dividuals who went about, living queerly, saying unusual and disconcerting things, inciting people to behave strangely, threatening divine anger, foreboding evils. There ᵃ a disposition to buy them off with a sort of reverence—
ᵃᵃregard. Inferior and unhappy people might find an

312

interest and excitement in their strange announcements and suggestions. But rulers did not like them, comfortable people disliked and feared them. They irritated, they terrified contented people. They seemed perverse, and many of them plainly were perverse. If they went too far mankind turned on them and they were ill-treated and mobbed and ridiculed; they were cast into prisons; beaten and killed.

The ones that mattered most seemed always, by our present standards, to have had something to say that was at once profoundly important and yet not quite true or not quite truly said. Disciples, sometimes in great multitude, respond to their enigmatical utterances. When they died or were killed men were left asking, 'What exactly did he say? What exactly did he mean?' The inspired words became very readily riddles for interpreters and matter for pedantry. They were phrased and rephrased, applied and misapplied, tried out in every possible and impossible way.

Nowadays we find a common quality in all these madmen, prophets, teachers and disturbers of the mental peace. The species was learning to talk and use language. The race was, as it were, trying to think something out; was attempting to say something new and enlarging to itself. It was doing this against great resistance. Its intellectual enterprise was playing against its instinctive fear of novelty. Some of these teachers died terribly, were flayed or burnt or tortured to death. One hung on a cross and died of physical weakness some hours before the two felons who were his hardier fellow sufferers, leaving a teaching compounded of such sweet and fine ideas of conduct, such mystical incomprehensibleness, such misleading inconsistency, that it remained a moral stimulus and an intellectual perplexity, a jungle for heresies and discoveries, for millions of souls for two millennia.

Vainly does one try nowadays to put ourself into the mind of the prophet led to execution. We know the value of what he did, it is true, but what did he think he was doing? The secret of such personifying, urgently seeking brains seems hidden from us now for ever.

313

In the busier and more prosperous social phases of history such disturbers are less evident; in times of change, and especially when there was also a release of social energy, when conflicting traditions ground and wore upon each other, these troubled and troublesome minds seemed to have multiplied. The days of the vast unstable Roman imperialism abounded in efforts to say something new and profound about life. Everywhere there were new worships, because a worship still seemed the only form in which a new idea and way of life could be conveyed from mind to mind. Everywhere the puzzled sprawling human race was trying to say something, some magic word to resolve its perplexities and guide it to peace.

With the Renascence of learning and the onset of organised science the actual number and the actual proportion of enquiring and innovating minds increased greatly. The effort of the racial mind to master the conditions of its being was renewed on a multitudinous scale. But now the disturbers of equanimity no longer appear as wild-eyed prophets; they no longer claim that the Word of the Lord is upon them. Abstract and logical thought has pervaded the mind of the race and such personification is no longer needed. They do not denounce the old gods; they analyse them. Moreover, now that we approach modern times and deal with more and more abundantly recorded events, we begin to realise with a living understanding and sympathy what was going on in the minds of the innovators and to feel in touch with the immeasurable heroisms and innumerable tragedies of those later pioneers, those rebels, critics, revolutionaries who were thrusting, more or less intelligently, against the acceptances and inertias amidst which they lived, towards a saner, more comprehensive and more clearly apprehended racial idea.

So far no completely masterly digest has been made of the millions of biographies and tons of other material that tell of the mental seething of the world from the seventh century of the Christian Era onward. If the old-prophets are too rare and remote for our under-

314

standing, the modern revolutionaries are almost too close and abundant for us to stand back and see them clearly. Vast studies have been organised of various portions of the field; Roger Cuddington and his associates' *Studies of Protestant Thought in Holland, the Rhineland, Switzerland and Britain from the Seventeenth to the Nineteenth Century* give, for instance, a picture of one wide area and period, in which the fermentation arose first in a religious form and owed much to the clash of Jew and Gentile; while Margrim's *Early Forms of Anarchism and Socialism* is a very successful attempt to realise the ideas and personalities from which the modern criticism of rule and property derived. With the help of such works as these, and with some luck among the biographies, we do contrive at last to get down close to an imaginative participation in those individual reactions which in the aggregate remade the human community in the form we know to-day.

Every one of these personal stories, if it were told completely, would have to begin with a child, taking the world for granted, believing its home, its daddy and mummy to be right and eternal. It confronted a fixed and established world with no standard of comparison in past or future. It was told its place in life and what it had to do. Bad luck, discomfort, some shock or some innate unrest was needed to put a note of interrogation against these certainties. Then for those whom destiny had marked for disturbance comes the suspicion: 'This that they have told me isn't true.' Still more disturbing came the possibility: 'This that they do and want me to do isn't right.' And then with a widening reference: 'Things could be better than this.' So the infected individual drifted out of easy vulgar living with his fellows, out of a natural animal-like acceptance of the established thing, to join the fermenting and increasing minority of troubled minds that made trouble.

He began talking to his fellows or he made notes in secret of his opinions. He asked awkward questions. He attempted little comments and ironies. We could conjure up hundreds of thousands of pictures of such doubters beginning to air their opinions in the eighteenth-century world, in the little workshops of the time, in shabby, needy homes, in market-places, in village inns, daring to say something, hardly daring to say anything, unable often to join up the vague objections they were making into any orderly criticism. But in the brown libraries and studies of the period other men were sitting, poring over books, writing with something furtive in their manner, while the pride of contemporary life brayed and trumpeted along the roadway outside. 'What is being told to the people is not true. Things could be better than this.' Men ventured on strange suggestions in university classes; brought out startlingly unorthodox theses.

The infectious interrogations spread. Constituted author-ity got wind of these questionings and itself came question-ing in search of heresy and sedition, with rack and thumb-screw. When we read the books and pamphlets of that awakening phase, writings which seem amidst profuse apologies to half say next to nothing, we get the measure of the reasonable timidities of the time. Men might pay in sweating agony and death for that next-to-nothing they had said.

At first they raised not so much the substance as the form of an interrogation. In the sixteenth century you would have found a number of local accumulations of heresies, but hardly any inkling of the Modern State. Except for some scholar's echo to the *Republic* or *Laws* of Plato, there was no one at all reading and comparing in the field of social and political structure before the seventeenth century. The eighteenth century was, in comparison with its predecessor, an age of voluminous revolutionary thought. Men began calling fundamental ideas and political institutions in ques-tion as they had never been challenged since the onset of Christianity. They went into exile for their innovations; their books were burnt; censorships were established to suppress these new ideas. Still they spread and multiplied. The authoritative claim of aristocracy, the divinity of ~archy, tarnished, dwindled, became ineffective under ~ripping notes of interrogation. Republics appeared and the first embryonic intimations of socialism.

In our account of the first French revolution and the re-volutionary perturbation of the eighteenth century [*No traces of this account are to be found in Raven's papers.*— ED.] we have had to discriminate between the economic and social forces that were forcing political readjustment on the one hand, and the influence of new ideas on the other. We have shown how little these formal changes were planned, and how small a share in these events is to be ascribed to creative intention or mental processes generally. Neverthe-less the questioning was drawing closer to reality and the scope of the planning was spreading. We will not tell again of the profound change in men's ideas about private pro-perty, private freedom and monetary relationship, that began to find expression in the socialist and communist movements of the age. Our concern here is to emphasise the billions of small wrangles that were altering the collective thought, to summon out of the past, for an instant, an elfin clamour of now silenced voices that prepared the soil for revolution, the not-at-all-lucid propagandists at street corners, the speakers in little meeting-houses, in open spaces and during work intermissions; to recall the rustle of queer newspapers that were not quite ordinary newspapers; and the handicapped book publications that were everywhere fighting traditional and instinctive resistances. Everywhere the leaven of the Modern State was working—confusedly.

As we have seen, the new conception of a single world society did not come at one blow, perfect and effective, into the human mind. It was not completed even in outline until the days of De Windt, and before that time it was repre-sented by a necessary confusion of contributory material, incomplete bits of it and illogical and misleading extensions of those bits. It had to begin like that; it had to begin in fragments and rashly. There was always a fierce disposition manifested to apply the new incomplete ideas, headlong and violently. The more the sense of insufficiency gnaws at a man's secret consciousness, the more he is in conflict with an inner as well as an outer antagonist, the more emphatic,

317

dogmatic and final he is apt to be. That disposition to bring the new ideas to the test of reality, the urge to assert by experiment, was the chief source of trouble for these ever increasing multitudes of innovating minds. Constituted authority, established usage, have no quarrel with ideas as such; it is only when these ideas become incitation, when they sought incarnation in act and reality, that conflict began.

So all over the world throughout the nineteenth century men were to be found contriving trouble for authority and devising outrages on usage. The light of world reconstruction lit their souls, but often it filtered through thick veils of misconception and had the colourings of some epidemic hate. They dreamt of insurrections, of seizures of power, of organised terror; in practice their efforts dwindled down too often to stupid little murders—often completely irrelevant murders—to shouting and swarming in the streets, to peltings and window-breaking, to blowing in the front doors of government houses and embassies, to the casting of explosives amidst the harmless spectators at public ceremonies.

Before the French revolution there was not nearly so much of such sporadic violence as afterwards. There were a few assassinations by religious or racial fanatics, but usually the older type of political crime was definitely connected with some conspiracy to change the personnel rather than the nature of a régime. The 'Anarchist' outrages of the nineteenth century, however clumsy, were by comparison social criticisms. Behind them, even though vague, exaggerated and distorted, was the hope of a new world order.

Linked inseparably with all these premature expressions of the desire for a new life were the activities of more extensive revolutionary systems: printing-presses in cellars, furtive distribution of papers, secret meetings, the savage discipline of fear-ruled illegal societies, the going to and fro of emissaries—men often with narrow and ill-assorted minds, but nevertheless men with everything to lose and little to gain or hope for by such activities. After we have

318

allowed for every sort of resentment and bitter impulse in them, the fact remains such men were devotees. They were a necessary ferment for the spread of thought.

That increasing revolutionary ferment, in all its tentative aspects, used to be called The Extreme Left. There had never been anything quite like it in the world before. For the most part these men had broken not only with the political and social order of their time, but with its religious beliefs. Between 1788 and 1965, hundreds of thousands of men and thousands of women, far braver than any Moslem fanatics, sustained by no hope of a future life, no hope of any greeting after the sudden blankness of their untimely deaths, and, so far as we can gather now, not even with a clear vision of the full and ordered social life for which they died, stood up sullenly or with a certain sad exaltation to face the firing party or the halter. A hundred times as many endured exile, prisons, ostracisms, beatings, gross humiliations and the direst poverty for the still dimly apprehended cause of human liberation.

They had not even the assurance of unanimity. They were all convinced that there had to be a better world, but they had not the knowledge, they had not the facilities for free and open discussion, to clear up and work out the inevitable outline of their common need. They formulated their ideas dully and clumsily; they went a certain way to truth and then stopped short; they suspected all other formulae than the ones they themselves had hit upon; they quarrelled endlessly, bitterly, murderously, among themselves. Nearly all sooner or later were infected by hate. Often it happened that two men, each of whom had roughly half the justice of things in him, killed each other, when indeed they needed only to put their prepossessions together to get the full outline of a working reconstruction.

Da Silva has called all those who made the revolutions and revolutionary efforts that occurred between 1788 and 1948 the 'revolutionaries of the half-light'. His studies of the tangled history of the new social concepts that broke through to open popular discussion only after the establishment of the Soviet régime in Russia in 1917 constitute a very brilliant work of elucidation and simplification. It is a history of twilight that ends at dawn. In the twenties and thirties of the twentieth century the ordinary man in the street was discussing, cheaply perhaps, but freely, ideas, possibilities and courses of action that no one would have dared to whisper about, would scarcely have dared to think about, two centuries before. He scarcely knew a single name of the pioneers, fanatics and desperadoes who had won this freedom for his mind.

The nature of the conflict was changing. That was very plain by 1940. Where there had been pioneers, there were now systematic explorers and surveyors; the teeming multitudes of our race were still producing devoted and sacrificial types, but the half-light was now a cloudy daylight and the ordered analyses and plans of such men as De Windt were making understandings and co-operations possible that would have been incredible in the nineteenth century. In the nineteenth century revolution was suspected, forbidden, dark, criminal, desperate and hysterical. In the twentieth century it became candid and sympathetic. The difference was essentially an intellectual one; after a vast period of stormy disputation the revolutionary idea had cleared up. The sun of the Modern State broke through.

Revolution still demanded its martyrs, but martyrdoms were henceforth of a different character. Biographies of revolutionists before the Great War go on by night, amidst a scenery of back streets, cellars, prisons, suspicions and betrayals. Biographies of revolutionists in the final struggle to establish the Modern State go on in full daylight. It is reaction now which has taken to the darkness, to plots, assassinations, and illegal measures. The Modern State propagandist became less and less like an insurgent individual of some alien subject race; he became more and more like a missionary in a savage country, ill-armed or unarmed, and at an immediate disadvantage, but with the remote incalculable prestige of a coming power behind him.

The later death-roll of revolutionaries has fewer and fewer executions in it and an increasing tale of assassinations and deaths in public conflict. A larger and larger proportion of those who died for it were killed either by mobs or in fair and open fighting. And soon the idea of the Modern State had become so pervasive that the battles ceased to be for it or against it; they became, rather, misunderstandings between impatient zealots with a common end. In many conflicts the historian is still perplexed to determine which side, if either, can be counted as fighting for the Modern State.

The analyses of De Windt made immense charities of understanding possible. Creative-minded men, though they hardened against the liar and the cheat, became less and less willing to fight the puerile adherent and the honest fanatic with a tiresome but honestly intended formula. 'There,' they said, 'but for certain misconceptions and resolvable obsessions, go our men,' and set themselves at any risk or loss to the task of conversion. Just as Fascism in its time seized upon the ancient terroristic and blackmailing Mafia in Sicily and partly annexed it, partly changed it and so superseded it, just as the Nazi movement incorporated large chunks of the Communist Party in its efforts to reformulate Germany, so now the Modern State fellowship grappled with the world-wide series of organisations which had superseded democratic institutions nearly everywhere, made every effort to capture the imaginations of their adherents, and showed the most unscrupulous boldness in seizing their direction whenever it could. The Modern State Movement differed from every preceding revolutionary movement in its immense assimilatory power, due to the clearness of the objectives it set before men's minds.

The difference between the revolutionary before the Great War and the revolutionary after that illuminating crisis is closely parallel to the difference between the old alchemist and the modern man of science; the former haunted by demons, goblins and spirits, warped by symbolic obsessions and cabalistic words and numbers, terribly alone with himself, obsessed with religious fears, by fear of the inquisitor, by fear of the ruler above and of the rabble below, perpetually baffled in his attempts to achieve great things, but full of a dangerous unpremeditated knowledge of poisons and mischievous devices; the latter with a mind released by centuries of analysis and simplification, re-assured by the incessant tale of scientific victories, stoically indifferent to popular misrepresentation and equally sure of his universe and himself.

§ 5. *The First Conference at Basra:* 1965

The conference of scientific and technical workers at Basra in 1965 is regarded by historians as a cardinal date in the emergence of the Modern State. It was organised by the Transport Union, which had begun as a loose association of the surviving aeroplane and shipping operators for mutual aid and protection. The ideas formulated at this conference —and even those were still formulated with a certain tentative or tactful incompleteness—had been gathering force and definition for some time. But this conference was the first to draw up a definite plan of the general human outlook and initiate an organisation to carry it out. It marked the transition from thought to action in general affairs.

The idea of using air transport as the combining and directive force for a new synthesis of civilisation was already an old and familiar one. It had been in men's thoughts for at least thirty years. A popular story published in 1933, *Man's Mortality* (by the English romancer Michael Arlen, 1895–1990), for instance, is an amusing fantasy of the world dominated by an air-transport syndicate. It is still a very readable book and interesting in showing the limitations of the educated imagination at that time. The belief in the possibilities of invention is unbounded; air velocities and air fighting are described on a scale that still seems preposterously exaggerated to-day; while on the other hand the inflated stock buying and selling of that period. although it had grown from the merest germ in about a century and a half, is represented as still going on unchanged, and the world's air dictators are gambling dishonestly in stock, and at last 'crash' financially and bolt as though they were just contemporary politicians and mystery men rather than lords of the whole power of the air. In a world of incredible metals, explosives and swiftness, the Stock Exchange, the Bourses, still survive. And there are still Power and Foreign Policies! Nothing could illustrate better the inability of people at that time to realise the economic and political changes that were then actually tumbling upon them. For some obscure reason mental and moral progress and institutional invention seemed absolutely impossible to them.

An interesting little London periodical of the same time, *Essential News*, has recently been reprinted for graduate students of history in the *Students' Reprint Series*. Its fourth issue (February 4th, 1933) contains a summary of contemporary thought about World Air Control. It cites a complete scheme for the 'International' control of aviators, drawn up by a small French group at the suggestion of M. Henri de Jouvenal under the presidency of M. Pierre Denis. A *Union Aéronautique Internationale* is proposed, a cosmopolitan air transport company. Linked with this and controlled by the poor League of Nations, an 'Air Force for Mutual Assistance' was to police the atmosphere. The proposals are so plainly Utopian and impracticable in the face of the sovereign state system as to seem insincere. It was only thirty years later, after the common suicide of the sovereign Powers of Europe, that the assembled technicians at Basra could revive the broad conception of this proposal.

This first conference at Basra was distinguished from its predecessors first by its universality and then by the extremely bold and comprehensive proposals for united action it accepted—proposals which were in effect, if not in form, the project for the modern World-State. It was the first of these gatherings attended by considerable American, Chinese and Japanese contingents, as well as the customary European representatives, and the Russian technicians were present in unprecedented strength and unexpectedly united and independent of the political controllers who accompanied them. New Zealand also had reappeared in the world's affairs. There were even two representatives (two schoolmasters in the Social Psychology section) from Iceland, which for most practical purposes had been cut off from the world for over five years. And one has only to compare the agenda of this and previous assemblies to feel at once the stride forward in the scope and courage of scientific and technical thought that had occurred.

It was a young gathering; the average age is estimated by Amen Rihani as about thirty-three, and five or six women attended in the social and educational branches. A third but very significant feature was the extensive use of that simple and convenient *lingua franca* of the aviators, Basic English. Even the native English-speaking people present did their best to keep their speeches within the limitations of that ingenious idiom.

The master section was still that of General Transport. The body which had organised the gathering was, as has been said already, the Transport Union, originally a purely business body, but the inspiration was that of the Modern State movement, and technicians in medicine, education, agriculture and every main type of industrial production were present. There was much discussion of the upkeep of the world routes and the administrative tasks arising out of that. Nothing could give the student a more vivid sense of the derelict state of the world at that time than the boldness with which this Control took possession of things and pushed its activities into new fields. It was decided, for instance, that all existing aerodromes and landmarks, lights and lighting fields, should be directly under its management.

There was no question of purchase; it took them over. Every aeroplane in the world was to be registered, was to carry a distinctive number, respect the common tariff of charges and pay a registration fee to the Control. Airships and aeroplanes which did not do this were to be treated as pirates, denied the use of aerodromes and filling stations, and 'driven out of the air'. They were to be driven out of the air if necessary by an 'air police' which the Control was to organise. Aerodromes or regions that harboured such recalcitrants were to be boycotted.

These proposals were not accepted without discussion. But there was very little protest against what was certainly, from the older point of view, an illegal usurpation of authority. The political members of the Russian contingent offered the chief resistance, and what other opposition appeared was not from aviators, engineers, chemists, biologists or men of that type, but from sociologists and economists of the less advanced schools. The main objection took the form of a question: 'But what will governments say to this?' So far as the Westerners and Chinese were concerned there was a disposition to disregard the possibility of political intervention. 'Wait till it comes,' they said cheerfully. But Soviet Russia and Soviet Japan were at that time much more rankly political than the rest of the world, and they at least had politicians as well as men of skill and science present at this gathering. A long speech was made by the commissar Vladimir Peshkoff, full of the menace of later trouble. He denounced the projected Control as an insidious attempt to restore a capitalist trust in the world. Its psychology would be bourgeois and capitalist. Moscow would never consent to the passage of controlled machines over the vast territories under Soviet control nor allow the exploitation of the resources of Russia in oil and minerals by any outside organisation.

'And how will Moscow prevent it?' asked Ivan Englehart, a Russian aviator and aeroplane builder, rising as Peshkoff sat down. 'Is it in nationalism of this sort that the Third International is to end?'

By way of reply Peshkoff leant towards him and spat out in Russian, 'Wait until you return to Moscow.'

'I may have to wait a little time,' said Englehart. 'I am a citizen of the world, and I shall go back to Russia in my own time and in my own fashion.'

'This is treason. Wait until Moscow hears of this!'

'And how and when will Moscow hear of this?'

'Very soon.'

Englehart was standing a few yards from Peshkoff. He shook his head with a sceptical smile. He spoke gently, like a man who had long prepared himself for such an occasion.

'You flew here, Tavarish Peshkoff, in my squadron. How do you propose to return?'

Peshkoff rose to his feet, realised the blank want of sympathy in the gathering, spluttered and sat down again in unconcealed dismay.

Englehart waited for a moment or so and then went on, choosing his words with quiet deliberation, to assure the meeting of the adhesion of the Russian technicians to the projected Control. 'That phantom Proletarian of yours fades with all the other empires and kingdoms,' he said to the political delegates, his colleagues. 'We are only giving shape to a new world order that is already born.'

His speech set the key for most of the subsequent debate.

That establishment of the Control was the backbone discussion, but it was no more than the backbone of a plan that covered the whole future organisation of society; upon it was articulated a whole framework of structural proposals. The central section dealt not only with the air network but with the organisation of every type of communication. The lighthouses, lightships, sea marks, channels and harbours of the world were suffering from a decade of economy, a decade of wartime destruction and a decade of chaos and decay. The meteorological services were no longer operative. All this had to be restored. The definite abandonment of every type of railroad was accepted as a matter of course. Railways were buried at Basra for ever. And the restoration and reconstruction of production in a hundred essential industries followed also as a necessary consequence of these primary resolutions.

The more the reader scrutinises the agenda, the more is he impressed by the mildness of the official title of the gathering: 'A Conference on Scientific and Mercantile Communications and Associated Questions'. It is clear that the conveners resolved to press on with their task of world reorganisation as far as they possibly could, without rousing the enfeebled and moribund political organisations of the past to obstruction and interference. The language throughout is that of understatement; the shape of the projects is fearlessly bold. A committee of experts had prepared a very good general survey of the natural resources of the planet, including those of the already suspicious Russia, and the conference set itself unhesitatingly to work out the problems of a resumption of production generally, with an entire disregard of the various proprietary claims that might arise to challenge the realisation of these schemes. There was no provocative discussion of these claims; they were ignored. The Air and Sea Control evidently meant to take effective possession not only of all derelict ports, aerodromes, coalmines, oil wells, power stations and mines, but to bring those in which a certain vitality still lingered into line with its schemes by hook or by crook, by persuasion or pressure. Its confidence in its solidarity with the skilled men working these latter establishments was absolute. Such a solidarity would have been inconceivable thirty years before. Financial adventure had been washed out of the minds of the new generation of technicians altogether. They simply wanted to 'get things going again'. Ideas of personal enrichment were swamped in their universal convictions that their class must now either work together and master the world, or leave it.

So with a modest air of logical necessity, of being driven rather than driving, the Conference spread its planning far beyond the material and mechanism of world intercommunication.

What is this reconstructed transport to carry? How is it

to be fed—and paid for? About the air-ports everywhere were tracts and regions sinking back to that primordial peasant cultivation which had been the basis of all the barbaric civilisations of the past. The question of the expropriation of the peasant and the modernisation of agricultural production was taken up at Basra at the point where Lenin and Stalin had laid it down, defeated. The Conference was lucidly aware that upon the same planet at the same time you cannot have both an aviator and a starveling breeding peasantry, toiling endlessly and for ever in debt. One or other has to go, and the fundamental objective of the Conference was to make the world safe for the former. The disappearance of the latter followed, not as a sought-after end but as a necessary consequence. And the disappearance of as much of the institutions of the past as were interwoven with it.

In the ideas of their relations to each other and to the world as a whole, these Basra technicians were all what the nineteenth century would have called socialistic. They were so fundamentally socialistic that they did not even raise the question of socialism. It is doubtful if the word was ever used there. They took it for granted that this Control that was growing like a limitless polyp in their minds would be the effectual owner and exploiter of all the aeroplanes, routes, industrial townships, factories, mines, cultivations that were falling into place in their Plan. It would have seemed as unnatural to them that a new Ford or a new Rockefeller should arise to own a factory or a mine personally as that anyone should try to steal the ocean or the air. There it was for the common good, and just as much was industrial plant for the common good.

All these men, it must be remembered, almost without exception, were men of the salaried type of mind. They had been born and brought up in a tradition in which money was a secondary matter. From the beginning of the mechanical age, the men of science, the technical experts, the inventors and discoverers, the foremen and managers and organisers, had been essentially of the salariat. Some few had dabbled in finance and grown rich, but they were exceptions. Before the World War indeed these sort of men had been accustomed to accept the acquisitive and gambling types, the powerful rich and owning people, as a necessary evil. Now they were manifestly a totally unnecessary evil, and without the least vindictiveness or animosity plans were made to do without them and prevent their return. The Basra Conference would as soon have considered a return of Foreign Offices or of Kings or Divinities.

But they had to consider—and this was the work of a powerful section upon which the Americans were exceptionally active—how the wealth of the world that they meant to restore had to be distributed for consumption, and how a close-knit world organisation was to be reconciled with personal freedom and particularly with artistic and literary initiatives. This was entitled the Section of Wages, Charges and Supply.

There seems to have been the completest agreement that the only way of combining service with private liberty is by the use of money. Without money there is necessarily a dictation of consumption and a dictation of movement to the worker. He would be given 'what was good for him'. But money generalised the claim of the worker as worker, and the claim of the citizen as shareholder in the commonweal, upon the goods, pleasures, facilities and liberties of life. You take your money and you buy this or that, or go here or there, or do whatever you please. But there were dangers in this invention; twice in history money had failed mankind and a money-linked order had crashed. This time, they thought, mankind had learnt its lesson, and a new money had to be devised that would be, in any large sense, foolproof, sneak-proof and scoundrel-proof. So much lay beneath the intention of the Section of Wages, Charges and Supply.

This section carried the question of money into regions that would have seemed quite outside its scope thirty years before. In the Twenties and Thirties of the century, and indeed into the war troubles of the Forties, there had been a great volume of discussion about money. Men had realised its dangers and set themselves, with the energy born of a sense of crisis, to the analysis of its processes and the invention of new methods that should prevent the gross accumulation of ownership, the mischievous manipulation of credit, the relative impoverishment of the worker and the strangulation of enterprise that had wrecked the second monetary civilisation. Gradually it had been realised that there could be no Theory of Money that was not in fact a complete theory of social organisation. The Conference set itself now to a prepared and simplified task.

The interdependence of monetary theory with the general theory of property and social structure, which had hardly been suspected by their fathers, now universally recognised. There was a considerable contingent of young lawyers present, though it would have amazed the previous generation beyond measure to find them in the ranks of technologists and men of science. They knocked the dust of centuries off the idea of ownership in these very pregnant debates. We have already mentioned the surprise of Nicholson at the new sort of law schools he found in America. At Basra the products of these schools were very much to the fore, together with several older teachers from the London School of Economics, which flourished until the landslide of 1968. These new lawyers, with their fundamentally scientific habits of mind, were amazingly unlike their professional predecessors—those obstinate, cunning and terrible old sinners who played so large a part in the economic strangulation of the United States and the frustration of all the high hopes of their founders. They had completely abandoned the pretence that the business of the law was to protect private property, exact debts and maintain a false appearance of equity between man and man. They knew that justice without equality of status and opportunity can be nothing more than a sham, and their ideas were already completely based on our current conception of law as the regulative system in the network of relationships between

330

the human commonweal and its subordinate corporations and individuals. They were entirely contemptuous of any claims, contracts, rules and precedents that impeded the free expansion of human welfare. Among all the various types that gathered at Basra, these younger lawyers, in close touch with the new economists on the one hand and the group psychologists on the other, and inspired by a political constructiveness of the boldest sort, were certainly the most remarkable.

It is chiefly to them that we owe the firm assertion by the Basra Conference of the principle that in a modern community there can be no individual property in anything but personal belongings and money. This was thrown out as something too obvious to discuss. Houses and lands were henceforth to be held on leases of a not too lengthy period, life tenure being the longest. All other tangible things, they assumed, belonged inalienably to the world commonweal—in the usufruct of which every human being was manifestly a shareholder. And it was these younger lawyers also who did the greater part of that task of disentanglement and simplification, which reduced money to its present and only proper use as a check for consumable goods and services, either paid out to the individual, or, in the case of minors and incapables, to the individual's guardians, either as a part of the racial inheritance or else as wages for work in the common service. The world was to be reborn without usury or monetary speculation.

The monetary methods of the world at that time were in a state of such complete chaos that there was no effective system in working order anywhere to present an immediate resistance to the operation of the new ideas. Every region was running its own, often very arbitrary and primitive system of tokens and checks. But the revival of communications that had made Basra possible was already giving an increasing prestige to what was known as the 'air-dollar'. This was not a metallic coin at all; it was a series of paper notes, which represented distance, weight, bulk and speed. Each note was good for so many kilograms in so much

331

space, for so many kilometres at such a pace. The value of an air-dollar had settled down roughly to a cubic metre weighing ten kilograms and travelling two hundred kilometres an hour.

This was already an energy unit and not a unit of substance, such as the old-world standards had always been. It marked very definitely that the old static conceptions of human life with limited resources were giving place to kinetic ideas of a continually expanding life. The air-dollar was a unit of energy in terms of transport, and its transformation into the energy dollar of our daily life to-day was already sketched out clearly by the Basra experts, although the actual change over was not accomplished until ten years later.

It was the plain, if unformulated, intention of the new Air and Sea Control to gain possession and exploit all the available sources of energy in the world as soon as possible, to frame its human balance sheet, scale its wages and declare its dividends as the common trustee of mankind, but manifestly if the threat of Peshkoff materialised, and the Russian Soviet system (or indeed any other owning group) was able to remain in effective control of its territorial wealth, the energy dollar would afford a just unambiguous medium for whatever trade was necessary between the competing administrations.

The planning of a new political, industrial and monetary world scheme still does not measure the full achievement of this First Basra Conference. There was also a strong and vigorous educational section working in close touch with the technicians and the social psychologists. It made plans not only for the co-ordination of the surviving colleges and technical schools in the world and for the revivification of those that had lapsed, but it set itself definitely to the task of that propaganda of the idea of the Modern State which is the substantial content of our existing fundamental education. This was dealt with by the Section of Training and Advertisment. Basic English was to lay the foundations of a world *lingua franca.* Evidently wherever the influence of the Air and Sea control extended, a new propaganda, a new Press, and new common schools were to extend. There can be little doubt that most of the teachers at Basra already saw quite clearly ahead of them in the world-wide mental and social order in which we live to-day. They knew what they were doing. They went back from this gathering encouraged and confirmed, to give themselves to the terrific and exalting adventure before them, to the evocation day by day, and idea by idea, of a new civilisation amidst the distressful, slovenly and still living wreckage of the old.

When the conference at last dispersed two new realities had appeared in the world, so unobtrusively that it was only slowly that the mass of mankind realised their significance. One was the Central Board, known also as the Air and Sea Control, consolidating the Transport Union, linking with it the other controls and sections and having its permanent offices at Basra; the other was the Police of the Air and Sea Ways, at first a modest organisation with about 3,000 aeroplanes, a handful of seaplanes, a hundred patrol ships, and a personnel of about 25,000 men. It was a small body judged by the standards either of preceding or subsequent times, but at that period it was by far the most powerful armed force in the world.

§ 6. *The Growth of Resistance to the Air and Sea Control*

For nearly ten years the new Air and Sea Control was able to grow and extend its methods and influence without any general conflict. The little breeze between the Russian political control and the technicians did not rise to a storm; instead it died away. Russia was learning wisdom at last and weakening in her resolve to subordinate the modern scientific type of man to his old-fashioned demagogic rival. She had suffered so severely by the miscalculations and convulsive direction of her party chiefs, she was still so ill equipped mechanically, and so poorly provided with aviators, that the old and now mentally weary dictatorship recoiled from a new struggle with these and their associated technical experts. It is to be noted that, in spite of the closest espionage, the creed of the Russian aviators, engineers, and men of science was already the Modern State and not the Dictatorship of the Proletariat, and that her political rulers were beginning to understand this.

So that the new Air and Sea control, sustained by a multitude of nuclei on De Windt's pattern scattered throughout the world, very much as the Bolshevik political organisation had been sustained by the Communist Party, came into existence and spread its ever-growing network about the planet without an immediate struggle. Its revolutionary nature was understood by few people other than its promoters. It grew rapidly. As the Esthonian proverb says: 'One must be born before one's troubles begin.'

The recovery of human prosperity in that decade between 1965 and 1975 was very rapid. It went on side by side with the expansion of the Transport system. By 1970 the Transport Control, the chief of the subsidiaries of the general Air and Sea Control, was running world-wide services that had as many as 25,000 aeroplanes aloft at the same time; it had possessed itself of shipyards on the Tyne, in Belfast, Hamburg and a number of other points, and was building steel cargo ships by the score; it was creating a new system of high roads for which a number of the old main railway tracks were taken over, and it was running water-power stations, substituting our present chemical treatment of carboniferous strata for the terrible hand coalmining of the older economy, and it was working oil. It had developed a subsidiary body, the Supply Control, which was rapidly becoming a vaster organisation than its parent. This was engaged in producing iron and steel, producing or purchasing rubber, metals, cotton, wool and vegetable substances, and restoring the mass production of clothing of all sorts, electrical material, mechanisms and a vast variety of chemicals of which the output had been dormant in some instances for twenty years or more.

Never very clearly cut off from the Supply Control was the Food Control, which began ostensibly with the victualling of the Transport Services, and was soon carrying on a vast barter in food materials, its own surplus supplies and commodities generally throughout the world. In all its ramifications these three bodies were in 1970 employing about two million people, to whom wages were paid in the new modern dollars, energy dollars, good for units in transport, housing and for all the priced commodities handled by the Controls.

The property of all these Controls vested in the Modern State Society, which consisted at this time of about a quarter of a million Fellows, who had to be qualified up to a certain level of technical efficiency, who submitted to the Society disciplines during their years of active participation, and received wages varying by about 200 per cent above or below a mean standard, according to their standing. About a quarter of the other employees were student apprentices aspiring to fellowship, and of these the proportion was increasing. The Society had already developed the organisation it was to retain for a century. The Fellows were divided into faculties for technical purposes; they voted by localised groups upon local issues and they had a general vote for the faculty delegation to the central council of the Society, which had its first seat at Basra contiguous to the central offices of the Three Controls. The relation of the Society to the Controls was not unlike the relation of the Communist Party to the Moscow Government in the early days of the Soviet system; it was a collateral activity of much the same people.

It was the Society itself which at first directed the educational activities of the Modern State Movement. Wherever it had either its own 'nuclei' or found employees of the

Controls, it provided an elementary education of the new pattern, which involved a very clear understanding of the history and aims of the Modern State idea, and wherever it had works and factories and a sufficient supply of students, it founded and equipped science schools and technical schools, which included psychology, medicine, group psychology and administration. Gradually a special section of Training and Education was developed under the Air and Sea Control, and this grew into a separate Educational Control. But it never became as distinct from, and collateral to, the Modern State Fellowship as the rest of the Control organisations. One may figure the whole of this world system as a vast business octopus, with the Air and Sea Control as its head and the other Controls as its tentacles. The account-keeping of this octopus centred at Basra, but a rapid development of subsidiary record and statistical bureaus also occurred. Side by side grew the intelligence and research services. By 1970 the world meteorological service was far in advance of anything that had ever existed before.

But already this restoration of communications and circulation was producing effects far beyond the Fellowship and the power of employment of the associated Controls. The ebb in the vitality of human life had already passed its maximum, and now began a restoration of activity everywhere, a fresh movement in the decaying towns, a new liveliness upon the countryside, a general reawakening of initiative, that were to confront the direction of this fast growing nexus of the Modern State with challenges, difficulties and menaces that grew rapidly to tremendous proportions.

It had been comparatively easy to spread throughout a prostrate and bankrupt world the new system of air and sea communications and trading that had been evolved. That world was too exhausted by war, famine, and pestilence and too impoverished to support extensive and aggressive political organisations. It was altogether another problem, even with the spreading 'nuclei', the new schools and propaganda, to control and assimilate the populations that

336

now, no longer living in want and insecurity, were beginning to feel a fresh strength and a renewed vigour of desire.

Let us review the world situation about 1975. The Transport Control had usurped a monopoly of air and sea transport and was also monopolising the use of its own new great roads. This gave it a practical ownership of the trade in staple products throughout the world. It was turning all the surplus products of its activities back, when its salaries had been paid, into strengthening its grip upon the general economy of mankind. By 1975 the Modern State Society counted just over a million Fellows, and in addition it was employing and training two million candidates, it was simply employing another three million, and it had between seven and eight million youngsters in its new schools. They were all, we may note, not only given a sound training in physical science and biology, but were learning world history and so acquiring a world outlook in the place of the more limited views that had hitherto framed the ordinary political imagination, and they were being taught Basic English as a *lingua franca*. In ten wonderful years the Transport Control had grown far beyond the scale of any of the great Trusts or Controls of the opening years of the century. It had created a world currency. But it was still far from 'owning the earth'. Its own produce did not exceed an eighth of all the outside stuff that it bought and sold. Its own production was mainly fuel, metals and mechanisms. Food it bought, timber, vegetable oils, crude rubber, for example. Several hundred millions of human beings were still self-subsisting, quite out of its scheme, or dealing with it only for a few manufactured articles and mass-produced commodities. And other hundreds of millions were rapidly developing, or rather recovering, a collateral productivity in relation to or in rivalry with its activities.

The chief difficulties before the Modern State Movement arose out of this parallel to its own rapid success. It was calling into existence a mass of exterior prosperity far beyond its immediate power of assimilation. Propagandists and teachers, advisory traders and competent directive

337

agents are not made in a day. The strain upon the supply of ability, loyalty and complete understanding in the movement was already being noted in 1970. In 1972 we hear of a 'scrutiny of qualifications', and new rules were made for the lapsing and expulsion of incompetent unsatisfactory Fellows. The controlling staff had to be enlarged continually, and the supply of men with the necessary character, knowledge of group psychology and understanding of the constructive theory of the movement was limited.

'Let us serve,' said Fedor Galland, who was already becoming a leading spirit upon the World Council, in a speech that was circulated in 1973; 'let us not fall into factions; let us not group ourselves. We cannot afford bickering; we must not thwart and waste each other. We have done no more as yet than make a start. Remember the strangulation of Russia by Stalin. Remember those excellent chapters of De Windt against the spirit of opposition. The struggle for the Modern State has only begun.'

Here we have the clearest indication that growth strains were already apparent within the structure of the still infantile Modern State.

But if the movement found difficulty in sustaining its internal unanimity, there was at least this in its favour, that outside it there was no single world-wide framework in which antagonisms could concentrate. The old international banking system was dead and gone, and the new order issued its new money and was free to create and dominate the financial organisation of things. The old armament-dealing interests were dead and buried. The old nationalist Press systems were dead and already forgotten. It is extraordinary with what rapidity this latter aspect of social life was forgotten, seeing that up to 1940 at any rate it was the primary medium of collective thought and opinion. To-day a copy of a newspaper of any date between 1890 and 1970 is a rare and precious thing, which has to be protected from carbonisation in an air-proof wrapper. The Central Board controlled most of the new paper supplies as well as the now rapidly reviving telegraphic, telephonic and air transmission systems.

The resistances and antagonisms it had to encounter, within its organisation and without, were certainly immense, but they were extremely various; the dangers they developed never came together into one united danger, never rose to a simultaneous maximum and produced a supreme crisis. In this respect or that the advance of the Modern State might be fought to a standstill and held, but it was never put entirely upon the defensive, and since it held trade, money and its ever-spreading efficient common schools in its hands, time was always on its side. 'If not to-day, to-morrow,' said Arden Essenden. 'But better to-day,' said Fedor Galland.

The rapidity with which the Transport Control of 1965 expanded into the Modern State octopus of 1975 accounts for quite another group of difficulties, as well as this initial difficulty of creating a personnel to keep pace with the perpetually elaborated task. This second group of troubles came from the fact that in habit and spirit the old order of things, the old ideas, the old methods, had not had time to die. That old world, blinded and enfeebled by its own errors, had staggered and fallen down in the Thirties and Forties, had lain in a coma in the Fifties. Throughout the Sixties the new world had come into existence. But in the brains of all the men and women alive who were more than forty years old, and in a great majority of those younger, more or less of the old world survived. The revival of human vitality in the Seventies involved not merely a renascence but a restoration. Old things came back to find their habitations still very imperfectly occupied by the new.

Let us consider what form this opposition had taken and what were the more serious survivals of the old order—old 'state of affairs' rather than 'order'—still in active existence about 1975. We shall then have a clue to the history of the next seventy-five years.

The task before the Air and Sea Control was essentially to leaven the whole world to its own pattern. Within its far-flung tentacles it embraced and sought to permeate with its own nature, with the concepts and methods of a commonweal of mutual service, a mass of some thousands and a half million human beings, still carried on by inertias established during thousands of generations. Morowitz calculates that in 1976 about sixty per cent of this mass was living directly upon the seasonal cultivation of the soil, and that two-thirds of this, throughout the temperate zone, was producing mainly for its own consumption and not for trade. He thinks this was a relapse from the state of affairs that obtained about 1910-20. An emancipation from the soil, an abolition of the peasant, had then been in progress for more than a century. Large-scale production, with an abundant use of machines, had so increased the output per head as to liberate (if it can be called liberation) a growing proportion of hands for industrial work or unemployment. But this process had been reversed after 1940. From that date onward there was a drift back of workers to the land, to live incompetently and wretchedly.

The abolition of the self-subsisting peasant had been the conscious objective of Lenin and Stalin in Russia. The cultivator, with increasing ease, was to produce fundamental foodstuffs far beyond his own needs and to receive for his surplus an ever increasing variety of helps, comforts and amenities. Millions of the cultivators in 1910 were cultivating entirely for the market; they produced cotton, hemp, rubber or what not, and were as dependent on the provision shop for their food as any townsman. The social crash had ended all that. In the Famished Fifties, as Morowitz says, everyone was 'scratching for food on his own patch'. In the Sixties the common way of life throughout the world was again immediate production and consumption. Only under the direction and stimulus of the Transport Control did the workers upon the soil begin to recover the confidence and courage needed to produce beasts only for sale and crops only for marketing.

The ambition of the Modern State Fellowship was to become the landlord of the planet and either to mine, afforest, pasture and cultivate directly or to have these tasks performed by responsible tenants, or groups and associations

340

of tenants under its general control. But at the outset it had neither the personnel nor the power to carry out so fundamental a reconstruction of human affairs. The comparative failure of the two Five Year Plans in Russia had been a useful warning against extravagant propositions.

The Modern State did not mean, as the old saying goes, 'to bite off more than it could chew'. Its chief missionaries were its traders. They were more abundant than, and they did not need the same amount of training as, the Modern State schoolmasters and propagandists. They went offering contracts and prices to existing or potential food growers, cotton growers, rubber planters and operable mines; the Control did its best to guarantee sales and prices to any surviving factories, and it trusted to the selective power it had through transport, the new monetary issues, research and technical education to strengthen its grip as time went on and enable it to establish a general order in this worldwide mélange of bankrupt producers and impoverished customers it was restoring to activity.

At first it made no enquiry as to the ownership of goods that were brought to its depots; it paid cash and observed its contracts; it attempted to discriminations between man and man so long as they delivered the goods and traded square. Its nuclei and schools were still propagandist schools in 1975 and quasi-independent of the trading, transport and industrial organisations that endowed them. But this was only the first stage in the Modern State undertaking. The next was to be more difficult.

The student of history must always keep in mind the importance of lifetime periods in social and political change. Between 1935 and 1975 was only forty years. Everywhere old systems of ideas were still dominating men's brains and still being transmitted to the young. Old habits of thought, old values, old patterns of conduct, that had been put aside, as it were, just as jewels and fine clothes and many polite usages had been put aside, during the days of dire need and immediate fear, returned with returning self-respect. During the Famished Fifties the full creative scheme of the Modern State won its way to dominate the imagination of at most a few score thousand minds, whose scientific and technical education had prepared them for it. After that the propaganda had been vigorous, but still, even after the Conference of Basra in 1965, the number of brains that could be reckoned as primarily Modern State makers probably numbered less than a couple of hundred thousand.

The subsequent propaganda was still more swift and urgent, but the new membership was not always of the same thorough quality as the old. The society wanted the services of every man or woman it could incorporate with its Fellowship, but it did not want an inrush of half-prepared adherents, refugees from moral perplexity requiring guidance, ambitious careerists. Every new religion, every church, every organised movement has known this conflict between the desire for expansion and the dread of dilution. On the one hand the Modern State recalled the headlong shallow mass conversions of Christianity and Islam, which had reduced those great faiths to a mere superstitious veneer upon barbarism, and on the other there was the more recent warning of Soviet Russia, morally and intellectually sterilised at last by the eternal espionage, censorship and 'purges' of the G.P.U. The Central brain of the Modern State octopus had to steer its world system or organisation between the extremes of rash receptiveness and black suspicion. It had to go steadfastly and discreetly and yet it had to go swiftly. If, on the one hand, it found presently that its own fellowship was not altogether as free as it had been at first from reactionary weaknesses and traditional sentiments, on the other it found that its leading ideas, by virtue of its material successfulness and of continual statement, were spreading far beyond the limits of its nuclei and its organised teaching.

In the economic realm there appeared, even from the first, intimations of a revival of prosperity, a number of developments that the Society, had it had the necessary resources, would gladly have nipped in the bud. It wanted to deal

342

directly with every primary producer. To-day that is how things are. But so soon as there was a new demand for cotton, for rubber, for pork, wheat, rice and the like, a multitude of obliging intermediaries appeared between the Negro cotton growers in America, the Sudanese cotton growers, the local folk who went into largely abandoned rubber plantations to collect rubber again, the wheat farmers and swineherds and ranchmen, and set themselves to collect and handle the produce for the Control buyers and to distribute Control goods by retail in return.

These people, the former business men of the world, emerged from the slums of decaying towns, from municipal offices, from their own reluctantly cultivated corners of land, from the dingy retreats of predatory bands, from small local trading establishments, full of the sense of trade revival. They organised loans to the peasants, contrived advances of material to them, advised them shrewdly, went officiously to the Control agents for instructions.

This sort of intervention did not stop at individuals, nor with advices and promises. In many parts of the world, in townships and counties and small states, where a Town Council or Workers' Soviet or Mayor or Lord of the Manor was in authority, or where mines or plantations lay abandoned and neglected, the reviving breeze of buying produced a violent desire in the minds of men to set other people working for their profit. They were 'Getting to Work Again' fêtes in America in 1969 to 'stimulate local business'.

By 1975, from Manchuria to Cape Colony and from Vancouver to Java, the old state of affairs—peasants in debt, peasants working to pay rent, peasants bringing in goods in arrears, fishermen, miners, factory and gang workers generally, collectors and hunters, the old immemorial economic life of mankind—was recovering vigour. Debt serfdom was returning everywhere. Rents were rising everywhere. Everywhere the increasing surplus product was being intercepted according to time-honoured patterns. Even slavery was reappearing in thinly disguised forms.

343

It had always been a strong tendency in the old order to utilise the labour of offenders against the law. Forced labour seemed so just and reasonable a punishment that whenever the possibility of using it profitably appeared the authorities set themselves to multiply indictable offences and bring luckless people into unpaid servitude. In the 'classic' age most mines were worked and most galleys propelled by convicts. In the late Middle Ages the Mediterranean shipping waited on the magistrate, and if offenders did not appear in sufficient numbers they had to be sought for. Out of the dimness of the Fifties and Sixties into the returning publicity and activity of this phase of recovery there appeared everywhere local bosses, chiefs, and political gangs inciting and driving people to the production of marketable goods. The Supply Control Report of 1976 on 'Conditions of Labour Supplying Goods to Us' notes the existence of convict labour in North and South America on the West Coast of Africa, in Soviet Russia, Central India, North China, Japan, Java and elsewhere, and states that in many districts it is hardly distinguishable from kidnapping.

'The cheapness of human beings,' runs the Report, 'is once more impeding the efficient organisation of mechanical production. Outside the range of our own services and factories, there are vast and increasing masses of people now living at a standard of life too low and under stresses too urgent for them even to begin to understand the objectives of the Modern State, and, drawing its sustenance from their degradation, there is rising again an intricate tangle of exploiting classes, entrepreneurs, wholesalers, retailers, moneylenders (lending the local coinages and exchanging against our notes), politicians, private and corporation lawyers, investors and landowners, of the most varied types, but all having one common characteristic, that they put profit before service and will resist and drive as hard a bargain as they can with our expanding organisation. These things are returning about as fast as we are growing.'

The Transport Control Report of the same year notes another system of troubles arising. Here the attack on

Modern State development was more direct. 'We are finding the question of wayleaves an increasing difficulty in the extension of our road net for local and heavy traffic. The world, we are told more plainly every day, is not ours to do with as we like. Everywhere claimants are springing up, renascent corporations, local authorities or private individuals who profess ownership of the soil and demand rents or monetary compensation from us. In some cases, where the local authority was of such a character as to afford a reasonable hope of its ultimate absorption by our organisation, we have been able to come to an arrangement by which it has taken over the making and maintenance of the route within the area of its alleged jurisdiction, but in the majority of instances the resistance is much more frankly in the nature of a hold-up. The enquiries of our social psychologists show a widespread desire for simple or disguised bribery on the part of the obstructives, though it has to be admitted that there are many genuine cases of quite disinterested stupidity. Few of them realise clearly that they are demanding bribes or exacting blackmail. They are obsessed by old-fashioned ideas of property; almost anything in existence they imagine can be appropriated as a man's "own", and then he has an absolute right to do what he likes with his "own", deny its use to the commonweal, destroy it, let it at a rack rent, hold it for some exorbitant price.

'Rarely have these obstructives the wholehearted support of their communities behind them—so much has to be conceded to the propaganda of the Modern State and to the general diffusion of our ideas and the spontaneous appearance of fresh and kindred idea systems. We are preparing a schedule of obstructives. They vary in scale from the single tiresome litigious individual with an old-fashioned clutching mind, through a long range of associations, cities and provincial councils, to the resuscitated sovereign governments of the war period. Two royal families have been exhumed from their retirement in the German-speaking part of Europe and more, it is said, are to follow. On various of our routes, notably on the Bordeaux–Black Sea road, the old Chinese claim for "likin" has reappeared. Our lorries have been held up at Ventimiglia, where a "dogana" has been erected by the Fascist government in Rome, a barrier has been put across the track, and payments have been demanded in the name of the King of Italy. There have also been demands for Octroi dues outside some French and Italian towns.

'A legal committee of the Modern State Faculty of Social Psychology is taking up the question of these new impediments to world revival and unification, and it will prepare a plan of action in the course of the next month. This attempt to revive the proprietary strangulation which ended the old order is irritating and may develop into very grave obstruction. The former world system of ownership and administration was in complete liquidation before 1960, and we have no intention of buying it out at anything above scrap rates. We deny absolutely any claim to enhanced values created by our restoration of production and commerce.'

§ 7. *Intellectual Antagonism to the Modern State*

The earliest known histories are dynastic. They are little more than lists of priest-kings and kings and tribes and contributions. With Herodotus history became political. It was only in the eighteenth century (C.E.) that economic processes came into the story, and only after the time of Karl Marx that their essential importance was recognised. Later still, climatic, biological and geographical changes were woven into the historical tapestry. Not until the last hundred years have education, cultural influences and psychological sequences generally been given their proper role in the human drama.

The most difficult thing in our understanding of the past is to realise, even in the most elementary form, the mental states of those men and women, who seem so deceptively like ourselves. They had bodies on exactly the same pattern as ours, if not so well exercised, well nourished and uniformly healthy; they had brains as capable as ours and as complicated. It is only when we compare their conduct with ours that we realise that, judged by their contents and their habits of reaction, those brains might almost have belonged to another species of creature.

We read incredulously about the public burning of religious heretics, of the torture of criminals to enforce confession, of murders and outrages, of the offence of rape, of the hunting and tormenting of animals for 'sport', of men and women paying money for the pleasure of throwing sticks at a tethered cock until it died, and it is hard to resist the persuasion that our ancestors were insane. Most of us, were we suddenly put back into the London of King Henry VIII, would be as frightened, and frightened in the same way, as if we were put into a ward of unattended criminal lunatics. But the brains of these people were no more diseased than ours. Their mental habit systems had been built up on a different framework; and that is the whole difference.

It was perfectly sane men who made the World War, who allowed the private capitalist system to smash itself to fragments in spite of reiterated warnings, and who came near to destroying mankind. If the reader were sent back only for the hundred and seventy years between now and 1933, he would still feel a decided uneasiness about what people might or might not do next. Yet as he fought down his alarm and went about among them he would have found them as completely satisfied of the sanity of their own mental shapes as he was.

Presently he would have found himself trying to adapt himself to those mental shapes. In the end he might come to realise that in his own case also it might be that the

347

things he felt compelled to believe and do, and the things he found impossible to believe and do, though they had served his everyday purposes in his own time fairly well, were no more final in the scheme of things than the ideology that framed the motives and acts of a Roman emperor or a Sumerian slave.

The difficulty in the comparison and understanding of past mental states with our own increases rather than diminishes as we approach the present, because the differences become more subtle and more interwoven with familiar phrases and with values we accept. We cannot keep in mind that meanings are perpetually being expanded or whittled away. We live to-day so saturated in our circumstances, so full of the security, abundance and vitalising activity of our world-commonweal, that it is hard to realise how recently it was possible for minds of the highest intelligence to call the most fundamental conceptions of our present order in question. Even in the middle twentieth century ideas that now seem so natural and necessary to us that we cannot imagine them disputed appeared extravagant, impossible and offensive to brains that were in their essential quality just as good as the best alive to-day.

In the early half of the twentieth century a great majority of educated and intelligent men and women had no faith whatever in the Modern State; they hated it, feared it and opposed it, and it is doubtful whether the balance was redressed until the twenty-first century was well under way. The Modern State was built up by comparatively mediocre men, upon whom the necessary group of ideas happened to strike with compelling force. As H. Levy insisted in his *Universe of Science* as early as 1932 (Historical Documents: General Ideas Series, 192,301), science is a 'social venture' rather than an accumulation of individual triumphs. Both the scientific idea and the idea of the human community were not individual but social products. And the Modern State prevailed because its logic steadily conquered not this man in particular nor that man in particular, but the sense of fitness in the general human intelligence.

Maxwell Brown, in his monumental studies of the growth of the Modern State idea, has made a fairly exhaustive review of the art and literature of the early twentieth century. Except in the writings of a few such sociologists as J. A. Hodson, Harry and Mary Elmer Barnes, James Harvey Robinson, C. A. Beard, Raymond B. Fosdick and a few American and English journalists, and in such alarmist fantasies as Aldous Huxley's *Brave New World*, there is no sense whatever of the immense revolutionary changes that were occurring in the social structure. Bernard Shaw, for example, though classed as a revolutionary writer, never, except in his preposterous *Back to Methuselah*, anticipated. The mass of his work was a witty and destructive commentary upon contemporary things, ending in that petition in bankruptcy, *Too True to be Good*. He had to a supreme degree the opposition mentality of the Irish.

This estrangement of literature from the Modern State Movement became more marked throughout the Nineteen Twenties and Thirties. As reality became urgent, as war and insolvency descended upon social life, literature, art and criticism recoiled into studies and studios and their own bitter and peculiar Bohemia; they became elaborately stylistic and 'rare', or brilliantly or brutally smutty.

This decadence of literature, says Maxwell Brown, was an inevitable expression of the economic decadence of the Thirties and Forties. He draws an illuminating contrast between the type of mind primarily directed towards aestheticism and the type of mind primarily directed towards science. The 'aesthetic producer', he insists, is dominated by acceptance; he writes for response. The scientific worker aims at knowledge and is quite indifferent whether people like or dislike the knowledge he produces. Aesthetic life therefore is conditioned by the times; science conditions the times.

Literature and art are necessarily time-servers, either abjectly so or aggressively and pretentiously so. They reflect real moods or speculate upon possible moods in the community. It is no good writing books that people will not read or painting pictures from which they merely turn away. Psychology in those days had not developed sufficiently to permit of a scientific analysis of creative work, and such criticism as there was, when it was not a simple release of spite, was essentially an effort either to persuade or to browbeat people into buying books and pictures or listening to music of a type fancied by the critic. It was more bitterly partisan and more propagandist than political discussion.

In the expansive phase of the later nineteenth century the general confidence of the prosperous classes was reflected in a large, hopeful, forward-looking complacent literature, and every critic was, so to speak, an uncle, a prosperous uncle, sitting by the fire, but the sense of contraction and advancing dangers that troubled the patrons of art and literature as the twentieth century unfolded threw a defensive quality over the intellectual world, outside the spheres of science and invention. The progressive note was no longer. The reading offered to the people was pervaded by a nagging hostility to new things, by lamentations for imaginary lost loyalties and vanished virtues.

It was not so much that the writers of the time desired civilisation to retrace its steps, as that they wished that no more steps should be taken. They wanted things to stop— oh, they wanted them to stop! The underlying craving was for consolidation and rest before more was lost. There was little coherent system in the objections taken; it was objection at large. Mass production was very generally reprehended; science rarely got a good word; war—with modern weapons—was condemned, though much was to be said for the 'chivalrous' warfare of the past; there were proposals to 'abolish' aeroplanes and close all the laboratories in the world; it was assumed that hygiene, and especially sexual hygiene, 'robbed life of romance'; the decay of good manners since the polished days of Hogarth, Sir Charles Grandison and Tony Lumpkin was deplored, and the practical disappearance of anything that could be called style. As one nineteenth-century American writer lamented, in suitably archaic English:

350

'How life hath cheapened, and how blank
The Worlde is! like a fen
Where long ago unstainêd sank
The starrie gentlemen:
Since Marston Moor and Newbury drank
King Charles his gentlemen.'

That was the dominant note.

Maxwell Brown gives a volume of material, quotations (*Literature Hangs Back*; Historical Documents: General Ideas Series, 311,002) from about four thousand representative books and papers.

As the world emerged again from the sheer desolation of the Famished Fifties and the great pestilence, this purely opposition mentality revived in hundreds of thousands of elderly literate people whose brains had been fitted and turned round in that way for good. It revived because it was all there was to revive in them; and it met with all too ready and natural an acceptance among those endless myriads of cleverish active people who were now trying to get private businesses and private profit systems going before it became too late for ever, between the expanding system of the Transport Control and its collaterals above, and the inarticulate and still needy masses below. They did not realise how much the revival of prosperity was due to the new organisation. It was not in their type of mind to want to account for revivals of prosperity. What they desired to do was to take advantage of the 'turn of luck'. To them from the first the Transport Control appeared as a formidable competitor, harsh in spirit and still harsher in method, which had set itself to prevent smaller brighter folk making hay while the sun shone. They were only too eager to see it as a huge, cheap, nasty, vulgar menace to all the jolly little profits and rewards and assurances that were peeping up again in life. For the loyalty and obedience of servants, it offered them ingenious mechanical arrangements; for the labour of respectful toilers, it suggested indifferent and dangerous power machinery. Are we not wise and virtuous enough in

351

ourselves they asked, that this World Control should come 'tidying us up'?

Manifestly the new order was resolved to 'incorporate' (hateful word!), if it could, all these would-be privileged, would-be irresponsible people. Its face was hard towards them. Its hygienic and educational activities threatened an increasing regulation of their lives. It proposed to rob them of the natural excitements and adventure of gambling and speculation; to deprive them of the legitimate advantages of their foresight and business flair. It threatened them with service; service and ever more service—a role, they insisted, that would be unendurably 'monotonous'. They wanted to be good sometimes and bad sometimes and jump from this to that. A 'soulless uniformity' became the bugbear of these recalcitrant minds.

The workers often resented Modern State methods almost as much as their immediate employers. Men have always been difficult to educate and reluctant to submit themselves to discipline, and there was a curious suggestion of the schoolmaster about these fellows of the Modern State nuclei. Dislike of what was at hand helped to conjure up fears of what might lie beyond. Once freedom of business had gone, what rules and regulations might not presently enmesh the wilful individual under the thumb of this one world employer? For instance, the Modern State centres were talking of a control of population; it was easy to see in that a hideous invasion of the most private moments in life. Weights and measures and money to-day, and wives and parentage to-morrow!

These widely diffused repugnances, fears and antagonisms were enhanced by the difficulties put in the way of aspirants to the Modern State Fellowship and to positions of responsibility in the service of the Controls. Jobs were not for everyone. Rejected candidates to the Fellowship were among the most energetic of Modern State antagonists. By 1970, all over the world, wherever the remains of the old prosperous and educated classes of 'independent' and business people were to be found, appeared associations to

352

combat the activities of the Modern State nuclei. They were Liberty Clubs and Free Trade Associations; there were Leagues and Citizens, Trade Protection Chambers and 'Return to Legality' societies. There were organised religious and patriotic revivals. The Modern State schools were discovered to be immoral, unpatriotic and anti-religious. It was extraordinary how the money-changers hurried to the deserted temples and clamoured for the return of Christ.

Every town and city found someone or other—as often as not it was some elderly lawyer or politician from the old days—keen to revive and protect its privileges. The world heard once more of the rights of people and nations to be free and sovereign within their borders. A hundred different flags fluttered more abundantly every day about the reviving earth in the sacred name of freedom. Even men who were engaged in organising debt-serf cultivation and debt-serf industrialism in the American cotton districts, in the old rubber plantations and in the factories of India, China and South Italy, appeared as generous supporters of and subscribers to the sacred cause of individual liberty.

The behaviour of the inferior masses showed a wide divergence of reactions. The widespread communist propaganda of the War Years and the Famished Fifties had intensified their natural hostility to the profit-seeking bourgeoisie, and there was little chance of their making common cause with them; but the Modern State Society, with the lessons of Russia before it, had no disposition to exacerbate the class war for its own ends. It knew quite clearly that to appeal to the mere insurrectionary impulse of the down-trodden was to invite the specialist demagogue, sustained by his gang and his heelers, his spies and secret police, to take the chair in the council chamber.

De Windt had driven that point well home. 'Creative revolution cannot co-operate with insurrectionary revolution.' There was to be no flattery of ignorance and inferiority as though they were the keys to an instinctive wisdom; no incitement to envy and jealousy against knowledge and ability.

The Modern State meant to abolish toil, and that meant to abolish any toiling class, proletariat, labour mass, serf or slave, whatever it was called, but it had no intention of flattering and using the oafish mental as well as physical limitations it meant to liberate from existence altogether. It took the risk that the forces of reaction would organise strikes and mass resistance against its regulations, its economies of employment, its mechanisation, its movements of population and the like, among the other inevitable difficulties of its task.

So the world-stage was set for the triangular drama of the late twentieth and early twenty-first centuries, in which re-action in a thousand forms, and Modern State organisation in one, struggled against each other to subjugate or assimilate the more or less passive majority of mankind.

We write in outline, and necessarily in an elementary history it is only the primary lines that can be given. But just as when we enlarge our scale of observation, the broad divisions of a map vanish and countries and divisions become hills, valleys, buildings, forests, roads, and at last, when we come to earth, stones, pebbles, blades of grass and flowers, so this rough division of humanity into three intermingled and intensely interacting multitudes was in reality qualified by a thousand million individual complications.

On the whole the content of people's minds was far more intricate then than it is now. That is a principle the student of history must never forget. The intellectual progress of mankind had been a continual disentanglement and simplification leading to increased grasp and power. These closing decades of the Age of Frustration were still, in comparison with our own time, a time of uncertainties, inaccuracies, mixed motives, irrational surprises and bitter late realisations. There was scarcely an unskilled toiler in the world who was really no more than a passive clod in the hands of his exploiters and employers. There was scarcely a re-actionary who did not in some fashion want tidiness and efficiency. And, conversely, there was hardly a Fellow of the Modern State organisation, man or woman, who had not

354

spasms of acute self-seeking and vanity, who could not be doctrinaire, intolerant and vindictive on occasion, who could not be touched by the sentimental and aesthetic values of the old order, and who did not like, love and react to scores of people incurably shaped to the opposition pattern.

The New Fiction of the Eighties and Nineties is enormously preoccupied with this universal battle of ideas and mental habits in people's mind. The simpler novels of the earlier past and the novels of the present day tell of individual character in a set battle between good and bad in a world of undisputed standards; but the novels of those years of social conflict tell of wild confusion between two sorts of good and two sorts of bad and of innate character distorted in a thousand ways. It was a difficult age. Life still has its endless ironies and ambiguities, but they are as nothing to those amidst which the men of 1970 had to steer their courses.

§ 8. *The Second Conference at Basra:* 1978

The second Conference at Basra, though many of its prominent figures had already played leading roles in the earlier gathering in 1965, was very different in scale, scope and spirit from that assembly. It was an older gathering. The average age, says Amen Rihani, was a full ten years higher. Young men were still coming into the Fellowship abundantly, but there had also been accessions—and not always very helpful accessions—of older men who had been radical and revolutionary leaders in the war period. Their frame of experience had shaped them for irresponsible resistance. Their mental disposition was often obstructively

355

critical and insubordinate. Many had had no sort of technical experience. They were disposed to throw an anarchistic flavour over schools and propaganda.

Moreover, the great scheme of the Modern State had now lost something of its first compelling freshness. The 'young men of '65' had had ten years of responsible administrative work. They had been in contact with urgent detail for most of that period. They had had to modify De Windt's generalisations in many particulars, and the large splendour of the whole project no longer had the same dominating power over their minds. They had lost something of the professional *esprit de corps,* the close intimate confidence with each other, with which they had originally embarked upon the great adventure of the Modern State. Many had married women of the older social tradition and formed new systems of gratification and friendship. They had ceased to be enthusiastic young men and they had become men of the world. The consequent loss of a sure touch upon primary issues was particularly evident in the opening sessions.

Moreover, the atmosphere of the 1965 gathering had been purely a Modern State atmosphere. Except for the Russian political representatives, there had been no antagonism at all to its general purposes, and there had been few people in Basra who were not Fellows of the Modern State Society or closely sympathetic with its aims. But now the reviving nationalisms, the resuscitating social and commercial interests of the moribund old-world system, were acutely aware of the immense significance of events at Basra, and there had gathered an assemblage of delegations, reporters, adventurers, friends and camp followers of every description, far exceeding the numbers of the actual Fellows. They crowded the Control rest-houses that clustered about the aerodrome, they invaded the offices and residences of the Controls, they stimulated the private enterprise hotels and restaurants that had recently sprung up among the date palms and rice fields of the environs, to an unprecedented congestion and liveliness, and multitudes of them had to be accommodated in tents and houseboats. A number of thirty-year-old hulls of passenger liners were fitted for their accommodation. Observers were reminded of the tourist period of the First Age of General Prosperity when they saw these uninvited visitors, chaffering with the old-world Bagdad carpet traders and Arab nomads who had also been attracted by the gathering.

There would probably have been a far greater multitude drawn to Basra if the Transport Control had not realised in time the social and hygienic dangers of too great a gathering, and had refused passages and limited bookings. Casual individuals were eliminated as much as possible, and all over the world groups of stranded pilgrims found themselves unable to get farther on the journey.

The most serious of these invaders were the delegations of enquiry sent by the reawakening sovereign governments of the old order. These were half diplomatic, half official-expert, teams, and they came with the declared intention of challenging the activities of the Controls in their several territories. They proposed to legalise and regulate the Controls. They had no formal standing in the Conference; they had invited themselves and given the Conference organisers notice of their coming. 'Better now than later,' said the Modern State officials, and accepted notice and provided accommodation. 'We have to have things out with them,' Williams Kapek wrote to Isabel Garden (*The Kapek Garden Letters*. Historical Documents Series: Basra II, 9,376).

Beside these 'old government' agencies there were a number of parties claiming to represent various new business combines and interests that were setting up in frank competition with the Control monopolies. There were a number of lawyers of the older type, men in sharp contrast and antagonism to the younger legists of the new American school. The contrast of the two types, the older all pomp and dodges and the younger all candour and science, is dwelt upon lengthily by Kapek.

'This Conference is essentially a Conference on Scientific and Mercantile Communications and Associated Questions,

357

similar to that held at Basra in 1965'; so ran a printed notice circulated to all the visitors who could claim any representative status. 'Its discussions are open only to the Fellows of the faculties of the Modern State Society. They are not public discussions and their reports are for the use of Fellows only. But it would be disingenuous to deny that the decisions arrived at may affect the general welfare of mankind profoundly, and since you come to present criticisms, claims and proposals presumably in that interest, the committee or organisation of the Conference will do all it can to facilitate meetings between your group and the faculty or faculties affected. Unfortunately the accommodation for meetings in Basra will be greatly strained by the needs of the actual Conference, and the committee can do little to arrange conferences between the immense variety of accredited bodies that have made an appearance, much less to arrange for their pleasures and comforts during the period of this assembly. The committee regrets that it does not consider the proposal of the committee of Bagdad citizens, claiming to represent the government of Irak, to police this unexpected World Fair with 300 Arab policemen, a camel corps of seventy-nine men and six machine-guns, as a practicable one. It has removed this body painlessly to comfortable quarters in the Island of Ormuz, and the Police of the Air and Sea Ways in its recognisable uniform will be alone responsible for order in the ancient province of Bassorah.'

Explicit details of information bureaus, hospital organisation, supply and available accommodation followed.

It is difficult to see how else the Central Control could have dealt with this unexpectedly abundant eruption of the old system, but the various delegations and commissions professed to be extremely indignant at their reception. They were of such various and unequal value that they found it impossible to fall into any combined scheme of action. Since their theory was that the Controls of the Modern State organisation were nothing more than a sort of world co-operative society, none of them could behave as diplomatic missions to a sovereign power. And consequently they could not regard each other as diplomatic missions. Their powers and authorisations were extremely ill-defined. The bland refusal of the Conference authorities to concede them meeting-places and anything but a very limited use of telephonic, cable and radio communications embarrassed them extremely.

'I met Sir Horatio Porteous, the British Imperial representative, in the street,' writes Williams Kapek. 'He was very eager to get my advice upon a point of etiquette. It seems that we have seized the province of Bassorah from the government of Irak and made prisoners of an alleged local police—those fifty lousy camels and the rest of it I told you about in my last—and that Irak is a mandatory protectorate under Great Britain. He wished to put in a protest somewhere. "But *where*?" said he.

'I adopted a sympathetic tone. "You see," said Sir Horatio, "this Central Control of yours isn't any damned thing at all! If it was a provisional government or something ..."

'I suggested a call on the Air and Sea Police.

' "But they are acting under orders. Who gives the orders? It's all so damned irregular!..." '

There was a flutter of calls between the delegations, some 'serious talks' and much drafting of more or less futile minutes, reports and protests. The weather was exceptionally hot and dry and such space and apparatus as was available for exercise and recreation was monopolised by the more energetic Fellows who were taking part in the Conference proper. It was difficult to keep cool, difficult to keep calm; still more difficult to keep well and hopeful. Some few of the intrusive delegates and commissioners took to drinking hard, but the supply of alcohol was severely limited and the police had turned practically all the professional ministers of pleasure out of the province. On the other hand, the Transport Control, in a mood of friendly indulgence, started a special service of pleasure steamers to Bubiyan, outside the jurisdiction of its police, and there a floating little mushroom town of cafés, restaurants, houses of pleasure, music halls and shows of every sort speedily sprung up to minister to the unofficial overflow of the Conference.

'Bubiyan is draining us quite pleasantly,' wrote Williams Kapek, 'and they say there is quite a boom in entertainment for man and beast in Babylon and Bagdad. The old British institution of the *long week-end* flourishes and Babylon gets more and more Babylonian.'

But there were still plenty of outsiders left in Basra to keep the faculties busy.

Meanwhile the Conference was going on behind closed doors. It was clearly recognised that this curious mélange of agents, delegates and officials from without its organisation was only the first intimation of the confused antagonisms that were gathering against the new order. The policy of expansion and quiet disregard had lasted long enough. The pretence of being a Conference upon communications and associated matters had to be dropped. The time had come for the Modern State to define itself and clear up its relations to the past out of which it had arisen and to all this world of tradition which was now rapping at its doors.

'Before we disperse,' said Arden Essenden, who presided at the first plenary session, 'we must admit some at least of these delegations, hear them and give them answers to take home with them. But first we have to know our mind much more clearly. What are we now and what do we intend to do? The days before us begin a new chapter in human history. It is for us to choose the heading and plan that chapter now.'

§ 9. 'Three Courses of Action'

There was no dominant individual of the De Windt character and quality at the second Basra Conference. There was no prophetic direction of the deliberations. But there was no want of what used to be called 'leadership', and a number of interesting personalities, the politic Hooper Hamilton; the frank, emphatic William Ryan; the intricate Shi-lung-tang; M'bangoi, the East African biologist; Rin Kay, the social psychologist—perhaps the finest mind in the gathering; Mohini L. Tagore; Morowitz, the mystical humanist; and Arden Essenden, the fanatic of action, gave point and definition to the differences of opinion.

They were interesting rather than outstanding men, because the general level of intelligence was a high one. The gathering had a personality of its own, wary, resolved to be well informed and to weigh considerations, but essentially determined. The presence of that miscellany of delegations and commissions which besieged the Conference dramatised the world situation and pressed for decisions. 'I feel like one of those old-world jurymen,' wrote Williams Kapek, 'who used to be locked up together until they returned a verdict. And you cannot imagine how hot and dry Basra can sometimes contrive to be.'

De Windt and his school of writers had planned the framework of a new world and shown to what social elements one had to look for its evocation, but he had given only the most scanty suggestions for getting rid of the body of the old. Already in 1965 the Modern State people had had a fairly distinct vision of our present order. But few of them had anticipated the diffused toughness of the old corpus and its capacity for counter-revolutionary exertion.

361

That had become oppressively evident by 1975.

Reports on the general situation had been very carefully prepared. They dealt with the various centres at which the spirit of opposition was being organised. Most serious of these were those former sovereign governments and legal systems which had seemed effaced, moribund or prostrate during the desolation of the Famished and Fever-stricken Fifties. In 1965 the only government actively antagonistic to the Controls had been the Soviet government in Russia. That antagonism, curiously enough, was not so great as it had been at first. The technicians of the sovietised regions were ousting the politicians; there was now indeed a working co-operation of Russian transport, communications and production with the world system under the Controls, and there seemed a reasonable prospect of ultimate assimilation. There was no objection being made to people nominally Communists who were also Fellows of the Modern State, and many Russian scientific and technical workers were Modern State Fellows and not members of the Communist party at all. The reports discussed hopefully and analytically the possibility of some similar process in America and the Far East. There also the political and legal structures did not present insurmountable obstacles to assimilation. The decline of humbug in America was bringing out the fundamental constructive energy of that great synthesis of Western people. But elsewhere there was increasing evidence that the sovereign state system and the system of private ownership were fundamentally irreconcilable with the new conceptions.

The reports gave information, which was in many particulars new to most of the assembled Fellows, of the very strenuous attempts that were being made by the reviving national governments in Germany, France, Italy and Great Britain to resume the manufacture of aeroplanes and war material. Whether there was a common agreement among them was doubtful, but the intention to put up air forces and organise aerodromes that should be able to ignore the regulations and refuse the service of the Air and

362

Sea Control was quite plain. They were finding great difficulty in securing the services of competent engineers, mechanics and aviators, but the thing was going on. Every student in the technical schools of the Control who failed a test or an examination, or was penalised for misbehaviour or rejected from the Modern State Fellowship, would turn up presently as a national government expert. And the governments were now setting up their own national technical schools and attempting to bring the schools and laboratories of the Control into the 'national' educational organisation. Not only was there a disposition to set up a competing system side by side with the Controls system, but there was a growing tendency to annex the organisations, roads, plant, mines, factories, aerodromes, schools, colleges, laboratories and personnel of the Control that chanced to be within the jurisdiction of the sovereign government concerned. The new Bavarian government, the Windsor Parliament and the government in Rome were all 'arranging to take over' these things within their territories. They were becoming more explicit about it every year. They persisted in regarding the interlocking Controls as a dangerous international Trust.

This was the burthen of the national missions of observation and enquiry which were stewing in the sunshine outside the doors of the Conference—'in a state of tentative menace', as Williams Kapek put it.

The minor delegations representing groups of owners and organised local interests had this much in common with the national missions, that they proposed more or less frankly to resume possession of properties the Controls had taken hold of and revived, or to impose burthensome charges. They varied like the inmates of a zoological garden in scale and power, but they had one quality in common: and obstructive litigiousness.

In the frankness of its privacy behind its closed doors, the Conference sized up these antagonisms and discussed their treatment. 'There are just three lines of treatment possible,' said Ryan brutally. 'We can treat with 'em, bribe 'em or rule 'em. I'm for a straight rule.'

'Or combine those ingredients,' said Hooper Hamilton.

The method of treaty-making and a *modus vivendi* was already in operation in regard to Russia. There indeed it was hard to say whether the Communist Party or the Modern State Movement was in control, so far had assimilation gone. And the new spirit in the old United States was now so 'Modern' that the protests of Washington and of various state governors against the Controls were received hilariously. Aeroplanes from Dearborn circled over the capital and White House and dropped parodies of the President's instructions to dissolve the Air and Food Trust of America. All over that realist continent, indeed, the Controls expanded as a self-owned business with a complete disregard of political formalities. But the European situation was more perplexing.

'Most of these European sovereign governments are no more than scarecrows,' said William Ryan. 'There's no living people behind them any longer. Leastway, no living people that matter. Call their bluff on them and you'll hear no more about them.'

It was Shi-lung-tang who argued against defiance and stated the case for Bribery.

Bribery in his suave exposition, bribery combined with treaties and tact, became a highly moral amelioration of direct action. He asked the Conference to realise how specialised and rare as yet was its new forward-looking habit of mind. When all the work of the propaganda and schools had been accounted for, it was doubtful if a twentieth part of the race accepted, or if a tenth understood, even in the most general terms, the difference between minds trained to creative conceptions and minds brought up in an atmosphere of defensive acquisitiveness and property accumulation. It would take three or four generations to convert the world to a forward-looking attitude. Either the Modern State movement had to seize power openly now and inaugurate a tyranny that would have to last as long as it took to turn round the great majority of intelligences into the new direction, or it had to propitiate, compromise and persuade these outer masses—*upon their own lines.*

'These people will never see things as we see them,' he insisted, making strange gestures and repeating his words to emphasise their importance. 'They have to live and die, *on their own lines.* It is not just to impose too much upon them. It is only as they die out that the Modern State form of mind can hope to be in a dominant majority. Their mental vices are incurable. Meet them half-way, make things easy for them. You will save the world three generations of suffering and bitter conflict.'

He unfolded his Machiavellian project. A greedy acquisitiveness was part of the make-up of every energetic old-world type. They were as incurably voracious as dogs. And yet we made good friends and helpers out of dogs. Their loyalties were at best gang loyalties; they were none the less greedy because they did at times hunt in packs. But they had no fundamental instinctive hostility to the Modern State. It was only when the Modern State thwarted their established habits of behaviour that they snarled at it and began to fear it. They could never make a solid front against the Modern State. They could always be played off against each other, one against another; they could be neutralised. The lesson of Russia's harsh repression of her bourgeoisie and professional classes in the Twenties and Thirties was a warning against the miseries and social damage of too sudden and forcible an attempt to change ideals of behaviour. Let the Modern State go more softly and more kindly.

He went on to detailed suggestions. With Russia, Spain and America, bribery need play but a minor role. The ruling mentality in these countries was now such that the present working agreements would pass naturally into assimilation in a little while. Elsewhere there was really no permanent harm in recognising the old claims to sovereign and proprietary rights, and securing such a hold upon leading men that they would keep their hands off the Modern State propaganda and schools and be content with handsome

365

subsidies from the Control services and industries. It would be cheaper than war. 'If they want a little war now and then among themselves——'

In spite of Shi-lung-tang's smiling face, there was audible disapproval at this point.

When he had done, his case for tact and insinuating corruption was knocked to pieces by Rin Kay. 'If we were a Society of Moral Supermen,' he said, 'we might venture to be as disingenuous as this.' But Mr. Shi-lung-tang forgot that every Fellow in the Modern State society had two enemies: the acquisitive man outside and the acquisitive man within. The point their Chinese friend missed was the fact that it was much more natural to adopt the behaviour patterns of the old world than to acquire those of the Modern State. The old dispositions were something that was; the new dispositions were something that had to be made and sustained. The inner life of a Modern State Fellow was a sustained effort to be simple and serve simply. That should take him all his time. He could not afford to be intricate and politic. 'We have a difficult enough task before us just to do what we have to do, plainly and honestly. We cannot afford to say and do *this* and mean *that*.' William Ryan supported that with vigour, but Hooper Hamilton spoke long and elaborately on the other side. The spirit of the society was plainly with Kay.

M. L. Tagore, an economic botanist, introduced a new line of thought into the discussion, or rather he revived the line of thought of nineteenth-century mystical liberalism. He said he was equally against bribery, insincere treaties or any use of force. He was old-fashioned enough to be a democrat and a believer in the innate wisdom of the unsophisticated man. And also he believed in the supreme value of truth and inaggressiveness. We must not outrage the sense of right in man, even if that meant the abandonment of our immediate objectives. We had to persuade him. And we had no right to assume that he did not hold himself to be right because his conception of conduct differed from ours. Let the Modern State society go on with the scientific organisation of the world, yes, and let us go on with the propaganda of its doctrines in every land. But let it not lift a hand to compel, not even to resist evil. He appealed to the missionary successes of early Buddhism and Christianity as evidence of the practical successfulness of spiritual urgency and physical passivity. He concluded in a glow of religious enthusiasm that did not spare him the contemptuous criticisms of the social psychologists who fell upon him tooth and nail so soon as he had done.

These speeches, which are to be found in full in the Basra Conference Reports, vols. 371 and 372, were the three salient types of opinion in that gathering. The immense majority were for the active line, for frankness and rule. A not inconsiderable minority, however, wavered behind the leadership of Hooper Hamilton. They felt that there were elaborations and refinements that did not find expression in the more aggressive speeches, that the use of force could be tempered by tact, and that lucidity towards an objective was compatible with kindliness and concession.

In a number of speeches some of them tried to express this rather elusive conception of compromise; some of them were not too skilful as speakers, they went too far in the opposite direction, and on the whole they tended to drive the movement towards a harder assertiveness than it might otherwise have expressed. The problems of the Russian system and American were abundantly discussed. Russia now was represented only by technicians, and there was abundant evidence that the repressive influence of the Og-pu had waned. Ivan Englehart was again a leading figure. He assured the Conference that there would be no trouble from Moscow. 'Russia,' he said, 'is ready to assimilate. Is eager to assimilate.'

Arden Essenden spoke late in the general discussion; he spoke with a harsh enthusiasm and passionate faith; he carried all the younger men and most of the older ones with him, and he shaped the ultimate decisions.

Some of his phrases are, as people used to say, 'historical'. He said, 'The World-State is not a thing of the Future. It is here and now. It has always been here and now, since ever men said they had a common God above them, or talked, however timidly, of the brotherhood of mankind. The man who serves a particular state or a particular ownership in despite of the human commonweal is a Traitor. Men who did that have always been Traitors and men who tolerated them nursed treason in their hearts. In the past the World-State had been torn up among three-score-and-ten anarchies and a countless myriad of proprietors and creditors, and the socialists and cosmopolitans, the true heirs of the race, were hunted like criminals and persecuted and killed.

'Now, through the utter failure of those robbers even to maintain their own social order and keep at peace among themselves, the world has fallen into our hands. Power has deserted them, and we, we here, have Power. If we do not use it, if we do not use it to the fullest, we are traitors in our turn. Are we to tolerate even a temporary revival of the old system? In the name of reason, why? If their brains have got into the wrong grooves—well, we can make fresh brains. Are we to connive with and indulge this riff-raff that waits outside our doors? Go out and look at them. Look at their insincere faces! Look at their furtive hands. Weigh what they say. Weigh the offers they will make you!'

To us to-day that seems platitudinous and over emphatic, but it conveyed the sense of the Conference and it led directly to the general decisions with which its proceedings concluded. The most significant of these was the increase of the Police of the Air and Sea Ways to a million men, and the apportionment of a greatly increased amount of energy to the improvement of their equipment. There was also to be a great intensification and speeding up of Modern State education and propaganda. Provision was also made for the enlistment of auxiliary forces and services as they might be needed for the preservation of order; these auxiliaries were to renounce any allegiance except to the Transport or other Control that might enlist them. The Controls were re-organised, and a central committee, which speedily became known as the World Council, was appointed by them to act as the speaking head of the whole system. The ideas of treaties and contracts with exterior administrations and of any diplomatic dealings with dissentients were abandoned. Instead it was determined that this central committee, the World Council, should openly declare itself the sole government of the world and proceed to make the associated Controls the administrative organisation of the planet.

Accordingly a proclamation was prepared to this effect and issued very widely. It was broadcast as well as printed and reprinted from a multitude of centres. It was 'put upon the ether' everywhere to the exclusion of other matter. For now the world had its wireless again in as great abundance already as in the early Thirties. So simultaneously the whole planet received it. It whipped up the waiting miscellany at Basra into a foam of excited enquiry. All over the world city crowds or solitary workers received it open-mouthed. At first there was very little discussion. The effect was too stunning for that. People began to talk after a day or so.

We give it as it was issued : a singularly poor piece of prose when we consider the magnificence of its matter. It seems to have been drafted by Arden Essenden, with some assistance from Hamilton and amended in a few particulars by the Council.

'The Council for World Affairs, constituted by the Air and Sea Control and its associates, declares :

'That between 1950 and 1965 this planet became derelict through the incapacity of its ostensible rulers and property owners to keep the peace, regulate production and distribution, and conserve and guide the common life of mankind;

'That chaos ensued, and

'That it became urgently necessary to build up a new world administration amidst the ruins.

'This the Air and Sea Control did.

'This administration has now been organised about a Central Council for World Affairs, which is making this statement to you.

'It is the only sovereign upon this planet. There is now no

369

other primary authority from end to end of the earth. All other sovereignty and all proprietary rights whatever that do not conduce directly to the general welfare of mankind ceased to exist during the period of disorder, and cannot be revived.

'The Council has its air and sea ways, its airports, dockyards, factories, mines, plantations, laboratories, colleges and schools throughout the world. These are administered by its officials and protected by its own police, and the latter are instructed to defend these organisations whenever and wherever it may be necessary against the aggression of unauthorised persons.

'In every centre of population there are now Modern State nuclei and Control agents conducting the educational work of the Council and in reasonable contact with the local economic life, with local enterprises, local authorities and individuals not yet affiliated to the Modern State organisations. The time has come for all these various quasi-independent organs of business and administration to place themselves in orderly relations to the new Government of the Whole World.

'We are constituting a Bureau of Transition, for the simplification and modernisation of the business activities, the educational and hygienic services, production, distribution and the preservation of order and security throughout our one home and garden, our pleasure ground and the source of all our riches—the earth, our Mother Earth, our earth and yours.

'Without haste or injustice and without delay, with a due regard to your comfort, your welfare and your wishes, the Bureau will set itself to bring your life into sound and permanent correlation with the one human commonweal.'

'It is usurpation!' cried a voice, when the declaration was put to the vote as a whole.

'You decide upon Force,' said Shi-lung-tang. 'I did my best——'

'But this means War!' cried Tagore.

370

'No,' said Arden Essenden. 'There is no more War. This is not War—nor Revolution. This is the recognition of a Revolution and Government again.'

§ 10. *The Life-time Plan*

It is still a debatable question how far that hard decisive declaration of the Socialist World-State at Basra was not premature. There are those who consider it the most timely of acts; there are some who believe it should have been made as early as the first Conference in 1965. The discussion became involved with the intellectual and moral conflicts that went on under the Air Dictatorship. It mingles with the controversies of to-day. But certainly, from 1978 onwards, the Modern State movement lost something of its pristine mental freshness, lost openness, lost much of that almost irresponsible adventurousness that had flung the network of transport and trading controls so swiftly about the earth. 'We have swallowed the world, but now we have to digest it,' said Arden Essenden. The old defiant repudiation of the past was replaced by a firm and sometimes rather heavy insistence upon the order of the future.

There was nowhere any immediate uprising in response to the proclamation of a World Government. Although it had been plainly coming for some years, although it had been endlessly feared and murmured against, it found no opposition prepared anywhere. Thirteen years had wrought a profound change in Soviet Russia and the large areas of China in association with Moscow. The practical assimilation of Soviet Transport and Communications was almost tacitly accepted. The details of the amalgamation were

371

entrusted to committees flying between Moscow and Basra. All over the world, wherever there was any sort of governing or managing body not already associated with the Modern State System, it fell to debating just how and to what extent it could be incorporated or how it could resist incorporation. Everywhere there were Modern State nuclei ready to come into conference and fully informed upon local or regional issues. The plain necessity for a systematic 'renucleation' of the world became evident. The 'Section of Training and Advertisement' had long since worked out the broad lines of a *modus vivendi* between the old and the new.

That *modus vivendi* is called variously The Life-time Plan or—with a memory of that pioneer effort in planning, The Five Year Plan of the Russian Dictatorship—The Thirty Year Plan. Independent businesses that respected certain standards of treatment of the workers, which would accept a certain amount of exterior control, technical and financial, and which maintained a certain standard of efficiency, were to be accorded not simply tolerance but a reasonable protection. Even if their methods were suddenly superseded by new devices, they were to be kept running until they could be wound up, their products were still to be taken by the Controls. This was far better treatment than was ever accorded superseded producers under the smash-and-grab conditions of the competitive system. In the same way, whenever possible the small owning peasant or the agricultural tenant was not dispossessed; he was given a fixed price for his output, counselled or directed in the matter of improvements and so merged by bearable degrees into the class of agricultural workers. This, as Rupert Bordinesco put it (*Brief Explanation:* Historical Documents Series 1969), gave them 'time to die out'. Because it was an integral part of the Life-time Plan that the new generation should be educated to develop a service mentality in the place of a proprietary mentality. There were to be no independent merchants or independent cultivators under twenty in 1980, none under thirty in 1990 and none under forty in 2000. This not only gave the old order

372

time to die out; it gave the new order time to develop the more complex system of direction, mechanism and delivery it needed soundly and healthily. The lesson of the mental discords and tragic disproportions in the headlong development of the first Russian Five Year Plan—disproportions as monstrous and distressful as the hypertrophies and atrophies of the planless 'Capitalist System' of the nineteenth century—had been marked and learnt.

It did not trouble the World Council that to retain millions of small businesses and tens of millions of small cultivators the whole world over for so long meant a much lower efficiency of production. 'These older people have to be fed and employed,' wrote Bordinesco, 'and now they will never learn or be able to adapt themselves to a novel routine of life. Help them to do their job a little better. Save them from the smart people who want to prey upon them— usurers, mortgagers, instalment salesmen, intimidators, religious or secular; and for the rest—leave them in peace.'

The *Brief Explanation* also drew a moral from the 'Period of Glut' in the Twenties, which precede the collapse of the Thirties, when the whole world was full of unconsumed goods and unemployed people. This, Bordinesco pointed out, was the inevitable consequence of an unregulated progressive system of private enterprise. 'There is no sense in throwing a man out of an employment, however old-fashioned, unless there is a new job for him. There is no sense in bringing children into the world unless there is education, training and useful work for them to do. We have to see that each new generation is arranged numerically in different categories of training and objective from those of its predecessor. The Russians learnt this necessity in their great experiment. As we progress towards a scientific production of primary substances, the actual proportion of agricultural workers, miners, forest wardens, fishermen and so forth in the community must fall. So also the proportion of ordinary industrial workers must fall. The heavy industries will precede the light in that. A certain compensation will be caused by a steady rise in the standard of living

373

and particularly by what De Windt called 'the rebuilding of the world', new cities, new roads, continually renewed houses everywhere.' (This was foreshadowed to a certain extent by the French plan for '*Outillage National*' and the German housing schemes in operation as early as the late Twenties, plan and schemes ultimately strangled by the budget-balancing fanatics.) But even that diversion of energy from the production of basic materials and small commodities to big structural undertakings would not suffice to use up the continually released human power in the community. At this point appeared what Bordinesco called the 'enlarging categories', which were to consume more than they gave. There had to be increasing numbers of people engaged in education, in the developing and ordering of knowledge, in experimental science, in artistic production, in making life more abundant and ample. To that expansion no limit could be set.

'We men have a lease of this planet,' runs the *Brief Explanation*, 'for some millions of years. It is foolish not to press on to better life, but it is more foolish to hurry frantically and cruelly. The history of the past two centuries is one sustained warning against the disemployment of men and women for whom there is no other use. Before we teach, our teachers have to learn; before we direct comprehensively, we must have experience in direction. We must always be attempting a little more than we can do, but we must not be attempting the impossible. We must advance without needless delay, but without waste, hurry or cruelty. Do not be fearful or jealous of the advent of the new conditions. No honest worker, man or woman, has anything to fear from the coming of the Modern State.'

§ 11. *The Real Struggle for Government Begins*

But the rulers of the new World State, as their enlargements of the Air and Sea Police made manifest, were under no illusion that the new order could be established in the world by declarations and 'Brief Explanations', and hard upon its proposals for conferences and assimilations came the organisation of its local constabularies and the regulations that made the reorganised nuclei the sole means of communication of independent local authorities, businesses and individuals with the central Controls. In nearly every part of the earth the nuclei had prepared a personnel of sympathisers and auxiliaries, varying in character with local conditions, outside the ranks of the Fellowship. The khaki uniform of the street and road guardians, differing very little then from the one familiar to us to-day, appeared as if by magic all over the world, and the symbol of the winged disc broke out upon aeroplanes, post offices, telephone and telegraph booths, road signs, transport vehicles and public buildings. There was still no discord with Russia; there the blazon of the wings was put up side by side with the old hammer and sickle.

Nowhere at first was there any armed insurrectionary movement. We realise from this how complete had been the collapse of the organised patriotic states of the World War period. They had no national newspapers, no diplomats, no Foreign Offices any more. There had been no paper for the former and there had been no salaries for the latter. Lacking vocal organs, nationalism as such was silenced. There were, however, protests, in a considerable variety of ineffectiveness, from local self-appointed bodies, and much passive resistance and failure to comply. But even the

375

removal of the winged sign was infrequent, and usually where that occurred nothing further ensued when the air police came whirring out of the sky to replace it.

This phase of tacit acquiescence was, however, only temporary, until the opposition could gather itself into new forms and phases and discover methods of organisation. The elements of antagonism were abundant enough. The Fascist garrison in Rome, claiming to be the government of all Italy, was one of the earliest to make its challenge. It had a number of airmen, unlicensed for various reasons by the Transport Control, and it now sent a detachment of its Black Shirts to occupy the new aeroplane factory outside the old Roman town of Turin, and to seize a small aerodrome and whatever air material was to be found in it at Ostia. The winged disc at these two places was replaced by the national fasces. A proclamation was made and disseminated as widely as the restricted means of publication permitted, calling for an assembly of the old League of Nations and reviving a long-defunct phrase of President Wilson's, 'the self-determination of peoples'. The King of Italy, after a diligent search, was found inoffensively farming in Piedmont, and the long-closed palace of the Quirinal was reopened and made habitable for him.

The new air police had been waiting with a certain impatience for provocation of this sort. It had been equipped with a new type of gas bomb releasing a gas called Pacificin, which rendered the victim insensible for about thirty-six hours and was said to have no further detrimental effect. With this it now proceeded to 'treat' the long-resented customs house at Ventimiglia and the factory and aerodrome in dispute.

At Ostia the police planes found a complication of the situation.

An extraordinary ceremony was in progress in the aerodrome. Three new aeroplanes had just been brought thither from the Turin factory, and they were being blessed by the Pope (Pope Alban III).

For the still vital Catholic Church had always been given

376

to the blessing of implements, shops, boats, bridges, automobiles, flags, guns, battleships, new buildings and the like.
It was a ceremony that advertised the Church, gratified the
faithful and did no perceptible harm to the objects blessed.
And this particular occasion had been made something of a
demonstration against the World Council. The Pope had
come; the King and the reigning Duce were present. Sound
films made only a few minutes before the arrival of the air
police show a gathering as brilliant, with its uniforms and
canonicals, as anything that might have occurred before the
World War. Choristers in cassocks and charming little lace
collars chant, acolytes swing censers; the venerable Holy
Father sits on a throne under a canopy, on a large crimson-
draped platform. There was a muster of at least three
thousand Black Shirts.

The action of the Council commander, Luigi Roselli, was
precipitate.

The subsequent enquiry intimates pretty clearly that he
betrayed anti-clerical bias. He had been chosen for this task
because he was himself an Italian, and so, it was thought,
less likely to exacerbate any latent nationalist feeling. (It is
an interesting sidelight on the times that the Fascist com-
mandatore on the ground was Mario Roselli, his elder half-
brother.) His general instructions had been to seize the aerodrome and the aeroplanes with as little violence as possible.
The Pacificin was only to be used in case of armed resistance. But the sight of the cassocks, the birettas, the canopies
and ornaments and robes, the sound of chanting and the
general ecclesiastical atmosphere were too much for the
young man's prejudices. His squadron circled in formation
over the aerodrome. The ceremony proceeded with dignity
in spite of the noise of his propellers. For it seemed incredible that any human being would dare to gas the Pope.

'Let go,' said Luigi Roselli, too malicious to realise the
brutality of his outrage.

The gas containers came crashing into the arena.

'Just for a moment,' says one of the aviators concerned,
in a memorable letter, 'the chanting rose louder. They

showed pluck, those priests. Hardly one of them broke ranks. Then they crumpled up in their places, drifting down on their knees for the most part. It was queer the way you saw the gas spreading among them; it was like a bed of flowers dying and the death spreading out from a lot of centres. The old boy on the throne didn't turn a hair. He had his hands together and his head bowed. You couldn't tell when it took him. The Fascist guard and the King's party weren't anything like so dignified. They gesticulated, they yelled. They were defiant and all that. And some ran about a bit before the stuff got them.

'Of course, you must understand, the whole lot thought they were being killed. None of them could have known anything of this new stuff. *We* didn't know until a fortnight ago.

'We had no gas masks on our bird, so I didn't take part in the landing party which seized the new 'planes.

'The last I saw of that aerodrome, it looked like some old Turkish carpet, gone threadbare in places but still with some brightish patches. Perfect garden of sleep. I hope nobody robbed any of them before they came to. But Roselli, I believe, dropped proper instructions about it all in Rome....'

Unhappily the raid had not been so completely bloodless as this young man supposed. A youthful priest, Odet Buanarotti, had been struck on the head by one of the glass containers and killed outright. He was subsequently canonised; the last saint and martyr to be inscribed in the Latin hagiography.

[*At this point Raven's written transcript breaks off abruptly.*]

BOOK THE FOURTH

THE MODERN STATE MILITANT

§ 1. *Gap in the Text*

So far I have been transcribing, with very little correction and no alteration, the text of Raven's dream book as he left it fully written out. But at this point, that fully written out history breaks off. The record of the next seventy or eighty years is represented only by an untidy mass of notes in the perfectly abominable private shorthand Raven used. Then comes the concluding chapter fully written out again.

I cannot say with any certainty why Raven left this very vital part of his story obscure and confused while he went on to the very last part of all. But I have my own ideas of what happened in his brain. In the first place he had a very human impulse to realise the issue of this world revolution that was unfolding in these notes, and it was easier, therefore, because it was more attractive, for him to write out the later part first. And in the next the intervening matter was really much more intricate for him to handle. It had, if I may use the expression, 'come through his mind' with difficulty and against resistances. His general ideas had been prepared for the new wars, for the post-war breakdown and for a world rule based on air power, and they had also been prepared for the steadily progressive World-State of the final phase. But they had not been prepared for the profound and complex mental and spiritual struggles of three-quarters of a century which inaugurated the new order. Those he had not thought out.

Whether it was really a clairvoyant vision he had of a real future textbook of history, or whether all this matter was an eruption from his subconscious mind, hardly affects the manifest fact that all this part came against the grain. One of the strongest arguments for the view that this Outline of the Future was evolved by Raven from his inner consciousness is the fact that there are several passages in which he seems to argue with himself, and that the quiet unhurrying assurance of the earlier and later narratives is not sustained in these middle parts.

I do not think it was mere chance that pulled him up precisely at the point when he came to the gassing of the Pope and the martyrdom of Saint Odet of Ostia. I think that this incident struck him as cardinal, as marking a supremely significant corner which humanity was turning. It was something that had to happen and it was something he had never let his mind dwell upon. It ended a practical truce that had endured for nearly three centuries in the matter of moral teaching, in the organisation of motive, in what was then understood as religion. It was the first killing in a new religious conflict. The new government meant to rule not only the planet but the human will. One thing meant the other. It had realised that to its own surprise. And Raven, with an equal surprise, had realised that so it had to be.

Nearly a year earlier the One World-State had been declared at Basra. There already it had been asserted plainly that a new order must insist upon its own specific education and that it could not tolerate any other forms of training for the world-wide lives it contemplated. But to say a thing like that is not to realise its meaning. Things of that sort had been said before, and passed like musical flourishes across the minds of men. The new government did not apprehend the fullness of its own intentions until this unpremeditated act of supreme sacrilege forced decision upon it. But now it had struck down the very head of Catholic Christianity and killed an officiating priest in the midst of his ministrations. It had gripped that vast world organisation, the Catholic Church, and told it in effect to be still for evermore. It was now awake to its own purpose. It might have retreated or compromised. It decided to go on.

Ten days later air guards descended upon Mecca and

closed the chief holy places. A number of religious observances were suppressed in India, and the slaughter-houses
in which kosher food was prepared in an antiquated and
unpleasant manner for orthodox Jews were closed throughout the world. An Act of Uniformity came into operation
everywhere. There was now to be one faith only in the
world, the moral expression of the one world community.

Raven was taken unawares, as the world of 1978 was
taken unawares, by this swift unfolding of a transport
monopoly into a government, a social order and a universal
faith. And yet the experiment of Soviet Russia, and the
practical suppression of any other religion than the so-
called Communism that had been forced upon it, might well
have prepared his mind for the realisation that for any new
social order there must be a new education of all who were
to live willingly and helpfully in it, and that the core of an
education is a religion. Plainly he had not thought out all
that such a statement means. Like almost all the liberal-
minded people of our time, he had disbelieved in every
form of contemporary religion, but he had tolerated them
all. It had seemed to him entirely reasonable that minds
could be left to take the mould of any pattern and interpretation of life that chanced upon them without any serious
effect upon their social and political reactions. It is extraordinary how such contradictory conceptions of living still
exist side by side in our present world with only a little
mutual nagging. But very evidently that is not going to be
accepted by the generations that are coming. They are
going to realise that there can be only one right way of
looking at the world for a normal human being and only
one conception of a proper scheme of social reactions, and
that all others must be wrong and misleading and involve
destructive distortions of conduct.

Raven's dream book, as it unfolded the history of the last
great revolution in human affairs to him, shattered all the
evasive optimism, all the kindly disastrous toleration and
good fellowship of our time, in his mind. If there was to be
peace on earth and any further welfare for mankind, if

383

there was to be an end to wars, plunderings, poverty and bitter universal frustration, not only the collective organisations of the race but the moral making of the individual had to begin anew. The formal revolution that had taken place was only the prelude to the real revolution; it provided only the frame, the Provisional Government, within which the essential thing, mental reconstruction, had now to begin.

That precarious first world government with its few millions of imperfectly assimilated adherents, which now clutched the earth, had to immobilise or destroy every facile system of errors, misinterpretations, compensations and self-consolations that still survived to confuse the minds of men; it had to fight a battle against fear, indolence, greed and jealousy in every soul in the world, the souls of its own people most of all, and win. Or it had to lapse. It had to do that within a definite time. If it did not win within that time, then dissension and relapse were inevitable and one more century of blundering and futility would have to be added to the long record of man's martyrdom. This new régime had to clean up the racial mind or fail, and if it failed then in all probability it would leave the race to drift back again to animal individualism, and so through chaos to extinction. Failures in the past had been possible without general disaster because they were partial and local, but this was the decisive world effort.

§ 2. *Melodramatic Interlude*

I have remarked already how impersonal is this school history of the year 2006 in comparison with the histories of our own time. Politicians and statesmen pass like the shadows of general forces, royalties peep and vanish like

mice behind the wainscot. They vanish at last altogether—
unobtrusively. Now and then this history picks out individuals, Henry Ford for instance, or De Windt, Winston
Churchill or Woodrow Wilson, not as heroes and leaders
but as types and witnesses. They manifest streams of
tendency in the social brain, systems of ideas at a point of
maximum effectiveness.

Then suddenly at this point the history lapses into something like melodrama. For a phase personalities assume
such an importance as to seem to dominate the world's
affairs, as Caesar and Cleopatra did or Mirabeau and Marie
Antoinette. I think some explanatory links must be missing
here, some comments that might have pointed the value of
this episode in illuminating the play of motive that led to the
Air Dictatorship. But let me give it as it came to me.

The Air and Sea Control and the organisation of the
associated subsidiary Controls had been the work of a
group of keen young men, moved to action by the growing
disorder of life and directly inspired by De Windt and his
school of writers. They had been full of generosity, enthusiasm and confidence. The first World Council elected in
1978 included most of these leaders of '65, now coming to
middle age, one or two older acquisitions and only two
additions from among the younger men. Arden Essenden,
with his vigour of initiative, was not only the chairman but
the natural leader of the first World Council. Only Ivan
Englehart could compare with him in power of personality.
There were finer and nobler minds present, but none others
so emphatic and so available for the crude uses of popular
admiration.

There was, it seems, a curiosity in the world about Essenden; his name was better known than any of his colleagues;
his portrait, though indeed through nothing worse than
acquiescence on his part, got into circulation, as newspapers
began to abound again. It was the method of the new World
Government to have no presidential or secretarial signatures
to its public announcements; it was stated simply that the
'Control', whichever it was, or the Council suggested, stated,

proposed or had decided, and the World-State seal with its winged disc authenticated the document. But the idea spread by impalpable means that Essenden, who was known to have made the decisive speech for immediate world government at the second Basra Conference, might well have put his name whenever that seal appeared. His prestige grew and came back to his ears. There can be no doubt that his consciousness of a vague exterior support affected his attitude towards his colleagues and their common task.

The historians of our textbook, so far as some difficult passages in the stenography can be deciphered, weigh the good and bad effects of this reinforcement of Essenden's natural impatient decisiveness. They bring in other instances and compare him with other dictators. Indisputably there are crises in human affairs so urgent that many worthy considerations and qualifications are better disregarded and overborne rather than that action should be delayed. These critics of our time study the amount of justification that can be made out for Mussolini, for Stalin, Kemal, Hitler and the various other dictators during the economic débâcle of the West, and I find this judgment of posterity very discordant with my own profoundly liberal and Anglo-Saxon prejudices. They stress the hopeless indeterminateness of the preceding parliamentary régime more than I should do.

They do not extend anything like the same charity to Essenden that they do to the earlier dictators. He played the 'strong man' role half a century too late. The pattern of development, they decide, had been fully provided by De Windt and his fellow theorists. Essenden, they insist, did not so much lead as 'speak first', and with a needless haste, when the general decision was imminent. He induced the committee to strike too soon and too harshly at the old religious and political traditions that seemed to stand in the way of the Modern State. He found some of his colleagues slow in grasping things that seemed obvious to him. He was impatient and overbearing.

Quite early after the declaration of world sovereignty

there were altercations in the committee meetings between him on the one hand and William Ryan and Hooper Hamilton on the other. Shi-lung-tang also becomes an inexplicable thorn in Essenden's side, an enervating influence full of insidious depreciation. We find Rin Kay intervening with a gentle firmness in these disputes and Englehart fretting openly at their dissensions.

This new world government, one must realise, was carrying on under conditions that were often saturated with emotion. There was still much uncertainty in the outlook; and this perhaps let in adventure and romance. The World Council was in effective possession of world power, but not in unchallenged possession. Even in 2000 C.E., nineteen-twentieths of mankind were still unassimilated to the organisation. If the world was not rebellious it was mutinous, and there were plenty of alert and intelligent people in opposition, estranged people or people shaped to forms of thought altogether uncongenial to the reconditioning of human affairs on Modern State lines.

It was inevitable that these disharmonies between the leading figures at the centre of things, and the similar veins of discord that broke the solidarity of the Fellowship with a thousand intricate streaks and patches of weakness, should find echoes and misinterpretations in the greater world outside the machine. That greater world was still prepared for heroes and villains, ready for blind partisanships and storms of suspicion. It wanted drama in its government. A legend came into being which exaggerated a supposed want of sympathy on the part of Essenden for the 'priggishness' and 'petty tyrannies' of the various Controls. He was supposed to be nobler stuff. He was credited with the intention of taking things into his own hands altogether and ruling the world in a more generous and popular spirit. As the history puts it: 'An autocrat has always been the imaginative refuge of the crowd from hard and competent aristocracy.'

That Arden Essenden ever plotted to realise these dreams there is no evidence at all. No word, much less any deed, is on record to show that he was unfaithful to the Modern State. But there can be no doubt that he felt that he was a fine figure and very necessary to the World Republic. He felt, as Stalin had done before him, that men could not do without him.

And then abruptly women come back into the history. We find a love intrigue flung across the stream of history. I did not notice until I came to this part of the world story how small a part women had played in the drama that began with the World War. In most countries they had been emancipated and given equal political rights with men before that disaster. That achieved, they vanish out of the picture throughout four decades of violence. There were indeed women leaders in the early stages of the Russian revolution, but none filled a decisive role. And for all the leadership women exercised between the Twenties and the Eighties they might have been every one of them in kitchen, nursery, hospital or harem. They lost what little political significance they had when queens went out of fashion. A considerable proportion of the Modern State Fellowship was feminine, but no women occupied decisive positions in the scheme. There were none on the World Council. They were doing vitally important work, educational, secretarial, executive and the like, but it was ancillary work that did not lead to individual distinction.

But at this point the historian of the year 2106 breaks his inadvertent taboo and two women's names appear, the names of Elizabeth Horthy and Jean Essenden, and we find the threads of human destiny running askew about a story of passionate love and passionate misbehaviour.

Elizabeth Horthy, who caused the downfall and execution of Arden Essenden, was evidently a woman of splendid appearance and unfaltering conduct. She was an air pilot, and she seems to have liked to wear her uniform on occasions when most women would have been in a robe. She knew, says the history, what suited her. She was tall and evidently beautifully made; she 'lifted her chin', it seems; she had a 'broad brow' and a 'serene' face. This I learn from

388

quotations that are given from Essenden's letters to her. They are the letters of a man quite artlessly in love. But there is nothing in the notes to tell us whether she was dark or fair, what colour of eyes looked out from under that 'broad brow', nor what sort of voice she had. Her love letters seem to have been pithy and extraordinarily indiscreet. Of her charm and distinction there can be no doubt. She was one of those women who seem radiant to men. She was 'like sunshine'; she was 'like heartening music'. Again I quote Essenden. She made men her friends, except for Hooper Hamilton, who manifestly felt some obscure resentment against her.

Now this young woman, with her obvious 'bravery' and a powerful disposition for romance, seems to have come to Basra in the train of William Ryan. It is possible but improbable that she was his mistress. Apparently she took little or no interest in the immense task of the World Revolution except as a suitable background for her exciting personal adventure. She seems to have fallen in love with Essenden at sight and he with her. It may be she came to Basra intending to do that. Something theatrical about him was not too theatrical for her. They were both theatrical. She liked things to be magnificent, and perhaps her taste for magnificence was stronger than her critical powers.

She seems to have given herself to him without hesitation or qualification or concealment. Theirs was—again I quote those artless letters of his—'the sort of love that flaunts itself like a flag'.

But there was a third principal in this primitive drama, the wife of Essenden, a woman of great energy, great possessiveness and obtrusive helpfulness. It had been her vanity to 'inspire' Essenden. And in the cast of the drama was Ryan, loudly resentful at Essenden 'stealing' his 'air girl', and Hooper Hamilton, inexplicably malignant. We are left to guess at the incidents and details of the drama, which was after all a very commonplace drama, only that it was magnified to the scale of the world stage. It culminated in Jean Essenden bringing a charge before the World Council against her husband of being concerned in a reactionary plot against the Modern State. She had, she said, intercepted letters, though none were ever produced. The historian of the year 2106, reviewing the particulars of the case, declares that there was no real evidence at all of any guilty associations of either Elizabeth Horthy or Essenden with the widespread movement that certainly existed for a monarchist and individualist reaction. But at the time the accusation was all too plausible. In some of her scrawled notes to him it seems Elizabeth called him 'my King'.

Moreover, Jean Essenden repeated the most incredible conversations with her husband: boasts of future glory, dark threats at his colleagues, strange replies to her remonstrances. She at least was an inflexible Modern Republican. Afterwards in a storm of remorse she retracted all this evidence, but only when it was too late. Probably it was half true. Probably it was reality a little refracted in her mind.

It was Hamilton who sealed Essenden's fate. He presided over the Special Court that had been formed to try the case. 'Some of the evidence may be given with a motive,' he said, looking at the white face of the accusing wife. 'But it is a small matter that Essenden should or should not be a party in this conspiracy. His real offence is that he should have allowed this situation to develop, that he should have permitted his attention to wander from the services of the Republic to personal gratifications—personal gratifications and displays. At least he had been guilty of egotism. He has sacrificed himself and the interest of the world that has wrapped about him to an intensely personal drama. The question of his specific guilt is an altogether minor matter. The question before us is not, "What has Essenden done?" but, "What are we going to do about Essenden?" There is need for repression coming; civil war and bloodshed are plainly upon us. This is no time for Great Lovers. Essenden has become ambiguous. He cannot lead us, and—how can we do without him? Things have come to this, Essenden, you are *inconvenient*. Apart from this quarrel of the women, *you are in the way.'*

The notes quote these words from the gramophone records of the trial. For it appears that the historian of the year 2106 could sit at his desk and listen to the steel-band record of the proceedings; note the speeches and mark the inflexions of the voices.

There was a pause, and then Essenden cleared his throat. 'I see that I am in the way.'

It was decided that there should be no open trial and condemnation. That would have precipitated a revolt. A tabloid was to be given to him, and he was to take it privately. He might 'sit in the spring sunshine amidst flowers and green trees' and take it in his own time.

The record was cut deep, it seems, by the scream of Jean Essenden, protesting that that last half-hour should not be spent by the two lovers together.

Through all the years to come those steel ribbons will preserve the shrill intonations of those distressful moments. 'I can't bear *that*!' cried Jean Essenden—down to the end of time.

'No,' Elizabeth's actual words are given; 'there is no need for you to be hurt any more. Don't be distressed, Jean, any more. It's over. It's all over for ever. I will go now. Out of the court now. I never meant to hurt Arden in this way. How was I to know? There is no need at all for us two even to say good-bye or be together any more. Jean, you couldn't help yourself. You had to do what you have done. But I never meant to hurt you. Or him.'

Those are her words as the shorthand notes give them, but we shall never hear the sound of them. But the man who wrote them down, a century after they were spoken, heard them as he wrote, heard her voice weaken, if it weakened. Was she speaking or was she making a speech? We are left guessing how far these words of hers betrayed her sense of drama or whether it had indeed the simple generosity it may have had.

There is no description of the last moments of Arden Essenden, the man who had drafted the proclamation that

391

founded the World-State. Possibly he did sit for a while in some sunlit garden and then quietly swallowed his tabloid. He may have thought about his life of struggle, of his early days in the years of devastation and of the long battle for the World-State for which he had fought so stubbornly. Or perhaps according to all the rules of romance he thought only of Elizabeth. Much more probably he was too tired and baffled to think coherently and sat dully in the sunshine staring at those flowers which made the colophon to his story. Then the book closed for him. He died somewhere in the North of France, but the notes do not say precisely where.

They are more explicit about the fate of Elizabeth Horthy, who killed herself that day. There was no tabloid for her. She took her nearest way out of the world by flying her machine to an immense height and throwing herself out. She went up steeply. It was as though she was trying to fly right away from a planet which had done with romance. 'The aeroplane ceased to climb; it hung motionless, a quivering speck in the sky, and then began to waver and fall like a dead leaf. It was too high for anyone to see that its pilot had leapt free from it and was also falling through the air. A mere tattered rag of body was found amidst the branches of a little thicket of oak near Chantilly.'

A fortnight after Hooper Hamilton also succumbed to 'egotism' and took an overdose of sleeping-draught at his summerhouse in the Aland Isles.

And with that this novelette-like interlude ends. It is elementary in its crudity. It is out of key with all that precedes it and all that follows. We are told there were other 'stories' about the men of the First Council, but those other stories after this one sample are left to our imaginations. Its immense irrelevance tears the fabric of our history. But through the gap we see the pitiful imagination of humanity straining for a supreme intensity of personal passion.

Did that young woman as she stepped out upon nothingness above the cirrus clouds feel that her life had been worth while? The history calls her 'that last romantic'.

§ 3. *Futile Insurrection*

The notes show the historians of 2106 convinced that there was no real complicity between Elizabeth Horthy and the leaders of the Federated Nationalists who now broke out into open revolt. The impression of her character made by her recorded words and deeds is, they argue, quite incompatible with the idea that, if she had indeed been a revolutionary, she would have abandoned her fellow conspirators for a melodramatic suicide because of the execution of Essenden. Far more like her would it have been for her to fly to the rebels in Germany and give herself passionately to avenge and vindicate his memory. But plainly she did not care a rap for the monarchist conspiracy, and it is possible that she did not know of its existence. Both she and Essenden, there can be little doubt, lived and died loyal, in intention at least, to the Modern State.

But it suited the revolt to seize upon her tragedy and use her as one of its symbols, and it was long believed that Essenden had retracted the socialist cosmopolitanism of the Basra Conference in favour of Federated Nationalism. It is interesting to find the legend of the poor old League of Nations presently become more powerful than its living reality, and ironical that it should supply the formula for an attempt to divide up the world again into 'sovereign' fragments. The declaration of the so-called Prince Manfred of Bavaria put the League into the forefront of his promises. Alternatively he spoke of it as a World Federation of Free Peoples, and he promised Freedom of Thought, Freedom of Teaching, Freedom of Trade and Enterprise, Freedom of Religious Profession, Freedom from Basic English, Freedom from Alien Influence everywhere. As a foretaste of

393

these good things, he released a little pogrom in the Frankfurt district where a few professing Jews still lingered.

[*From this point to another which I shall indicate when I reach it I am able to give a fairly trustworthy transcription of the notes.*—ED.]

There was never anything that amounted to actual war during this period of disturbance; nothing that could be called a battle. The World Council had the supreme advantage of holding all communications in its hands, and, as military and naval experts could have told the rebels, there is no warfare without communications. Prince Manfred issued some valiant proclamations 'to the World' before he took his tabloid, but since Basic English was repudiated by his movement, they were translated into only a few local languages, printed on stolen paper by hidden hand-presses, and sought after chiefly by collectors. The jamming of the public radio service was mischief rather than revolt. At first there was a certain revival of the manufacture of munitions in factories that had been seized by rebel bands, but generally these ended their output after at most a few weeks under the soporific influence of Pacificin. There were a few deserters from the Air Police and a certain number of small private aeroplanes in nationalist hands; but the network of registration, vigilant police patrols and the absence of independent aerodromes soon swept rebellion out of the air.

There remained the bomb, the forbidden pistol, the dagger and the ambush. It was these that made the revolt formidable, forced espionage, search raids, restriction of private movement and counter violence upon the World Control, and rendered the last stages of the struggle a grim and indeed terrible chapter in human history. In narrow streets, in crowds and conferences, in the bureaus of administrations and upon the new roads, lurked the death-dealing patriot. He merged insensibly with the merely criminal organisations of blackmail and crime.

It was this murder campaign, the 'Warfare of the Silenced and Disarmed', as Prince Manfred put it, which stiffened the face and hardened the heart of the Modern State for half

a century. It took to 'preventive' measures; it began to suspect and test; that horrible creature, the *agent provocateur*,
was already busy again before 2000. He was busy for
another decade; he did not certainly vanish from the world
until the Declaration of Mégève in 2059, but there is no
record of his activity after 2030. And the government which
had begun its killing with Arden Essenden and Prince Manfred came to realise the extreme decisiveness and facility of
the lethal tabloid. For the grosser forms of execution had
given place to this polite method, and every condemned
man could emulate the Death of Socrates, assemble his
friends if he chose, visit some lovely place or retire to his
bureau. In vain the veteran Rin Kay protested in the committee that, just as he had argued long ago that men were
not good enough to be Machiavellian, so now he declared
they were not good enough to be given powers of life or
death, incarceration or relief over their fellows. 'You murder
yourselves when you kill,' he said.

The rebels, however, were killing with considerable
vigour and persistence, and their victims had no such calm
and grace in their last moments. They were stabbed, shot,
waylaid and beaten to death.

'For a terror,' wrote Kramer, 'death must be terrible.'

'For murder,' said Antoine Ayala, 'death must be inevitable.'

In the end the penal code did seem to achieve its end.
There were 5,703 political murders in 2005, and 1,114 in
2007. The last recorded occurred in 2034. The total is over
120,000. But during these twenty-nine years there were
47,066 political executions! Rihani estimates that more
than seven per cent of these were carried out upon anonymous, circumstantial or otherwise unsatisfactory evidence.
Most were practically sentences by courts martial. The
millennium arrived in anything but millennial fashion.

§ 4. *The Schooling of Mankind*

And now again the shorthand notes are troubled, disturbed and almost unreadable, and the resistances of Raven rise up and mingle with proper text.

It was the age-long issue between faith in compulsion and faith in the good will of the natural man that had invaded the record. It affects me as I transcribe now; I do not see how it can fail to affect any contemporary writer or reader. I get again that flavour, that slight but perceptible flavour of—what can I call it but *inhumanity*?—in the historian's contribution. These men whom we anticipate here are different in their fundamental ideas. This short transition of a hundred and seventy years is marked by a subtle change in the human heart. I wonder if the same kind of difference might not arise if we could bring a good contemporary mind of the early eighteenth century into untempered contact with our thoughts to-day. Would not such a mind find us nowadays rather hard and sceptical about things respected, rather harshly frank about things biological, rather misshapen in our sentimentalities?

It is an old joke to revive such literary characters as Dr. Johnson or Addison and make them discuss contemporary things, but generally the fun goes no farther than clothing modern reactions in old-fashioned phrases and costume. But in the light of my own response to the harshly lucid, cold and faintly contemptuous criticism of our present resistances by the writer or writers of this 2106 document I find myself reviewing these old juxtapositions. I see that if we could indeed revive Johnson he would not only strike us as an ill-mannered, offensive, inadaptable and tiresome old gentleman who smelt unpleasantly and behaved worse, whose comments on life and events would be wide of the mark and discoloured with the echoes of antiquated controversies, but we should find that his contact with us would be pervaded by an incurable distress at our pace, at our strangely different values, our inhuman humanitarianism, as it would have seemed to him, and our cruel rationality. He who had sat so sturdily against his background of accepted and acceptable institutions, customs and interpretations would find that background vanished and himself like a poor martyr in the arena with eyes upon him from every direction. Of course he would be hustled off to meet Mr. G. K. Chesterton, and that might prove the most painful of all his encounters. For Mr. Chesterton, who is posed so often as an avatar of the old doctor, belongs to his own time quite as much as the most futuristic of us all.

I am a hostile critic of present conditions and a revolutionary in essence; nevertheless, I can get on with the people about me because, even though my song is a song of revolt, it is in the same key and tempo as theirs; but I perceive that if I were transferred to this infinitely happier and more spacious world the history of Raven's reveals I should be continually and irreparably, in small things and great things alike, discordant. I should find nobody to get the point of my intelligent observations; I should laugh incomprehensibly, fail to see the jokes that pleased these larger, more vigorous people, and the business of life would hurry past me. All sorts of things I had hoped for and forecast might be there—but in some essential way different and alien to me.

It is one of the things that Raven's notes have taught me that a human mind, an adult human mind anyhow, is much less easily transplanted to a new time and climate than I had been wont to assume. To me, the story of Arden Essenden's bold leadership, his acute self-consciousness, and his uncontrolled love for Elizabeth Horthy seem matter for such another story, let us say, as Meredith's *Tragic Comedians*; but the historian of the year 2106 finds him and her only material from which to dissect out the treacherous egotism

397

of passion. Something in me rebels against that, just as it rebels against the assumption that the World War was a process of sheer waste, its heroisms and sacrifices blind blundering, and its significance out of all proportion less than the social and economic dislocations that caused it.

And now that I come to these disconnected records of the harshly rational schooling of human motives under the Air Dictatorship, records that even Raven found no zest in copying, my distaste is as ineradicable as it is unreasonable. I feel that, but for 'the accidents of space and time', I should have been one of the actively protesting spirits who squirmed in the pitilessly benevolent grip of the Air Dictatorship. But whether it suits my temperament or not, this story, as it came through Raven to me, has to be told.

The men who made the great revolution and unified the world between 1965 and 1978 were men of practically the same mental assumptions as our own. They were in direct mental and moral continuity with our contemporaries. While the reader turns the page, if there is any truth in this history, De Windt, still absolutely unknown, must be working either in Berlin or London upon that Theory of the Nucleated Modern State which was the decisive plan of that final consolidation, publishers must already have read and rejected the preliminary scheme of his great work, and in a year or so from now some Mrs. Essenden will be choosing the name of Arden for her boy. It is as close to us as that. The men of the first World Council, therefore, saw both sides of the business and wavered in feeling between our tradition and the new order they were creating. But the subsequent generation which constituted the Air Dictatorship had been shaped from the beginning in the aggressive bright new schools of the Modern State nuclei, they had fed on a new literature, they looked out upon fresh horizons, and their ideology had been determined more than anything else by the social psychologists and 'new lawyers' of the American school. They were starkly constructive. Nuance to them was obscurity and compromise weakness.

It is plain that so far as the future was concerned the first

World Council with its rivalries and politics was far less effective- than the unobtrusive Educational Control which worked under it during its régime and gradually drew together police, hygiene, schooling and literature into one powerful nexus of direction. While the World Council was fighting for and directing and carrying on the unified World-State, the Educational Control was remoulding mankind. With the opening years of the twenty-first century (C.E.) the erstwhile leading figures of the revolution fall back into secondary places or vanish from the limelight altogether, and a simpler-minded, more determined group of rulers comes to the front.

[*I resume my transcription here.*]

'The world is various enough without artificial variety,' was a leading maxim of the Educational Control which created the men of the Air Dictatorship; and a variant of this maxim was: 'It does not increase the interest of the human assembly to suffer avoidable mental cripples and defectives.' So this body of teachers set themselves to guard new lives, beginning even with pre-natal circumstances, from what they esteemed to be physical and mental distortion. There was no shadow of doubt upon this score for the Educational Control. Every possible human being had to be brought into the new communion. Everyone was to be exposed to the contagion of modernity. Every year now increased the power of the Modern State Fellowship; by 2000, it numbered five million; by 2010 thirteen. Every increase enabled the Educational Control to thrust its enquiring and compelling fingers more and more intimately into the recesses of human life. It had more men and women made to its pattern and a greater force of teachers and inspectors it could trust.

There can be no denying the excellence of the immediate physical results. *Historical Scenes in a Hundred Volumes* witnesses from 1990 onward, not only to the resumption of the advance in the technique of picture-making and the abundance of pictures, but to the restoration of physical welfare. As the student turns over the pages he sees man straighten himself again, grow physically, become more alert. The slouching foot-dragging men and women, the aimless faces, the fattish and lumpish figures of improperly nourished people, the wretched clothing and ignoble make-shift gear of the Second Decline and Fall, disappear; after 1990 clothing is fresh and simple, and after 2010 it begins to be austerely beautiful.

And this was being achieved very largely through what the liberal thought of the nineteenth century would certainly have called 'persecution'. It is plain that the earlier World Council was all too disposed to leave great areas of the planet that did not 'give trouble' alone. The new World Council, which is known also as the Air Dictatorship, would have none of that. There began a systematic attack upon the 'lapsed regions', as they were called from the year 2006 onward. The government set itself in that year to 'tidy up' the still half-barbaric peasant populations of Hayti, Ireland, West and Central Africa, South Italy, American Georgia and its associated states, Georgia in the Caucasus, Eastern Bengal, regions where traditional superstitions, secret societies, magic cults or sacrificial practices showed an obstinate persistence. There was a definite hunt for medicine men, sorcerers, priests, religious teachers and organisers of sedition; they would be fined or exiled, and parents and others would be fined for 'impeding' the education of their children at the cosmopolitan schools.

Many critics of the Air Dictatorship are of opinion that this was a needless pursuit of dying customs and beliefs that might well have been left to fade out into mere fantasies and affectations. But the new generation of rulers took life too seriously for that. It is an issue that can never be settled, since we can only know what actually occurred.

The old Catholic Church, it seems, was still in existence in these days, the last surviving Christian organisation, but it was greatly impoverished, and it had suffered severely from schisms, evidently the result of imperfect communications throughout the dark decades. There was a Pope in Dublin and another in Rome and a coloured Pope in

Pernambuco. From the legal point of view the Irish Pope was the most legitimate successor of St. Peter. He had been duly elected by the Conclave, but the Fascist organisation objected that he was not of Italian origin, his orginal surname being O'Dowd and his Italian accent imperfect, and the cardinals were intimated into a new election. Some feud between rival gang organisations in America seems to have been involved in this split, but the details are obscure and need not occupy the student's time here. There was in consequence a division of the American Catholic world between the Dublin and the Roman Communion, and this led to a murderous series of feuds, riots and small local wars. 'Down with the Wop Pope!' said the Irish. One is reminded of that earlier splitting of the Church through the rivalry of the French monarchy and the Central European imperial system that set up a rival Pope in Avignon.

Ireland was the last stronghold of Christianity. The Catholic religion had been compulsory in South Ireland from 1944 until 1980, and the Erse language, although that was largely corrupted by unavoidable English words and locutions, had also been made obligatory. Overt Birth Control knowledge had been successfully banned, though this produced no effect in the decline in population, and the Modern State nuclei had been boycotted more effectually there than in any other part of the world. The Dictatorship found itself fighting one of its most difficult battles for power with this tenacious people. The Irish came out in revolt all over the world. In Ireland after the maculated fever the population never rose above two millions, but there was a widespread Irish tradition throughout the English-speaking world. Some of the more brilliant and formidable antagonists of this schooling and drilling of our race that was going on, Paidrick Lynd, Arthur Fitzgerald and Bernard O'Dwyer for example, came from Ireland. Oddly enough none of these three was a Catholic, and Fitzgerald at any rate had suffered a term of imprisonment for blasphemy, but the spirit of opposition was either innate in them or it had become ingrained in their natures.

Let the student note the open alternative at the end of the preceding paragraph. It raises a question that remains unsettled to this day. It is the clue to our contemporary moral problem. The Air Dictatorship, with what was still a very under-developed science of social psychology at its disposal, had come upon one of the obscurest and most debatable of educational problems, the variability of mental resistance to direction and the limits set by nature to the ideal of an acquiescent co-operative world. De Windt, preoccupied by his gigantic schemes for world organisation, had treated the 'spirit of opposition' as purely evil, as a vice to be guarded against, as a trouble in the machinery that was to be minimised as completely as possible. The Air Dictatorship was carrying out and did carry out its world settlements on those assumptions. One may well believe that the world could have been unified into one enduring Pax Mundi in no other way. And yet they were faulty assumptions, and in the end they had to be abandoned for subtler and better conceptions of social interaction.

As every practising teacher understands, resistance is a necessary factor in teaching. Soft non-resistant material takes an imprint very readily only to lose it again very quickly. Easy pupils make teaching slipshod. The difficulty but also the soundness of teaching increases with the amount of reaction in the learner. And also resistance involves a certain element of collaboration; the thing learnt becomes a resultant, incorporating elements introduced in the struggle. It is easier to carve cheese than a good piece of wood; every piece of wood has a bias, it has to be dealt with on its own terms, it has to be managed and humoured, but in the end there is no comparison in quality and interest between carved cheese and wood-carving. These are the commonplaces of our educationists. But the defence of the work of the Educational Control is that its repressive measures were aimed not at intrinsic but at artificial resistances left over from the pre-revolutionary age.

In the old world of the early twentieth century there was a vast amount of crude generalisation about what were called 'racial' characteristics. There were generalisations about arbitrarily chosen agglomerations of mixed population—the Spanish for example, or 'the West', 'Russia' or the Jews; such generalisations were always unjust and inaccurate and often extremely mischievous. Nowadays we do not write of races any more, but recognise groups of characteristics, evidently transmitted en bloc as a rule by associated genes, and anthropologists are steadily developing a scientific classification of human types. In few aspects do human beings vary more widely than in their recalcitrance. It is not a simple case that some people are more resistant and some less. There is a wide variation in the life cycle in this respect. Recalcitrance varies with age and sex. It varies with diet. Some types are obdurate as children but afterwards become more reasonable. Some reach a maximum of insubordination in adolescence. Generally speaking, passive resistance, unteachableness and obstinacy, but not insurrectionary energy, increase rapidly with age. And in certain populations, of which the Irish was one, there was a powerful access of resistance after adolescence in the male. It rose to the level of absolute refractoriness.

Now the apologists for the 'persecutions' of the Air Dictatorship maintain that its missionary teachers were already quite prepared with the sympathy and finesse needed to teach every type of human being they would encounter in the world. So long as resistance was personal between teacher and learner they welcomed it. At least they said they welcomed it. But when it came to the systematic organisation of young people who would otherwise have had indifferent minds, so as to present a mass resistance and subversive opposition to the world order, the Educational Control, it is argued, was justified in hindering and suppressing books, meetings, teachings, agitations. It had the whip hand, and it would have been a sin not to have made use of that advantage. 'We do not suppress individuality; we do not destroy freedom; we destroy obsessions and remove temptations. The world is still full of misleading doctrines, dangerous imitations and treacherous suggestions, and it is the duty of government to erase these'; so ran the uncompromising memorandum issued by the Educational Council in 2017.

'We have to get a common vision of existence, a common idea of right and wrong, established throughout the whole population of the world, and *speedily*,' this memorandum declares. 'Natural instinct is no help in a labyrinth of artificialities. It has to be supplemented by either training or discipline. The better we train, the less need for oppression; the more thoroughly we crush out false presentations and agitations, the more freely, as well as safely, men can live. Things are rushing back headlong to prosperity, and we cannot face abundance and leisure with the present morale of the race. It has to be stiffened up; it has to be drilled to keep ranks.'

In 1955 humanity was suffering throughout the globe from disorder, famine and pestilence; its numbers were declining, and it might well have been supposed that it was driving towards extinction. The change of fortune was swift beyond precedent. As early as 2017 we have this clear intimation that its guides and rulers were contemplating the advance of plenty and an excess of leisure with terror.

EDITOR'S NOTE

I think that it may make things clearer for the reader here if I give a compact summary of the political forms assumed by the developing world government between 1965 and 2106. The writer of this history of Raven's, writing for his contemporaries, assumed them to be familiar with many institutions for which the readers of this book will be altogether unprepared. Fortunately the relations of the Communist and Fascist Parties to their respective governments give us a helpful parallel to the relations to the World Council, the actual world government after 1965, of what was called the Modern State Movement. It was its incentive and its conscience.

404

The political structure of the world developed in this fashion:

After the chaos of the war (1940–50) and the subsequent pestilence and 'social fragmentation' (1950–60) there arose, among other attempts to again reconstitute a larger society, a combine of the surviving aviators and the men employed upon the ground plant of their trade and transport. This combine was called *The Transport Union*. It does not appear to have realised its full potentialities in the beginning, in spite of the forecasts of De Windt.

It initiated various conferences of technicians and at last one in 1965, when it was reorganised as *The Air and Sea Control* and produced as subsidiary organs *The Supply Control, the Transport (and Trading) Control*, an *Educational and Advertisement Control* and other Controls which varied from time to time.

It was this Air and Sea Control which ultimately gave rise in 1978 at the Second Conference of Basra to the *World Council*. This was the first declared and formal supreme government of the world. The Air and Sea Control then disappeared, but its subordinate Controls remained, and coalesced and multiplied as ministries do in existing governments, under the supreme direction of the World Council.

There was no further change in essential political structure between 1978 and 2059, but there was a great change in the spirit and method of that supreme government, the World Council. A new type of administrator grew up, harder, more devoted and more resolute than the extremely various men of the two Basra Conferences. These younger men constituted what our historian calls here the Second Council, though it was continuous with the first. There was a struggle for power involving the deaths of several of the earlier councillors, but no formal change of régime; there continued to be a World Council constituting the supreme government of the world. This Second Council is also referred to as the Air Dictatorship in its earlier years, and later on as the Puritan Tyranny. These are not exact constitutional terms but loose descriptive phrases. The membership of the World Council changed by individuals coming and going, but its character remained singularly uniform for over forty years. It grew more elderly in spite of a few youthful accessions. In 2045 its average age was 61.

This Second World Council endured until a Conference at Mégève in Savoy (2059) reconstituted the world government on lines which are drawn out fairly plainly in the following chapters.

And now for the relations of this series of governing bodies to the World-State Movement.

The ideological developments that inspired these changes were initiated by a group of writers of whom De Windt was the outstanding figure. He built up the project for a World-State in all its essentials in a book on *Social Nucleation* published in 1942. The intrinsic quality of this book has been entirely overshadowed by its importance as a datum point in history. It is a slow laborious book.

It was the seed of the Modern State Movement which furnished the plans of the Air and Sea Control. The Modern State Movement was never a formally constituted government nor anything in the nature of a public administration; it was the propaganda and development of a system of ideas, and this system of ideas produced its own forms of government. The 'Movement' was initially a propaganda and research, and then a propaganda, research and educational organisation. Its active full members were called Fellows; it had a class of dormant members, whose relationship to the active category varied under different conditions and at different periods; and it had a class of neophytes or apprentices, as numerous or more numerous than its active Fellows. It ultimately incorporated the mass of adult mankind (and womankind) in its Fellowship.

It was never divided up into regional bodies. Its Fellows were acceptable at any local centre they happened to visit. Naturally it began mainly as localised nuclei, but those localisations were merely for convenience of propaganda, teaching and local purposes. The effective subdivision of the Fellowship was into *faculties*, and these again were subdivided into sections and departments. There was to begin with a faculty of scientific research, a faculty of interpretation and education, a health faculty, a faculty of social order, a supply and trading faculty, a number of productive faculties, agricultural, mineral and so on. There were splits and coalescences among these faculties. Their splits and coalescences had a frequent relationship to the splits and coalescences of the Controls, because it was obviously a mental convenience for a faculty or faculties to correspond with one or more Controls.

The faculties and their subdivisions, their sections and departments, possessed electoral central councils, but there never seems to have been a general directorate of the Modern State Movement after the early days in which it was one simple system of propaganda and enquiry nuclei; its nuclei almost from the outset differentiated naturally into faculties, each viewing human affairs from its own angle; the movement as a whole did not require a continuing directive council; there were only conferences when concerted action between diverse faculties was desirable.

There never seems to have been any difficulty in the way of a man or woman belonging to two or more faculties at the same time, and this greatly facilitated the melting of one faculty into another. The Modern State Movement was an 'open order' attack on social structures; it was a solvent and not a mould. The moulds were the Controls.

The faculties and their sections, departments and so forth developed very unequally; some dwindled to insignificance, and some on the other hand grew to unanticipated proportions and created their own distinctive organisation and machinery. This was particularly the case with the social psychology department of the faculty of science, which annexed the whole faculty of training and advertisement by a sheer community of subject. This social psychology department of the faculty of science was given the legal and responsible direction of the Educational Control.

This body of social psychologists and their associates became a great critical and disciplinary organism side by side with the World Council, which ultimately, as will be explained in the following chapters, it superseded.

The world then ceased, it seems, to have any single permanent government at all. It remained under a series of primary Controls dealing with each other by the method of conference, namely the Controls of transport, natural products, staple manufacturers, population (housing and increase), social sanitation (police and medicine), education (these two latter were later merged as the Behaviour Control), and the ever expanding activities of scientific research and creative work. So the world which had once been divided among territorial Great Powers became divided among functional Great Powers.

Later a Bureau of Reconciliation and Co-operation seems to have grown up, which decided upon the necessity and method of inter-Control conferences. It was something rather in the nature of a Supreme Court than of a ruling council.

Most of the old faculties of the Modern State Movement dissolved into technical organisations under these Controls, with the one exception of that former department of the science faculty the department of social psychology, which by 2106 had become, so to speak, the whole literature, philosophy, and general thought of the world. It was the surviving vital faculty of the Modern State Movement, the reasoning soul in the body of the race.

In the end it becomes something like what the early nineteenth century used to think existed under the name of Public Opinion, the consensus of active thought and imagination throughout the world. It is plain that by 2106 this rule by a pervasive intelligence had become an unchallenged success. It was all that was left by way of King, President or Supreme Government on earth.

This assembling and clearing-up of statements which are otherwise scattered rather perplexingly through the text under consideration will not, I hope, annoy such readers as have already grasped what I have summarised here. I will now return to that text itself.

§ 5. *The Text Resumes: The Tyranny of the Second Council*

The Air Dictatorship is also called by some historians the Puritan Tyranny. We may perhaps give a section to it from this point of view.

'Puritan' is a misused word. Originally invented to convey a merely doctrinal meticulousness among those Protestants who 'protested' against the Roman version of Catholicism, it came to be associated with a severely self-disciplined and disciplinary life, a life in which the fear of indolence and moral laxity was the dominant force. At its best it embodied an honourable realisation: 'I shall do nothing worth while and nothing worth while will be done unless I pull myself together and stiffen up my conduct.' If the new Air Dictatorship was schooling the world with considerable austerity, it was certainly schooling itself much more so.

The code of the first makers of the World-State had been a simple one. 'Tell the truth,' they insisted; 'maintain the highest technical standards, control money and do not keep it, give your powers ungrudgingly to the service of the World-State.' That seemed to leave them free for a good deal of refreshing self-indulgence, and it did. They ate, drank and were merry, made love very freely, envied and competed with one another for power and distinction, and set no adequate guard upon the growth of rivalries and resentments. Our history has glanced at the fall and death of Essenden, but this is only one episode in the long and complicated history of the private lives of the first world committee. Slowly the details are being elucidated and analysed by a body of historical students. Except that the victims are dead, and cannot hear, the results are as pitiless as the old Christian fancy of the Recording Angel and his Book on Resurrection Day.

They appear as very pitifully human; their sins happened to them, they were taken unawares in phases of fatigue, by resentment, by sensuality or flattery. Women were attracted by their prestige and offered the reassurance of love in their weaker moments. In many cases the moral downfall was due to the very limitlessness of the devotion with which they first gave themselves to their world task. They worked without rest. Then they would suddenly find themselves worn bare, bankrupt of moral energy. They had made no proper balance between the public task and the inward desire. Outbreaks of evil temper would follow, or phases of indolence or gross indulgence. The Fellowship was disconcerted; the outer world ran with scandal. 'These Fellows,' said their critics, 'are no better than the pretenders and rascals of the the the old régime. Rin Kay, the wise, is consumed with affection for his little friend, and Ardasher of the experimental aeroplanes makes his young men do dangerous stunts to please a girl. Morowitz is collecting Persian miniatures quite unscrupulously and Fedor Galland spends half his time now making a garden at Babylon.'

The ambitous young men who were little boys when the first conference at Basra was held were educated by teachers who were none the less harshly zealous because they were doing relatively inconspicuous work and had no little friends nor miniatures nor gardens to amuse them. These teachers had a lively sense of their leaders' defects and of their own modest but real moral superiority. The youngsters under their teaching were saturated with constructive enthusiasm, but they were trained also to judge and condemn the weaknesses of their spent and tired predecessors. They learnt that the brightness of this new world that had been made for them was in danger from the very men who had made it. The technically more skilful and intensive teaching that had been given them had made them more self-conscious and wary in their behaviour, and far more capable of managing the detail of their lives. They were simple in principle and hard in detail. They had a modern wisdom about diet and indulgence; they regarded lack of fitness as a crime.

The difference is evident in *Historical Pictures*, where one usually sees the older generation dressed either carelessly or picturesquely and often either self-consciously or gracelessly posed, while the younger men and women in the simpler and plainer clothing that was coming into fashion carry themselves like athletes. Austerity has become a second nature to them. Devotion and the sacrifice of the individual they carried to such a pitch that, for instance, it was considered unseemly for them to have portraits made, and there was no record kept of the names of the chairmen and the movers of motions in the central committee during their ascendancy. It has needed special research to rescue some of the names of this second generation of world rulers, who set up the Puritan Tyranny and made the Socialist World-State secure. One of the moving spirits was certainly Han H'su and another Antoine Ayala.

They ousted their predecessors without any coup d'état, one by one, through sheer superiority in energy and working power. The great revolution was over; the World-State was in being. But it was not secure. It was a time for just such continuous detailed work as only a naturally able and energetic type with a hard training could hope to do. They were not selected by any voting or politics to fill the Council, they were selected by their own staying and driving power. The milder or subtler types could not keep the pace and fell into less authoritative positions. The influence of certain teachers and groups of teachers was very considerable. Three schools, the Unamuno Foundation at Coimbra, the Columbia University of New York, and the Tokio Social College, accounted for more than a third of the World Council in 2017.

For nearly forty years the new Council, with occasional renewals, worked and kept a whole generation of men and women working. As Aldous Huxley (1894–2004), one of the most brilliant of reactionary writers, foretold of them, they 'tidied up' the world.

There can be no denying the purification and rarefaction of the human scene that was achieved during their sway. They tightened up the disciplines of the Modern State Fellowship, and nevertheless the proportion of the fellowship increased until it bade fair to become the larger moiety of adult mankind. The mental habits of the Fellowship, its habitual bearing, extended through the whole population. The Tyranny, says Vordin, altered the human face for ever. It closed the mouth and made the lips firmer, made the eyes steadier and more candid, opened the brow, altered the poise of the head, obliterated a number of wrinkles and habits of expression. Portraits of the earlier and later time confirm this generalisation. One type of odd-character after another became rare and began to disappear from the human comedy. Rascals and recalcitrants grew old, sat in the sun for a time rather protestingly and vanished. They took many disagreeable and some whimsical casts of countenance with them. Sexual prostitution ceased and eliminated a characteristic defiance from feminine carriage. The trader found he had nothing to trade with and came into the employment of the Supply Control, gambling, horse-racing, sport, generally went out of fashion, and those queer oblongs of pasteboard, 'playing cards', retired to museums, never to emerge again. Every one of these vanishing interests or practices took its own scores of social types, of 'reaction systems', to use the modern phrase, away with it. Faces ceased to be masks.

Every year the world grew safer for the candid. The need for cunning and wary self-restraint diminished enormously, the habit of making a face a 'mask'. Humanity was extroverted. A lively self-forgetful interest in external things becomes more and more patent. The 'worried' look of the introspective habit of mind disappears. 'Everyone must know plainly,' said the new rulers. 'Men must be perplexed no more.' The old religions could not emulate the moral prestige of the new cult, and even the resentments of the persecution that deprived them of their last shreds of

412

educational influence could not preserve them. For nearly forty years this rule of the new saints, this resolute simplification and smoothing out of life, went on.

History becomes a record of increasingly vast engineering undertakings and cultivations, of the pursuit of minerals and of the first deep borings into the planet. New mechanisms appeared, multiplied, and were swept away by better mechanisms. The face of the earth changed. The scientific redistribution of population began. Yet there was little likeness to the world of to-day, as we know it. No age in human history has left us such strange and uncongenial pictures.

Costume was not unpleasant during this period, because of its simplicity; the human figures in the scene at least are tolerable; but these scientific Puritans also produced some of the clumsiest architecture, the most gaunt and ungainly housing blocks, the dullest forests, endless vistas of straight stems, and the vastest, most hideous dams and power-stations, pylon-lines, pipe-lines, and so forth that the planet has ever borne. But at any rate they flooded the Sahara and made the North African littoral the loveliest land in the world. The productivity of mankind was now advancing by leaps and bounds, in spite of the severe restraint presently put upon the introduction of fresh labour-saving devices; and yet these Puritans were consumed by an overwhelming fear of leisure both for themselves and others. They found it morally necessary to keep going and to keep everybody else going. They *invented* work for the Fellowship and all the world. Earth became an ant-hill under their dominion, clean and orderly but needlessly 'busy'. So harshly had they reacted against the weaknesses of their seniors and so unable were they to mitigate their own self-imposed severities.

Let us cast up the good mankind can attribute to this strange phase of sternness and grim repression. For all the faint masochist and sadistic flavour of its closing years, the good was beyond all measure greater than the evil. 'The obliteration of out-of-date moral values' (the phrase is Antoine Ayala's) 'and the complete establishment of a code

413

of rigorous and critical self-control, of habitual service, creative activity, co-operation, of public as well as private good manners, and invariable truthfulness, were achieved for all time. We grow up so easily now into one free, abundant and happy world that we do not realise the effort still needed even in the year 2000 to keep life going upon what seem now to us the most natural and simple lines possible. We find it almost impossible to imagine the temptations to slacken at work, loiter, do nothing, "look for trouble", seek "amusement", feel bored and take to trivial or mischievous "time-killing" occupations, that pursued the ill-trained, under-vitalised, objectless common citizen before 2000 C.E. Still more difficult is it to realise how subtly these temptations were diffused through the mass and how hard they made a well-directed life. We have to trust the psychological experts about that.'

The New Puritans 'disinfected' the old literature, for example. It is hard to see that now as an urgent necessity. These old stories, plays and poems seem to us to convey the quaintest and most inexplicable systems of motivation conceivable, and we cannot imagine people being deflected by them; they might as easily be led astray by the figures on a Chinese screen or an Hellenic sarcophagus; but before the persecution those books were, as one censor called them, 'fever rags'. They stood then for 'real life'. They provided patterns for behaviour and general conduct. That queer clowning with insults and repartees, that insincerely sympathetic mocking of inferiors, that denigration of superiors, which constituted 'humour' in the old days, strikes us as either fatuous or malicious. We cannot understand, for instance, the joy our ancestors found in the little blunders and misconceptions of ill-educated people. But then they also laughed at the cripples who still abounded in the world! Equally distasteful now is most of their 'romance' with its false stresses, its unnecessary sacrifices and desperations. 'Romance,' says Paul Hennessey, 'is essentially the violent and miserable reaction of weak spirits to prohibitions they cannot fairly overcome.'

414

We find the books glorifying war and massacre, and the tangled masses of suggestion that elaborated the innate hostility and excitement caused by difference of racial type, so unconvincing that it is difficult to believe that they ever gripped. But they did grip and compel. They drove innumerable men to murders, lynchings, deliberate torture. They dressed the foulest and cruellest of crimes in heroic colours. There had to be a break with these traditions before they could be seen as we see them now. It needed the heroic 'priggishness' of the Air Dictatorship, putting away the old literature and drama for a time, suppressing the suggestion systems of the old religions and superstitions, jailing and segregating men and women for 'hate incitement', ruthlessly eliminating sexual incitation from the lives of the immature and insisting upon a universal frank sexual hygiene, to cleanse the human mind for good and all and inaugurate the unconstrained civilisation of to-day. There was no other way to renaissance.

Joseph Koreniovsky has called the Puritan Tyranny 'the cold bath that braced up mankind after the awakening'. Man, he says, was still 'frowsty-minded' and 'half asleep' in the early twenty-first century, still in urgent danger of a relapse into the confused nightmare living of the Age of Frustration. You may call it a tyranny, but it was in fact a release; it did not suppress men, but obsessions. None of us now can fully realise the value of that 'disentanglement from tradition', because now we are all disentangled.

And next to this ruthless 'mental disinfection' of the world, and indeed inseparable from it, we must put the physical disinfection of mankind to the credit of the Air Dictatorship. Between 2000 and 2040 every domicile in the world was either destroyed and replaced, or reconditioned and exhaustively disinfected. There was an immense loss of 'picturesqueness' in that process, and we shiver nowadays when we look at pictures of the white bare streets, the mobile rural living-boxes, the bleakly 'cheerful' public buildings, the plain cold interiors with their metallic furniture, which everywhere replaced the huts, hovels, creeper-

415

clad cottages and houses, old decaying stone and brick town halls, market houses, churches, mosques, factories and railway stations in which our tough if ill-porportioned and undersized forefathers assembled about their various archaic businesses.

But between the same years the following diseases, the names of which abound in the old histories, and the nature of which we can hardly imagine, vanish from the human records: catarrh, influenza, whooping cough, sleeping sickness, cholera, typhus, typhoid, bubonic plague, measles and a score of other infectious scourges. (Only yellow fever remained as a serious infection after 2050. That demanded the special effort of 2079 for its extirpation.) Syphilis, and indeed all those diseases known as venereal, were stamped out completely in two generations; they were afflictions so horrible and disgusting that their description is not now considered suitable for the general reader. There was a similar world-wide attack on plant diseases and distortions, but of that the student will learn in his Botanical History.

The psychologists who are rewriting human history have still many open questions to settle about the training and early influences that gave the world this peculiar group of rulers, and so the account of its hardening and deterioration remains incomplete. They admit that the Tyranny was in essence a liberation, but they insist that it left vitally important desires in the human make-up unsatisfied. Old traditions and mischievous obsessions were rooted in these desires, and the Tyranny had not been content with an eradication of the old traditions. It had denied the desires. It had pulled up the soil with the weeds. It had exalted incessant, even if pointless, activity above everything else in life.

Overwork, a strained strenuousness, has been a common characteristic of the rulers of mankind in the past. It shows through the Edicts of Asoka, for example, and particularly in Rock Edict VI (*Asoka*, D. R. Bhandarkar, 1932, Classical Historical Studies, 21–118). 'I am never satisfied,' runs the Edict, 'with the exertion or with despatch of business.

The welfare of the whole world is an esteemed duty with me. And the root of that, again, is this, namely, exertion and despatch of business.' A great majority of the successful Caesars and Autocrats from Shi-Hwang-Ti to Hitler have the same strenuousness—Alexander the Great perhaps was the chief exception, but then his father had done the work before him. Mussolini, the realiser of Italian Fascismo, in his *Talks* to Ludwig (Historical Documents Series 100,319) betrays an equal disposition for single-handed accomplishment and an equal disinclination to relinquish responsibility.

All the chief figures of the Air Dictatorship betray, upon scrutiny, signs of the same drive to do too much and still to do more. They display all the traits of a collective weary conqueror, unable to desist and think and adapt himself. They went on ruling and fighting when their victory was won. They had tidied up the world for ever and still they went on tidying. After their first real successes they manifest an extreme reluctance to bring new blood into the responsible administrative task. They had arisen to power as a group by their usefulness, because they were unavoidably necessary to those original founders of the World-State whom they first served and then by sheer insistence upon performance pushed out of authority and replaced. The three virtues in a ruler according to Han H'su were puctuality, precision and persistence. But it was a dictum of Paidrick Lynd's that 'indolence is the mother of organisation'. They had none of that blessed gift of indolence. When the legacy of work that the first world revolution had left them was exhausted, they brought things at last to the necessity for a final revolution through their sheer inability to organise a direct succession to themselves or to invent fresh undertakings.

That final revolution was the most subtle of all the substitutions of power that have occurred in human affairs, the most subtle and so far the last. The Dictatorship could suppress overt resistance; it could impose obedience to its myriads of injunctions and rules. But it could not suppress

417

the development of general psychology nor the penetration of its own legislative and administrative activities by enquiry and criticism..

The Department of General Psychology had grown rapidly until it had become the most vigorous system of activities in the scientific faculty of the Modern State Fellowship. In its preparatory stages it had taken the place of the various 'Arts' and Law curricula of the old régime. It was the modernisation of the 'humanities'. The founders of the World-State had given this particular department of the scientific faculty almost as great a directive and modifying power over both the Educational and Legal Controls as it exercises to-day. Even then it was formally recognised as the responsible guardian in the theory of Modern State organisation. It more than realised the intentions of De Windt. It became the thought, as the World Council had become the will, of mankind acting as a whole. And since the education and legal adjustment of the World-State was thus under the direction of a department of research continually advancing, they differed diametrically in character from the education and teaching of the old-world order.

The student cannot keep this difference, this flat contrast, too clearly in mind. He will never understand the historical process without it. The Old Education existed to preserve traditions and institutions. Progressive forces arose as a dissent from it and operated outside its machinery. In the eighteenth, nineteenth and early twentieth century education was always a generation or so behind living contemporary ideas and the schoolmaster was a drag on mankind. But the New Education, based on a swiftly expanding science of relationship, was no longer the preservation of a tradition, but instead the explanation of a creative effort in the light of a constantly most penetrating criticism of contemporary things. The new schoolmaster showed the way, and the new education kept steadily ahead of contemporary social fact. The difference of the New Law and the Old Law was strictly parallel. If a man of the year 1900 had been told of a progressive revolution led by lawyers and schoolmasters inspired by scientific ideas, he would have taken it as a rather preposterous joke, but to-day we ask, 'How else can the continuity of a progressive revolution be sustained?'

The failure of the German revolution of 1918 and the relapse of that unfortunate country into the puerility and brutish follies of Hitlerism was entirely due to the disregard of the elementary principle that no revolution could be a real and assured revolution until it has completely altered the educational system of the community. Every effective old-world revolution was a revolt against an established education and against the established law.

The role of the modern Education Control in preserving, correcting and revivifying the progressive process in human affairs had already been manifested by the supersession of the leading personalities of the Basra Conference in the World Council by their successors who became the Air Dictatorship. Now these men in their turn found the instruments of government becoming recalcitrant in their hands and obeying the impulse of unfamiliar ideas. They had cleared and cleansed the site while social science had been preparing the idea of the new structures that were to stand upon it, and now they found themselves confronted by an impulse towards creation and enrichment entirely discordant with their habits of administration. Their subordinates began to send back the instructions given them as 'insufficient and not in accordance with the psychology of the workers'—or other people—'concerned'. Schemes were condemned by those to whom they were entrusted as unnecessarily toilsome or needlessly ungracious. Workers took matters into their own hands and demanded more pleasant processes or more beautiful results. The committee was disposed at first to insist upon unquestioning obedience. Thereupon the Education Control produced a masterful argument to show 'the social harmfulness of unquestioning obedience'.

There could be no greater contrast in the world than that between the older revolutionary crises in human affairs and this later conflict of wills. The old revolutions were at best

419

frantic, bawling, sentimental affairs in which there was much barricading of roads and destruction of property; people were shot abundantly and carelessly and a new régime stumbled clumsily to responsibility on the ruin and reversal of its predecessor. Such revolutions were insurrections of discontent against established institutions. But this last revolution was the cool and effectual indictment of the world executive by a great world-wide educational system. It was not an insurrection; it was a collateral intervention. The new order arose beside its predecessor, took matters out of its hands and replaced it.

The need for an intolerant militant stage of the World-State had passed. The very reason for the disciplines of the Puritan Tyranny had been dissolved away in the completeness of its victory. But the last men to realise this were the old men who now sat trying to find tasks to keep humanity out of mischief in the bureau of the World Council.

§ 6. *Aesthetic Frustration: The Notebooks of Ariston Theotocopulos*

It is a growing custom of historians, and we have already followed it freely, to vivify their general statements by quotations from contemporary descriptive writers. As histories have disentangled themselves from their primitive obsession about rulers and their policies, they have made a more and more extensive use of private memoirs, diaries, novels, plays, letters, sketches, pictures and the like. Once upon a time washing bills and memorandum books were below the 'dignity of history'. Now we esteem them far above acts of parliament of diplomatic memoranda. And certainly there is no more convenient source of information about current ideas and feeling under the Air Dictatorship than the cipher Note Books of that gifted painter and designer Ariston Theotocopulos (1997–2062). For thirty-seven years until his death, he wrote in these books almost daily, making his own shrewd comments on current events, describing many odd and curious occurrences, noting very particularly his own emotional reactions, and adorning them all with a wealth of sketches, dreams, caricatures and the like, which make the full edition in facsimile, with a translation, among the greatest delights of the book-lover. The bulk of this matter does not concern the student of general history at all, and yet it is possible to pick out from it material for a far clearer realisation of life under the second Council than could be derived from a score of abstract descriptions.

The earlier of these volumes are coloured by the irritation of the writer with three particular things: the restrictions upon private flying, his difficulties in finding scope for his genius, and the general want of beauty and graciousness in life. At that time there were no privately owned aeroplanes and no one could act as an air pilot who was not an active Fellow of the Modern State organisation and subject to its rules and disciplines. Theotocopulos had an anarchistic soul, and his desire to wander freely above the mountains and clouds, to go whither he liked at his own sweet will, unhampered by any thought of immediate 'service', became an obsession with him. 'If they would let me alone I would give the world something,' he scribbles. 'But what on earth is the good of those blighted old Master Decorators telling me to do this and that? Did I come into the world to imitate and repeat things done already?'

And in another place he notes: 'Some damned official flying overhead on his way to preventing something. It spoilt the day for me. I couldn't *think* any more.'

Then comes a cry of agony. 'The lay-out of all this terracing is wrong. What is the good of putting me to do a frieze of elephants on a wall that ought to come down again? If I do anything good that wall will stay where it is.

The better I do it, the more likely they are to keep that wall. And it's wrong. It's wrong. It's wrong.'

A few pages on, one word is all alone by itself: '*Elephants!*'

Then follows a string of caricatures of that animal which Li has characterised as acute biological criticism. Theotocopulos had been vividly interested in elephants, but now he had tired of them. He represents them as diaphanous or altogether transparent, and reveals the distresses of their internal lives. And there is a whole page of incredibly wicked elephants' eyes.

He was working on the rather deliberate decoration of the main-road system then in course of construction, running from Cape Finisterre through North Italy and along the North Black-Sea Dyke to the Crimea and Caucasia. That system has since been deflected from the Ligurian coast northward, but at that time it was made to follow by the sea to Genoa, and thence passed in a great cutting through the mountains to the plain of the Po and so to the still existing Chioggia viaduct. It was one of a not very ably conceived system of world roads that was greatly modified before its completion in our own time, and it was carried out with a massiveness and a solidity of ornamentation that witness to the World Council's incapacity to realise that Change was still going on. Those roads seem to have been planned for all time. They indicate mental coagulation.

Theotocopulos was engaged upon the coast section between the old town of Nice to the old port of Genoa. It was driven in a series of flattened curves that straightened out in places to a right line, cutting brutally through headlands and leaping gulfs and bays in vast viaducts. Above and below the slopes were terraced with natural or imitation marble walls and the terraces were planted with oranges, lemons, vines, roses, olives and agaves. These terraces went up, as Theotocopulos says, 'relentlessly' to the old Corniche Road above, broken only by a few masses of evergreen trees. The ruins of the villas and gardens of the Capitalist era and most of the towns along the coast that Titus Cobbett had visited and described seventy-odd years before had now been cleared away; a few groups of residential buildings occurred here and there, and pretentious staircases, which were rarely used because of the lifts they masked, led down to beaches and holiday places and harbours for pleasure boats and fishermen. These holiday places and the residential buildings were low and solid-looking, after the fashion of the time, and they provoked Theotocopulos to frenzy. He caricatured them and spotted his drawings with indecent words. It is amazing how truthfully he drew them and how ingeniously he distorted them. He represented them as cowering into the earth like the late buildings of the war years, from which they certainly derived their squatness.

'We still dream of air raids and war in the air,' he said, and he speaks elsewhere of 'the inmates of those fortifications.... If only I could get hold of an aeroplane and a bomb! Perhaps after all there is some sense in keeping intelligent people like me out of the air, with this sort of stuff about.'

His task unhappily kept him in close contact with all this squat architectural magnificence. He had won distinction at an unusually early age for his brilliant drawings of men and animals; he had a grotesque facility for seeing into bodies and conveying his sense of internal activities; before his time the only anatomy known to artists had been muscular anatomy; and he was set to 'decorate' an ungainly stretch of wall near Alassio with a frieze of elephants. It is necessary to explain that in those days there was the completest divorce in people's minds between aesthetic and mechanical considerations. First you made a thing, they thought, and then you decorated it. It seems almost incredible now, but the engineers of the Air Dictatorship were supposed and expected to disregard all thought of beauty in what they did. If they made something frightful, then the artist was called in to sugar the pill. There, as in so many things, the restless sensitive mind of Theotocopulos anticipated the ideas of to-day. 'Engineers ought to be artists,' he says, 'anyhow;

and artists ought to be engineers or leave structural work alone.' This wall of his still exists; his decoration has preserved it, even as he foresaw. It just remains for his sake, a lesson for students and a monument to his still incomparable talent.

'Took a holiday,' he notes one day, 'and rowed about five miles out to sea. These disproportions grow worse as one gets away from them. Never before have I seen anything that got uglier as it receded in perspective. This coast does. The road is too broad and big. There will never be that much traffic. The population of the world isn't increasing and on the whole it rushes about less than it did. One hundred and twelve metres of width! What is this coming torrent of traffic from Finistere to God knows where? Not a sign of it as yet. Nor ever will be. The little lizards get lost across that glassy surface and die and dry up. Artless earthworms crawl out upon it and perish. One sees them by the thousand after wet weather. No shade for miles. The terraces are badly spaced and the walls that sustain them look gaunt. There is no sympathy in all this straight stuff with the line and movement of the hills behind. They *live*. And this accursed habit of building houses close to the ground! Damn it, don't we build to get away from the ground?'

And then suddenly in big capitals comes one word 'PROPORTION!'

After that he meditated with his pencil in hand, jotting down his thoughts. 'The clue to life. Not simply beauty. There is no evil but *want of proportion*. Pain? Pain arises out of a disproportion between sensations. Dishonesty? Cruelty? It is all want of proportion between impulse and control....'

It is interesting to trace in the notebooks how he tries over ideas that are now familiar to everyone. He worries between the ideas of proportion and harmony. Then he hits on the discovery that all history is a record of fluctuations in proportion. To-day, of course, that is a commonplace. We have told the economic and political history of the twentieth century, for instance, almost entirely as the story of an

424

irregular growth of the elements of life, hypertrophy of economic material going on concurrently with a relative arrest of educational, legal and political adjustment. The first dim realisations of these disharmonies were manifested by the appearance of 'planning', those various crude attempts to make estimates of quantities in social life of which the Russian Five Year Plan was the first. After 1930, the world was full of Plans, and most of them were amazingly weak and headlong plans.

We learn from these notebooks of Theotocopulos how imperfectly this idea of really deliberate quantitative preparation in the activities of our species was apprehended even in the early twenty-first century. Just as the war complex ran away with men's minds in the war period, so now political unity and uniformity and an extravagant concentration of enterprise upon productive efficiency had outrun reason. The interest of these notebooks lies exactly in the fact that they are not the writings of a scientific social psychologist, but of a man who was, except for his peculiar genius and energy of expression, a very ordinary personality. They tell us how common people were taking the peculiar drive of the times, how the general mind was puzzling out its new set of perplexities and asking why, after having abolished war, restored order, secured plenty, defeated the fears and realised the wildest hopes of the martyr generations, it was still so far from tranquillity and happiness.

'Growing pains,' he writes abruptly. 'That was old Lenin's phrase. Is a certain want of proportion unavoidable?'

After that flash in the pan, the notebook wanders off into a dissertation upon Levels of Love, of no importance for our present purpose. But that idea of 'Growing Pains' was working under the surface all the time. Suddenly appear pages of sketches of strange embryos, of babies and kittens and puppies, all cases of morbid hypertrophy. 'Is want of proportion inevitable in all growth? Nature seems to find it so, but she always has been a roundabout fumbler. She starts out to make a leg, and when it comes out a wing she

425

says, "Eureka! I *meant* to do that." But in *designed work*? In engineering for example?'

His mind goes off to the making of castings, the waste in grinding, the problems that arise in assembling a machine.

'Nature corrects the disproportions of growth by varying the endocrines,' he reflects. 'And when a house has got its frames set up and its walls built, we turn out the masons and put in the plasterers and painters. So now. A change of régime in the world's affairs is indicated. New endocrinals. Fresh artisans.'

This particular entry in the notebook is dated April 7, 2027. It is one of the earliest appearances of what presently became a current phrase, 'change of régime'.

The preoccupations of Theotocopulos with the physical and mental aspects of love, his extraordinary knack of linking physiological processes with the highest emotional developments, need not concern us here, important as they are in the history of aesthetic analysis. For a year or so he is concentrated upon his great 'Desire Frieze' in the Refectory of the Art Library at Barcelona, and he thinks no more of politics. He likes the architects with whom he is associated; he approves of the developments at Barcelona, and he is given a free hand. 'These fellows do as they like,' he remarks. 'A great change from all those damned committees, "sanctioning" this or asking you to "reconsider" that.' Then he comes under the influence of that very original young woman from Argentina, also in her way a great artist, Juanita Mackail. Sketches of her, memoranda of poses and gestures, introduce her. Then he remarks: 'This creature thinks.' So far he has never named her. Then she appears as 'J' and becomes more and more frequent.

'There is something that frightens me about a really intelligent woman. Was it Poe or De Quincey—it must have been De Quincey—who dreamt of a woman with breasts that suddenly opened and became eyes? Horrid! To find you are being looked at like that.'

Following this a page has been torn out by him, the only page he ever tore out, and we are left guessing about it.

426

An abrupt return to political speculation in the note-books follows. A number of entries begins, 'J says', or end, 'This is J's idea.'

Then some pages later he repeats: 'This creature thinks. Do I? Only with my fingers. Language is too abstract for me. Or is it true, as she says, that I am mentally lazy. *Mentally lazy*—after I had been talking continuously to her for three hours!'

'It seems all my bright little thoughts don't amount to anything compared with the stuff these social psychologists are doing. I have a lot to learn. I suppose J would school-mistress anybody.'

The notebooks keep the fragile grace and mental vigour of Juanita Mackail alive to this day. She was the sort of woman who would have been a socialist revolutionary in the nineteenth century, a commissar in Early Soviet Russia or a hard worker for the Modern State in the middle twentieth century. Now she was giving all the time her strongly decorative idiosyncrasy left free to the peculiar politics of the period. It is plain that before she met Theotocopulos she was already politically minded. She had had a feeling that the world was in some way not going right, but her clear perception of what had to be done about it came only with her liaison with him. The notebooks with their frankness and brutality tell not only a very exceptional love story, but what is perhaps inseparable from every worth-while love story, a mutual education. Theotocopulos was her first and only lover. To begin with he had treated her as casually as he had treated the many other women in his life, and then it is plain that, as he began to find her out, his devotion to her became by degrees as great or greater than her devotion to him.

He studied her. He made endless notes about her. We know exactly how she affected him. How he affected her we are left to guess, but it is plain that for her there was at once the magnificence of his gifts and the appeal of his wayward childishness. The former overwhelmed her own. It is plain in her surviving work. The earlier work is the best. He asks twice, 'Am I swamping J? Her stuff is losing character. She is borrowing my eyes. That last cartoon. Am I to blame? It *was* such lovely stuff. Once upon a time.' And he writes: 'This maternity specialisation is Nature's meanest trick on women. If they are not going to be mothers, if they *can't* be mothers, why on earth should they be saturated with motherhood? Why should J think more about getting me a free hand to do what I please than she does about her own work? She does. I haven't asked her. Or have I, in some unconscious way, asked her? No, it's just her innate vicious mothering. I am her beloved son and lover and the round world is my brother, and every day her proper work deteriorates and she gets more political and social-psychological on our account.'

From that point onward the trend of these notebooks towards politics becomes very strong. The early volumes express the resentments of an isolated man of extreme creative power who finds himself singlehanded and powerless in an unsympathetically ordered world. The late show that same individuality broadening to a conception of the whole world as plastic material, sustained by a sense of understanding and support, coming into relationship and co-operation with an accumulating movement of kindred minds. At last it is not so much Theotocopulos who thinks as the awakening aesthetic consciousness of the world community.

'The change of régime has to be like a chick breaking out of its egg. The shell has to be broken. *But the shell had to be there*. Let us be just. There is proportion in time as well as in space. If the shell is broken too soon there is nothing to be done but make a bad omelette. But if it isn't broken at the proper time, the chick dies and stinks.'

The forty-seventh notebook is devoted almost entirely to a replanning of the subject of his early animadversions, the Ligurian coast. That notebook proved to be so richly suggestive that to-day some of his sketches seem to be actual drawings of present conditions, the treatment of the Monaco headland for example, and the reduction of the terraces.

But his dreams of orange-groves are already quaint, because he knew nothing of the surprises in tree form that the experimental botanists were preparing. The forty-ninth notebook is also devoted to planning. 'Plans for a world,' he writes on the first page. 'Contributions.' He seems to have amused himself with this book at irregular intervals. There are some brilliant anticipations in it and also some incredible fantasies. Occasionally, like every prophet, he finds detail too much for him and lapses into burlesque.

There is a very long note of a very modern spirited discussion about individuality which he had with Juanita when apparently they were staying together at Montserrat. The notes are the afterthoughts of this talk, 'shots at statement' as he would have called them, and they bring back to the reader a picture of that vanished couple who strolled just sixty years ago among the tumbled rocks and fragrant shrubs beneath the twisted pines of that high resort, both of them so acutely responsive to the drift of ideas that made the ultimate revolution—she intent and critical, holding on to her argument against his plunging suggestions, like someone who flies a kite in a high wind.

'The individual is for the species; but equally the species is for the individual.

'Man lives for the State in order to live by and through —and in spite of—the State.

'Life is a pendulum that swings between service and assertion. Resist, obey, resist, obey.

'Order, discipline, health, are nothing except to make the world safe for the aesthetic life.

'We are Stoics that we may be Epicureans.

'Exercise and discipline are the cookery but not the meal of life.

'Here as ever—PROPORTION. But how can proportion be determined except aesthetically?

'The core of life is wilfulness.'

So they were thinking in 2046. Have we really got very much farther to-day?

§ 7. The Declaration of Mégève

Theotocopulos and his Juanita were present at the Conference at Mégève which wound up the second World Council. They both seem to have been employed upon the decoration of the temporary town that was erected for this purpose on those upland meadows. The notebooks, in addition to some very beautiful designs for metal structures, contain sketches of various members of the Council and some brilliant impressions of crowd effects in the main pavilion. There is also a sketch of a painting Theotocopulos afterwards made; it appears in all our picture-books of history: the tall presence of old Antoine Ayala, standing close to the aeroplane in which he departed for his chosen retreat in the Sierra Nevada; he is looking back with an expression of thoughtful distrust at the scene of his resignation. The pilot waits patiently behind him. 'Well, well,' he seems to say. 'So be it.' The sinking sun is shining in his eyes, so that they peer but do not seem to see.

The drawing of nine of the World Councillors listening intently to the statement of Emil Donadieu, the secretary of the Education Faculty, is almost equally well known.

It was the most gentle of all revolutions. It might have been a thousand years away from the fighting and barricading, the pursuits and shootings and loose murderings, of the older revolutionary changes. The Council suffered not overthrow but apotheosis. Creation asserted itself over formal construction and conservation. For a decade and more the various Control had been showing a greater and greater disregard of the Central Council; they had been dealing directly with one another, working out their immense co-operations without the intervention—which was more and

430

more inhibition—of the overriding body. It was the Education Faculty of the Control of Health and behaviour that had at last provoked the gathering. It had in its own authority set aside the prohibitions on naked athleticism which had been imposed by the Council in its 'general rules of conduct' thirty years before. The matter was a trifling one, but the attention of the Council was drawn to it; and it was decided to choose the occasion for a definite assertion of the Council's authority. Was there still a Supreme Government in the world? was the question posed by the veteran ruling body. Probably it seemed to them quite imperative that there should be a supreme overriding body, and the bland exposition of Emil Donadieu which dispelled this assumption must have been an illuminating revelation to them on the march of human ideas since those days of youthful zeal and vigour when they found themselves directing the still-militant World-State.

In those days the need for concentrated leadership had prevailed over every other human consideration. It had been necessary to fight and destroy for ever vast systems of loyalties and beliefs that divided, misled and wasted the energies of mankind. It had been necessary to replace a chaos of production and distribution for individual profit by an ordered economic world system. But once this vast change-over was made and its permanence assured by the reconstruction of education on a basis of world history and social science, the task of a militant World-State was at an end. The task of the World Council was at an end.

'But then who is to govern the world?' asked Eric Gunnarsson, the youngest and most ambitious member of the Council.

'No need to govern the world,' said Donadieu. 'We have made war impossible; we have liberated ourselves from the great anti-social traditions that set man against man; we have made the servitude of man to man through poverty impossible. The faculties of health, education and behaviour will sustain the good conduct of the race. The controls of food, housing, transport, clothing, supply, initiative, design,

431

research, can do their own work. There is nothing left for a supreme government to do. Except look up the world it has made and see that it is good. And bless it.'

'Yes,' said Eric Gunnarsson, 'but——'

These words are registered in the phonograph record of the debate. And with these two words Eric Gunnarsson, the ambitious young man who may have dreamt at one time of being President of the World, vanishes from history.

Donadieu went on to a brief history of government in human affairs, how at first man could only think in personifications and had to conceive a tribal God and a tribal King because he could not conceive of organised co-operation in any other way; how Kings remained all too individual and all too little social for anything but the narrowest tribal and national ends, and how therefore they had to be controlled and superseded by councils assemblies and congresses, which in their turn became unnecessary. These ruling bodies clamped men together through the ages of discord until at last the race could be held together in assured permanence by the cement of a universal education.

But the gist of that debate was embodied in the 'Declaration of Mégève' with which the Conference concluded its deliberations.

'The World-State now follows all the subordinate states it swallowed up to extinction; the supreme sovereign government, which conquered and absorbed all minor sovereignties, vanishes from human affairs. The long, and often blind and misdirected, effort of our race for peace and security has at length succeeded, thanks to this great Council that now retires. It retires with the applause and gratitude of all mankind. And now in serenity and security we can survey the property it has redeemed from waste, this planet and its possibilities, our own undeveloped possibilities too, and all the fullness of life that lies before us. This is the day, this is the hour of sunrise for united manhood. The Martyrdom of Man is at an end. From pole to pole now there remains no single human being upon the planet without a fair prospect of self-fulfilment, of health, interest and freedom.

There are no slaves any longer; no poor; none doomed by birth to an inferior status; none sentenced to long unhelpful terms of imprisonment; none afflicted in mind or body who are not being helped with all the powers of science and the services of interested and able guardians. The world is all before us to do with as we will, within the measure of our powers and imaginations. The struggle for material existence is over. It has been won. The need for repressions and disciplines has passed. The struggle for truth and that indescribable necessity which is beauty begins now, unhampered by any of the imperatives of the lower struggle. No one now need live less nor be less than his utmost.

'We must respect the race and each other, but that has been made easy for us by our upbringing. We must be loyal to the conventions of money, of open witness, of responsibility for the public peace and health and decency: these are the common obligations of the citizen by which the commonweal is sustained. We must contribute our modicum of work to the satisfaction of the world's needs. And, for the rest, now *we can live*. No part of the world, no work in the world, no pleasure, except such pleasure as may injure others, is denied us. Thanks to you, Heroic Council; thanks beyond limit to you.'

THE MODERN STATE IN CONTROL OF LIFE

§ 1. *Monday Morning in the Creation of a New World*

With the Declaration of Mégève in 2059 C.E. the Age of Frustration, the opening phase of the Era of the Modern State, came to an end. Let us recapitulate that history in its barest outline. The World-State had appeared dimly and evasively, as an aspiration, as a remote possibility, as the suggestion of a League of Nations, during the World War of 1914–18; it had gathered experience and definition throughout the decades of collapse and disaster; it had formally invaded human politics at the Conference of Basra in 1965 as manifestly the only possible solution of the human problem, and now it had completed its conquest of mankind.

The systematic consolidation of that conquest had begun in earnest after the Second Conference of Basra in 1978. Then the World Council had set itself to certain tasks that had been so inconceivable hitherto that not the most daring sociologists had looked them in the face. They had contented themselves with pious aspirations, and taken refuge in the persuasion that, if they were sufficiently disregarded, these tasks would somehow do themselves. They were tasks of profound mental reconstruction, reconstruction going deeper into the substratum of the individual life than anything that had ever been attempted before. In the first place traditions of nationality had to be cleared away for good, and racial prejudice replaced by racial understanding. This was a positive job against immense resistances. Next a lingua-franca had to be made universal and one or other of the great literature-bearing languages rendered accessible

437

to everyone. This again was not to be done for the wishing. And thirdly, and most evaded of all three obstacles that had to be surmounted, issue had to be joined with the various quasi-universal religious and cultural systems, Christianity, Jewry, Islam, Buddhism and so forth, which right up to the close of the twentieth century were still in active competition with the Modern State movement for the direction of the individual life and the control of human affairs. While these competing cultures remained in being they were bound to become refuges and rallying-shelters for all the opposition forces that set themselves to cripple and defeat the new order of the world.

We have told already how that issue was joined, and shown how necessary it was to bring all the moral and intellectual training of the race into direct and simple relations with the Modern State organisation. After 2020 there is no record of any schools being open in the world except the Modern State schools. Christianity where it remained sacerdotal and intractable was suppressed, but over large parts of the world it was not so much abolished as watered down to modernity. Everywhere its endowments had vanished in the universal slump; it could find no supply of educated men to sustain its ministry; the majority of its churches stood neglected and empty, and when the great rebuilding of the world began most of them vanished with all the other old edifices that lacked beauty or interest. They were cleared away like dead leaves.

The story of Islam was closely parallel. It went more readily even than Christianity because its school organisation was weaker. It was pinned very closely to the teaching of Arabic. The decadence of that language shattered its solidarity much as the disuse of Latin disintegrated Western Christianity. It left a few-score beautiful mosques as Christianity left a few-score beautiful chapels, churches and cathedrals. And patterns, legends, memories remained over in abundance, more gracious and lovely by far than the realities from which they were distilled.

There had been a widespread belief in the tenacity and

438

solidarity of Judaism. The Jews had been able to keep themselves a people apart, eating peculiar food and following distinctive religious practices, a nation within the nation, in every state in the world. They had been a perpetual irritant to statesmen, a breach in the collective solidarity everywhere. They had played a peculiar in-and-out game of social relationship. One could never tell whether a Jew was being a citizen or whether he was being just a Jew. They married, they traded preferentially. They had their own standards of behaviour. Wherever they abandoned their peculiarities aroused bitter resentment.

It might have been supposed that a people so widely dispersed would have developed a cosmopolitan mentality and formed a convenient linking organisation for many world purposes, but their special culture of isolation was so intense that this they neither did nor seemed anxious to attempt. After the World War the orthodox Jews played but a poor part in the early attempts to formulate the Modern State, being far more preoccupied with a dream called Zionism, the dream of a fantastic independent state all of their own in Palestine, which according to their Babylonian legend was the original home of all this synthesis of Semitic-speaking peoples. Only a psychoanalyst could begin to tell for what they wanted this Zionist state. It emphasised their traditional wilful separation from the main body of mankind. It irritated the world against them, subtly and incurably.

On another score also the unpopularity of Israel intensified in the early twentieth century. The core of the slump process was manifestly monetary. Something was profoundly rotten with money and credit. The Jews had always had and cultivated the reputation of a peculiar understanding and cleverness in monetary processes. Yet in the immense difficulties of that time no authoritative direction came from the Jews. The leading minds of the time who grappled with the intricate problems of monetary reconstruction and simplification were almost all Gentiles. It was natural for the common man to ask, 'Where are the Jews?'

It was easy for him to relapse into suspicion and persecution. Were they speculating unobtrusively? It was an obvious thing for Gentile speculators to shift suspicion to this race which gloried in and suffered by its obstinate resolve to remain a 'peculiar people'.

And yet between 1940 and 2059, in little more than a century, this antiquated obdurate culture disappeared. It and its Zionist state, its kosher food, the Law and all the rest of its paraphernalia, were completely merged in the human community. The Jews were not suppressed; there was no extermination; there were world-wide pogroms during the political and social breakdown of the Famished Fifties, but under the Tyranny there was never any specific persecution at all; yet they were educated out of their oddity and racial egotism in little more than three generations. Their attention was distracted from Moses and the Promise to Abraham and the delusion that God made his creation for them alone, and they were taught the truth about their race. The world is as full as ever it was of men and women of Semitic origin, but they belong no more to 'Israel'.

This success—the people of the nineteenth century would have deemed it a miracle—is explicable because of two things. The first of them is that the Modern State revolution was from the first educational and only secondarily political; it ploughed deeper than any previous revolution. And next it came about under new and more favourable conditions. In the nineteenth century the family group had ceased to be the effective nucleus in either economic or cultural life. And all the odd exclusiveness of the Jew had been engendered in his closed and guarded prolific home. There is an immense collection of fiction written by Jews for Jews in the early twentieth century, in which the relaxation of this immemorial close home-training and the clash of the old and modernising generations is described. The dissolution of Israel was beginning even then.

The task of making the mind of the next generation had been abandoned almost unconsciously, for Jew and Gentile alike, to external influences, and particularly to the newspaper and the common school. After 1940 this supersession of home training was renewed in an extensive form. The Modern State movement had from the outset gripped the teachers, re-created popular education after the dark decades upon its own lines and arrested every attempt to revive competing schools. Even had he desired it the Jew could no longer be peculiar in the food either of his body or his mind.

The complete solidarity of mankind in 2059, the disappearance of the last shadows of dislike and distrust between varied cults, races and language groups, witnesses to the profound truth of what Falaise, one of De Windt's editors, has called the Mental Conception of History. The Age of Frustration was essentially an age of struggle to achieve certain plainly possible things against the resistances of a muddled human mind. The Declaration of Mégève was not simply an assertion of victory and freedom for the race, it was the demonstration of its achieved lucidity.

As the curtain of separatist dreams, racial fantasies and hate nightmares thinned out and passed away, what was presented to that awakening human brain? A little sunlit planet, for its external material, bearing what we now realise is not a tithe of its possible flora and fauna, a ball crammed with unused and unsuspected resources; and for the internal stuff of that brain almost limitless possibilities of mental achievement. All that had been done hitherto by man was like the scribbling of a little child before eye and hand have learnt sufficient co-ordination to draw. It was like the pawing and crawling of a kitten before it begins to see. And now man's eyes were open.

This little planet of which he was now at last in mentally untroubled possession was not simply still under-developed and waste; its surface was everywhere scarred and disfigured by the long wars he had waged so blindly for its mastery. Everywhere in 2059 the scenery of the earth still testified to the prolonged war, the state of siege to establish a unified mastery, that had now come to an end. If most of the divisions and barriers of the period of the sovereign states had disappeared, if there were no longer castles, fortifications, boundaries and strategic lines to be traced, there were still many indications that the world was under control and still not quite sure of its own good behaviour. The carefully planned system of aerodromes to prevent any untoward developments of the free private flying that had been tolerated after 2040 was such an indication, and so was the strategic import plainly underlying the needlessly wide main roads that left no possible region of insurrection inaccessible. From the air or on a map it was manifest that the world was still 'governed'. The road system was like a net cast over a dangerous beast.

And equally visible still was the quality of recent conquests in the social and economic fields. As Theotocopulos complained, the Second Council overdid its embankments, it was distrustful even of the waters of the earth. Its reservoirs and rivers had, he says, 'a bullied air'. If the jostling little fields and misshapen ill-proportioned farms, the untidy mines, refuse-heaps, factories, workshops, slums and hovels and all the dire squalor of competitive industrialism had long since disappeared from the spectacle, there was still effort visible at every point in the layout of twenty-first-century exploitation. The stripping and burning of forests that had devastated the world so extensively in the middle decades of the preceding hundred years had led to strenuous reafforestation. Strenuous is the word. 'Grow,' said the Council, 'and let there be no nonsense about it.' At the end of the Age of Frustration a tree that was not lined up and lopped and drilled was an exception in the landscape.

Everywhere there was still this suggestion of possible insubordination and the sense of an underlying threat. Man had struggled desperately and had won, but it was only now that he was finding time to consider any but the most immediate and superficial possibilities of his planet.

The air-view as the dispersing delegates from Mégève saw it forty-seven years ago was indeed in the vividest contrast to the world garden to which we live to-day. That clumsy rationality, that real dread of aestheticism, that had haunted the Council to its end, had made the artificial factors in the landscape inelegant and emphatic almost without exception. Bridges and roads 'got there', as Theotocopulos said, 'like charging rhinoceroses'. True that the disposition to squat forms, which came from the age of the air raids, no longer prevailed, but there was a general tendency to make buildings too solid and too big; they had sometimes a certain grandiose boldness, but more often than not there was a touch of military stupidity in the appearance of their piled-up masses. They stood to attention. There was a needlessly lavish abundance of pylons, and they were generally too sturdy.

The enrichment of vegetation which is now world-wide was in operation at that time only in a few experimental areas; in most regions there was still hardly more forest or cultivation than had existed a century and a half before. If the devastation of fellings and fires during the last wars had been replaced by the new straight-ruled squared-out forests, there was as yet no perceptible rise in the level of the plant community anywhere; what had previously been forest was plantation or forest again, and what had been prairie was still prairie, differing only from the grass prairies of older days in the dwindling contingent of weeds and wild flowers. In spite of the self-complacency of the forestry department of that time, many trees distorted by disease survived, and most were by our standards stunted. To young eyes to-day this world of our fathers, as they see it in picture book and panorama, has not merely a regimented but a barren look, and its cultivation seems laborious and poor.

Yet compared with the landscape of two centuries ago its aspect was relatively prosperous, spacious and orderly. There is something very touching in the freely expressed response of the nineteenth-century folk to both urban and country landscape and to natural scenery generally. They did not dream how meagre their descendants were to find the spectacle before them. They had, at any rate, as good

443

cloudscapes and sunsets as we have, and such natural coast scenery as that of Western Scotland was practically the same then as it is to-day. They would endure irksome travel to see sunlit snowy mountain masses or get to some viewpoint that caught the rhythm of a distant chain. They loved water and woodlands and distant fields in a wide view, and towns they admire chiefly as piled up accumulations seen from a distance. Also they delighted very greatly in the close brightness of flowering hedges, sheets of bluebells, primrose ridges, green moss and tendrils and any sort of flower. They pick these things out for appreciation so persistently in their literature and paintings that it is only with an effort we realise how much they were 'picked out', and how dull and repetitive were endless miles of their normal roads and countryside and how flatly forbidding the ordinary aspects of their habitations.

So far as we can reconstruct it now the prevalent note of the nineteenth century scene was weak insipidity, degenerating very easily into a distressful means ungainliness. America was frost-bitten in the north and slovenly in the south and unkempt everywhere. Happily the shorter-lived, not very healthy or vigorous folk of these days had no standards of comparison, and actual intimations of discontent with nature and the countryside were rare. There is scarcely an admission in nineteenth-century literature that the larger part of the world was gaunt, unsatisfactory and utterly unsympathetic. Writers and poets did not dare to admit as much because they had neither the hope nor the energy to make things better. They would not see it in obedience to an elementary psychological law.

But under the Second Council, the criticism not only of man's achievement but of natural insufficiency had become voluminous because neither was felt any longer to be final. It was not only the heavy engineering, the massive buildings and the over-emphasised roadways that those returning delegates threatened with their minds. Much of the land was still unsettled. They looked down on areas of marsh and scrub, bare wilderness of rock, rainless regions, screes and avalanche slopes. For them as for us it was a world of promise still to be fulfilled.

'Now we can begin on all this,' they said. 'Now we have really to begin.'

§ 2. *Keying up the Planet.*

It had long been known that the vegetation of earth and sea, on which the volume and vigour of all other life depends, was not nearly commensurate with the available moisture and sunlight. As early as the nineteen thirties it was being pointed out by an English economic botanist, Frederick Keeble (1870–75, *Collected Works* in the Science section of the Reprints), that there were delays and arrests in the multiplication of diatoms, seasonal grass crops and other extensive primary vegetable growths, arrests due to the fact that while all other conditions were favourable the supply of assimilable nitrogen was too slow to keep up the growth process. He applied the agricultural lesson of manuring to the whole spectacle of life and insisted that we were living in a 'nitrogen-starved world'. Nitrogen is yielded up by the inorganic world to the uses of life with extreme reluctance. This observation of Keeble's threw a new light for most people on the alleged bounty of nature. Other workers in the same field spread their observations to other elements. Carlos Metom (1927–2014), in a striking passage, compared life on our planet to 'a starveling foal on a barren patch that has never learnt to look for green pasture'.

This fundamental poverty of terrestrial existence can be traced through most of the geological record. Life has been a stinted thing. There were a few periods of exuberance, the period of the Coal Measures for example, when life seemed really to pour upward; but for most of recorded time life nibbled round the outside of a ball of limitless mineral wealth to which it had no key. No individual intelligence could ever penetrate that hidden hoard of plenty. It was only when the collective mentality of Science had arisen and was going on deathlessly from one clarification to another that a far more abundant vegetable basis for animal and human existence came within the range of possibility, and only now that the waste of human energy in warfare and unco-ordinated trading and money-getting was at an end for ever, that the realisation of that possibility could be attempted. But hundreds of thousands of brains are now alight with the prospect of evoking such a plenty and wealth of life on our planet as the whole universe had never dreamed of before this time.

The Second Council, in the beginning of its long reign, had not a sufficient knowledge of the latent powers of applied biology to anticipate this fundamental enrichment of life. It conceived its role to be the working-out of the logical consequences of mechanical invention during the nineteenth and twentieth centuries. The greatest of these consequences were the abolition of distance and the super-session of toil by power machinery. The goal of the Council was to confirm and establish human unity for ever, and to set up a frame of progressive public activities that should provide universal employment and universal purchasing power in the face of a continually increasing industrial efficiency. At first it was preoccupied by the persecuting activities that were needed to secure the world against any reaction towards private monopolisation, romantic national-ism, religious eccentricism and social fission. Then, as its success in this direction passed beyond challenge, as the world community was plainly assured, it found itself con-fronted by an ever more portentous problem of leisure.

It seemed a natural outlet for the surplus of human energy to provide among other things for an enormous development of scientific research and an exploration of the deeper mineral resources of the earth's crust. The Council assigned something like a third of the resources available for science to biological work, and it does not seem to have occurred to these rulers of the world, preoccupied as they were with the suppression, the excessive suppression, the obliteration even, of deleterious and antiquated separatist doctrines and the refashioning of economic life, that this huge growth of biological enquiry would result in anything more than the extinction of plant and animal diseases, and improvements and economies in cultivation. It was outside the range of their imaginations to anticipate a spate of biological invention that put the spate of mechanical invention which revolutionised the conditions of human life in the nineteenth and twentieth centuries altogether in the shade. Biological knowledge outgrew them just as aesthetic sensibility outgrew them.

From the thirties of the twenty-first century onward the conservatism of the Second Council had held back an increasing amount of scientific discoveries from practical application. The world was unified; it was supporting its population (which was being kept well below the modest safety line of 2,000 million) with absolute ease; its health was at a higher level than nature had ever known before; and it was, so far as the powers in being could manage it, marking time. It was like an adolescent who is still treated as a child. Even the new possibilities of exuberant vegetation were not being released. The areas needed for food supply could have been halved before 2050, but the Council decided that the consequent dislocation of the population would be likely to strain social order, and it kept four or five million people at the healthy but not very entertaining work of agricultural production, while it promoted enquiries for the 'industrial application of marginal excesses of foodstuffs'. It was not only producing, but distributing, staples in 2050 on precisely the lines adopted in 2020. It was restraining educational developments and innovations in building. It had made the world safe for humanity, and it meant to keep the world at that.

In 2047 Homer Lee Pabst published his remarkable researches on the effect upon chromosomes of certain gases derived from the old Sterilising Inhalation made from Permanent Death Gas. These gases are known now as Pabst's Kinetogens, and there is a whole series of them. Their general effect is to produce mutations of various types. They bring about, abundantly and controllably, a variability in life which has hitherto been caused only with comparative rarity by cosmic radiations. By 2050 the biological world was confronted by a score of absolutely new species of plants and—queer first-fruits in the animal world—by two new and very destructive species of rodent. The artificial evolution of new creatures had come within the range of human possibility.

Limitless possibilities opened before the human imagination. The Council gave way to panic. It saw the world it had taken such pains to put in order given over to uncontrollable vegetable and animal monstrosities. A nightmare of evil weeds and strange beasts dismayed it. Even the human type, it realised, was threatened. The laws restraining experiments upon animals were extended, and every animal novelty produced by Pabst was to be reported upon and destroyed. Plant novelties of decorative or economic value were, however, to be tolerated. Within his laboratory and experimental grounds Pabst ignored these prohibitions, and the faculty of science increased the endowment of the new experimental genetics. And now that the Supreme Council could no longer interfere, the Transport and General Distribution Control, the newly developed section of the Behaviour Control and the Health Services took up Pabst results and arranged a conference (2060) for their proper exploitation. A general plan for the directed evolution of life upon the planet was drawn up, a plan which, with various amendments, is in operation to this day.

Most of the 'wild beasts' of our ancestors are now under control in their special enclosures and reservations. There are fifteen Major Parks of over five hundred square miles in which various specially interesting faunas and floras flourish without human interference, except for the occasional passage of some qualified observer on foot or the transit of a specially licensed aeroplane overhead. Adventurous holiday-makers are excluded. The creatures in these areas are less affected by man than were their predecessors. They form a valuable reserve control of the genetic tentatives that are being made upon their more or less captive brethren. The most startling result of these experiments is Dumoric's claim to have restored, by means of carefully bred crosses and the cultivation of atavistic types, extinct ancestral forms of the fallow deer.

One beneficial result of the preoccupation of the Second Council with the problem of employment for idle hands and minds had been the very great advances made in both mineralogical and meteorological science. It did not realise that the systematic observation of winds and rainfall could possibly upset its orderly world. Indeed, the prospect of forbidding the wind to blow where it listed was entirely after the Council's heart. So, too, the possibility of controlling or drying up volcanoes and earthquakes appealed very strongly to it. Before 2000, man's knowledge of the composition of what he used to call the earth's 'crust' and the mineral resources of the planet beneath that crust was extraordinarily superficial. Geologists relied almost entirely for their knowledge upon surface features, chance exposures and industrial excavations. But the ever increasing resources available for research made a systematic probing and exploration of the deeper layers increasingly possible. The student will find in any contemporary textbook of Geology an account of the series of beautiful contrivances such as the Shansi borer, the Hull and Watkins 'diviner' and the Noguchi petrograph, which have now made, so to speak, hidden things visible to a depth of twenty-five miles, and there too he will find a description of a score of ingenious devices for isolating blocks of deep-lying rock and bringing their desirable ingredients to the surface. Until a hundred years ago nothing of this sort was even imagined. Instead of employing the energy imprisoned underground to drive what was needed to the surface, the scanty product of the old-world mines was *hauled* up by human or mechanical powers from above and the ores and coal and salt were actually hewn out *in situ* by hordes of sweating, underpaid human beings.

Equally rapid was the progress of meteorology once the Second Council gave its mind to that subject. Practical meteorology was of very recent date. Except for a little work with the barometer from 1643 onward, forecasting began only in the nineteenth century and was not systematically attempted until 1850. An infinitesimal tampering with the composition of the air began in the early twentieth century. Then man found himself able to withdraw nitrogen from it, but this was done only to provide fertilisers, and in such small quantities as to make no appreciable effect upon the composition of the atmosphere. Little more was attempted until the last war, when the local use of substances like the so-called Permanent Death Gas was carried out on a sufficiently big scale to amount to a transitory readjustment of the air over the region poisoned. Then in the thirties of the twenty-first century there was an extensive use of gas on a large scale to destroy locusts, rodents and various insect pests. Considerable enthusiasm was shown at the time, but one or two unfortunate accidents cooled the zeal of the Council. It was realised that air-mixing for anything but stimulating and purifying purposes must wait upon the achievement of wind control. Air-mixing was put back into the pigeonholes with a gathering number of other gifts from science that the Council deemed premature.

The Joint Commission for replanning the world found itself therefore with three correlated groups of possibility challenging its spirit of adventure. A new flora of several thousand species was awaiting release from the experimental grounds, and this was only the easiest of the apparently limitless possibilities of animal and vegetable variations that experimental biology was taking up. A huge and hitherto unsuspected wealth of mineral substances was ready to come out of the deep-lying rocks and refresh the rather limited and jaded resources of the contemporary soil.

And alterations in the composition and movements of the atmosphere were no longer inaccessibly beyond human effort. The obstruction of individual ownership and localised governments had been swept away for ever. In that respect the Second Council had beyond question triumphed. But the very vigour with which it had done its task for man and the world as they were, and still in effect are, had cleared the ground for such an unprecedented inventiveness as is now rapidly altering not only the face but the very substance of life.

The Replanning Commission set about its task with the leisurely energy of a body under no stress of necessity. 'Life is quite good as it is,' runs the Introduction to its Draft plan. 'But it is part of the fundamental goodness of life that we have as much incessant novelty as we desire at our disposal. Due proportion must be our perpetual care. Want of proportion in the development of new things was the general cause of the great bulk of human suffering and frustration during the past five centuries. We have now an organisation of Controls that can restrain anything like the spasmodic mercenary enterprise, without plan or balance, that let loose disaster in the early twentieth century. We can afford to look before we leap and measure within quite close limits the tale of consequences we set going. In the end we may find that there was very considerable justification for the restraint put by our Supreme Council upon the immediate application of recent inventions, and particularly of recent biological inventions, which might otherwise have precipitated very similar but even more fundamental and catastrophic disproportions to those which overwhelmed the capitalist civilisation of the nineteenth century.

'The particular field in which we propose a continuation of restraint is in the application of the rapidly advancing science of genetics to the increase of variability so far as human beings, and probably some other of the higher mammals, are concerned. We believe that the general feeling of the race is against any such experimentation at present. Under the Second Council the painless destruction of

451

monsters and the more dreadful and pitiful sorts of defective was legalised, and also the sterilisation of various types that would otherwise have transmitted tendencies that were plainly undesirable. This is as far, we think, as humanity should go in directing its racial heredity, until our knowledge of behaviour has been greatly amplified. For an age or so we can be content with humanity as it now is, humanity no longer distressed and driven to cruelty by overcrowding, under-nourishment, infections, mental and physical poisons of every sort. There is a rich mine of still greatly underdeveloped capacity in the human brain as it is, and this we may very happily explore by means of artistic effort, by scientific investigations, by living freely and gaily, for the next few generations. Normal human life can be cleansed, extended and amplified. With that we propose to content ourselves. Even upon this planet we have millions of years ahead before there can be any fundamental change in our environment.

'Directly we turn from humanity to other forms of life it is manifest that a most attractive realm is opening to us. We may have new and wonderful forests; we may have new plants; we may replace the weedy and scanty greensward of the past by a subtler and livelier texture. Undreamt-of fruits and blossoms may be summoned out of non-existence. The insect world, on which so much of the rest of life depends, may be made more congenial to mankind. The smaller fry of life and the little beasts and the birds can be varied now until they all come into a tolerable friendship with ourselves. As our hands lose their clumsiness we may interfere more and more surely with the balance of life. There is no longer fear of abundance now that man is sane.

'Our planning of human activities for the next few generations will involve no fundamental changes at all for humanity. It will be a keying-up of the sort of life for which our race, however darkly, confusedly and unsuccessfully, has always striven. At present deliberate weather-control is too big a task for us, but we believe that a sure weather calendar for a year or so ahead is now becoming possible.

An immense series of enterprises to change the soil, lay-out, vegetation and fauna, first of this region and then of that, will necessitate a complete rearrangement of the mines, deep quarries, road network and heavy sea transport of the globe. None of this need be ugly or repulsive, even in the doing; it can all be made intensely interesting. Engineering structure, which was once clumsy and monstrous, is now becoming as graceful as a panther. Industrial enterprises that formerly befouled the world with smoke, refuse and cinder heaps, are now cleaner in their habits than a well-trained cat. The world lay-out of the Second Council, designed apparently for a static society, will be to a large extent swept aside by our new operations. And no doubt our achievements in their turn will give way to still bolder and lovelier enterprises.'

So ran the Introduction to what is known as the Keying-up Plan of 2060. To-day we are most of us still immersed in its realisation. It has given the world occupation without servitude and leisure without boredom. When we have had enough of our own work for a time we fly off—or walk round the corner—to see what other people are doing. The world is full of interest and delight, from the forest gardens of the Amazons with their sloths, monkeys and occasional pumas and alligators to that playground of the world, the snowfields of the Himalayas. We can arrange to take a turn with the meteorological observers in the upper air, or tune our lungs for a spell in the deep-sea galleries below the rafts of Atlantis. There we can see the great cephalopods of the middle levels coming for their food or watch the head-long growth of a giant pearl.

We are already so accustomed to grace, beauty and variety in all the details and general forms about us that it is only by turning over the pictures and records of seventy years ago that we realise how relatively uneventful were the first decades of human unity. At first man seems to have been so exhausted by his escape from massacre, disease, economic waste and general futility, and so terrified by the thought of any relapse into the old confusions, conflicts and

453

economic cannibalism, that he was capable of nothing but order. But he gathers courage. It is not only our world that is being keyed up, but ourselves.

§ 3. Geogonic Planning

Among the 'deferred projects' that lie behind our current activities, and second only to the system of schemes for inducing and directing a great increase in human variability, is the complex of plans that have been drawn out to alter the terrestrial contours. Here again is something far too great and dangerous for our present wisdom, but something which it seems inevitable our race will ultimately attempt.

At present, and for many generations yet, we are still the creatures and subjects of geography; the oceans and great mountain chains condition our lives. They determine habitats, which again determine the human type best adapted to live for the greater part of its life in this or that region. Every kind of us, dark or fair, thick-set or slender, black or buff, has its own distinctive best place in which to rear its children and work and rest. It may roam the earth as it will, but only in certain regions is it altogether at home. No type is at home everywhere. There is no universal man. A universal type of man would be possible only on a flat and uniform earth. There is a necessary variety in humanity which no one now desires to diminish.

But the question the modern geographer puts to us is whether there is not a classification of habitats possible, into very desirable, undesirable and inimical, and whether a certain modification of the planet-levels operating in conjunction with the restoration of forests now in progress

454

would not greatly increase the desirable habitats, by a redistribution of rainfall, a change in the fall of the surface waters, protection from winds and so forth. A not very considerable rise in the Apennines, for instance, would bring them up to the permanent snow-line and change the character of the entire Italian peninsula. And an increase in desirable habitats may bring with it an increase in the variety of desirable human types.

Yesterday this sort of thing was called 'chimerical', to-day it is impracticable and unnecessary, because of the volcanic forces that might be released. So for the present the geogonist, like the geneticist, must content himself with dreams—in his case dreams of moulding a fire-spouting, quivering planet closer to the expanding needs of man. His turn to remodel the world will come perhaps in a thousand years or so. There is plenty of time for that.

§ 4. *Changes in the Control of Behaviour*

The past forty-eight years have seen very great modifications in the social control of individual behaviour. There has been a very great increase in the science, skill and quality of the teachers throughout the world, but quite apart from that the character and purpose of education and police have changed profoundly.

Education as we understand it to-day began about the middle of the twentieth century. It had only the slenderest continuity with the education of the preceding age, just as the education of Christendom had only the slenderest continuity with the education of the pagan world. Reading, writing and counting were taught in all three systems, but

455

beyond that the very objectives were different. Modern education began as propaganda after the time of De Windt, as the propaganda of the Modern State. It sought to establish a new complete ideology and a new spirit which would induce the individual to devote himself and to shape all his activities to one definite purpose, to the attainment and maintenance of a progressive world-socialism, using an efficient monetary system as its normal medium of relationship.

This seemed, and was, a gigantic undertaking. It faced colossal obstacles in ordinary human nature. But it was supremely necessary if human civilisation was to continue. The alternative was a relapse through chaotic barbarism to animal casualness and final extinction. Thought and behaviour patterns had to be shaped therefore to subserve this objective, to the relative disregard of any other conceivable purpose. The Modern State became the whole duty of man. This propaganda passed necessarily into a training for public service and a universal public education. The Modern State Fellowship was a trained body pledged to impose its own type of training upon all the world. It proposed to be the New Humanity. It would accept no compromises. It made the whole educational framework militant. No other type of school and no other system of teaching was tolerated for more than half a century. Never before was man so directed and disciplined.

The educationists of this period of the First Council and the Air Dictatorship were particularly sedulous to restrain what they called 'aberrant motives'. Austerity in eating and drinking, hardiness, severity in exercise, a jealousy of leisure and a profound distrust of aesthetic and sensuous gratification, and particularly of sexual excitement, marked the educational ideals of these men who set out to remodel the world. In the early stages of progressive and revolutionary thought in the nineteenth century there had been considerable laxity of private conduct. There had been a revolt against what was called 'Christian morality', and a disposition not simply to condone but encourage indulgence in forms that had hitherto been prohibited. Most of this 'liberalism' in conduct had vanished from revolutionary circles by the second or third decade of the twentieth century. The Modern State Movement, as it developed, was pervaded by a disapproval of every sort of sensuous or emotional affection. The business in hand could not suffer it. It wasted time; it wasted energy. It let in too much intrigue. It undermined the common loyalty. Not even Christianity in its most militant stages was so set against the dissipation of energy in this direction. The new sexual puritanism differed from the old in its toleration of birth control, its disregard of formal marriage and a certain charity towards the first excesses of youth, but it insisted with even greater vigour upon public decency and upon the desirability of sexual seriousness, enduring connexions and complete loyalty between lovers. As a result the world was far more monogamous, more decorous and decently busy after 2000 C.E. than it had ever been before.

Many critics to-day are disposed to consider the repressions of that time excessive. We are now in a different phase; the militant age is past. They allege that there was a vast amount of secret and solitary vice and moral and mental distortion beneath the cold surface of things during these disciplined years, and they consider that the undeniable harshness and obstinacy of the Second Council as it grew old was a direct result of its puritanism. They do not hesitate to use such terms as masochist and sadist. But this is by no means a unanimous opinion. Equally reputable authorities deny that there was any such seething pit of stifled desires and thwarted motives under the orderly and healthy activities of the constructive time as this new school pretends. In no psychological problem are we still so inadequately informed as in the quantitative estimate of sexual impulse and restraint.

Our investigators work at literature, biographies, diaries, pictorial art, police reports in their intricate attempt to recover the vanished mental states of these departed generations. There seems to be a sort of rhythm in these things.

The contrast between present conditions and conditions seventy years ago is paralleled in history by the contrast between English social life in 1855 and 1925. There also we have a phase of extreme restraint and decorum giving way to one of remarkable freedom. We can trace every phase. Every phase is amply documented. There are not the slightest grounds for supposing that the earlier period was one of intense nervous strain and misery. There was a general absence of vivid excitation, and the sexual life flowed along in an orderly fashion. It did not get into politics or the control of businesses. It appears in plays and novels like a tame animal which is not to be made too much of. It goes out of the room whenever necessary. By comparison England in 1920 was out for everything it could do sexually. It did everything and boasted about it and incited the young. As the gravity of economic and political problems increased and the structural unsoundness of the world became more manifest, sexual preoccupations seem to have afforded a sort of refuge from the mental strain demanded by the struggle. People distracted themselves from the immense demands of the situation by making a great noise about the intensifications and aberrations of the personal life. There was a real propaganda of drugs and homosexuality among the clever young. Literature, always so responsive to its audience, stood on its head and displayed its private parts. It produced a vast amount of solemn pornography, facetious pornography, sadistic incitement, resexualised religiosity and verbal gibbering in which the rich effectiveness of obscene words was abundantly exploited. It is all available for the reader to-day who cares to examine it. He will find it neither shocking, disgusting, exciting nor interesting. He will find it comically pretentious and pitifully silly.

It is small wonder that the scattered workers for the Modern State, who were struggling heroically with the huge problems of social dislocation and social reconstruction, developed an antipathy against these aesthetic and sexual preoccupations which robbed them of the help and service

458

of so many hopeful youngsters. The Modern State Movement was unobtrusively puritanical from the outset. After the romantic lapses of the First World Council it became oppressively puritanical.

It was the precedent of the moral disorder of the early twentieth century to which the Educational Control appealed, a hundred and twenty years later, to justify its sustained regulation of private morals and repression of stimulation. It failed to realise the profound difference of the new conditions. The florid ebullition of sexual troubles, sexual refinements and sexual grossnesses in the Age of Frustration had been a natural consequence of frustration. Everywhere in the face of challenges too huge to face, rich and poor alike found themselves aimless, unoccupied, menaced. Ill health was increasing. Drugs, alcohol and sex were available to excite and soothe and deaden their distressed nerves. Good-looking youth, which could not sell its brain or labour, could still find a market for its person. About every nucleus of unjustly acquired wealth or demoralised power prostitution and parasitism festered. What else was there to do in that ugly, unhappy and dangerous world? But the world of 2040 was a busy, keenly interested and healthy world again.

We cannot detail in this general review of history the reluctant lifting of one prohibition after another. We may now go naked, love as we like, eat, drink and amuse ourselves with our work or as we will, subject only to a proper respect for unformed minds. And no harm has been done at all. When the Puritanical Tyranny began, its directors felt they had imprisoned a tiger that would otherwise consume all the plenty and safety they achieved. Very reluctantly indeed, bit by bit and after endless disputes, were their prohibitions relaxed. And no tiger appeared. Properly nourished people do not take to gluttony, properly interested people are not overwhelmed by sex. Instead of a tiger appeared a harmless, quiet, unobtrusive and not unpleasing pussy-cat, which declined to be in any way notable.

Humanity was changing. The threatened outbreak of

459

pornography, abnormality and sex excitation did not occur. But anyone who studies the fiction and drama of the past half-century and compares it with the similar literature of the old world will realise that there are far more personal love and far more happy lovers than ever before, and that physical love to demonstrate loyalty, show preference, enrich association and seal friendship was never so direct and beautiful. Jealousy we have, but it is rarely malicious; desire, but it is rarely vicious. In this as in so many other things progress has meant simplification. The souls we read about of two centuries ago strike us as grotesquely tangled, tormented and nasty souls. Hate mingled with their desires; mercenary considerations were an ever present defilement; they paired dishonestly and mated insincerely.

But while there has been this release from the straitlaced sexual morals of the militant period, in another field there has been no relaxation. The new order can tolerate no tampering with the monetary-property system that holds us all together. Not only is our police incessantly alert against robbery and cheating as the old world understood it, but many gainful practices that 1920 would have considered tolerable or even admirable are suppressed, and are likely to be suppressed for all time. Gambling, the mean desire and device to get the spending of someone else's earnings, is punished as heavily as the forgery of money checks; and all those speculative activities which seemed to be the very texture of the nineteenth-century social order dare not reappear now in any disguise at all. Money is a check for our personal needs, or for the giving of graceful presents. There must be no misuse of money to gain an advantage over another human being, even with that other human being's connivance. There we are still bound. That sort of thing is the vice of cannibalism. Beyond that liberty increases daily.

With a sound education of mind and body and a rigorous and exact protection of property and money from dishonourable impulses, we have found that it is possible to give every human being such a liberty of movement and general behaviour as would have seemed incredible to those militant socialists who ruled the world during the earlier decades of the last century. But it is just because of their stern and thorough cleansing of human life that we can now live in freedom. We may go anywhere in the world now, we may do practically anything that we can possibly desire to do.

§ 5. *Organisation of Plenty*

Just as it becomes increasingly difficult for the teacher of history to convey to each new generation what human feelings and motives were like in a world of morbid infections and unwholesome bodily habits or in a heavily sentimentalised atmosphere of general distrust and insecurity, so also he has to make a most vigorous imaginative effort to recover even the faintest shadow of the pervading vexation, humiliations and straining anxiety that resulted from an almost universal deficiency of common things. Everybody, except a small minority, went short until the close of the twentieth century. Even the rich had to be wary, cunning buyers to satisfy all their fancies and desires. The simplified economic order of our world to-day runs so smoothly that we hardly think at all about our ordinary needs. Housing, food and clothing wait upon us wherever we go. It is so easily done that we fail to realise the immense cleansing away of obstructive difficulties that had to occur before it could be made so easy.

One of the results of abundance that our ancestors would have found paradoxical is the abolition of encumbrance. But the less there was in the past the more you had to have

461

and hold. Men had to appropriate things because there was not enough to go round. Your home was not simply the place to which you retired for solitude or intimacy; it was a storehouse. In the sixteenth or seventeenth century it was even fortified by bars, locks and bolts against robbers. You got with difficulty, and what you got you kept. The successful man of those days was imprisoned and smothered in accumulations upon which he dared not relax his watchfulness and grip. They were as indestructible as he could make them, for once destroyed or ignored they might prove irreplaceable. Everybody was keeping things, keeping them rather than using them. If they were not wanted now they might be wanted presently. If that successful man desired to vary his urban life he had to possess a country house. In these establishments there had to be a miniature social economy. Much of the food was not only prepared in the personal household, but produced on the private estate. All this had to be managed and watched to prevent waste, slackness and dishonesty. All the clothes the prosperous man might want to wear had to be stored and preserved in presses and wardrobes; his household needed gear against any possible emergency; and all his accumulations had to be guarded against robbers. It was almost as anxious and wearing a job to be rich as to be poor in those days of general insufficiency. And if the rich man travelled, he had to travel in his own coach with his attendants, taking a great burthen of clothing and general luggage with him.

In the relatively plentiful days of the later nineteenth century which in so many details foreshadowed and yet failed to complete and generalise the conditions of our own time, there was for the prosperous at least a certain alleviation of the burthen of property. The temporary achievement of a limited cosmopolitanism of money and credit, the multiplication of the bourgeoisie, the liquidation of ownership by joint-stock undertakings, the increased facilities for communication and movement, made successful people less disposed to sit down amidst their possessions. There was a sustained general effort, which we now find grotesque and irrational, to keep property and at the same time not to be bothered by property. The ideal of success, was no longer concrete ownership but purchasing power. Houses, furnishings and so forth changed hands with increased readiness.

Instead of living in great complete houses and dining at home, people lived in smaller houses or flats and dined in collective dining-rooms or restaurants. They gave up having country houses of their own and travelled freely and variously, evoking a vast industry of hotels and hired villas. They travelled lighter—in comparison with preceding centuries, that is. As retail trade organised itself upon big-business lines, the need for the private storage of gear diminished. People bought things when they wanted them, because now they could do so. The big 'stores' of the early twentieth century carried an enormous and greatly varied stock.

In the days of Shakespeare new clothes, new furniture, new houses, new things of all sorts were infrequent; in the early twentieth century there were already intimations of the general fresh newness of our own times. The facilities for scrapping were still poorly developed, and there was much congestion and endless litter about, but renewal and replacement for those who had purchasing power were already well developed. If it had not been for the social catastrophe due to ignorance, individualism, monetary deflation and nationalism that overwhelmed that phase of civilisation, the distributing organisation of the world might very probably have developed straight on from the system of linked stores as it flourished in America in 1925 to our present conditions. And similarly there was an expansion of hotel life and a belated beginning of portable country houses, clearly foreshadowing our current arrangements.

After the disasters and new beginnings of the middle decades of the twentieth century it was to the patterns of big business at the close of the First Age of Abundance that the direction of the Transport Union recurred. We have told how easily and necessarily that Union became the trading monopoly and finally, as the Air and Sea Control, the

463

actual government of the renascent world. Its counting-houses issuing and receiving its energy notes became the New Banking; its Trading Council became the New Retailing; its Supply Control took over, at last, the productive activities of the world. From the first the new powers were instinct with the idea of mobility. They had no vestiges in their composition of the skimping and saving traditions of the ages of insufficiency. They set about providing as ample and various accommodation for everything as the ever-increasing production of the planet permitted.

The great distributing stores of the previous age provided the patterns from which the new distribution developed in that age of recovery. Wherever old towns and cities were being reconstructed or new ones appearing about new centres of productive activity the architects of the Air and Sea Control erected their great establishments, at first big and handsome after the old fashion and then more finely planned. At first these stores sold things according to the old method, then gradually in regard to a number of things, to clothing for example, they organised the modern system of exchanging new things for old; the new shoes or garment would be made and fitted to the customer and the old taken away and pulped or otherwise disposed of. Nothing is cobbled nowadays; nothing is patched or repaired. By degrees this method abolished that ancient institution the laundry altogether. That line of fluttering patched and tattered garments so characteristic of old world village scenery vanished from the earth. New rapid methods of measuring and fitting replaced the tape, scissors and sewing of the old days. In the time of the Hoover Slump men would wear their underclothes for years, having them painfully washed out, dried, ironed and returned weekly, and they would wear their complex outer garments with all the old fastenings, buttons, straps, buckles and so forth, sometimes for many years. They had to be made of dark fabrics with broken patterns to conceal their griminess. The clothing of the Middle Ages was still filthier. Nowadays the average life of our much simpler and brighter outer garments with their convenient zip fastenings is about a week, and such light underclothes as we wear last about three days. We keep no wardrobes of them; the stores are our wardrobes. If the weather changes the stores are ready for us everywhere with wraps or heavier or lighter materials. It must be a remote expedition indeed that needs a change of raiment. We wear less clothing than our ancestors, partly because of our healthier condition, partly because we do not like to hide lovely bodies, but mainly because in the past men wrapped themselves up against every contingency. They wore hats whenever they were not under a roof, socks inside their boots, buttons on their sleeve-cuffs, collars and ties. It seems as though these elaborations became necessary to social prestige because of the general shortage. In an age of scarcity it was a testimonial to one's worth to be fully clad. In the nineteenth century the well-to-do wore gold watch-chains and gloves, which they carried in their hands in hot weather, as further evidence of substantial means.

Housing again, under the Air and Sea Control, took off from the point where the hotel-flat had left it in 1930. There was never any attempt to resume the building of those small permanent houses which were spread so abundantly over England, for example, after the World War. The first task of the new world control was mainly sanitary. Infection lurked everywhere; four decades of social disorder had made every building a decaying disease-trap for the young that were born into it. The Housing Control rebuilt the housing quarters of the rotten old towns in the form of blocks of dwellings, clean, spacious and convenient, but, to our eyes now, very squat and dull. They were from ten to twelve stories high, and very soundly and honestly made. Everywhere they had water, lighting, heating in the colder climates and sanitation. The picturesquely clustering rural villages were replaced all over the earth by the same type of concentrated house-block, the style and material varying only so far as conditions of climate required it. The villages were literally swept up into these piles. Even where small private cultivation was still going on, the concentration into these mansions occurred and the peasants bicycled out to their properties. Every block had its crèche, its school, its store and its general meeting-rooms.

As we look back on it this supersession of the single separate unlit, undrained and waterless hut or hovel, cottage or little steading seems to have been a swift business, but in reality it took from 1980 to 2030, much more than half the average lifetime, to spread this new conception of housing over most of the world, and by that time in the more advanced regions the older blocks were already being replaced by more beautiful and convenient creations.

Historical Pictures shows us the whole process. We see the jumbling growths of the early phase of the twentieth century; towering apartment-houses and hotels struggling up, far above the churches, mosques, pagodas and public buildings, out of a dense undergrowth of slums. Then come arrest and decline. The pictures become as full of ruins, sheds and makeshift buildings as the drawings of Albrecht Dürer. Amidst these appear air-raid shelters with their beetling covers, first-aid pillars with their chequered markings and anti-aircraft forts. Further ruin ensues and we see life disorganised by the Great Plague.

Then suddenly these stout, squat, virtuous new blocks thrust into the scene and the battered past vanishes. A new Age has begun. The towns grow larger, finer and more varied. The housing blocks are grouped with the expanding stores, public clubs and hotels in parks and gardens near to the aerodrome, and convenient for whatever industry gives the agglomeration its importance. The public club became prominent after 2000 C.E., both architecturally and socially. That again was the revival of two old ideas; it was a combination of the idea of the English or American club with the idea of the Baths to which the Roman citizens resorted. Here from the start were grouped the gymnastic and sport halls, dancing-floors, conference rooms, the perpetual news cinema, libraries, reading-rooms, small studies, studios and social centres of the reviving social life.

The twenty-first century rediscovered an experience of the

nineteenth and of the first centuries of the Christian Era, a discovery that was also made by Alexander the Great, that it is much easier to build great modern cities in new places than to modernise the old centres of activity. And the more vital these old centres remained the more difficult was their reconstruction, because it meant the interruption and transfer of important activities to new quarters. New York was typical of this lag in rebuilding. Up to quite recently Lower New York has been the most old-fashioned city in the world, unique in its gloomy antiquity. The last of the ancient skyscrapers, the Empire State Building, is even now under demolition in 2106 C.E.!

This was not because New York has fallen out of things, but, on the contrary, because it was in the van of the new movement. We have already quoted Nicholson's account of its reviving importance in 1960. A year or so later it became the headquarters of the American branch of the Air and Sea Control, a western equivalent to Basra. The swiftly expanding activities of the new government needed immediate housing, and the gaunt surviving piles of Lower New York were adapted hastily to its accommodation. This kept them going for a time, and then arose a prolonged controversy between rival schools of planning for the reconstruction of that strangely vital city. It is not only true that the poorer the world was the more it was encumbered by property, but also that the more vigorously a place or a building is being used in progressive work the more difficult it is to keep it up to date.

Since the middle of the twenty-first century there has been a worldwide reappearance of the individual home, more particularly on the countryside, by the sea, and amidst forests and mountain scenery. But it has reappeared in a new form. It is not really the same thing as the old cottage and country house.

The idea of a home made of portable material, constructed at some convenient industrial centre and sent to any desired site, was already in the minds of such restless innovators as Henry Ford before the Decline and Fall. The country college, the country house, is an imaginative outlet. For great numbers of men and women comes a phase when the desire for that little peculiar place, with its carefully chosen site, its distinctive long-coveted amenities, its outlet upon the woods, the mountain, the jungle or the sea, has an overpowering appeal. There they will live, dream, work and be happy. Few of the many who had that dream could satisfy it in the old days. Some rare, rich persons were able to buy land, build elaborately after their desires, make gardens. When they died or became bankrupt other people without the leisure to make their own homes bought the abandoned home. They would far rather have made a place for themselves, but there stood the predecessor's desire in brick or stone, solid and irremovable, and they did what they could, by means of alterations, to eliminate the taste of him.

But as plenty and mechanical power increased, as the new road system made more and more of the earth accessible, as power-cables and water supply spread everywhere, it became easy not only to clear away and obliterate the traces of houses that were done for, but to bring a pleasant individualised country house within the purchasing power of an increasing proportion of the population. The mastery of power in our time is manifested almost as much by its swift scrapping and scavenging as by its limitless productivity. Nowadays a man or woman may hit upon an unoccupied site, spend a few pleasant weeks planning and revising projects and designs, and give his order. In a month his home is ready, in a day or so more the foundation has been laid, and in three or four weeks the dream is realised; the house stands as he wished it to stand, connected to the power mains, supplied with water, furnished to his taste, smiling and ready. It is hardly more trouble than ordering an aeroplane or an automobile.

In its earlier stages the evocation of the preconstructed house was not so rapid, but from the first it was far quicker than the laborious piling up of the old-world builder.

And with an equal facility now a house is cleared away.

We no longer think it meet to wear another man's abandoned house any more than we think it proper to wear the clothes of the dead. Clearing away, says Michael Kemal, is the primary characteristics of the Modern Age. The Age of Frustration was essentially an age that could not clear away, either debts, sovereignties, patriotisms, old classes, old boundaries, old buildings, old scores or old grievances. It is only in the past century that man has learnt the real lesson of plenty, that far more important than getting things is getting rid of things. We are rich universally because we are no longer rich personally.

We have mentioned the travelling wealthy man of the seventeenth century, for then only the wealthy aristocrats could travel freely, and we have glanced at the cumbersome impedimenta of his voyage. Compare him with any ordinary man to-day who decides to take a holiday and go to the ends of the earth. He may arrange with a travel bureau overnight for one or two special accommodations, then off he goes in the clothes he wears. He takes a wallet with his money account, his identification papers and perhaps a memorandum book. He may wear, as many people do, a personal ornament or so that has taken a hold upon his imagination. He may carry something to read or a specimen he wants to show. Whatever else he is likely to want on his way he will find on his way. He needs no other possessions because his possessions are everywhere. We have solved the problem of socialising property, the problem the early twentieth century was unable to solve. We have the use and consumption of material goods without the burthen of ownership.

§ 6. The Average Man Grows Older and Wiser

The numbers and the quality of the human population have changed very greatly in the past two centuries. Always these things have varied; every animal and vegetable species fluctuates continually in the numbers and quality of its individuals; but it is only recently that these movements have been recorded and examined systematically. The anti-progressives of the early twentieth century loved to assert that 'human nature' never altered; to imagine that the men of the Stone Age felt and thought like bank clerks picknicking in a cave, and that the ideas of Confucius and Buddha were easily interchangeable with the ideas of Rousseau, Karl Marx or De Windt. They were not simply ignorant but misinformed about almost every essential fact in the past experiences and present situation of the race. Only when the twenty-first century was well under way did any consciousness of the primary operating forces in human biology appear in the discussion and conduct of world affairs.

In the year 1800 the total population of the world was under 900 millions, and the average age was about 22. In 1900 the population had doubled and the average age had risen by nearly ten years. In 1935 a maximum was attained of 2,000 millions and the average age had mounted to nearly 40. In a hundred years the facilities for intercommunication and physical reaction had increased beyond all measure. But the statesmen, educators and lawyers of that age, as we have shown very plainly in this history, were unaware of any of these differences that had occurred since their methods were developed. They drooled along according to precedent. A set-back for adjustment was therefore inevitable. We have told the broad facts of the crash that began with the war massacres of 1914–18 and culminated in the cycle of pestilences before 1957. In thirty years the population of the earth fell to about one thousand million or less, and the average age receded to something about 23. This was a stupendous recession, not merely in numbers but in the maturity of the average mind.

Then came the Air and Sea Control and the First and the Second Council with their restoration of hygienic conditions and their scientific planning. The increase of population was watched and restrained for a century, but the average age extended until now it is 62 and still rising. The population total crept back to 1,500 millions in 2060 and reached 2,000 millions again in 2085. It has become manifest that such a population is no longer unwieldy, and that with the scientific education and behaviour control we now possess, a considerable further increase can be contemplated without dismay.

The population of the earth is now 2,500 millions, and it will probably be let up to 4,000 millions as rapidly as the world is keyed up for its full support and happiness. The danger of such a population swarming dangerously or getting into panics, mental jams, crushes and insanitary congestions grows less and less. The opinion of contemporary authorities is that 4,000 millions is an optimum, and that before many decades have passed it will be possible to keep most of those born actively and happily alive to something like 90 years of age. But the question of the possibility and advisability of prolonging the individual life more than three or four decades beyond the 'three-score and ten' of the Biblical barbarian is still an open one. It is possible that there is a limit to the memories a brain can carry and to its power of taking new interest in fresh events. There may be a natural death for most people in the future about the age of a hundred or a little more, as painless and acceptable as going to bed and sleeping after a long and interesting day.

These quantitative biological alterations involve the profoundest differences in the quality of every life concerned.

471

It is not simply that each individual has now a justifiable faith that he will live out his life to the end, but that the conditions in which he lives call out quite a different re-action system from that evoked in the past. Before the Middle Ages people thought of their grandparents as older and mightier people, but we think of our ancestors as younger and feebler people. Those earlier generations were like fresh-water fish, living in shallow, saline and readily dried-up water, in comparison with others of the same species living in a deep, abundant, well-aerated and alto-gether congenial lake. They were continually uncomfort-able, constantly stranded by circumstances; they flapped about widely and died early. Although they were the same in essence, their behaviour, their very movements, were like the behaviour of a different species of being.

Consider the existence of a young man in Shakespeare's time. If he did not die young he aged rapidly. He would be heavy, old and pompous at forty. A swarm of ailments lay in wait for him to emphasise and accelerate his decay. Youth was stuff that would not endure. The beauty and vitality of women were even more evanescent. So they snatched at love and adventure. The world was full of Romeos and Juliets at the crest of their passionate lives in their teens, who nowadays would be in the college stage of education, a score of years away from any conclusive drama. The literature of the time witnesses to a universal normal swift transitoriness. The simple precipitate love story, the jealousy, the headlong revenge and so on makes the substances of drama, romance and poem. That and the grab at spendable wealth: El Dorado, treasure trove or robbery attempted and defeated. A career was made or marred by a week's folly, and there was little time to recover it before the end. It is extraordinarily interesting to note all the things in life that are left out by the Elizabethan litera-ture, and so to measure that smaller brighter circle of interest in that age.

The changing biological conditions between 1840 and 1940 mirror themselves faithfully in the art and reading of the decades. The novel, which is at first pervaded by a gay hello to life, which accepts everything as cheerfully as a young animal, which laughs, caricatures and incites, becomes reflective, analytical, purposeful. Life no longer ends at the first rush. The proportion of novels to other books diminishes. The penetration of the individual consciousness by the great social and economic processes that were going on becomes more and more evident. When literature revived at the close of the twentieth century it was an adult literature, expressing the mentality of readers and writers who were fully grown men and women in a planning world that had ceased to be accidental and incoherent. In the novel as it then reappeared there is much more about personal love and the interplay of character, but far less (and the proportion continues to diminish) about the primary love adventure.

That diminution of haste and avidity, of the quick egotism and swift uncritical judgment of youth, still continues. The deliberation, serenity and breadth of reference in the normal life increase. The years from thirty to seventy were formerly a sort of dump for the consequences of the first three decades; now they are the main part of life, the years of work, expression and complete self-discovery, to which these earlier stages are the bright, delightful prelude. There was a time when the man or woman over forty felt something of a survivor; he was 'staying on'; relatively the world swarmed with youth, with the swiftness, rivalries and shallowness of youth; the fitness of the ill-protected body had gone already; the elderly people who were 'getting on for fifty' moved slowly and had duller if sounder apprehensions. But now most of us are in the graver years with our bodies and apprehensions unimpaired, and there is no longer the same effect of being rather in the way of a juvenile treat. The Juvenile Treat, the age when even the old aped the young, ended in the World War and the economic collapse. After that came a struggle, at first unconscious and then open and declared, between youth and mental maturity.

In the bad years after the World War for a couple of generations there was a very unhappy relapse towards youthful predominance. The old people had failed to avert the collapse, the legitimate seniors for the new period were dead and broken and morally disorganised, and there was a sort of poetic justice in the stormy release of puerility that ensued. Italy was scourged by its hobbledehoys in black shirts; Russia was ruled by the blue-chinned Young; Ireland was devastated by hooligan patriots; presently Germany, after brooding over its defeat for ten years, had a convulsive relapse to fiercely crazy boyishness in the Nazis. Indian patriotism had a kindred immaturity. The tender years of many of the young revolutionaries executed by the British, outrage our standards of toleration. Everywhere was youthful ignorance with lethal weapons in its hands, conceited, self-righteous, exalted, blind to the tale of consequences.

Breaking up things is the disposition of youth, and making is not yet in its experience. Liberalism and the middle-aged had a phase of unprecedented ineffectiveness. There seemed to be no judgment left in the world, and the young, in masks and requisitioned cars, making nocturnal raids, indulging in punitive cruelties, beating, torturing, displaying in equal measure physical recklessness and moral panic, came near to wrecking the whole civilising process.

It is an interesting task to trace the gradual maturing of these adolescent organisers that seized so much of the control of the world in that age of transitional disorder. There are voluminous books in which Fascism in 1920, Fascsm in 1930 and Fascism in 1940, or again Communism in the same decades, is elaborately compared with itself. After all their impatience and sentimentality, their rank patriotism and reactionary cant, we find these youth movements unobtrusively sneaking back to planning, discipline and scientific methods. Millions of young men who began Fascist, Nazi, Communist and the like, blind nationalists and irrational partisans, became Modern State men in their middle years. They became at last instruments to realise the

474

plans and visions of the very men they had hunted, mal-treated and murdered in the crude zeal of their first beginnings.

But now youth is well in hand for ever, and when we speak of a man to-day we really mean a different being from a nineteenth-century man. Bodily he is sounder and fitter, almost completely free from disease; mentally he is clear and clean and educated to a pitch that was still undreamt of two centuries ago. He is over fifty instead of being under thirty. He is less gregarious in his instincts and less suggestible because he is farther away from the 'home and litter' mentality, but he is far more social and unselfish in his ideology and mental habits. He is, in fact, for all the identity of his heredity, a different animal. He is bigger and stronger, more clear-headed, with more self-control and more definitely related to his fellow creatures.

This is manifest everywhere, but it is particularly visible in such regions as Bengal and Central China. There we find the direct descendants of shrill, unhappy, swarming, degenerate, under-nourished, under-educated, underbred and short-lived populations among the finest, handsomest, longest-lived and ablest of contemporary humanity. This has been achieved without any attempt at Positive Eugenics; it has resulted from the honest application of the Obvious to health, education and economic organisation, within little more than a hundred years. These populations were terribly weeded by the pestilences of the age of disorder and grimly disciplined by the Tyranny. They are now, after that pruning and training, bearing as fine flowers of literary and scientific achievement as any other racial masses.

§ 7. *Language and Mental Growth*

(I print this section exactly as Raven wrote it down. It is,
the reader will remark, in very ordinary twentieth-century
English. Yet plainly if it is a part of a twenty-second-cen-
tury textbook of general history it cannot have been written
originally in our contemporary idiom. It insists upon a
refinement and enlargement of language as if it had already
occurred, but no such refinement is evident. It must have
been translated by Raven as he dreamt it into the prose of
to-day. If he saw that the book of his at all, he saw it not
with his eyes but with his mind. The actual page could
have had neither our lettering, our spelling, our phrasing
nor our vocabulary.)

One of the unanticipated achievements of the twenty-first
century was the rapid diffusion of Basic English as the
lingua franca of the world and the even more rapid modification, expansion and spread of English in its wake. The
English most of us speak and write to-day is a very different
tongue from the English of Shakespeare, Addison, Bunyan
or Shaw; it has shed the last traces of such archaic elaborations as a subjunctive mood; it has simplified its spelling,
standardised its pronunciation, adopted many foreign locutions, and naturalised and assimilated thousands of foreign
words. No deliberate attempt was made to establish it as the
world language. It had many natural advantages over its
chief competitors, Spanish, French, Russian, German and
Italian. It was simpler, subtler, more flexible and already
more widely spoken, but it was certainly the use of Basic
English which gave it its final victory over these rivals.

Basic English was the invention of an ingenious scholar
of Cambridge in England, C. K. Ogden (1889–1990), who

devoted a long and industrious life to the simplification of expression and particularly to this particular simplification. It is interesting to note that he was a contemporary of James Joyce (1882–1955), who also devoted himself to the task of devising a new sort of English. But while Ogden sought scientific simplification, Joyce worked aesthetically for elaboration and rich suggestion, and vanished at last from the pursuit of his dwindling pack of readers in a tangled prose almost indistinguishable from the gibbering of a lunatic. Nevertheless he added about twenty-five words to the language which are still in use. Ogden, after long and industrious experimentation in the reverse direction, emerged with an English of 850 words and a few rules of construction which would enable any foreigner to express practically any ordinary idea simply and clearly. It became possible for an intelligent foreigner to talk or correspond in understandable English in a few weeks. On the whole it was more difficult to train English speakers to restrict themselves to the forms and words selected than to teach outsiders the whole of Basic. It was a teacher of languages, Rudolph Boyle (1910–59), who contrived the method by which English speakers learnt to confine themselves, when necessary, to Basic limitations.

This convenience spread like wildfire after the First Conference of Basra. It was made the official medium of communication throughout the world by the Air and Sea Control and by 2020 there was hardly anyone in the world who could not talk and understand it.

It is from phonetically spelt Basic English as a new starting-point that the language we write and speak to-day developed, chiefly by the gradual resumption of verbs and idioms from the mother tongue and by the assimilation of foreign terms and phrases. We speak a language of nearly two million words nowadays, a synthetic language in fact, into which roots, words and idioms from every speech in the world have been poured. K. Wang in a recent essay has shown that there are still specialisations of vocabulary. The vocabulary of a score of recent writers of

Italian origin chosen haphazard shows a marked preference for words derived from the Latin, in comparison with twenty Eastern Asiatic writers whose bias is Chinese and American. Yet they can all understand one another and they are all in one undivided field.

There are few redundancies in the New English of to-day and to-morrow, and there is an increasing disposition to take synonyms, and what used to be classified as 'rare' or 'obsolete' terms, and re-define them to convey some finer shade of meaning. Criticism, in the form of the Dictionary Bureau, scrutinises, but permits desirable additions. One can feel little doubt about the increasing delicacy and precision of expression to-day if we compare a contemporary book with some English classic of the eighteenth century or nineteenth century. That is still quite understandable to us, but in its bareness and occasional ineptitudes it seems half-way back to the limitations and lumberingness of Early English or Gothic.

The fuller the terminology the finer the mind. There can be very little doubt that the brain of a twentieth-century man compared with the brain of an ordinary man to-day, though in no way intrinsically inferior, was a far less polished and well-adjusted implement. It was warped by bad habits, cumbered with a tangle of unsound associations, clogged with unresolved complexes; it was like a fine piece of machinery in a state of dirt and neglect. The modern brain is far more neatly packed and better arranged, cleaner and better lubricated. It not only holds much more, but it uses the larger keyboard of our contemporary language more efficiently. The common man to-day is apt to find the philosophers and 'thinkers' of two centuries ago unaccountably roundabout, tedious and encumbered. It is not so much that he finds them obscure, but that when at last he has dragged the meanings out of their jungles of statement into the light of day he finds he has thought all round them.

An interesting and valuable group of investigators, whose work still goes on, appeared first in a rudimentary form in the nineteenth century. The leader of this group was a certain Lady Welby (1837–1912), who was frankly considered by most of her contemporaries as an unintelligible bore. She corresponded copiously with all who would attend to her, harping perpetually on the idea that language could be made more exactly expressive, that there should be a 'Science of Significs'. C. K. Ogden and a Fellow of Magdalene College, I. A. Richards (1893–1977), were among the few who took her seriously. These two produced a book, *The Meaning of Meaning*, in 1923 which counts as one of the earliest attempts to improve the language mechanism. Basic English was a by-product of these enquiries. The new Science was practically unendowed, it attracted few workers, and it was lost sight of during the decades of disaster. It was revived only in the early twenty-first century.

Then Carl Ratan became the centre of a group of workers inspired by the idea of making English more lucid and comprehensive and a truly universal language. His work has expanded into the voluminous organisation of the Language Bureau as we know it to-day. The work of that Bureau has been compared to the work of the monetary experts who finally made money exact a hundred and fifty years ago. Just as civilisation was held back for some centuries by the imperfections of the money nexus, so we begin to realise to-day that our intellectual progress is by no means so rapid as it might be because of the endless flaws and looseness of the language nexus.

An interesting compilation in hand, which promises to become a veritable history of philosophy and knowledge, is the *Language Discard*. This project was originally set going by the Dictionary Section of the Language Bureau, as a mere account rendered of obsolete or obsolescent terms or terms which have become greatly altered from their original meaning; but the enquiry into the reasons for these changings and preferences and abandonments led very directly into an exhaustive analysis of the primary processes of human thought. A series of words, '*soul, spirit, matter, force, essence*', for example, were built into the substance of Aryan and Semitic thought almost from their beginnings, and it was only quite recently that the exhaustive analyses by Yuan Shan and his associates of these framework terms made it clear that the processes of Chinese and Negro thinking were by no means parallel. Translation between languages, in all matters except matters of material statement, is always a little loose and rough, but between the ideology underlying the literature of Eastern Asia or the attempts of Africans to express themselves and that embodied in the ruling language of to-day the roughness approaches violence. That clash, as it examined, is likely to produce very extensive innovations in our philosophical (general scientific) and technical nomenclature. We are speaking and writing a provisional language to-day. Our great-grandchildren will no more think of using many of our terms and turns of expression to-day than we should think of resorting again to the railway train, the paddle steamboat and the needle telegraph.

This rearrangement of the association systems of the human brain which is now in progress brings with it—long before we begin to dream of eugenic developments—the prospect of at present inconceivable extensions of human mental capacity. It will involve taking hold of issues that are at present quite outside our grasp. There was a time when early man was no more capable of drawing a sketch or threading a needle than a cow; it was only as his thumb and fingers became opposable that the power of craftmanship and mechanism came within his grip. Similarly we may anticipate an enormous extension of research and a far deeper penetration into reality as language, our intellectual hand, is brought to a new level of efficiency.

There is not only this sharpening and refinement of the brain going on, but there has been what our great-grandparents would have considered an immense increase in the amount, the quality and the accessibility of knowledge. As the individual brain quickens and becomes more skilful, there also appears a collective Brain, the Encyclopaedia, the Fundamental Knowledge System, which accumulates, sorts,

480

keeps in order and renders available everything that is known. The Encyclopaedia organisation, which centres upon Barcelona, with its seventeenth million active workers, is the Memory of Mankind. Its tentacles spread out in one direction to millions of investigators, checkers and correspondents, and in another to keep the educational process in living touch with mental advance. It is growing rapidly as the continual advance in productive efficiency liberates fresh multitudes of workers for its services. The mental mechanism of mankind is as yet only in its infancy.

Adolescence perhaps rather than infancy. It is because the mind of man is growing up that for the first time it realises that it is young.

§ 8. *Sublimation of Interest*

Not only is the average man to-day, an older and graver creature than his ancestor of three centuries ago, but he is very differently employed. There has been a great diversion of his interest from the primary necessities of life.

Three centuries ago, well over ninety per cent of the human population was absorbed either in the direct production of necessities or in the scramble to get them from their original producers. Direct producers, the peasants and toilers, the entrepreneurs and their managers and directors, and direct distributors accounted for upward of eighty per cent of the human total; the rest were the millions of interveners, usurers, claim-makers, landowners, rentiers, solicitors, speculators, parasites, robbers and thieves who were deemed necessary to ginger up the economic process. The forces of law, order and education, excluding temporary

481

conscription and levies for military ends, took up five per cent of the residue, and a small minority, something under five per cent of the total population, supplied all the artistic effort, the scientific enquiry, the social and political thought, the living soul of the entire social body.

The systems of interest of most people were therefore restricted almost entirely to work and the struggle to possess. They had to think continually of the work they did either for their own profit or for the personal profit, comfort or fantasy of some employer. They had to think of keeping their jobs or getting fresh ones, and this, in the days of narrowing employment after the Hoover Slump, became at last a monstrous obsession of the brain. What they earned they had to spend carefully or guard carefully, for the rascaldom of business was everywhere seeking to give nothing for something. Sometimes, sick of their narrow lives, they would gamble in the desperate hope of a convulsive enlargement, and for most of them gambling meant disappointment and self-reproach. Add to these worries a little love, a good deal of hate, and a desperate struggle to see it all in a hopeful and honourable light, a desperate hunger to be flattered and reassured, and you have the content of ninety-nine per cent of the human brains that made the world of 1930. They could no more escape from this restricted circle of urgently clamorous interests, hardly ampler than the circle of an animal's interest, than the animals can.

The Modern State has broken this cramping circle of interests for every human being. We are still creatures with brains like our forefathers, corresponding ganglia to ganglia and fibre to fibre, but *we are not using those brains for the same purposes*. The Modern State, by ensuring plenty and controlling the increase of population, has taken all the interests of the food-hunt and the food-scramble, and all the interests of the struggle to down-and-out our human competitors, away from the activities of the individual brain. A relatively small number of specialised workers keep the necessary Controls of these primary preoccupations going.

We worry about food, drink, clothing, health and personal freedom no more. The work we *must* do is not burthensome in amount, and it is the most congenial our educational guardians can find for us and help us to find. When it is done we are sure of the result; nobody is left in the world to cheat us or to rob us of our pay. We are still competitive, more so perhaps than ever; jealousy still wars with generosity in us; the story of our personal affections is rarely a simple story; but the interest we feel in our work is a masterful interest and not a driven interest, and our competition is for distinction, appreciation and self-approval and not for mutual injury. There has been a release of by far the larger moiety of the mental energy of the normal man from its former inescapable preoccupations.

This steady obliteration of primary motives is manifested most illuminatingly by the statistics of what used to be 'Crime and Punishment', figures of the offences, insubordinations and deliberate outrages upon social order and the consequent punishments and corrective proceedings that are issued by the disciplinary organisation of the Behaviour Control. Statistics for the years of decadence are not forthcoming, but there is plentiful material from the comparatively orderly and prosperous period between 1890 and 1930. Great Britain then constituted the healthiest and most law-abiding community in the world, but the figures that emerge to the student of history present what seems to us an appalling welter of crime. Stealing, cheating of every sort, forgery, burglary, robbery with violence, poisoning and other forms of murder, occurred daily. It did not seem as though that thick defilement of wrongdoing about property could ever cease. Innumerable suicides occurred through pecuniary worry. Yet now all these crimes, which filled the jails, arising out of the scramble for money and property in an age of insufficiency, have almost completely vanished from human life. The Behaviour Control Report for 2104 (2105 is not yet available) records 715 cases of stealing for the whole world. In nearly every case the object stolen was some personal work of art, some small jewel, a piece of embroidery, a pet animal, several children—in one instance—the bulb of a new variety of lily that aroused the instinct to possess and care for it. It is doubtful whether there were many undetected or unreported thefts.

There has not, however, been anything like the same abolition of personal offences. They have diminished. But while the property offences have diminished to the scale of one-ten-millionth of the old-world figures, these others show a reduction in the nature of single instances to former hundreds. Many tpyes in our population are still very easily turned towards sexual lawlessness. Beautiful and attractive people and particularly attractive children are not yet perfectly immune from undesired solicitation, personal persecution, annoying assault and resentful injury. Jealousy is still a dangerous passion, more particularly below the age of forty. The Behaviour Control ascribes nearly 520,000 offences to this group of urgencies, mostly assaults of varying degree of malignity, culminating in 67 murders. There were also 2,192 suicides in the total. These figures show only a slight improvement upon the annual average for the previous decade.

Another difficult class of offence which finds no exact parallel in the criminal statistics of former times, unless the British offence of 'malignant mischief' is to be put in this group, are acts of annoyance, destruction, assault and so forth, due to competitive jealousy and the expansion aroused, often quite unwittingly, by the bearing or achievements of one's fellow creatures. This sort of misbehaviour varies in degree from the black hatred and fury of an uncontrolled egotism to what verges in some cases upon justifiable criticism of slightly fatuous or self-complacent behaviour. Four murders, some hundreds of assaults and acts of wanton destruction in this category witness to the fact that this world is still not a Paradise for every type of individual. Either they are bitter by some inner necessity or they have been embittered. Yet when we take the grand total of every misdeed that had to be dealt with last year, counting even the most petty occasions for restoration, warning or reproof, and find it is just three quarters of a million in a world of 2,500 million people, we have a quantitative measure of human progress in two brief centuries that justifies a very stalwart confidence in the human outlook. The imagination of man's heart is no longer evil continually. It is only evil occasionally, and the practical task of our social psychologists is to reduce those occasions and provocations.

The abundant release of brain-stuff, the mental plenty which has resulted from the organisation of material plenty, is of necessity being directed into new channels. That meagre half per cent or less of creative workers of the old régime, the few curious men who played about with novel ideas, the odd men of leisure who collected 'rarities' and inventions, has grown into a mighty body of enquiry, experiment, verification and record which is becoming now the larger part of the world's population.

We know now certainly what the people of three centuries ago never suspected, that the human brain released from hunger, fear and the other primary stresses is very easily amenable not only to creative and directive desire but also to kindly and helpful impulses. Almost all the people who kept our productive, our distributing and transport services going are there because they find the work entertaining, because they like making the machine work well and helping people. There is a satisfaction in being able to do things skilfully for others that they could not do nearly so well for themselves. The barbers, shoemakers, tailors, dressmakers, hatters, outfitters and so forth in the great stores to-day are very different people from the rather obsequious, deferential 'inferiors' who made our great-great-grandfathers presentable to the world. Their essential interest is to make their customers sightly and comfortable and not to earn a profit for an employer. The old literature reeks with contempt for barbers and tailors and cobblers, often the contempt of profound resentment. If the common man despised the cobbler, the cobbler pinched his toe and chafed his heel. The barber, it seemed, did no more than cut hair rather badly, and the tailor cut clothes. Except by accident, the barber had ceased to be a barber-surgeon. But nowadays the old-world barber would scarcely recognise himself in the barber-dentist, the kindly expert who sees to our coiffure, gives attention to our teeth, scrutinises our mouth, hair and skin to detect any evidence of failing health, and sends us on our way refreshed, encouraged or warned. Often his friend the tailor or dressmaker will call in while he deals with us to consider our general bravery and improvement, and suggest variations of our exercise and habits.

The old distributing trades have lost their sharp demarcation from the advisory professions. They are in touch with the guardians of development who have replaced the schoolmasters, nurses, governesses, tutors and so forth of the old time, and with the general advisers who have taken on the tasks of the family solicitor, religious minister, private confessor and general practitioner of the past. These advisory and directive professions probably number two or three times as big a proportion of the whole population as the lawyers, educationists and doctors of the nineteenth century. They merge again into another stratum, the specialist teachers, concerned with developing and imparting skills and building up and maintaining the common ideology. This class again passes by insensible degrees into the worlds of technical work, art, literature and scientific research.

The primary producers and elaborators of material, our agriculturalists, engineers, chemists, transport men and industrial directors, also do their work because they like doing it. It satisfies them. They like their materials, they like their difficulties, they like the order of their days. In spite of an increasing output per head of population and an increasing variety and elaboration of the things we use, socially or individually, the numerical proportion of this section of the human population does not increase. Efficiency still outruns need and desire. The two and a half years of compulsory public service, which is an integral part of our education, supplies a larger and larger proportion of such toil as is still unavoidable.

This release of human energy from primary needs is a process that seems likely to continue indefinitely. And all the forces that have made our world-wide social life and keep it going direct that released energy towards the achievement of fresh knowledge and the accumulation and rendering of fresh experience. There is a continual sublimation of interest. Man becomes more curious, more excited, more daring, skilful and pleasantly occupied every year. The more we learn of the possibilities of our world and the possibilities of ourselves, the richer, we learn, is our inheritance. This planet, which seemed so stern a mother to mankind, is discovered to be inexhaustible in its bounty. And the greatest discovery man has made has been the discovery of himself. Leonardo da Vinci with his immense breadth of vision, his creative fervour, his curiosity, his power of intensive work, was the precursor of the ordinary man, as the world is now producing him.

§ 9. *A New Phase in the History of Life*

From the point of view of the ecologist the establishment of the Modern State marks an epoch in biological history. It has been an adaptation, none too soon, of our species to changing conditions that must otherwise have destroyed it. The immense developments and disasters of the nineteenth and twentieth centuries show us mankind scrambling on the verge of irreparable disaster.

The infinite toil of millions of tormented brains, the devotion and persistence of countless forgotten devotees, gave form and clear purpose in time to what were at first mere flounderings and clutchings towards safety. The threatened race did not fall back into that abyss of extinction which has swallowed up so many of the bolder experiments of life. In pain and uncertainty it clambered past its supreme danger phase, and now it has shrugged to such a level of assurance, understanding and safety as no living substance has ever attained before.

By means of education and social discipline the normal human individual to-day acquires characteristics without which his continued existence would be impossible. In the future, as the obscurer processes of selection are accelerated and directed by eugenic effort, these acquired characteristics will be incorporated with his inherent nature, and his educational energy will be released for further adaptions. He will become generation by generation a new species, differing more widely from that weedy, tragic, pathetic, cruel, fantastic, absurd and sometimes sheerly horrible being who christened himself in a mood of oafish arrogance *Homo sapiens.*

The difference of the coming man from the man of the past will be multitudinous and intricate, but certain broad lines of comparison appear already. We have noted already the difference in the age cycle between ourselves and our ancestors, which has prolonged the youthful phase and shifted on the valid years towards the thirty-five to eighty period, and we have cited also the completer physical development, due to the release of vital energy from the task of resisting various infections, poisons and morbidities of growth. We are probably only in the beginning of a very much more considerable physical modification. The aesthetic ideals of the past are likely to play a large part in determining the direction in which these modifications will take us. But these physical developments, important though they must ultimately be, are as yet much less imporant than the changes in moral form that are manifestly in progress. A brief consideration of these will make a fitting conclusion to this general outline of history.

Essentially they constitute a readjustment of the individual to the racial life. When we go back in time for a million years or so we find our ancestor species in a phase of almost fundamental individualism. Except where sexual life and the instinct system to protect offspring came in, the subman shifted for himself. He had no associates in the food hunt, no allies for defence. He was as solitary an animal as the tiger. From that he passed through stages of increasing sociability. The onset of these stages was made practicable by the retention of immature characteristics into adult life. The same thing is happening to the remnant of the lions to-day. They remain cubbish and friendly now to a much later age than they did a few-score thousand years ago. Man passed through a stage when he was as sociable as a modern lion and on to a phase when he was as sociable as a wolf or hunting dog.

But he did not rest at that. All the conditions of his life favoured the formation of still-larger communities and still-closer interdependence. He became a cultivator, an economic animal, and his communities expanded to thousands and scores of thousands of individuals held together by mutual service. He produced language and religion to bind the will and activities of these aggregations into an effective common policy. The history of mankind, we unfold it to the contemporary student, is a story of ever increasing communication and ever increasing interdependence. Insensibly the material side of individual freedom was modified into unavoidable co-operation with the community.

Stress must be laid upon that word material. The physical subjugation and socialisation of the human animal far outran his moral subjection. The history of mankind is also a history of education and compulsion. It is a record of give and take. Man almost up to the present day has remained at heart still the early savage, caring only for himself, for his sexual life, and, during the few years of their helplessness, his children. He has been willing to associate for aggression or for defence, but only very reluctantly for a common happiness. He has had to barter his freedom for the advantages of collective action, but he has done so against the grain, needing persuasion, pressure and helpful

489

delusions.

The history of mankind has had to be very largely the history of a succession of religious and emotional inventions and reconstructions, to override the inherent distaste in the individual for subordination and self-sacrifice. At every opportunity the individual has sought to recover its personal initiatives. Its egotism has battled instinctively of necessity to get the best of the bargain and receive with as little giving as possible.

Man's natural self struggles to do that now as strongly as ever he did. But he struggles now in a better light and more intelligently; he realises what is impossible, and the long conflict of individualism with society has arrived at a rational compromise. We have learnt how to catch and domesticate the ego at an early stage and train it for purposes greater than itself.

What has happened during the past three and a half centuries to human consciousness has been a sublimation of individuality. That phase is the quintessence of modern history. A large part of the commonplace life of man, the food-hunt, the shelter-hunt, the safety-hunt, has been lifted out of the individual sphere and socialised for ever. To that the human egotism has given its assent perforce. It has abandoned gambling and profit-seeking and all the wilder claims of property. It has ceased altogether to snatch, scramble and oust for material ends. And the common man has also been deprived of any weapons for his ready combativeness and of any liberty in its release. Nowadays even children do not fight each other. Gentleness in difference has become our second nature.

All that part of man's life and interests has been socialised entirely against his natural disposition in the matter. In all those concerns the whole race is now confluent; it is becoming as much a colonial organism as any branching coral or polyp, though the ties that link us are not fleshly bands, but infinitely elastic and invisible and subtle. In the later chapters of this world history we have examined and displayed, with particular attention because of its culminat-

490

ing character, the essential individualism of the World War process, and we have told how, with what difficulty and after what scourgings, our race has been brought to its present phase of organised self-control. This present phase is the victory of creative power working through the indi-vidualties of a more intelligent minority, in the face of uni-versal confusion, taking indeed advantage of that confusion to inaugurate our present order. That wilful minority has opened the gates to a power and abundance of existence beyond all former dreaming. But our Modern State has neither absorbed nor destroyed individuality, which now, accepting the necessary restrictions upon its material aggres-siveness, resumes at every opportunity its freedom and enterprise upon a higher level of life.

The individuality deprived, or relieved if you will, of its primary instinctive preoccupations with getting and keeping, disillusioned about precedence, personal display and such-like barbaric vanities, growing continually and swiftly in wisdom and knowledge has now to go farther afield to find itself. No longer a self-sufficient being, at war with all its kind, it has become a responsible part of a species. It has become an experiment in feeling, knowing, making and response.

The body of mankind is now one single organism of nearly two thousand five hundred million persons, and the individual differences of every one of these persons is like an exploring tentacle thrust out to test and learn, to savour life in its fullness and bring in new experiences for the common stock. We are all members of one body.* Only in

* This was the phrase of that interesting mystic St. Paul (Saul) of Tarsus (2–62 c.e. Epistles with analysis and commentary by Hirsch and Potter in the *Historical Reprints: Development of Ideas Series*), who did so much to pervert and enlarge the simpler cosmopolitan fraternalism of Jesus of Nazareth (–4–30 c.e.) before it was finally overwhelmed and lost in the sacrificial sacerdotalism of formal Christianity. For a brief period before it relapsed the Pauline cult had a curious flavour of Modern State feeling. There was, however, a politic disingenuousness in Paul which betrayed his undeniable intellectual power. He was ambiguous about blood sacrifices, im-

the dimmest analogy has anything of this sort happened in the universe as we knew it before. Our sense of our individual difference makes our realisation of our common being more acute. We work, we think, we explore, we dispute, we take risks and suffer—for there seems no end to the difficult and dangerous adventures individual men and women may attempt; and more and more plain does it become to us that it is not our little selves, but Man the Undying who achieves these things through us.

As the slower processes of heredity seize upon them and confirm these social adaptations, as the confluence of wills supersedes individual motives and loses its present factors of artificiality, the history of life will pass into a new phase, a phase with a common consciousness and a common will. We in our time are still rising towards the crest of that transition. And when that crest is attained what grandeur of life may not open out to Man! Eye hath not seen, nor ear heard; nor hath it entered into the mind of man to conceive. . . . For now we see as in a glass darkly. . . .

At this point Raven's copied-out manuscript comes to an end—it seems to me a little abruptly. But it is the end; he has written the word 'Finis' here. I will add only one word or so by way of comment. I have called that manuscript a dream book. Was it a dream or was it indeed, as he declared and believed it to be, a vision of the shape of things to come? Or—there is a third possibility. As dreaming, this book is far too coherent; as vision, incredulity creeps in. But was Raven, too busily employed and too obsessed by the sense of urgency to embark upon a detailed analysis of world development, was he trying nevertheless to sketch out in this fantastic form a general thesis at least

mortality, private property and slavery, to the eternal injury of the Christian movement. It was completely prostituted to usage before the first century was over. See Ivan Mackenzie, *General Elements of Religion* 2103. Mackenzie has an excellent chapter on the anticipation of Modern State ideas by ancient writers, and is particularly interesting on the Superior Person (Generalised or Super Man) of Confucius (551–478 B.C.) and the *City of God of St. Augustine* (354–430).

about the condition of things to come? If this is neither a dream book nor a Sibylline history, then it is a theory of world revolution. Plainly the thesis is that history must now continue to be a string of accidents with an increasingly disastrous trend, until a comprehensive faith in a modernised World-State, socialistic, cosmopolitan and creative, takes hold of the human imagination. When the existing governments and ruling theories of life, the decaying religious and the decaying political forms of to-day, have sufficiently lost prestige through failure and catastrophe, then and then only will world-wide reconstruction be possible. And it must needs be the work, first of all, of an aggressive order of religiously devoted men and women who will try out and establish and impose a new pattern of living upon our race.

THE END

DRAGONFLIGHT *by* ANNE McCAFFREY
— *Corgi S.F. Collector's Library Selection*

The Corgi S.F. Collector's Library is a series that brings, in uniform edition, many of the Greats of S.F.—standard classics, contemporary prizewinners, and controversial fiction, fantasy and fact . . .

DRAGONFLIGHT is Anne McCaffrey's novel which won both the Hugo and Nebula Awards. Set in a medieval world of the future, it tells of Holds, and Castles, and Keeps, and of a great flight of dragons, led by a golden queen and ridden by men sworn to the defence of their fantastic and incredible planet . . .

0 552 09236 3—35p   T82

FANTASTIC VOYAGE *by* ISAAC ASIMOV
— *Corgi S.F. Collector's Library Selection*

The Corgi S.F. Collector's Library is a series that brings, in uniform edition, many of the Greats of S.F.—standard classics, contemporary prizewinners, and controversial fiction, fantasy and fact . . .

FANTASTIC VOYAGE is the novel based on the 20th Century-Fox Motion Picture of a journey into a new dimension. Four men and one woman, reduced to microscopic size, are injected into the carotid artery of a dying man. Their mission—to fight their way into the cranium and destroy a blood clot. At stake—a man's life on which depends the fate of the entire world . . .

0 552 09237 1—35p   T83

A Corgi S.F. Collector's Library Selection

THE MENACE FROM EARTH
by ROBERT A. HEINLEIN

The Corgi S.F. Collector's Library is a series that brings, in uniform edition, many of the Greats of S.F.—standard classics, contemporary prizewinners, and controversial fiction, fantasy and fact . . .

THE MENACE FROM EARTH is the title story in this anthology, which also includes BY HIS BOOTSTRAPS, considered to be one of the best science fiction stories ever published. Robert A. Heinlein is acknowledged as one of the world's leading writers in the field of S.F. and in this collection his gift for providing fantasy-plus-feasibility is shown to the full.

0 552 09334 5—35p   T84

NEW WRITINGS IN S.F. 21
Edited by John Carnell

NEW WRITINGS IN S.F. brings to lovers of science fiction strange, exciting stories—stories written especially for the series by international authors. This edition features stories by Keith Roberts, Douglas R. Mason, James White, Sydney J. Bounds, Colin Kapp, H. A. Hargreaves and Michael G. Coney, and is the last edition to be edited by the late John Carnell.

0 552 09313 0—35p   T85